The Woman Who Shot Mussolini

The Woman
Who Shot Mussolini

FRANCES STONOR SAUNDERS

faber and faber

First published in 2010
by Faber and Faber Limited
Bloomsbury House
74–77 Great Russell Street
London WC1B 3DA

Typeset by Faber and Faber Limited
Printed in England by TJ International Ltd, Padstow, Cornwall

A CIP record for this book
is available from the British Library

ISBN 978-0-571-23977-1

1 3 5 7 9 10 8 6 4 2

For Fiona Burton

There is such a thing as a moral atmosphere.
VIOLET GIBSON

Contents

PART ONE

REVELATION

Everything begins in mysticism and ends in politics.
CHARLES PÉGUY

I

Now

Wednesday 7 April 1926

A glance. Duration, one, possibly two, seconds. In particle physics, an eternity. In history, the briefest of encounters, an infinitesimally small exchange. Two arms are raised, Benito Mussolini's in the Fascist salute, Violet Gibson's in the levelling of a pistol. The distance separating these two people, who have never met, is approximately eight inches. Close enough to breathe each other's breath. Murder can be a very intimate business.

Violet, daughter of a peer, looks like a pauper. She is wearing a black dress, shiny with wear; her grey-white hair is pinned up in an erratic bundle with straggles that have fallen loose, she is very thin. Mussolini, son of a blacksmith, is dressed like a stockbroker. Butterfly collar, black tie, spats, overcoat with velvet-trimmed collar – clothes picked out that morning by his Jewish mistress, who has spent the night with him. He hasn't slept very well, on account of a suspected stomach ulcer that causes him frequent discomfort. (Away from the crowds, it has become an everyday reflex for him to loosen his trousers and knead his stomach with his hands.) Violet, who has been preparing to kill Mussolini for some time now, hasn't slept well either, because she too suffers from stomach pains.

Until she raises the pistol and points it at Mussolini's face, it's been a normal Fascist morning. At eight o'clock Quinto Navarra, Mussolini's valet, arrived at his apartment in the Palazzo Tittoni on via Rasella. Shortly after, they got into a black Lancia, and were driven to Mussolini's office at Palazzo Chigi. His Excellency the Prime Minister Benito Mussolini, Il Duce, sat behind his desk, receiving his proconsuls and listening to their petitions. His staff and security services have been fine-tuning his schedule, issuing detailed orders for its flawless execution. The chief of police has just completed Security Order number 08473, detailing policing arrangements for the following day. Carbon copies of these security orders are despatched daily to those responsible for public order, including the heads of the Military and Political Police, the Interior Ministry and the royal protection squad. The chief of police has to cope with a poorly trained force that has no efficient telephone system, an almost complete lack of motor transport, and cramped and unhygienic local police stations. In a few hours, he will have to revise the order substantially. But, for the moment, everything is running as it should in the new Roman imperium.

Violet, in the meantime, is making her way from via Nomentana, a broad avenue of villas and apartments extending across what had been, until recently, a rural hinterland of Rome. Does she walk? Does she take the tram? Violet has no staff to draw up and attend to the minutiae of her schedule, which is probably just as well, for if the past were available to us in all its detail it would overwhelm the present. As the nuns at the convent where she is lodging will later testify, Violet rose at six, and appeared, veiled, for Mass in the convent chapel. She went out after breakfast, at 8.30 a.m. She was a little agitated, 'as if she was trying to control some inner emotion'. Asked if she would be back for lunch, she answered yes, with 'a half-smile'. Sister Riccarda was concerned. In the night, she had taken Violet some medicine for her stomach pains. The nun noticed that she had been reading an Italian newspaper, and had marked up some passages. 'I didn't realise that tomorrow I would have to be out for such a long time,' Violet said, her meaning, as always, elusive. As she sets out from the convent, she is unaware that the Mother Superior, Mary Elizabeth Hesselblad, is watching her closely from a window.

Violet passes through Porta Pia, Michelangelo's great travertine portal, and heads towards the church of Santa Susanna. Here, three days ago, on Easter Sunday, she attended Mass, seated beneath florid frescoes depicting the martyrdom of Susanna, the third-century saint who had consecrated her virginity to Christ. Violet, though not a virgin, is ready to embrace her own martyr- dom, because God has willed it so. In her right hand, which is tucked into a pocket, she carries a Lebel revolver, the standard- issue weapon of the French military, capable of firing six 8mm rounds loaded into a swing-out chamber. She has wrapped it in her black veil. In her room at the convent, where she has been practising with the empty revolver, gripping it with both hands for a steady aim, she has a box of twenty live bullets. In the left pocket of her spinsterly dress she carries a large stone, concealed in a black leather glove, with which she will smash the windscreen of Mussolini's car should she need to shoot him in the vehicle. These are the implements of her saintly geste.

What the Tourists See

Classical Rome, medieval Rome, Renaissance Rome, baroque Rome, eighteenth-century Rome, post-unification Rome. Foreign visitors (an estimated 150,000 of whom have arrived in the city to celebrate Easter) are venturing forth from hotels and *pensioni* to pace out their routes across all these Romes, two thousand years of history and confused memories squashed into rubble or sculpted onto soaring masonry. For many tourists, it's the last chance to rummage through their Baedeker or Murray's *Handbook of Rome* before beginning the exodus home. Edith Wharton loathed these 'red volumes which accompany the traveller through Italy', because they had 'so completely anticipated the most whimsical impulses of their readers that it is now almost impossible to plan a tour of exploration without finding, on reference to them, that their author has already been over the ground.' But Violet's impulses carry her along on a trajectory unmeasured by any guidebook.

Fascist Rome, great gusts of Roman glory, the sense of what Virginia Woolf identified as 'an age to come of pure, self-assertive virility'. The 'unmitigated masculinity' of the new Rome is per- sonified by its leader, Benito Mussolini, whose 'muscles' and 'extraordinary vitality' are a delight to Lady Asquith, wife of the former British Prime Minister (who offers, by contrast, an unconstructed physique and indoor skin). An estimated thirty million pictures of Il Duce in up to 2,500 different poses are in circulation.

He has been photographed swimming, fencing, boxing, riding, cutting corn shirtless, his chest glistening with sweat – unimaginable for most of his political contemporaries. Hitler, Stalin, Lenin, Baldwin, Chamberlain, Roosevelt, Blum and Franco are not visibly 'men' in this way, timidly keeping their bodies as private concerns. Mussolini's body, it is said, leaves 'after-images' of itself to arouse the faithful. Clementine Churchill, meeting Il Duce in March 1926, found him 'quite simple and *natural*, very dignified ... [with] beautiful golden brown, piercing eyes which you can see but can't look at.' As if looking at him were like looking at the sun. All in all, she concluded, 'one of the most wonderful men of our times.' She was delighted to take away a signed photograph in memento. Lady Oxford described his sonorous voice as one of the most beautiful she had ever heard. Lady Ivy Chamberlain, wife of Foreign Secretary Sir Austen, was an enduring fan who treasured her own Fascist party badge (and, while they lasted, the orchids Mussolini sent her). Lady Sybil Graham, wife of the British ambassador, was said to be equally charmed.

Tourist guides advise that Mussolini himself is among the sites to visit. 'Everyone who came to Rome wanted to have an interview with Mussolini,' observed an American journalist. 'To see him was as much a part of the long-planned trip to the Eternal City as it was to visit the ruins or to walk over the places where the heroes of antiquity had once walked.' Women travellers dream of tea with Mussolini – though he doesn't drink it, except for camomile, which he takes both orally and through the rectum, as a palliative for his stomach pains.

Sister Caterina Flanagan will testify that Violet had watched an official procession in September 1925, but came back indignant because Mussolini had not appeared. This was not surprising, the nun explained (ignorant of Violet's intentions), as many foreign guests at the convent who were great admirers of Mussolini's 'were constantly trying to catch a glimpse of him, and were disappointed if they failed'. How ridiculous, muses Foreign Secretary Dino Grandi, are these 'elderly widows and elderly deracinated ladies' – *pace* Miss Jean Brodie, a woman in her prime – who adore Il Duce and long to give him seed-cake.

What the Tourists Do Not See

They do not see the political prisoners, the castor oil, the *manganello* clubs, weighted with thick leather or lead; or the body of the murdered opposition leader Giacomo Matteotti, left to rot in a ditch outside Rome; or the three thousand dead and buried, bludgeoned or knifed or shot by Fascist squads. The tourists, as they settle into their wagon-lit trains (fully booked three weeks in advance, on account of Easter), do not see the prisoners transported to *confino*, internal exile, in cattle cars attached to third-class trains, chained, handcuffed, without food or air. The tourists do not see the smashed bones of the corpse of the anti-Fascist Catholic priest Don Giovanni Minzoni; or the contusions and internal bleeding of Socialist Party leader Giovanni Amendola, savagely beaten by Fascist thugs in July 1925. His broken body will

[7]

never recover. Nine months later, on this very day, Wednesday, 7 April 1926, it is cooling on a slab in a hospital morgue in Cannes. A normal Fascist morning.

The inflation of Mussolini is continuous and pervasive. All newspapers are obliged to give prominent place to his articles and speeches; typesetters have to print the word *DUCE* in capital letters. There is a rush on gold paint and leaf, for decorating the lictors' maces and fasces and Roman eagles and the throne that is being constructed for Mussolini to sit upon during the ceremony, in a few days' time, to mark his elevation as 'Caesar of the Modern Empire'. The fascination and élan of Fascism: but at its heart lies a rancour, a nervous fear. The regime is permanently readying itself for 'the muster, the march, the battle, the liquidation of foes who paradoxically never [lose] their menace . . . for another conflict, another test'. Mussolini gives 'fighting' speeches. 'War' is declared against cabbies, who are told they must shave ('Edict Bans Whiskers and Prescribes Hat, Collar and Tie'); against women who are dressed in 'immodest garb'; against bachelors who refuse to go forth and multiply little Fascists. On the walls of thousands of buildings Mussolini's historic slogans are daubed in indelible black varnish – *Credere, Obbedire, Combattere* (Believe, Obey, Fight); 'Mussolini is always right'; 'We shall shoot straight'.

Violet knows how to shoot a pistol, having once used one on herself. But her aim might be a problem, as the bullet she fired into her body a year ago – 'I wanted to die for the glory of God' – missed her heart and whizzed through her ribcage before coming to a halt in her shoulder bone.

Caput Mundi

At 9.30, after a meeting with the Duke d'Aosta, cousin of the king, Mussolini is driven the short distance from Palazzo Chigi to Campidoglio, the Capitoline. He isn't wearing the bowler hat his mistress handed to him before he left his apartment – too much, perhaps, under a brilliant April sun. (He later abandons the use altogether, when he realises that bowlers are worn by Laurel and Hardy in the Hollywood comedies he so enjoys watching). He gets out of the car at the foot of the wide, shallow steps leading up to the capitol of the capital of the world, and ascends them at full tilt, leaving his personal secretary huffing and puffing behind him. This place is the centre – political, religious, administrative – of all Romes. If Mussolini has his way, it will be the centre also of the new Roman Empire.

Michelangelo's exquisite geometry: a three-sided piazza of peach-coloured buildings in the middle of which Marcus Aurelius rides his bronze horse, centuries of stormy events swirling at his feet. On the west side is the Palazzo dei Conservatori, which Mussolini enters through the main door. He proceeds along the dizzying marble corridors, his heels clacking like castanets against the stone. In the Sala degli Orazi e Curiazi, he mounts the podium and launches into the inaugural speech of the Seventh International Congress of Surgeons. Hundreds of surgeons listen with satisfaction as Mussolini praises their art and thanks them for their many interventions on his own body after bits of it had been blown off or shattered in the Great War. The storm of steel that hit him was a misfired shell he himself had loaded, leaving him with scores of fragmentation and puncture wounds, a smashed right collarbone, a temporarily paralysed left arm and a severe laceration in his right leg which became infected, requiring an agonising scraping procedure down to the marrow of his shin-bone. As it turns out, these have proved to be useful wounds, virtuous punctuation marks in the progress of a modern saviour as he advances towards his triumph.

One early biographer of Mussolini wrote, in *Dux*, that he had so many war wounds he seemed like 'Saint Sebastian, his flesh pierced as if with arrows.' The author was Margherita Sarfatti, who as Mussolini's mistress was well qualified to trace the intimate details of his body. Mussolini collected near-death experiences like generals collect medals: duels (he fought at least two in

1919, and one in 1920), plane crashes (in March 1921 a plane he was piloting nosedived suddenly and crashed – he emerged with only scratches to his face and a twisted knee). And explosives. Shortly before the March on Rome, in October 1922, a bullet grazed his ear when a euphoric *squadrista* fired his gun into the air. As a newspaper editor in Milan, Mussolini used to keep several bombs and hand grenades on his desk, 'in case his political enemies should attack him', reported *Time* magazine. Once, while writing an editorial, 'he set fire to the fuse of one of these bombs by accidentally resting his cigarette upon it. An assistant noticed the smouldering fuse, screamed. Looking up, Editor Mussolini snuffed it out with his fingers, continued the writing of his editorial.' 'I like to live dangerously,' Mussolini was fond of saying.

Violet approaches Campidoglio. Perhaps the large crowd gathered there draws her to the place. This is not on her itinerary for today, not the scene she has chosen for a fatal encounter with Mussolini. In her pocket is a tiny scrap of paper, the tip of the lip of an envelope, on which she has written 'Palazzo del Littorio', the address of the Fascist Party headquarters where, according to the newspaper she has been reading, Il Duce will appear that afternoon. On Campidoglio, she approaches a tall, bearded man and asks if the King is present. No, not the King. Mussolini. She threads her way through the crowd and positions herself by one

of the two lamp posts just outside the Palazzo dei Conservatori. Nearby are two uniformed policemen. Directly in front of her are the liveried marshals of the Capitol in stiffly brocaded silk coats and plumed bicorn hats. Plainclothes secret agents are everywhere. She looks old and sad and bedraggled, with precarious spectacles – she stands in the golden section of this Fascist *tableau vivant*, and nobody notices her.

Here he is. Mussolini has left the building, and is making his way towards the statue of Marcus Aurelius, where his black Lancia is waiting with the engine turning over. It is 10.58 a.m. The Governor of Rome is in front of him, and doctors Bastianelli and Alessandri are alongside him. Behind them follow Quinto Navarra and other staff, led by the Foreign Secretary, Dino Grandi. A jostled photograph shows Mussolini striding forward confidently, chest puffed out like a cockerel. The crowd is swaying forward to get a closer look. The odd straggler pops out like a

Campidoglio, seconds before Mussolini emerges from the Palazzo dei Conservatori.
Violet (circled) is next to the lamp post.

hernia from behind police lines and is pushed back in. '*Viva il Duce!*' is the chant, which Il Duce acknowledges with a salute. He stops less than a foot away from Violet. A group of students bursts into a chorus of the Fascist anthem, 'Giovinezza':

The poets and the artisans,
The landlords and the peasants,
With pride at being Italian
Swear faith to Mussolini.
There is no poor quarter
That does not send its men
Does not unfurl the flags
Of Fascism the redeemer.

Mussolini turns his head slightly to acknowledge the students. According to one eyewitness account, the sound of the gun firing is like a stick thwacking a stone. Mussolini's saluting arm retracts, his hand clamps to his face, blood pours between his fingers. He staggers back, one step, two. But he is still on his feet. He looks up, astonished, and his eyes settle on Violet, who is also astonished, just as she pulls the trigger again.

Click.

A misfire. The pistol hammer strikes, but nothing happens. The bullet has stuck in the chamber. Several seconds pass, in which everybody is suddenly and unnaturally fixed, held to their positions as in a game of grandmother's footsteps. Silence without, and within the amplified thud of heartbeats.

Then uproar. Mussolini, once he realises he is not dead, summons more composure than anybody else at the scene. 'It's nothing, everybody stay calm,' he orders, and everybody panics. He brushes aside the famed physician Dr Bastianelli, who was standing behind him when the gun was fired and who now produces a handkerchief and is trying to press it to Mussolini's bleeding face. More screams from the crowd. 'Don't be afraid,' Mussolini commands. 'I'm here. This is a mere trifle.' He is right: Violet's first bullet has nicked the bridge of his nose, removing a tiny divot of flesh. But such is the loss of blood that Mussolini eventually yields to Bastianelli's suggestion that they go back inside the building to stem the flow and treat the wound.

As Mussolini is being hustled away, Violet is set upon by the crowd, which 'like flames of fire' leaps up into 'a frenzied rage', according to one excited report. A woman standing behind Violet strikes her, hitting her about the head with a handbag and pulling her hair. She will later boast of having been the first to land a blow. The pummelling is delivered with the added vigour of personal affront, for, as she tells it, Violet had nudged her out of her original spot and obscured her view. Of the two policemen who are within arm's length of Violet, one manages to knock the pistol from her hand, while the other punches her square in the face. This blow knocks Violet backwards to the ground, whereupon the mob jumps on top of her, kicking her about and tearing at her clothes.

Police superintendent Ermanno De Bernardini tries to gain control of the crowd. 'Leave her! Let us do our job!' he shouts. 'She's ours!' somebody replies. In the ensuing melee, Brigadier Lucarini, a uniformed officer, suffers cuts and bruises sufficient to merit a visit to hospital. This is now a massive brawl. Witness statements and police reports reveal the sheer number of agents present, the different departments involved in policing the event, and ultimately, the uselessness of all of them. Violet looks vacant, stunned. She does nothing, does not cry out for mercy or deflect the blows. Her rope of hair has loosened, adding to her dishevelled appearance. Her spectacles have been trampled on, and the holy medallions she was wearing around her neck – her protecting saints – have been yanked off. With great difficulty, the policemen drag her away from the scene before the crowd can tear her limb from limb.

Mussolini, meanwhile, is in a small storeroom, lying backwards across a chair with his feet in the air and his head hanging over the edge (so that it is lower than his heart), from which position he has an upside-down view of the chaos unfolding around him. If he is in danger, it is from the crush of hundreds of eminent surgeons all determined to save his life. '[They] almost killed me,' he later tells his wife Rachele. 'Those illustrious scientists, in the name of helping me, threw themselves across me and almost smothered me. I confess that in that instant I felt afraid. I defended myself energetically but with difficulty.' Outside, the crowd goes mad, some windows are smashed. Fifteen minutes later, Il Duce reappears with a large plaster spread across his nose and cheeks like an accidental butterfly. Once again he addresses the crowd and calls for calm, but the people press forward, knocking down the barriers and surging around him. With difficulty, he is manoeuvred towards his car, bundled into it and driven back to his apartment, where he can finally allow himself to be shocked. His mistress, Margherita, who has no idea of what has just happened, is there to receive him.

Violet has been taken into the courtyard of the Museo dei Conservatori, containing the fragments – head, hand, foot – of the colossal statue of Constantine the Great, the emperor who believed that Rome's future lay with Christianity. The toe of the foot is bigger than a man's waist. Against the gargantuan proportions of these marble remains, miniature Violet is like Alice in Wonderland. She is very confused. Nearby, the sound of shattered glass as a window is broken. Somebody sends for a brandy to calm her nerves. 'Drink me'. She does. She stammers out her name and two addresses in Rome, then refuses to speak further.

An hour or so later, when the square has been cleared and closed off as a crime scene, she is driven in a police car the short distance to the Mantellate prison, a vast complex on the west bank of the Tiber. She is seated in the back of the car, without handcuffs, between police superintendents Epifanio Pennetta and De Bernardini, both of the Political Police. She remains silent. At the prison, she is received by the nuns who run the women's section. She is photographed – two mug shots, one in profile, the other straight on – next to a criminal identification number, 14967. Her cheeks are flushed, a sign of incipient swelling from the punches she has taken. There are scratches and cuts on her face, as if she has just run pell-mell through a bramble bush. Her starched white collar is torn. The line of her mouth and lips is a thin horizontal, framed by two deep creases running down the inside of both cheeks. Her once fine facial structure – the raised cheekbones, the well-defined jawline – has suffered subsidence following the removal of most of her upper teeth some years previously. Her eyes are suffused with a kind of mist; her gaze is both terribly resigned and painfully direct. She looks out as if at a porthole, beyond which lies the vast wilderness of the world.

She is then fingerprinted, each digit of her left hand ink-pressed and held under the guiding hand of a police officer – a careful process, like rolling gnocchi in flour. She is handed over to the nun-jailers, who stripsearch her and confiscate her garter belt and

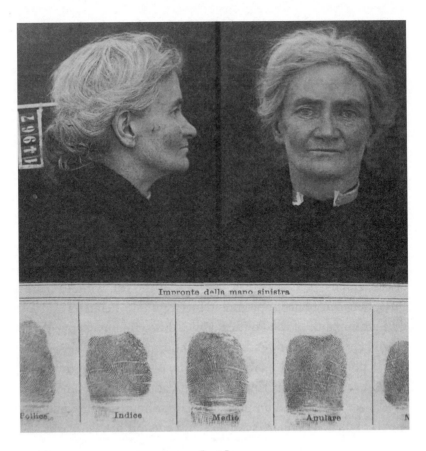

Impronte della mano sinistra

Pollice   Indice   Medio   Anulare

hair clips. A search of her clothes turns up the little scrap of paper on which she has written 'Palazzo del Littorio'. There is nothing else. No handbag, no money, no identity papers, no personal effects. Violet is then washed and taken to the infirmary so that the cuts and swellings on her face and body can be attended to.

Shortly afterwards, and still in the infirmary, Violet meets the men who will determine what will happen to her: the chief of police, the crown prosecutor, chief superintendent pennetta, and two investigating magistrates. There is an interpreter, because none of them yet knows whether she speaks Italian. She replies falteringly to their questions, in English with a light Irish accent, giving some personal details and confirming that she has been in Rome for some time. She tells them she tried to commit suicide last year, that she has not returned to England because she fears her family will put her in a lunatic asylum. She is shown the Lebel pistol, but says she doesn't know what has happened, she has never seen Mussolini before. The questions become more heated: 'I don't know anything. I don't remember anything.' And then, with a look of surprise: 'Mussolini? Are you sure it was me?'

II

Then

The Honourable Violet Gibson, daughter of Lord and Lady Ashbourne, is wearing a dress of white poplinette, with lace and chiffon fichus, fastened on the left side with a bunch of pink malmaison carnations, and a large white hat trimmed with chiffon and pink carnations, and bouquet of the same. She is twenty-four, a bridesmaid at her brother's wedding. This detail drops from a sepia-aged cutting from *The Times* that has been pasted into a hefty leather-bound album of newspaper clippings. There are several other volumes, held at the House of Lords archive, all devoted to the Ashbourne family, paterfamilias Edward Gibson, first Lord Ashbourne, Lord Chancellor of Ireland. Politically and socially, in Dublin and in London, the Ashbournes have made their mark, and they keep an assiduous record of it.

From the cuttings the outline of Violet's social curriculum can be traced. At eighteen she is presented as a debutante by her mother at the court of Queen Victoria, and thus gains the threshold of the belle-époque establishment. Thereafter she is a regular fixture in the society columns and court circulars. She attends a reception with her parents given by the Duchess of Devonshire at Devonshire House, Piccadilly; a luncheon given in Dublin by Lord Ashbourne in honour of the Lord Lieutenant and Countess Cadogan; the annual reception of the Marquess and Marchioness of Londonderry for the opening of parliament, regarded as the major event of the London season (some quipped that Londonderry was 'catering his way into the cabinet'). She is a guest at state concerts at Buckingham Palace ('Full Dress, Ladies with Feathers and Trains'), where, surrounded by the contents of *Burke's Peerage*, the *Libro d'oro*, the *Almanach de Gotha*, she listens to Sir Walter Parratt conduct flowery songs by Donizetti, Jensen, Liszt, Adam. She is reported by *The Times* to be with her parents and brother William in St Moritz, where the season is in full swing. There, together with the Duchess of York, the Duchess of Teck, the Duchess d'Aosta, the Comte de Turin and a potpourri of other European nobility, she watches her brother Harry, a keen sportsman and leading tobogganer of the Engadine, as he wins the Grand National race. (His book, *Tobogganning on Crooked*

Harry Gibson with fellow tobogganer

Runs, was reviewed as 'one of the best known works on that fascinating sport', though his use of 'the Queen's English' was considered 'rude and often positively reprehensible'.)

As the winter season ends in Switzerland, it continues in Dublin, where Violet gracefully assists at her mother's ball, 'attended, of course, by a large crowd of the elite'. The decoration, 'carried out in white Nile lilies, variegated tulips and smilax' suspended from the ceilings in enormous nosegays, is 'notably beautiful and abundant'. Violet wears a dress of pure white satin, the bodice completely covered with a network and fringes of pearls, and finished on the shoulders with clusters of violets and foliage. She sparkles amidst the '*triste* toilettes' of the Duchess of Buccleuch, Lady Inchiquin, and Lady Hastings, who all wear black. At another wedding, that of her sister Elsie in June 1893, Violet, a bridesmaid, wears a white bengaline dress with a full waistcoat of fine lace and a picture hat trimmed with lace and silk to match. 'She was the shyest of the bridesmaids, but she looked *so* nice!' Elsie writes in a letter from her honeymoon.

In a photograph published in the *Lady's Pictorial* in September 1897, Violet appears beautifully attired, her waist cinched to an impossible circumference, her long tresses of hair piled high under a hat decorated with fresh flowers. She looks anything but shy: she holds her head, tilted at a slight angle, in a dashing, thoroughbred way, confident, spirited. Extremely pretty, the embodiment of belle-époque fashion, she stands just feet away from the Duke and Duchess of York (the future King George V and Queen Mary) on their official visit to Howth Castle, which Lord Ashbourne had rented as a formal residence befitting the office of Lord Chancellor. Flanking the royal party are her parents, the archbishop of Dublin and the Lord Chief Justice of Ireland – the mentors of her youth, fixed in an exalted frieze, 'calmly conscious of a social and economic ascendancy which appeared theirs by right'.

This is the Honourable Violet Gibson in her youth, firmly and safely entrenched in a caste outfitted with privilege, topped with picture hats, and a title that signals her significance in the Anglo-Irish ruling elite. This is her life, before her thoughts turned against her, before the world as she knew it went all topsy-turvy.

LORD ASHBOURNE'S PARTY AT HOWTH CASTLE.

The royal party at Howth Castle, September 1897. Violet is on the right, next to her father.

*

In a key passage in *Mrs Dalloway*, Virginia Woolf's protagonist Clarissa meditates on the woman she can see moving around in the opposite house, about whom she knows nothing. Clarissa discounts deep metaphysical explanation – 'love and religion' – preferring to see in 'the midst of ordinary things', in life itself, a riddle. 'The supreme mystery . . . was simply this: here is one room: there another' – which stands for the nugatory knowledge we have of the lives of others. We see, but we see across an impassable distance, another human being, passing from one room to another. Violet Gibson: how little we know. We see her in one 'room', one state – levelling a pistol at Benito Mussolini. We see her in another 'room', another state – a slender debutante, smiling, radiant. The mystery is how this woman, so vivid to us in each state, each contradictory state, achieves the short, enigmatic journey – a lifetime and a moment – from the lighted room to the shadows of the one beyond.

III

Open, O Ye Heavenly Gates

Like the floral nosegays on the ceiling at her mother's ball, Violet Gibson was not expected to do much. Her life, as the daughter of Ireland's pre-eminent statesman, was lived at the heights, up there with the *sans pareil*. It was a genteel, sequestered existence, far removed from the blood and mire of Irish politics and the subsistence conditions in which most of the population lived. There were concerts, art galleries, lectures to be attended, salons for discussion and coquetting and drinking tea from bone china. There were carriage rides along the high-walled lanes of Dalkey, a fashionable Dublin suburb where the Gibsons maintained a residence; and, from their city home, walks to and around a tightly knit nucleus of institutions: the Royal Dublin Society, Trinity College, the National Library and the clubs around St Stephen's Green. Walking between them, or down Grafton Street, people constantly met one another. Society was small enough to know 'everybody', or their relations – genealogy was a second language, and nobody questioned the grandiose canopy of a family tree if it featured in *Burke's Landed Gentry of Ireland*, even though Sir Bernard Burke was lax in pressing for proper proofs of descent.

The Gibsons lived in a beautifully appointed Georgian house in Merrion Square, a coveted address for Dublin's elite. Violet's father, Edward, had been born here in 1837, the son of a wealthy solicitor who held the office of taxing master in Chancery. There was a family fortune, accumulated over four centuries since the Gibsons, English protestants, had settled in County Meath, and consisting primarily of cash rather than extensive land ownership (in 1885, the family registered holdings of less than two thousand acres). The practice of law being the principal profession of

Edward's forefathers, it would appear that British justice had served the family well in more ways than one. Edward, far into his own, well-remunerated career, received a substantial annual income from his father.

Edward was a sickly child, withdrawn from prep school because of his frail constitution and tutored at home. He achieved the rare distinction of winning a place at Dublin University's Trinity College when he was only fifteen. He read English History, English Literature and Political Science, became president of the Historical Society and left laden with prizes and 'a reputation at twenty that some men at forty vainly sigh for'. He then read for the Bar from chambers at Lincoln's Inn in London, taking silk in 1871, and for the next twelve years he practised tirelessly on the Irish circuit. Little is known about his legal career, probably because not much happened. His enemies claimed that he 'never had any practice worth speaking of'; others that 'possessed of ample means, he was placed above the necessity of slaving at his profession, and could afford to devote much time to public duties'. In 1875, at the age of thirty-seven, he was returned to the House of Commons as the Conservative member for the University of Dublin. It was an easy victory – the electorate for the seat was tiny, a couple of thousand at most, and most of them were allowed to vote twice, once as graduates of the university and again in their home constituencies; but from this moment Edward Gibson became a prominent figure in public life.

He was noted for his mass of prematurely snow-white hair and his florid 'Hibernian face', lit up by a pair of piercing black eyes; also his eloquence (though he could be windy, with speeches rarely lasting less than an hour) and chivalrous fairness, an unusual quality in Irish politics. He was, a journalist wrote, 'A man of even temper, of polished manners, of large scholarship, utterly devoid of spiteful feeling toward any class of his countrymen, having no quarrel with any of them, and wishing well to them all.' His wit, his pungent and decisive irony, delivered in a 'mellifluous voice just softened by the real Dublin brogue', made him a compelling figure in the House of Commons, where he was ranked as one of the 'hardest hitters' alongside Gladstone and Randolph Churchill.

He never fails in a great debate to rise to the occasion. He is one of the few speakers in the House who is listened to with attentive interest by both sides ... When the word is passed into the lobby or the tea-room that 'Gibson is up', there is invariably a rush inside.

Equipped with a little travelling air-pillow, Gibson shuttled between his Dublin chambers and Westminster on the Royal Mail Service via Holyhead and Kingstown, a sea passage of just over three hours. The mail packets were advertised as having 'unequalled First Class accommodation, Private Deck cabins, Lavatories, Smoking Rooms, and every modern improvement. They are lighted by electricity.' Cheaper fares were available for less commodious arrangements, and they were taken up by the tens of thousands of men, women and children who were part of the mass exodus from an Ireland in which few shared in Gibson's fortune. At least three million people left between 1845 and 1870, their misfortune the more typical lot in a country where the poverty of the many contrasted drastically with the wealth of the few, where laissez-faire economics and fractious politics saw wild oscillations between conciliation and coercion, curfews, martial law.

When Gibson first took his seat in the House of Commons, most Englishmen had forgotten about the Irish problem. Michael Davitt, the Fenian activist who was to lead the Irish peasants' revolt after 1877, was serving time in Dartmoor prison for 'treason felony', and the Home Rule MPs had not yet become more than 'minor nuisances on the fringe of Parliamentary life'. Conditions in Ireland being deemed peaceful, Disraeli's Conservative government, formed in 1874, was pursuing a policy of benign neglect. Initially, Gibson supported this inactivity. He dismissed as absurd those Home Rulers who were agitating for land reform in Ireland, and claimed that most Irish tenants (the majority Catholic population) were 'exceptionally prosperous', that 'the savings banks were teeming with the millions of the people'.

Before two parliamentary sessions were over he had made such an impression that Disraeli nominated him Attorney General for Ireland. Gibson turned this minor office (traditionally held as a stepping-stone to the judicial bench) into one of the most influential departments in the Irish government. He was even spoken of as the 'effective controller [of policy] at Dublin Castle' who gave the putative heads of government – the Lord Lieutenant and the Chief Secretary – their marching orders.

Gibson's position as Disraeli's Irish protégé came to an abrupt end when the latter died in April 1881. There followed a protracted power struggle in the Conservative party, and an alarming deterioration in Irish affairs. By the time Gibson was appointed Lord Chancellor of Ireland in June 1885, the country was 'fast merging into the conditions of anarchy'. Gibson's earlier comments about the prosperity of Irish tenants now appeared culpably glib. The countryside was convulsed by the Land War, a conflict between half-starved peasants and the old landed ruling class that was conducted in a feverish atmosphere loud with threat and vicious struggles with armed police. Nearly fifteen thousand tenants were violently evicted for non-payment of rents between 1879 and 1883, more than over the previous thirty years. 'The houses were ransacked, the furniture thrown out, the fires quenched, and a bit of thatch was taken possession of as a token in each case that the landlord had re-entered his rights. Then the inhabitants were turned adrift in the world.' In response, some landlords were assassinated, others were confronted by the famous no-rent policy of 'boycott' – so named after Captain Charles Boycott, one of the strategy's victims in Mayo – organised by the Land League ('the land of Ireland for the people of Ireland') with the backing of the Home Rulers whom Gibson so disparaged. In 1880 alone, 2,590 incidents of murder, assault (including ear clipping), intimidation, attacks on animals and other outrages were attributed to the Land League's militant activists.

Ireland was a confused and devastated place, suspended between two languages, between two conflicting ideas of who the country belonged to. The combination of an agricultural depression and a determined attempt to mount a challenge to the existing land-ownership structure resulted in something quite unprecedented: a fusion of radical protest in the countryside with disciplined parliamentary opposition in the shape of Charles Stewart Parnell's Irish Party. Parnell, who had spent time in jail and was accused of conniving at the infamous Phoenix Park murders of May 1882 (which claimed the two most senior imperial figures in Ireland), was himself an encumbered landlord. Impeccably conservative in his social attitudes, he wanted the peasants to own their land and Ireland to develop as a capitalist country. But he knew how to hint at the violence that could be unleashed if demands for land reform and Home Rule were not met. 'Ireland has been knocking at the English door long enough with kid gloves, and now she will knock with a mailed hand,' he told a meeting of supporters in 1885, his voice trembling with passion. Unionists (so-called for their allegiance to the 1800 Act of Union by which Ireland was politically joined to the United Kingdom) referred fearfully to 'a reign of terror', and imagined themselves into the menacing landscape of the gothic horror that Irish novelists made so convincingly their own (culminating in Bram Stoker's *Dracula*, whose early title, *The Dead Un-Dead*, was an appropriate metaphor for the impossible reality in which many Anglo-Irish found themselves).

Gibson, elevated to the peerage as the first Baron Ashbourne upon his appointment as Lord Chancellor, was swift to make his mark as 'the keeper of the Queen's Irish conscience'. It may have been the ominous sense of threat from an enveloping Catholic nationalism, or he may have undergone some genuine soul-searching since his curt portrayal of Irish tenants enjoying the locust years, or it may have been pure political calculation (Westminster was now dominated by long and highly combustible debates on Ireland), but within the space of a few days in early July 1885 he single-handedly drafted an act – the Land Purchase Act, soon commonly known as Lord Ashbourne's Act –

which conferred on Irish tenants opportunities of purchasing their holdings on favourable terms. This was Ashbourne's solution to the question of Home Rule: kill it with kindness. Governance from Westminster should continue, not by repression, but by gradual reform aimed at improving the circumstances of Ireland's people.

The Act sealed Ashbourne's reputation as a paternalistic conservative, a servant of the Crown devoted to the Act of Union but also to the inalienable rights (or at least some of them) of its subject population. Ashbourne had his detractors, of course – those who refused to concede that the Crown had the right to gift what didn't belong to it. Within Ashbourne's own family, the tension developed into a painful and unresolvable conflict, for prominent among those who disagreed with him was his own son and heir, Willie. As decided in his Irish nationalism as the father was in his Unionism, Willie loathed British rule with all its 'hideous, patronising, doctrinaire, all-for-Ireland's-good, little measured out globules of remedies', as Alice James memorably characterised it.

Edward Gibson had married the nineteen-year-old Frances Colles, of County Meath, in 1868. In that year, she produced his heir, William, followed by seven children within a decade – Henry (Harry), Elizabeth (Elsie), Edward, Ernest (known by his second name, Victor), Frances, Violet (Vizie), born in 1876, and finally Constance. In 1872, Gibson's father died, leaving him a very rich man. The value of the estate was published in the newspapers as £61,000 (roughly £4 million today), 'besides landed property'. 'What an awful lot of money I suppose you will have,' Frances wrote to her 'darling husband', who was away at the time. 'It really almost frightens me to think of it.'

Energised by his fortune, his professional success and his numerous offspring, Gibson was 'a thoroughly domesticated man', devoted to his wife and children, enjoying their company to an extent rare among the politicians of his generation. But, despite his desire to spend as much time as possible with them, events often forced the family to separate. In these periods, the children were pursued by a steady stream of letters from their anxious father. Reunions were joyous but emotionally tumultuous affairs, his presence inextricably associated with his absence. Interviewed in 1883, he was observed 'amusing his little daughters, one of whom [Violet] is sitting on his knees, and trying to divert his attention from the Parliamentary Reports of the last night's debate, to admire her doll'. Such diversionary tactics met with limited success. 'He has', another journalist commented, 'a wonderful power of abstraction, and conversation does not in the least disturb him.'

For Violet, especially, his abstraction was a void, a well of darkness in what Virginia Woolf described as 'that great cathedral space which was childhood'. To be simultaneously doted on and ignored was muddling, an unwanted extra confusion in the journeywork of growing up. Of all the children, Violet seems to have adopted the most striking strategies for dealing with this ambivalence. 'She showed signs, even as a little girl, of a peculiar temperament,' her younger sister Constance remembered. 'She was hysterical and impatient of restraint, would fly into the most awful tempers, over the least trifle, and often lost control of herself.' W. B. Yeats once observed that children 'weep, like geniuses, tears upon tears for some dead Orpheus of whom they have dreamt and pass with wondering indifference, like geniuses, among the sorrows of their own household'. Violet was never equipped with this wondering indifference.

Violet may have learned to stamp her feet to get attention (when Lucia Joyce did the same, her father James referred to her 'King Lear scenes'), but she also learned the ways befitting a young Honourable, the title she acquired, aged nine, when her father became a peer. She was a beautiful girl, very finely built with pre-Raphaelite features, diminutive proportions (her adult height was five feet one inch), thoughtful grey eyes. She sang well and loved art, both interests that she had the leisure to indulge. Her education, conducted at home by governesses, encompassed little else. There was also travel, to broaden the mind. When she was ten, she visited Italy for the first time, taking in Venice and the Italian Lakes, to which she returned regularly each spring for several years. In the summer months, the family decamped to a small estate near Boulogne-sur-Mer, taken by Lord Ashbourne on a long lease in the mid-1880s. Violet learned to speak excellent French, and encouraged her father in the same. Here was an opportunity, against the competing claims of her many siblings, for communicating with him exclusively, for harnessing his distraction to her own needs. But he never mastered the language.

When he became Lord Chancellor, the new Lord Ashbourne acquired a huge annual salary of £8,000 (equivalent to £640,000 today), a seat in cabinet, a family crest ('on a bank a pelican in her piety') and a motto, taken from the Psalms: *Coelestes pandite portae*, 'Open, O Ye Heavenly Gates'. Certainly, the Ashbournes knew little of the earth-floored slums north of the Liffey, or of the murky north-side suburbs later anatomised by James Joyce in *Dubliners*. Dublin's poor were among the worst-fed and worst-housed in Europe, with an adult mortality rate beaten only by cities like Trieste and Rio de Janeiro. Living conditions were 'spectacularly destitute', with twenty-five per cent of families living in one-room tenements occupied by more than four people. For the Lord Chancellor's family, 'immured behind the stockade of Protestant respectability', the immiseration, the upheavals in the countryside, the murders and mass arrests, were held at bay. They were the noises-off to a closed-circuit life of balls, entertainments and jollity, to which the house on Merrion Square was magnificently suited.

In the leather-bound albums (diligently compiled by Constance) is an article from *The World* captioned 'Celebrities at Home', in which the reporter describes a breathless tour of the Merrion Square residence, wondrously mapping out a house crammed with riches: Chippendale furniture, Empire writing-tables, Sheraton sideboards, ornate Italian stucco-work, Dresden china. At the top of the first flight of stairs was 'a delightful alcove especially built by Lord Ashbourne to receive the beautiful white Carrara marble statue of Paolo and Francesca da Rimini . . . an exquisite specimen of sculpture, and highly prized by Lord Ashbourne, who purchased it at the Milan Art Exhibition in 1872'. There were ceilings by Adam; Bartolozzi engravings, 'much prized by Lady Ashbourne, who is a keen collector herself'; a dining room in crimson and white seating forty; a library containing comfortable Chesterfield and easy chairs and a large desk. Books and bric-a-brac were everywhere, and there were cut flowers in profusion. The impression is of a house given over to formal entertaining, to the acquisition of beautiful objects, but also, in the less stuffy atmosphere of the library, to use by all the family, to relaxation and recreation.

The hallway gave evidence of another pastime. It was adorned with swords, muskets, pistols, blunderbusses 'and other less civilised weapons'. Violet's brother Harry was a first-rate shot with rifle and pistol. His old school magazine reported that 'he narrowly escaped having to fight a duel with a Frenchman, his opponent in a competition, because he had thoughtlessly fired with the left hand, which he could use equally well with the right'. Violet may have learned something about shooting from him, and from the array of arms that hung in the hallway at Merrion Square.

Violet at age seventeen, shortly before being presented at court as a debutante.

IV

The Problem of Being

The principal aspiration for Lord Ashbourne's daughters was that they should marry well and thus consolidate the family's Anglo-Protestant respectability. In this, Elsie and Frances both proved high achievers: Elsie married William, fifth Baron Bolton of Bolton Castle in 1893, and Frances married Alexander Horsbrugh-Porter, son of Sir Andrew Porter, in 1904. Unmarried daughters were expected to stay at home and look after their parents, a role the youngest daughter Constance, true to her name (or perhaps hostage to it), assumed with disciplined devotion. Violet, determined to escape either destiny, was to take an altogether different path.

The training for these roles was simple: education at home until the age of twelve; reading (not too much, as this could create an excess of independent thought); languages; social graces (a well-executed curtsey went a long way, as did a firm but good manner with servants). There was also needlework, an activity Virginia Woolf learned to loathe as symbolising a kind of mindless passivity. There were no seventeenth-century women poets, she argued, because Shakespeare's sister was too busy mending stockings or tending to the stew. Alice James, whose considerable literary talents were eclipsed by the fame of her brothers, confided to her diary the hobbling powerlessness of this passivity. She described how she 'tried to sit immovable reading in the library with waves of violent inclination suddenly invading my muscles taking on some of their myriad forms such as throwing myself out of the window, or knocking off the head of the benignant pater as he sat with his silver locks writing at his table'. Similar conditions prevailed at Merrion Square. From the 'Celebrities at Home' article in *The World*, we learn that 'Lord Ashbourne generally works in the midst of his family in the "green" room, which is most frequently used when they are all sitting together. Some of his most important speeches and judgments were written there.' The benignant pater, like Mr James, sat at his desk, his silver locks falling over his papers and notebooks while the young Violet struggled with the volcanic substrata of her emotions until they finally detonated in the 'most awful tempers', to the horror of her family.

Unlike her sisters, who enjoyed strong constitutions (Frances was a keen hockey player, a passion she ranked alongside 'mathematics and keeping pets'), Violet was an extremely frail child, condemned to observe energy rather than expend it. Ironically, the sheer frustration of this predicament most likely produced the energetic tantrums that were frowned on by medical (not to mention social) convention. Her illnesses – scarlet fever at five, prolonged peritonitis at fourteen, pleurisy at sixteen, rubella at twenty – made her different, set her apart from her siblings, creating the expectation that hers was to be a life of the swoon and the chaise longue on which she must lie 'like a piece of timber', as Virginia Woolf put it. Taking up this theme of life bypassing the invalid, Alice James railed against the contradictions produced by the combination of a lively intellect and a weak body:

I seem perfectly grotesque to myself, a wretched, shrivelled, alien enclosed between four walls, with such an extraordinary disproportion between what is felt and what is heard and seen . . . an emotional volcano within, with the outward reverberation of a mouse and the physical significance of a chip of lead-pencil.

Reflecting on this terrible disjunction, Florence Nightingale recorded that as a very young child she had 'an obsession' that she was 'not like other people'. She was 'a monster'; that was her 'secret which might at any moment be found out'. Her autobiographical novel *Cassandra* (written in 1852, but not published in her lifetime) was a scathing analysis of the stresses and conventions that drove so many Victorian women to silence, depression, illness, even lunatic asylums and death. Reading it in the late 1920s, Virginia Woolf thought it was more like screaming than writing.

The crushing suppression of possibility. What to do? More needlework? A jigsaw? Take up a book? At a time when women's rights were still a peripheral topic, few were able to break out. Nightingale, famously, lit the way, repudiating conventional society and the frustrations of the Victorian female role, as did the Irish aristocrat Maud Gonne after her. There were other rebels, who toiled to secure the status of licensed freethinkers. The Anglo-Irish cousins Edith Somerville and (Violet) Martin Ross, who refused their male suitors and earned their own living by writing (as Somerville and Ross, *The Real Charlotte, Some Experiences of an Irish R.M.*); who took photographs of each other naked on the beach, their cinched waists, twenty inches, showing their fascination with stays; and rode out to hunt – Martin, short-sighted but sans spectacles, getting completely lost, and rarely able to see the jumps until she was already flying through the air, and getting her hair painfully tangled in low-hanging branches and afterwards wishing she were bald. There was Eileen Gray, an Irish–Scots aristocrat born in County Wexford in 1878, who set off for Paris where she embarked on bisexuality and a distinguished career as a designer. And Freya Stark, whose early impatience with stuffy family rites (she would abscond from boring picnics on Dartmoor by galloping off on her pony) developed into adventurous solitary journeys in the Middle East and many acclaimed books.

But such adventures were, in the main, reserved for men, whose ambitions and desires the world was organised to satisfy. Violet's brothers, schooled at Wellington, Harrow, Trinity Dublin, Cambridge, Oxford, were accustomed to action. They were the elite corps of the 'Anglo-Saxon fraternity', bearers of a sacred trust, as the headmaster of Harrow, the Reverend Welldon, reminded himself: 'An English headmaster, as he looks to the future of his pupils, will not forget that they are to be the citizens of the greatest Empire under heaven . . . he will inspire them with faith in the divinely ordered mission of their country and their race.'

It was in this spirit that Victor Gibson left Ireland in the spring of 1900 to fight in the Boer War. A dashing thrill-seeker and man-about-town, Victor was the sergeant and founder of the 45th Dublin Company, or Irish Hunt contingent. The men of this hastily assembled mounted battalion, dressed in Norfolk jackets and felt hats, and paying their own passage to South Africa, were regarded as 'the social and political show-piece of the new Volunteer Army'. The Earl of Longford and Viscount Ennismore joined, as did two companies of Ulster Protestant Unionists including the Earl of Leitrim, a whiskey baronet, and a group of English and Irish gadflies who were happy to convert both them-selves and their hunting equipment – horses, clothing and sad-dlery – into assets in the British imperial cause.

What started as a great adventure for the twenty-five-year-old Victor quickly ripened into disaster. On 31 May, his company, along with the entire 13th battalion of the Imperial Yeomanry, was captured by the Boers at Lindley. 'There was a gallant Last Stand,' writes the historian Thomas Pakenham, a descendant of the Earl of Longford, whose textbook die-hard conduct ensured the debacle that followed. 'With blood streaming from wounds at the neck, face, and wrists, [Longford] ordered his men to fight to the end. "I knew it to be madness," Victor Gibson later said, "and so did everyone else, I think, but not a man refused."' The Boer bag totalled about 530 men, including the seriously wounded Longford, Lords Ennismore, Leitrim, and Donoughmore and the Honourable Victor Gibson. The whiskey baronet was killed, hopefully under the influence of his own malt. The wounded were left at Lindley, and the other prisoners were marched northwards to the eastern Transvaal, away from the twenty thousand British troops trying to rescue them.

In London and Dublin news of the Lindley fiasco was met with horror. 'The utmost anxiety now prevails', reported *The Times* on 7 June. Later that month, intelligence reached the War Office that the bulk of prisoners, including Victor, were 'stated to have been in good health'. For the Ashbournes, there was little to do but wait for further, scarce bulletins. In this atmosphere of nerve-racking suspense they resolved to press on with plans for the wedding of Edward, which event took place on 15 August 1900, with Violet as bridesmaid, clutching her bouquet of pink malmaison carnations. Victor excepted, the Ashbournes were all present, their family now enlarged by the marriage of Willie in 1896 to Marianne de Monbrison, of French Huguenot descent, and of Elsie to Lord Bolton in 1893, a union that had already produced three children. Three months after being captured, Victor and the remainder of his shattered battalion were finally released, sailing home on 26 September in the *Carisbrooke Castle*.

By this time, the Boer War was aligning Irish nationalism along a broad front. Decrying British policy in South Africa as a repeat of the colonisation of Ireland, nationalists like Maud Gonne advocated the bombing of British troopships. Together with her friend and collaborator Arthur Griffith, Gonne formed the Transvaal Committee, one of whose first acts was the vote to give the freedom of the city of Dublin to Paul Kruger, president of South Africa and the face of Boer resistance to the British. The committee later evolved into Cumann na nGaedhael (Society of the Gaels), and later still into Sinn Féin ('Ourselves' or 'Our Own Thing'). The war also deepened the furrows within the Ashbourne family. Where Lord Ashbourne was a conservative, a Unionist, a passionate exponent of British imperialism (in whose cause he had almost lost a son), Willie, his heir, was a nationalist who identified himself with its victims. He was everything the father was not: liberal, a Home-Ruler, pro-Boer.

Willie wanted to become Irish in a decolonised Ireland, to naturalise himself, as if his real nature could never be satisfactorily expressed until he did. To this end, in his early twenties he had adopted Gaelic dress – saffron cloak, green stockings, belt with large silver buckles and kilt, in the sporran of which, it was rumoured, he housed a tortoise. He wore his hair long to his shoulders, like a tribal chief of ancient lore. (Yeats, in London, wore the black cloak of a professional Celt, leading the satirist George Moore to quip that he looked like an umbrella left behind after a picnic). After meeting him for the first time, one acquaintance wrote: '[He is] a half hatched philosopher & saint who . . . has the eyes of a Melanchthon but the mouth & wit of a Paddy . . . He has the worst clothes of any philosopher I've met.'

Willie's chosen language, even for private prayer, was Gaelic – 'It is one of the chief trials of my life', he once said, 'to be called on to speak English.' George Bernard Shaw, on the other hand, liked to boast that, 'being an Irishman', he couldn't speak Gaelic, which he dismissed as one of the many 'Nationalist inventions [which] are not Irish at all'. Shaw enjoyed pointing out that the Gaelic League, which promoted the revival of an 'indomitable Irishry', was founded in London by Irishmen (including Willie) who had chosen emigration – hence 'Wild Geese' – over the scandals and low politics which convulsed their country. This was true. Willie's first marital home was near Dorking, Surrey, where he cut a strange figure striding across the fields in his kilt, or teeing off at the local golf course. But Ireland's pull was irresistible: the Wild Geese returned, either in person or in their imaginations, time and time again. Exile, for them, was the nursery of nationality – Oscar Wilde's years as a student in Oxford strengthened his conviction that an Irishman only discovers himself when he goes abroad. At home he 'had but learnt the pathetic weakness of nationality, but in a strange land realised what indomitable forces nationality possesses'. W. B. Yeats, who followed Wilde and Shaw to London in the 1880s, rapidly became depressed at how self-conscious Celts there were turned into mere entertainers, so he returned to Dublin and worked to shift the centre of gravity of Irish culture back to the native capital.

The Abbey Theatre (1904), the Gaelic League (1893), the Irish Literary Society (1891) and the Gaelic Athletic Association (1884): these were the constituent parts of the Irish Risorgimento, the 'return to the source' which sought to make Ireland once again interesting to the Irish. Shaw might dismiss the Gaelic League as a kind of stage Irish invention, where Irishness was idealised as barefoot children and turf fires, but it was arguably modern Ireland's first mass democratic organisation, dedicating itself not only to reviving the Irish language, but to workers' education (it was responsible for organising the first great industrial parades held on St Patrick's Day) and gender equality (the small but influential Irish feminist movement used Gaelicist channels). There were only six books in print in Irish at the founding of the Gaelic League, and most Irish speakers in the countryside were still illiterate. In just one year, the League sold fifty thousand textbooks and registered thousands in language classes. By 1904, its membership much boosted by the nationalist tide brought on by the Boer War, it had become a crucible for ideas about a culturally and politically revived Ireland, where national pride and economic prosperity could be recovered. Attending its meetings were Michael Collins, a post-office clerk who became one of the most lethal guerrilla commanders of the new century; Desmond FitzGerald, 1916 rebel and minister of the first Free State Government; Pádraic Ó Conaire, author of the first novel in the Irish language; Erskine Childers, Anglo-Irish author of *The Riddle of the Sands* who later ran arms for nationalist revolutionaries; and Willie Gibson, son of the Lord Chancellor of Ireland.

There were women, too. Constance Markiewicz, née Gore-Booth, with her sister Eva one of Yeats's 'two girls in silk kimonos' dreaming of 'some vague Utopia'. Markiewicz, a countess by marriage, was a Sinn Féiner who later took part in the 1916 Easter Rising, for which she earned a death sentence (commuted because of her sex). And Maud Gonne, Yeats's impossible love, who shuttled between London, Paris and Dublin – a dislocated, peripatetic, unstable existence. But her deep belief in self-sacrifice for the cause tied her inexorably to Ireland, as did her unwavering identification with 'the people' (her idea of which was based, as with many upper-class rebels, on memories of servants who had been kind to her). Gonne's antics earned her the derision of many of her class, to whom she exemplified a sort of *trahison des débutantes*. 'A great red-haired yahoo of a woman', they called her – unfairly, for she was well-bred and beautiful. But this was the price she paid for scorning the expectations of her class and sex.

Others travelled in different dimensions. At thirty, Florence Nightingale's Cassandra realises that her passion, intellect, and moral energy have been destroyed by

... the petty obligations, genteel rituals, and religious cant of a mindless social code. Inspired by a divine vision, she tries to emulate the life of Christ, to become the saviour whose suffering will awaken other women from their thrall. But society calls her mad and will not listen to her prophecies, and she dies unregarded.

Violet, a beautiful if fragile debutante, raised to be little more than an ornament, had already taken the first steps in this direction.

V

The New Mystics

On 1 February 1866, an American woman slipped and fell on an icy pavement in New Hampshire. Her name was Mary Baker Eddy, and she was to identify this event as the inauguration of Christian Science. Eddy, who was forty-five, claimed to have nearly died as a result of the fall – a claim strongly disputed in testimony from her attending physician – and to have been miraculously restored to life when 'the healing Truth dawned upon [her] senses'. Up to this point, Eddy, who had been chronically ill all her life, had been terribly misled as to the nature of physical illness. The truth that struck her on the icy pavement was that illness didn't actually exist: sickness, death, and even the body were only *imagined*. It was a 'scientific certainty that all causation rests with the Mind, and that every effect is a mental phenomena [*sic*]'.

Eddy claimed to have the power of healing, called Divine Science, though she never provided any tangible proof of it. But the idea that illness was an illusion that could be dispelled by mental adjustment and discipline in the form of daily prayer and exercise was a compelling incentive for many, especially women whose chief experience of life was one of lassitude, of lying about with folded hands, cosseting their listless or recalcitrant bodies. Craving a source of inner strength, many found it in Eddy's seminal work, *Science and Health*. 'I read the first chapter on Prayer. It was just like the conversion of St Paul,' recalled the Protestant Nancy Astor, who after years of ill health and 'nervous disorders' underwent a Damascene revelation. 'Here I found the answer to all my questions . . . If I was spiritual I would not have to suffer in the flesh, I learned. It was like a new beginning for me. My life really was made over.' Nancy took to taking cold baths in the

morning and standing on her head, and the regimen seemed to
work, her nervous afflictions relegated to the past. Visitors to
Cliveden did not escape her missionary zeal. Bibles would turn up
on the arms of their chairs, innocently marked with passages
thought relevant to Mrs Eddy's doctrines. Her children were subjected to a process of 'intense religious indoctrination', though
in the end it proved counter productive, largely owing to the
intransigence of its advocate. Her son, Michael, agreed with Mark
Twain's judgement that it was all 'Eddygush'. Yes. But by the
1910s, the Christian Science Church had made Mrs Eddy –
dubbed '*the* monumental hysteric' – the richest woman in
America, and boasted over a million members. Violet's mother,
Lady Ashbourne, became an ardent follower, perhaps drawn like
so many others by the promise of physical, as well as spiritual,
wellbeing. In the photograph taken at Howth Castle in 1897,
when she was thirty-eight, Lady Ashbourne appears strong – but
domestic life had apparently drained her health (or her will), as
hints a letter written by Elsie to Violet many years later: 'I think
she was fond of all of us, but there were so many and she wasn't
very strong.' The peculiar mélange of Protestantism and Christian
Science was accommodated in the Ashbourne household without
strain. One newspaper described Lady Ashbourne as 'an earnest
Christian Scientist' whose 'house is the meeting place of many of
the Irish adherents of that cult'.

Merrion Square was a rich setting for such activity, just as
Cliveden was. Frances, the hockey-playing daughter, was also a
member and worked for a time as the Dublin correspondent of
the *Christian Science Monitor*. Violet, with her depressing résumé
of maladies, seemed an ideal recruit. But she didn't like it. The
much-vaunted health benefits didn't materialise for her, and she
found the whole atmosphere surrounding Christian Science
insufferable. In this, her experience echoed that of Michael Astor.
His memories of the Cliveden of his childhood were of 'a place of
lyrical beauty'. But behind 'its brilliant social façade' he came to
see another world, one of 'moral abjuration', a world 'united

uneasily by the voice of parental authority', 'increasingly stultify-
ing', from which he was 'determined to escape'. For Violet,
Merrion Square became just such a place – queasy with frustration
and enclosure, crowded with family and cultists. No room to
move, just somewhere to move from. She came to loathe
Christian Science as a 'a small body of utterly unscrupulous liars'
who deserved to be 'swept off the face of the earth'. In time, she
would remove herself from her family in order to get away from it.

Violet's flight from Mary Baker Eddy's cult took her towards
another spiritual leader: Helena Blavatsky, the charismatic
founder of Theosophy. Blavatsky was a compulsive confuser of
fact with fiction, whose imaginative outline of her life included
claims to have ridden bareback in the circus, toured Serbia as a
concert pianist, opened an ink factory in Odessa, worked as an
interior decorator for Empress Eugénie, and fought with
Garibaldi's army in the Battle of Mentana. But the central event
of her *Wanderjahre* was a meeting with a dematerialising Tibetan
called Master Morya. It was this encounter that alerted Blavatsky
to the existence of the 'Secret Doctrine' – the key to the truth of
life itself. Who better to mediate this wisdom to the world than
Blavatsky herself? Hastily synthesising oriental religion, reincarnation, Western magic, Asian scripture and Rosicrucian, Masonic
and Templar mythology, in 1875 she came up with Theosophy, an
amalgam of rubbish wrapped up as an appealing obscurity. Its followers were ambitiously charged with the duty of collecting and
diffusing 'knowledge of the laws which govern the universe'. The
history of organised occultism in the West was born.

Realists, Oscar Wilde once complained, 'have sold our
birthright for a mess of facts'. The attraction of a mystical – or
magical – consciousness for people seeking relief from the oppres-
sion of mere facts supplied Theosophy with a rich recruiting
ground. The London Theosophical Society included many upper-
class neophytes, among them Lady Emily Lutyens (wife of architect Edwin Lutyens), and the Countess of Caithness, who lived in

a palace in Nice and dressed like Mary Queen of Scots, of whom she claimed to be the reincarnation. Anna Kingsford, president of Theosophy's London Lodge, was visited by Joan of Arc, the Virgin Mary, Anne Boleyn, and Swedenborg's wraith, who mentioned in passing that Jesus had revived Confucianism. Kingsford also had visions that came to her in trances or dreams. Sometimes she saw her own inner organs – a useful aid in diagnosing her illnesses (she had many, both organic and psychosomatic).

Helena Blavatsky settled in London's Holland Park in spring 1887, and there received a stream of distinguished guests, including W. B. Yeats, who took the revival of eastern wisdom very seriously and investigated a wide range of esoteric 'sciences' including cheirosophy (palmistry), celestial dynamics (astrology), chromopathy (healing by colours) and polygraphics (a form of automatic writing). Yeats's interest 'in life and its shadow', his rejection of empirical 'realities' in favour of 'truth' was wryly commented on by Virginia Woolf: 'Neither religion nor science explains the world. The occult does explain it. Has seen things. His coat hanger advanced across the room one night. Then a coat on it, illuminated; then a hand in it.' In 1890, he was asked to resign from the Theosophical Society after he organised a committee to raise the ghost of a flower from its ashes, an experiment deemed to be disruptive. He transferred his loyalty to a magical fraternity called the Hermetic Order of the Golden Dawn (of which Bram Stoker, a strong believer in the occult, was rumoured to be a member).

Fin de siècle, mal du siècle. Charles Darwin didn't invent doubt, but he certainly accelerated it, amplified its possibilities. His theories made impossible demands on a Christian belief system that held the world to have been created in six days. If God was leaving by the front door, moony-eyed Madame Blavatsky was rustling in through the back, promising to convert doubt into expectation. Much of her drawing-power rested on the sensational inducements of claims to occult communion with the Great White Brotherhood of Masters. (When asked how he was able to forecast turns in the price of stocks, the railway tycoon Cornelius Vanderbilt famously answered: 'Do as I do. Consult the spirits!') With its almost limitless claims to be the touchstone for the hidden phenomena of life, Theosophy readily serviced the suggestible, the hysterical, the unhinged. But it is also true that not all its adherents fit this stereotype. Many embraced the first object of its statement of purpose, the concrete aim of building a universal brotherhood 'without distinction of race, creed, sex, caste or colour'. It was a daring concept, one that intersected with contemporary radical thought. Feminists rallied to it as the one 'religion' that between the 1890s and 1920s consistently advocated equality of the sexes; and socialists and Fabians were happily pressed into its campaign against materialism (in *The Key to Theosophy*, Madame Blavatsky described Jesus and the Buddha as 'preaching most unmistakably Socialism of the noblest and highest type, self-sacrifice to the bitter end').

In this, Theosophy, more than Christian Science's cult of self-absorption, answered to Violet's longings, to her philosophical and political consciousness that, owing much to Willie's influence, was taking shape as a form of ethical socialism. Still held, if only by a thread of filial obedience, to both Protestantism and Christian Science, as soon as she turned twenty-one she embarked on a series of journeys to the Theosophical Society's 'lodges' in Switzerland, Germany and France. Helena Blavatsky had outlined the foundations of a New Jerusalem, and Violet wanted to be part of it.

VI

La Femme Qui Cherche

Theosophy established itself as a significant and enduring presence in Violet's psyche. But she never fully embraced it. Intellectually and emotionally, she was still reaching for something that lay beyond her grasp. She left no record of her travels in this period, of her discoveries and disappointments. We peer into a room and search for her. Here? No, not here. She has already passed through, leaving only the lightest impression of her presence. 'Here is one room: there another.' That is the mystery.

And then she reappears. On 28 July 1902, buried deep in a lengthy column in *The Times* titled 'Ecclesiastical Intelligence', is the announcement that Violet Gibson had become a Catholic. She was twenty-six. Thereafter – and as a direct consequence of this decision – her appearances in the society columns of *The Times* would be few. Indeed, until she shot Mussolini in 1926, there was to be very little about her that was deemed worth mentioning (in contrast to her sisters, Frances, Elsie and Constance, who continued to flower as society fixtures).

In the contemporary vernacular, Violet's was not a conversion, but a 'perversion', as in 'turning the wrong way' – a usage not necessarily linked to sexual deviance at that time, though in the context of attacks on Catholics it often was. *Palmer's Index to The Times* catalogues under the heading of 'perversion' seventy-six columns about the conversion to Catholicism of one or more notable persons between 1830 and 1902. There are an additional fifty-seven columns filed under 'Perverts to Rome' between 1843 and 1859. In one, 'perversion' is shown spreading to an entire family like an infection: 'The theological change was first completed in the minds of two daughters, who, with the zeal of new converts, never ceased until they had brought over their parents and the other members of the family'; or, in a column headlined 'A Pervert Converted', it is described turning back on itself in the double-helix story of an Anglican archdeacon who became and then unbecame a Catholic: 'The church of Rome was then only contemplated from without – he now sees it in all its error and defilement within.' When John Henry (later Cardinal) Newman embraced the Church of Rome in 1845, he was attacked by evangelical Protestants as having been drawn into too close an association with the seductive powers of papism (described in one much-circulated pamphlet as being as 'deadly' as 'prussic acid and arsenic'). His conversion was constructed as a form of violence, 'at the intersection of national invasion and rape'.

Ironically, it was Catholics who often viewed converts with the most circumspection. Like Dr Catacomb in Ronald Knox's story *Barchester Pilgrimage*, many English Catholics 'never thought of a convert but as a bird which had flown into the room by accident, to the embarrassment of the occupants'. Or Clive Heron in Antonia White's *Beyond the Glass*: 'I don't believe it's possible for anyone to *become* a Catholic . . . I don't approve of conversions . . . or de-conversions for that matter. One should remain in one's situation.' Catholicism, for the convert, was not cosy, safe, culturally sequestered; rather, it was hostile territory. 'I can quite see it can put one in the most agonising predicament,' Clive concedes. '"It is a fearful thing to fall into the hands of the living God". Yes, indeed.'

Violet's decision to embrace the Catholic Church was heavily influenced by her brother Willie, who had converted in 1890 while at Oxford University. Attaching himself to a group of liberal Catholic, or 'Modernist' thinkers, Willie took his adopted Church to task over its increasingly authoritarian and reactionary stance.*

---

* Willie was a founder of Oxford's Roger Bacon Society, closely identifying with the medieval English philosopher and scientist who was condemned and imprisoned by the Church for his heretical beliefs.

The Modernists saw themselves as defenders of the true faith as informed by the teachings of Gospels rather than the dictates of Rome – a faith they saw as best served by adaptation, rather than resistance, to the forces of progress. The Vatican responded by denouncing the Modernist challenge as a dangerous heresy and took steps to silence increasingly vocal dissidents, including the Irish Jesuit theologican George Tyrrell, who was an intimate friend of Willie's.

Tyrrell, a Dublin-born convert, argued that the Pope must not be an absolute autocrat, but rather a 'spokesman for the mind of the Holy Spirit in the Church'. Tyrrell also claimed 'the right of each age to adjust the historico-philosophical expression of Christianity to contemporary certainties, and thus to put an end to this utterly needless conflict between faith and science which is a mere theological bogey'. This was the Modernist case in a nut-shell, and for giving it unlicensed expression, Tyrrell was formally disciplined by the Vatican. More severe punishments followed: in 1896 he was unseated from his chair of philosophy at Stonyhurst College, and ten years later he was expelled from the Jesuit order and excommunicated. After his death in 1909 he was denied burial in a Catholic cemetery. A priest who was present at his interment made a sign of the cross over Tyrrell's grave, for which act he was censured by his bishop.

Tyrrell's reputation for integrity in the face of such violent sanctions earned him many followers across Europe (including the Italian Modernist, Father Ernesto Buonaiuti, whom Italian police later identified as a possible conspirator in Violet's attempt on Mussolini). His influence on Willie was deeply felt. In May 1899, Willie published a journal article in which he aired Tyrrell's criticism of Catholic apologetics as being irrelevant to the realities of the modern world. The following month, Cardinal Merry del Val, an ardent Spanish anti-Modernist, responded by challenging Willie's commitment to the Church, speculating that he seemed 'to be walking through [it] on his way elsewhere, like the people walk through S. Stefan's cathedral in Vienna, going in by one door and out by the other to make a short cut'. Some three decades later, del Val enjoyed the particular satisfaction of being sent in person by the Pope to congratulate Mussolini after Willie's sister had failed to kill him.

The Modernist cause was both a theological challenge and a social reform movement. Inspired by the doctrine of the Incarnation, which demonstrated Christ's compassion for the *whole* person, body and soul, it evolved into a Christian socialist mission to care for the poor. Willie, like many young men from Oxford and Cambridge who answered the call to become 'squires in the slums', entered warmly into social work in the London districts of Southwark and Kennington, areas crammed with ruinous tenements, workhouses, asylums and hospitals, where over a million people (equivalent to the entire population of Scotland) lived in 'pestilential human rookeries' whose horrors recalled those of the slave ships. This was the 'Darkest England' of Salvation Army founder William Booth's 1890 tract, *In Darkest England and the Way Out*.

Following Willie's example, even down to the choice of the priest who converted her, Violet worked hard at developing a social and political conscience within the context of Modernist belief. In London, she visited with Willie the most derelict areas and gave alms to the poor. Later, in Rome, she would do the same, this time on her own. *De haut en bas*, old habits die hard: unlike her contemporary, the Irish–Scots aristocrat Eileen Gray, who abandoned her title, deeming 'The Honourable' as suitable 'only for operettas', Violet persisted in using hers.

Willie was no St Francis. Well known and respected in London's slums – he was 'greatly loved by all', according to one admirer – he commuted with ease from Southwark to Mayfair, sometimes attending receptions with his parents who, though dismayed at his conversion, persisted yet in tolerating him in their world. Such leniency, while it lasted, was surprising. The Anglo-Irish elite was historically reluctant to compromise with Catholics, and its more conservative members were still psychologically in thrall to the 1792 declaration of the Dublin Corporation: 'We consider the Protestant ascendancy to consist of a Protestant king in Ireland, a Protestant parliament, a Protestant hierarchy, Protestant electors and government, the benches of justice, the army and revenue, through all their branches and details, Protestant.' But Willie was the Ashbourne heir, and perhaps his parents maintained the hope that he would eventually fulfil their expectations.

There was no quarter given to Violet, who was placed square in an agonising predicament. She had not intended her conversion to be a total negation of her parents' values, though it was certainly a refutation of the hybrid religious grid on which her mother pirouetted. Either way, she knew that the consequences would be extreme. Writing to her father, she described the painful and protracted difficulties that attended her decision:

For a whole year I have been bothering myself over religion, and can now see no way out of becoming a Catholic. I have had a terrible time since giving up Christian Science. For some months afterwards I did not miss it so much, because [a friend] discovered how unhappy I was and left nothing undone to make me happier. Sometimes he wrote twice a day to me. And so [. . .] he did not let me think too much.

In a rare confession of her wounds, she added, 'Nobody realised that I was in any trouble and required care. I can't bear to talk of that dreadful time of loneliness and weakness.'

For several years before her conversion, Violet had been living on her own, supported by a private income from her father. Willie, whom she adored, had taken her under his wing, tutored her in the philosophical and doctrinal debates of Modernism, involved her in his social work in London. But none of this could compensate for the paternal sympathy or understanding she yearned for. It was not forthcoming. Lord Ashbourne was horrified by her decision. 'I am *very* sincerely sorry if you will mind my becoming a Catholic,' she pleaded with him.

I hated the idea myself for a long time, but gradually saw that it was mere prejudice which was keeping me back. The two principal reasons on which I am going over are: 1. that the Church is *one*, *apostolic* and *united*, and that it bears good fruit; 2. that it is the religion of the *Incarnation*. I have come to the conclusion that the Incarnation is the *great* fact, a stupendous one, which Christian Science has not taken into consideration.

Religion can act as a psychological prop, a compensation for rootlessness and emotional disarray – and Violet certainly had experience of this. Her attempts, sometimes melodramatic (the temper tantrums as a child), to attract her father's love may have been displaced into a different paternal relationship – in place of filiation, affiliation with God as father. But there was also an intellectual hunger for a substantive truth, one that superimposed on intense personal cravings a set of non-negotiable obligations. As T. S. Eliot argues in 'Thoughts after Lambeth', 'Youth' will be more attracted to 'a difficult religion than to an easy one', a religion that has not been 'robbed of the severity of its demands'.

Lord Ashbourne was not – would never be – persuaded. His disapproval was deep and abiding. Violet's mooring knots were slipped, her safe anchorage in the Anglo-Irish ascendancy severed. The photograph taken at Howth Castle now memorialised the lost domain of her youth. She chose exile over 'the network of grudges, rejections and aspirations' that encouraged so many others of her generation to do the same. Another door was closed.

VII

L'Homme Qui Cherche

The private income Violet received from the age of twenty-one had enabled her to travel and live independently in lodgings in London or abroad. Her various addresses can be traced through Lord Ashbourne's notebooks. In 1902, the year of her conversion, he scribbled her address as Villa Pré Riant, Coppet, Lake Geneva.

Switzerland was where Violet's brother Harry spent much of his time, preparing for the annual Engadine race and, when tuberculosis attacked his lungs, airing them at lakeside resorts. It was where T. S. Eliot went with his wife Vivien to seek a cure for their nervousness. At Lausanne ('the waters of Leman') he sat down and wept. People went there to escape bad weather, accidie, taxation. In the magic mountains above Geneva, many nail-biters and hysterics – Ezra Pound's 'Dostoievskian duds worrying about their own unimportant innards' – sojourned in clinics and spas, ever mystified by their curious ailments and malaises.

These well-heeled consumptives and hypochondriacs relied on the services of maids, waiters, cleaners, bellboys, porters. This was the other Switzerland, the land of economic migrants, refugees from a life elsewhere that begrudged them even these menial roles. When Violet arrived in the dreary lakeside village of Coppet, in nearby Geneva a young man was sleeping rough on park benches, in a packing-case under a bridge, in a public lavatory, finding precarious work as a builder's labourer, or butcher's or wine-seller's boy. His name was Benito Mussolini.

Born in 1883 in the Romagna village of Dovia, near Predappio, Benito was the son of a blacksmith and a schoolteacher. So, despite his later claim that he was a 'child of the last peasant civilisation', the boast was scarcely true (he had no interest, in his youth, in developing an organic relationship with the land). At school, he was deemed violent and uncontrollable, and was eventually expelled. During one petty squabble, Benito, not yet eleven, pulled out a knife and stabbed a classmate in the hand. The future Duce was told by an outraged teacher that he had a soul as black as soot, and was then put out to sleep with the school dogs for the night, though a charitable teacher eventually rescued him. Notwithstanding these experiences – or perhaps because of them – he became a schoolmaster. His collar was nearly always dirty, his shoelaces undone, his hair long and unwashed. Pupils remembered him as '*il tiranno*', banging his fist on the desk and swearing at them. Some of them thought he was mad.

Singularly ill-suited to the profession of teaching, unable to receive or dispense the tutelage of authority, Benito began to drift. In 1902, aged nineteen, he went to Switzerland, a move which allowed him to escape military service: in Dovia, he had harangued conscripts as they marched off, singing, to do their national duty. Switzerland, 'the sausage-maker's democracy', was a haven for revolutionaries, intellectual exiles, economic migrants, and much of Benito's time there was spent with socialists and anarchists. Now was the period, to be remembered with advantage at appropriate moments thereafter (Mussolini's Agincourt, one of many), in which he had no roof over his head and did menial jobs – though often he was swiftly promoted to clerical work, and at least one contemporary noticed that this pseudo-worker's hands remained soft and white. 'I was a Bohemian in those days. I made my own rules and I did not even keep them,' Benito later bragged. His pockets were usually empty save for a nickel medallion of Karl Marx. But he didn't cadge crusts. In Geneva one day he attacked 'two English women sitting on a bench with their lunch – bread, cheese, eggs. I could not restrain myself. I threw myself upon one of the old witches and grabbed the food from her hands. If they had made the slightest resistance I would have strangled them!'

Biographers have struggled to identify the young Mussolini's belief system. Its chief characteristic has been rather grandly described as 'maximalism' – basically, a commitment to the act of revolution, as opposed to reform. State authorities being the natural enemies, it's no surprise that among Mussolini's experiences in Switzerland were trouble with the police, arrest, imprisonment, expulsion from one canton to the next, or, on one occasion, after ten days in the cells, over the border into Italy. He made his way back again and fell ill, very likely from hunger and the loneliness of exile. He read voraciously, a surfeit of Kropotkin, Marx, Schopenhauer, Nietzsche, Blanqui, Kant, Sorel (from whom he learned to style himself as '*un apostolo di violenza*'), Hegel, Spinoza – all devoured impatiently, haphazardly, so that 'his philosophical views were always the reflection of the book he had happened to read last'. It was an ill-digested macédoine of philosophy and political history, later regurgitated with disastrous consequences. As the Ukrainian socialist Angelica Balabanoff, who took Mussolini under her wing at that time, commented, 'No one could see in this bewildered and neurotic youth of twenty the man who was to rule Italy.'

And nobody could have known that the young Anglo-Irish aristocrat Violet Gibson, also exiled in Switzerland, also lonely, also traversing difficult terrain of philosophical enquiry and personal truth, would one day try to kill him.

VIII

Hoc Est Corpus Meum

Violet had gone to Switzerland in a state of anxiety and grief, following the disagreement with her parents over her conversion, and the death of the friend who had assisted her through her dark night of the soul. On the geriatric shores of Lake Geneva she found little to lift her spirits. Young, beautiful, confused, she made her way back to London, and tried to take up her former life. She bought new clothes, went to parties, even attended a few society events with her parents, who were keen to keep up appearances (and perhaps nurtured the hope that she might yet renounce her conversion). 'I was very naughty,' was her later judgement of herself. 'Worldly and sensual.' It was just as well, for the years to follow brought another heavy freight of sadness.

In April 1905, Victor's wife of just five months, Mary Wood, died suddenly. In December that year, Violet's beloved tobogganning brother Harry died, aged thirty-five, of tuberculosis. His last months had been wretched, as the disease moved to his brain. With the recently bereaved Victor in attendance at a hotel in Switzerland, he had become more and more confused, shouting out obscenities then falling into a kind of frozen swoon. 'My poor, poor brain, my poor brain', he would mutter, in between cursing his father as a 'murderer' who had leeched his lifeblood, and accusing Victor of 'using mesmeric powers and trying to kill him'. 'Poor Harry, I think he would be happier dead,' Victor wrote in a letter to Lord Ashbourne. Now he was. Shortly after, in February 1906, when the Conservatives lost the general election, Lord Ashbourne's career as Lord Chancellor of Ireland came to an abrupt end. Despite his membership of the Lords, the influence and trappings of high office were now forfeited.

In London, beset by grief and still held at arm's length by her parents, Violet drifted. She stumbled into the bohemian world of Chelsea, a place viewed with horror by Claude Batchelor in Antonia White's *Beyond the Glass* for its lurid behaviour and late-night drinking clubs, and there met a young artist, to whom she became engaged in 1908. Worldly and sensual – in Catholicism Violet had discovered the Word made Flesh; now she discovered her own incarnation as a sexual being. But in early 1909, her fiancé died suddenly. Nothing is known about him, not even his name.* Significantly, Violet never spoke about him, except in the generalised context, when interviewed by doctors or policemen, of her having had sexual relations with men. Further, her family was either ignorant of this liaison, or, more likely, inclined to dismiss it as another manifestation of Violet's waywardness. Constance, in 1927, will refer to it, but identifies the fiancé only as 'a man'. Another mystery, another empty room.

The death of this unknown artist marked the moment when Violet's romantic destiny was permanently fixed. She was thirty-three years old. There was to be no more sex, no husband, no children. Her life was to be turned over to other matters – in her own words, to 'charity and prayer'. 'I'm rather impressed by Roman Catholics,' says Richard Crayshaw in *Beyond the Glass*. 'They're so awfully in earnest about it. They let it interfere with their ordinary lives.'

It was in this earnest mood that Violet set out for Rome, to discover for the first time the holy sites of the one, true, and apostolic Church – the penitential steps, the purging votives, the ossified remains of saints displayed in glass cabinets, the miraculous virgins, the hooded processions, the drowsy chanting. Many Anglican

---

* A magazine article written in 1926 by an unidentified columnist who claimed to have known Violet at the time of her engagement (but whose knowledge of her was clearly unreliable) gives the name as Leonard Ross, an Irish amateur artist who 'dabbled' in Chelsea, but succumbed to dysentery and died in South Africa after being demobilised from an Irish regiment. If so, the dates don't fit. But it's possible Violet met Ross through her brother Victor, and that Ross died, later than 1902 (when the war ended), and as a result of illness contracted at that time. It has not been possible to find any trace of Leonard Ross.

visitors to Italy experienced this foreign ritual aesthetic as a kind of moral seduction – the Latin Mass, with its murmured incantations, the priest conjuring blood from wine, flesh from bread, his shoulders turned away from the congregation as he hunched over the unfolding miracle. The prolific anti-Catholic controversialist John Cumming recalled with a shudder that 'painfully aware as I was of the fearful principles that lurk beneath, I could scarcely help being charmed, fascinated, and arrested by the sublimity of their music, the impressiveness of their ritual, and the *tout ensemble* of a solemn and richly decorated service'. Henry James, after attending a vesper service in the church of Santa Cecilia in Rome, confessed in a letter to his mother that 'in spite of the crowded and fetid church and the revolt provoked in my mind by the spectacular Catholicism . . . I truly enjoyed the performance'.

For Violet, a pilgrim unequipped with this protecting scepticism, it was all too much. She fell ill and decided once again to return to England. By the time she reached Milan she was running a high fever and was so incapacitated that she had to telegraph home. Lord Ashbourne was alarmed enough by her report to offer to come out and retrieve her, but Violet, still bruised by his repudiation of her conversion, declined the offer. She accepted instead Constance, who shortly joined her in a hotel, where they put up for several weeks. 'My dearest Father,' Constance wrote,

Violet is much better today . . . The doctor is a quiet, practical Italian who talks English. He does not profess to understand what is wrong, but is dealing with her I think very much as he would with a case of Roman fever . . . I am reading out a life of Fra Angelico in French, which requires courage on my part and quickness of comprehension on hers to discover what on earth I am trying to say! She shows me photographs of his pictures as we go along which makes it very interesting.

Constance was blessed with a small imagination. For her, reading the life of Fra Angelico, the fifteenth-century friar who prayed in supplication before he took up a paintbrush, and 'never made a crucifix but he was bathed in tears', was a pleasant distraction. For Violet, it was an immersion in the drama of Christian mysticism, a focus for piety and the spiritual revelation of truth. 'When we read the lives of the Saints we are living in their atmosphere, and thinking their thoughts,' she wrote in a little black notebook. In the story of Fra Angelico, in his devotional paintings of Christ and the saints radiant in salmon and pomegranate and green and gold, Violet glimpsed a 'moral atmosphere' – it was in this atmosphere, she had decided, that she wanted to live her life.

A sturdy Constance took her brisk morning walks around Milan, stopping to admire statues of Cavour, d'Azeglio, Manzoni and Garibaldi, whose secular narratives she was more familiar with – 'I felt as though I was surrounded by my dearest and most intimate friends!' she wrote to her father – before returning to her mysteriously ailing sister. Violet would succumb five more times in the next year to a 'feverish illness' which doctors were unable to identify. Grief was never, apparently, considered as a possible somatic indicator.

The Italian doctor placed Violet's illness under the umbrella term 'influenza', a common designation for anything that presented as nervous exhaustion. Perceived by the male medical profession as mainly a female affliction, influenza drove many a woman to the couch. Virginia Woolf's diaries provide a running commentary: 'Her legs have gone,' she writes of Vivien Eliot. 'But what's the matter? No one knows. And so she lies in bed – can't put a shoe on.' On a holiday to Greece in 1906, Vanessa Bell became increasingly unwell and unable to cope with the journey, and spent much of the time inert. When she reached Athens she collapsed – it took a fortnight's rest and four glasses of champagne a day before she was well enough to be carried onto a boat bound for Constantinople and the Orient Express. Woolf herself was often to be found in bed, usually on her husband Leonard's instructions. At the first sign of a headache or insomnia he made her rest and stop writing. When she felt the 'Spirit of Delight', psychiatrists argued that she was in fact hypermanic after bouts of depression (as opposed, simply, to being gripped by the Spirit of Delight), and Leonard saw to it that Virginia was kept 'within the bounds of reality' – whatever that meant. But enforced rest, without writing, often made her insane with frustration, 'tied, imprisoned, inhibited'.

These nervous disorders were also diagnosed as 'hysteria', the very word making it an affliction of women. Illustrations of the nervous system in the nineteenth century were of female bodies, whereas illustrations of the muscular system were of male bodies. Nerves were inherently feminine, and women were inherently prone to nervousness. The hysterics in Sigmund Freud's and Josef Breuer's *Studies in Hysteria* (1895) were all women (though when Freud describes the talking cure as a collaboration, he refers to the hysteric as 'he', as if, in order to imagine his comrades in scientific enquiry, he must think of them as men). The Victorians turned the nervous system, as they did sexuality, into an economic model with an in–out ledger of income and expenditure. Each person had only a certain amount of nervous energy, an inherited capital fund that could more easily be depleted than replenished. 'Heedless overexertion, whether mental or physical, could drain an individual's supply, leaving an exhausted nervous system incapable of all endeavour. Failure of nervous power meant utter incapacitation.'

'Nervous'. This word started off in the language as a synonym for *strong, sinewy* and *energetic*. During the eighteenth century it had expanded to take on all the notions of an excitable, agitated, apprehensive and hypersensitive temperament. In 1869 the American physician George M. Beard came up with the term 'neurasthenia' to describe 'the morbid condition of the exhaustion of the nervous system'. As 'hysterics' began increasingly to populate the *fin de siècle*, the definition sharpened. The famous psychiatrist Henry Maudsley saw them as morally degenerate, 'believing or pretending that they cannot stand or walk', only to lie in bed all day asking for the sympathy of their anxious relatives. They were 'perfect examples of the subtlest deceit, the most ingenious lying, the most diabolic cunning, in the service of vicious impulses'.

By then, neurasthenia was clearly understood as a woman's disease, though most women patients did not name their own behaviour and feelings as nervous – more frequently the connection was made by a male relative. When men detected such nervousness in their wives or sisters or daughters, they marched them off to the nearest clinic or lunatic asylum, to be treated by nerve specialists. 'Sir Roderick Glossop . . . is always called a nerve specialist, because it sounds better,' wrote P. G. Wodehouse in *The Inimitable Jeeves* in 1923, 'but everybody knows that he's really a sort of janitor to the looney-bin.'

Woolf, Bell, Gibson, and many others like them – these women were not idle or malignant shirkers. On the contrary, they worked hard – on their politics, on their consciences, on their ideas – and they did so in a culture that demanded, contradictorily, the compliance and quiescence of the idealised feminine. Freethinking women lived on their nerves because theirs was a nervous enterprise – feeling the way, teasing out new possibilities, exploring the psychic frontiers, pushing at the perimeter fence. And if there was hysteria around, it was, as often as not, in the reaction of men who simply couldn't cope with the emergent 'new woman'.

*

By autumn 1911, Violet seemed to have found some peace, some distance from the death of her fiancé, of her brother Harry, of her sister-in-law Mary. After returning to England from Italy she tried to rally herself, not to submit to a life of systemic frailty. She moved to Buckfastleigh, in Devon, where she frequented the ancient Benedictine Buckfast Abbey and took long walks in the woods and along the banks of the River Dart. From there, she wrote to her father, thanking him for a framed photograph of him in his coronation robes (their friend from Howth Castle days, the Duke of York, had been crowned George V in 1910). The picture, she wrote, was 'simple and dignified'.

I am particularly pleased at being given [it] just now as I have been thinking lately how very much we children ought to value the name you have given us, and what a passport it is as we go through the world. I also am very grateful for the little fortune you have given me, as it makes me completely independant [sic]. Yours affectionately, Violet Gibson.

Lord Ashbourne's disapproval of her conversion was unshakable, but this was a rapprochement of sorts.

Violet's companion in Buckfastleigh was Enid Dinnis, a Catholic convert and writer of syrupy mystical fiction. ('Catholicism present-ed itself to me in the glory of a high romance', Dinnis once wrote in a short autobiographical note which aptly describes her out-put.) With her, Violet seems to have found a deep friendship based on emotional and intellectual like-mindedness, what Montaigne called 'the consonance of wills'. Tender and fragile, she found strength, a place of safety, in the friendship. At a time when she had few if any voluntary attachments, the bond acquired a special significance. Dinnis, in turn, was solicitous and protective of Violet.

Dinnis would later refer to the time in Buckfastleigh as the 'happy days'. It was a happiness rooted in contemplation, stillness, derived not from stimulation but from the avoidance of it. Violet lived modestly, seeking the ways of the hermits and anchorites – the 'life apart', the nurtured privacy – whose stories she was now avidly studying. She was financially independent, rich by most standards, but she chased few pleasures – unlike Edith Wharton, who was using her wealth to travel around Europe in a Panhard-Levassor motor car or charter expensive yachts; or Eileen Gray, similarly wealthy, who was living in Paris and making exquisite lacquer furniture; or Virginia Woolf, who thrilled at the sight of money in her purse. After her aunt died by a fall from her horse in Bombay,

... a solicitor's letter fell into the post-box and when I opened it I found that she had left me five hundred pounds a year for ever ... the greatest release of all came, which is freedom to think of things in themselves. That building, for example, do I like it or not? Is that picture beautiful or not? Is that in my opinion a good book or bad? Indeed my aunt's legacy unveiled the sky to me.

Violet may not have experienced the same frisson of excitement when she received her 'little fortune' from Lord Ashbourne, but she did pursue the new horizons it opened up for her. Despite her uncompromising commitment to Catholicism, she continued a serious inquiry into Theosophy, travelling to Munich in 1912 to attend a course at the Bavarian Theosophical Society. In the same year, she returned to Italy, and also spent time with her brother Willie, who had taken up residence in Compiègne, near Paris, with his wife Marianne.

*

Lord and Lady Ashbourne were taking a turn in London's Hyde Park. They walked in the brilliant midday sunshine with arms linked. This detail is included in newspaper reports of what happened next. Lord Ashbourne, aged seventy-six, stumbled then fell heavily to the ground, striking the back of his head on a paving stone. Lady Ashbourne cradled him in her arms. Her shrieks for help attracted some passers-by, who carried him in their arms the short distance across the park to St George's Hospital. Lady Ashbourne then rushed to 5 Grosvenor Crescent, their London address, to summon Constance to her father's bedside. Elsie, who normally resided at her husband's seat of Bolton Castle, in Yorkshire, happened to be in London, as was Willie. They too made for the hospital. Victor was in Ireland. At four o'clock in the afternoon of Thursday, 22 May 1913, Lord Ashbourne died.

Violet, who had returned from Buckfastleigh and was living alone in Putney Hill, was not there. Did the family try to reach her? Did she refuse to come? That evening she wrote to Constance: 'I have just now read the news in the evening edition, and all I can think of is "Constance Constance Constance".' The cadence of the *de profundis*.

Who knows if you were with him. Knowing you as I do I hope that you were, because I know the strength that you were able to instil in him in such an uncertain moment. You were for him the perfect daughter . . . And it is beautiful to be able to think what it is you always meant to him and of how much he loved you . . . How dearly I would like to be able to help you! Tell me if there is anything I can do . . . I do know what this means to you, because you loved him so very deeply.

Her words cast a line, full of compassion, between herself and Constance. But in the matter of her own reaction to the news of her father's death, there was only silence.

Lord Ashbourne's passing received extensive coverage in newspapers in England and Ireland. In due course, the obituaries and plaudits – together with a telegram of sympathy to Lady Ashbourne from the king and queen – were proudly pasted into the family albums by Constance. Conspicuously absent is an article headlined 'New Peer Disinherited', which appeared in the *New York Times* on 22 July 1913:

The late Baron Ashbourne, the noted Unionist leader . . . left a fortune of $450,000 to his second son, Edward Gibson, and only $4,000 to his eldest son, William Gibson. The latter is an enthusiastic Nationalist, wears the ancient Irish dress, speaks the Irish language, and is a convert to Catholicism.

A catalogue of sins, for which Willie now reaped the punishment.

The sterling value of Lord Ashbourne's estate was £100,000 (roughly £7 million at today's value). Under the terms of his will, Lady Ashbourne was to be the beneficiary in her lifetime of a large capital sum, plus the house in Merrion Square and the London residence in Grosvenor Crescent, complete with mews house and stabling. She also received diamond jewels – a tiara, necklace, earrings and coronet brooch – paintings, 'the old Great Seal of Ireland', and other treasures. Variously distributed were his claret jugs, silver cups, gold watch and chain, signet ring, 'two paintings by his mother in his bedroom' and much else. His private papers and correspondence he bequeathed to Edward and Constance, 'being confident that they will be solely anxious to act in reference thereto with reserve, prudence, and propriety'. Violet was the beneficiary of a capital fund invested in her name, set up by her father in 1911, from which she was able to draw a respectable annual income of roughly £300 (£21,000 today). Willie's share was a paltry one-off legacy of £800 (£56,000 today), the bulk passing in trust to the younger son Edward, who was living with his wife in Sandyford, County Dublin.

Publicly revered as fair and impartial, Lord Ashbourne revealed himself in death as a man ill-disposed towards those who crossed him. He had hoped for an eldest son like Nancy and Waldorf Astor's Bill, an heir who 'comprehended the mysteries of family institutions, of ritual and rite', a 'cultivated official'. Willie, clearly, did not fit the profile. To his father, he had become a figure of revulsion. The Gaelic League, of which he was a prominent member, had evolved from a cultural pressure group to a political hothouse, a refuge for those activists who demanded the Home Rule that Lord Ashbourne had laboured strenuously to prevent. In time, many of Willie's friends and associates in the League would become revolutionaries, the first martyrs for Irish independence who were to die in the streets and parks of Dublin during the Easter Rising of 1916. If Willie wanted to pursue his dream – and his father's incubus – he would have to do so without Ashbourne gold.

Lord Ashbourne was cremated at Golders Green on 26 May. His ashes were taken in a coffin to Ireland, accompanied by Lady Ashbourne, Willie and Marianne, Edward, Elsie, Frances and Constance. Victor travelled in the opposite direction, to represent the family at a memorial service at the chapel of Gray's Inn, of which Lord Ashbourne had been an Honorary Bencher. After a well-attended funeral (photographers jostled for shots of the new Lord Ashbourne in his kilt), he was interred in the family vault in Dublin's Mount Jerome Cemetery. Violet, too, was there, having made the crossing on her own – a powerful statement of her separation from the family. It was her first trip to Ireland since leaving in 1902. It was also to be her last.

IX

Holy War

The Ashbournes had few men to contribute to the war. Harry the toboganner was dead; Willie, at forty-six, was too old to serve (and would never, in any case, have taken a British uniform), as was Edward, forty-one. Victor, at thirty-nine, was also exempt but he compensated by raising and training a regiment, just as he had done for the Boer War. According to *The Times*, he 'decided to invite one hundred former university and public school men to unite in forming a company with a view to active service'. The company (commanding officer, Colonel Victor Gibson) was 'all of the well-to-do class', and paid its own expenses, including camp rations, tent accommodation, uniform and horses. Trained on Epsom Racecourse, the Public School Corps quickly swelled to two battalions. It was paraded for the first time in Hyde Park on 13 September 1914, its members wearing mufti, cloth caps or Homburgs, school or college colours, and accompanied by the band of the Scots Guards. Then off they went, singing 'Jerusalem', to be wasted at their own expense in the mud and blood and shit of the trenches.

In the first months of the war, the British forces experienced staggering death tolls in the battles of Mons, the Marne, Alsace and Ypres. As men poured into the frontlines, scores of women mobilised themselves into auxiliary roles. Edith Wharton opened a workshop in Paris for unemployed women, and founded American hostels to take care of Belgian and French refugees. She also set up four hospitals to care for tubercular patients, and established the Children of Flanders Rescue Committee. In Italy, the twenty-two-year-old Freya Stark volunteered as a nurse in a clinic in Bologna, and then returned to England to team up with a friend who was running an all-night sandwich and coffee stall for the troops at Paddington Station. At Cliveden, Nancy Astor turned the large covered tennis court and bowling alley into a hospital with six hundred beds, complete with operating theatres. An estimated twenty-four thousand casualties were treated there by the end of the war.

One consequence of the war was the declaration of an armistice between the British government and the suffragist movement. 'War was the only course for our country to take,' wrote Christabel Pankhurst. 'This was national militancy. As suffragettes we could not be pacifists at any price.' Christabel and her mother Emmeline suspended their political agitation, and in return the British government unconditionally released all suffragette prisoners, many of whom joined other women in the war effort. Mr Punch, of the eponymous satirical magazine, declared himself 'proud and delighted' at their resourcefulness:

It is quite impossible to keep pace with all the new incarnations of women in war-time – bus-conductress, ticket-collector, lift-girl, club waitress, post-woman, bank clerk, motor-driver, farm-labourer, guide, munition maker . . . Perhaps in the past, even in the present, [Mr Punch] may have been, or even still is, a little given to chaff Englishwomen for some of their foibles, and even their aspirations. But he never doubted how splendid they were at heart; he never for a moment supposed they would be anything but ready and keen when the hour of need struck.

Virginia Woolf, taking a dim view of the whole affair, recorded the shock of seeing 'the faces of our rulers in the light of the shell-fire. So ugly they looked – German, English, French – so stupid.' Many were the women who denounced the war, campaigning instead to raise a voice 'above the present hatred and bloodshed' and speak to the 'great ideals of civilisation and progress'. In late April 1914, the Women's International Congress held a peace conference at The Hague, 'to demand that international disputes shall in future be settled by some other means than war', and 'to claim that women should have a voice in the affairs of the nations'. The Fawcett Archive holds the list of 156 women of the British

General Committee of the Congress who were anxious to travel to The Hague. They include Lady Ottoline Morrell, Violet Gibson and Sylvia Pankhurst, who emerged as one of Britain's leading revolutionary anti-war agitators. 'We worked continuously for peace, in the face of the bitterest opposition from old enemies, and sometimes unhappily from old friends.' And indeed family: Sylvia's pacifism divided her from her mother Emmeline and her sister Christabel, who were playing an important role as speakers at meetings to recruit young men into the army. Both were vocal opponents of the Women's International Congress. In the event, only three British women were able to attend because Winston Churchill, then at the Admiralty, 'closed' the North Sea to British shipping in order to prevent the other delegates (only twenty-five of whom had been given passports) from sailing from Tilbury. Ottoline Morrell, one of those unable to travel, comforted herself with a trip to the Hydro spa in Buxton.

Frustrated at being prevented from going to the conference, Violet travelled instead to Paris and offered to work for various pacifist organisations propagandising against the war. She also travelled to Switzerland to study at the newly-founded school of Rudolf Steiner, the German polymath who, having broken from Theosophy after finding it too small to accommodate his grand vision of a new world order, had created his own, in the end far more durable sect, Anthroposophy. When Scotland Yard raided the London flat of a well-known pacifist in 1917, Violet's name was found amongst his papers. The Yard opened a file on her, in which her 'strong anti-British attitude' was noted. 'She appears to have been a member of the Anthroposophical Society,' it stated, 'an organisation largely composed of cranks, "advanced" people and pacifists, controlled by the late Rudolf Steiner, and used largely as a means of radiating German peace propaganda. Miss Gibson visited Steiner's wife at Dornach in Switzerland after the outbreak of war.'

The International Council of Women, the International Woman Suffrage Alliance, the Women's International League for

Peace and Freedom – these organisations, open to women of all continents, religions and political affiliations, worked on peace, labour legislation, the abolition of prostitution, and nationality (during the war, the practice of bestowing a husband's nationality on his wife had led to some women finding themselves enemy nationals in the land of their birth). Members had to undertake lengthy and expensive travel to attend meetings, serve as officers, participate in activities, so only those with independent means or sufficient national or international stature to attract subsidies could take part. Delegates to the Hague Congress footed their own bills. Thus it was generally aristocratic and/or financially independent women who became pathfinders for women's rights and a broad agenda of social reform. Edith Somerville, for example, after seeing the ways in which the police abused and manhandled working-class suffragettes, became convinced that it was the duty of aristocratic women to put their bodies on the lines at demonstrations. They were brave, intelligent women, these ladies of title and distinction, who dug deep into their own fund of privilege and money to create the political and social capital that future generations would inherit.

What had terrified Florence Nightingale was that middle-class Victorian women were Cassandras rendered so crazy and powerless by their society that they could rail and rave but never act. In a piercing insight, she observed that passivity transforms even altruism into hate: 'The great reformers of the world turn into the great misanthropists, if circumstances of organisation do not permit them to act. Christ, if he had been a woman, might have been nothing but a great complainer.' From complainers to campaigners: war had released Florence Nightingale from the chains of passivity, from going insane in the bosom of her family; it took another war to provide the same opportunity to her successors.

Violet, however, was unable to take advantage of the opportunity. Though little is known about her career as a pacifist, it signals the moment when she emerged from merely philosophical and spiritual enquiry into engagement in the world of political activism. It was a question of fighting the good fight, not floating down into acquiescence. But no sooner had she tasted the experience than it came to an abrupt end. In early 1914, aged thirty-eight, in the preparatory stages of the Hague congress, she was diagnosed with Paget's disease (a type of cancer). Surgeons removed her left breast in a mutilating operation that left a jagged nine-inch scar across her chest. Violet's response to this shock, to the post-operative pain and distress, was completely contra-indicated: instead of taking to the chaise longue again, she embarked on the punishing journey to Paris and work as a peace activist. Now, in the spring of 1915, she again fell ill and was forced to return to England. Unsurprisingly, her bad health continued.

On 18 May 1916, at age forty, she underwent a further gruelling operation in London, this time for acute appendicitis and peritonitis. The surgeons were aghast at the poisoned state of her intestines: they were fizzing with infection, 'so septic and so encased in adhesions that there was little to be done'. The lesions from this unsuccessful operation left her with chronic and often acute pain in the abdomen, near the scar area, for the rest of her life. No amount of willpower could be mobilised against this devastating blow: she was now virtually an invalid, barely able to rise from her bed – 'all the horrors of the dark cupboard of illness once more displayed for my diversion', as Woolf put it – all her plans for action dissolving in the misery and frustration of the inactive life.

A curious note surfaces in Violet's medical records. The doctor treating her at this time questioned 'her attitude towards the pain she suffered' and the fact that she appeared to be 'ignoring the means to alleviate such'. She seemed to think, the note reads, 'that her poor health was a sacrifice to be made for her religious beliefs'. This comment opens up a dreadful prospect: that the war inside Violet's body was a kind of visceral transaction of the war inside her mind.

The key to her self-abnegation might lie in an oblique scribble in Violet's little black notebook (later confiscated by Italian police, and still held in the state archives): 'Fr. John O'Fallon Pope, S.J., took me as his child on 12th August 1915.' On her return from Paris, she had not sought medical help, but spiritual guidance. By entrusting the health of her soul to a Jesuit who taught an uncompromising curriculum for a life guided by God, Violet set herself a compass-bearing that would draw her, more than a decade later, to the scene on Campidoglio.

John O'Fallon Pope was an American-born convert who had spent several years in Italy as a seminarian before being ordained in 1878, joining the Jesuits the following year. Between 1900 and 1915 he was Rector of the eponymous Pope's Hall in Oxford, during which time he was referred to, alongside Willie Gibson, as a Modernist. Most likely, it was Willie who introduced him to Violet. Known as a 'precise, sensitive scholar, with the habits of a recluse . . . a master in the spiritual life, well read in spiritual books, scholarly in his utterances and interests, and capable of inspiring high spiritual ideals', O'Fallon Pope agreed to be Violet's confessor when she visited him in Oxford in August 1915. A year later, in July 1916, barely two months after the failed operation on her intestines, Violet attended a long retreat given by him at Manresa House in Roehampton.

The retreat was based on the Spiritual Exercises of Saint Ignatius, founder of the Jesuit order, which require the retreatant to reflect on the relation between the Creator and his creature, and then to meditate on sin and the judgement and penalties due to it. Self-mortification was required, in the practice of which Jesuits employed a range of physical chastisements (wearing hair shirts, flagellating the body with barbed whips, fasting). The Exercises demanded conformity with God's will ('God, being truth itself and omniscient, possesses the requisite authority to be believed', O'Fallon Pope preached), personal love of Jesus, and the correction of 'every form of self-deceit, illusion, plausible pretext'. A 'mechanical, emotional, or fanciful piety' was not tolerated – the proof of genuine service was in deeds, not words.

True believers, O'Fallon Pope taught, were bidden to intervene, in God's name, in human affairs. This could be a dispiriting task.

Unfortunately, the disunion of Christendom may continue for long weary years. Scandals must needs come; ravening wolves will enter in among us, not sparing the flock; and of our own selves shall arise men speaking perverse things to draw away disciples after them; there must be schisms amongst us and there must be heresies. But each man who has the welfare of Christ's Mystical Body at heart should labour strenuously, unceasingly, and courageously to heal the wounds of Christendom so far as it is given him to do. He must sanctify himself and he must pray; but also he must act so as to affect directly his fellow men.

Violet hung on O'Fallon Pope's every word. She made notes:

The degree of holiness depends on the degree of mortification. Mortification means putting to death. We must refuse to give the body the satisfaction it asks for. *Keep the spirit of mortification alive.*

The mortified man will live out the present perfectly without looking ahead.

Father Pope finds many who serve our Lord for a time, but very very few persevere. Poor human nature.

He wishes that I should profit of every opportunity to mortify myself and renounce my will.

I must move my will to obey my intellect.

A saint is eminently rational. Why are we not saints? Because we do not act perfectly according to conscience. Also because we are not logical.

When our conscience forbids die rather than do it.

Mortify your memory and you will have peace.

An apostle *burns with zeal.*

Fr. P. is the embodiment of Our Lord's love of humanity.

To read the notebook is to witness the struggle for Violet's soul. 'I have no constancy or perseverance', reads a weary entry, one of many recording the effort to remove the stubborn stain of every bad thought, the difficulty – antagonism, even – of reconciling spiritual search with actual existence. The retreat was an exacting regimen, particularly for Violet, whose health, both physical and emotional, had taken many batterings. There is one entry that hints at O'Fallon Pope's awareness of her fragility, and the cost to her of trying to overcome it. 'You are not only a human being,' she records him telling her, 'but specifically a specially soft delicate *woman* human being. The softer the more satisfactory.' Had he seen in her an inclination towards excessive self-mortification? Was he concerned that Violet was taking his words too literally? But how else was she meant to take them? Here was a man who came across as knowing himself so surely that he could not think against himself, who presented himself as a conduit of true wisdom, next to which any other form of argument appears as a dangerous counterfeit.

If O'Fallon Pope tried to hold Violet back, he failed. She had already crossed a threshold, and it was he who had opened the door and pointed the way. In *The Art of the Novel*, Milan Kundera explains, defining the word 'border', that we think the border in our lives between happiness and tragedy is miles away – whereas, Kundera asserts, it is only inches away, the border that, once crossed, will change our lives irrevocably. Violet left the retreat in the apostolic condition, firm in the belief that the Divine plan required sharpshooters to carry it out.

X

Il Miglior Fabbro

On 22 February 1917, Corporal Benito Mussolini, an enlisted *bersagliere* (literally, 'sharpshooter') was instructing a group of soldiers in the use of mortars by firing shells into the Austrian lines high up on the Alpine front. Mussolini dropped the last bomb down the red-hot tube. It exploded immediately, scattering deadly shrapnel in all directions. Five soldiers died instantly, many others dropped wounded, including Mussolini. Hospitalised for several months (he had forty shards of metal in his body), he had time to think about the future, of the return to peace when there would be no more 'convulsions', but rather 'a "détente" of soul and body'.

After his two years' self-imposed exile in Switzerland, Mussolini had returned to Italy in 1904 where, despite his aggressive anti-militarism, he took advantage of an amnesty to deserters and belatedly signed up for his national service (the alternative, he said, would have been to emigrate to America). He still burned with scorn for authority, was pledged to Socialism and the overthrow of both king and parliament, farcical institutions which the '*virtuoso*' must one day destroy. He attacked lickspittle capitalists and the petite bourgeoisie; nationalists (the national flag was 'a rag to be planted on a dung-hill', 'The Fatherland is a spook . . . like God, and like God it is vindictive, cruel and tyrannical'); the Catholic Church ('that great corpse'), the Vatican ('a gang of robbers'), Christianity itself ('humanity's immortal stigma of opprobrium'). He delighted to report that, around his birthplace of Dovia, socialist 'baptisms' were gaining in popularity and very likely would soon replace the religious ceremony. In 1910, he published *The Cardinal's*

Mistress, a period bodice-ripper in which the Church was portrayed as a place of lust, hypocrisy and murder.*

Mussolini's journalistic nom de plume at this time was *L'Homme qui cherche*, and his imagined itinerary through life remained appropriately eclectic – 'I need to orient my ideas better and make them more precise.' In truth, it was not a question of precision, but of tailoring ideology to action. The only cause he ever recognised, said one contemporary, 'was his own', and his 'only use for ideas was to enable him to dispense with ideas . . . Only action counted.'

According to socialist theories, war – unjust, colonial, imperial war – demanded a general strike and resistance from all members of the working class. So, when Italy invaded Libya in September 1911, Mussolini urged this case without qualification, condemning the 'mock-heroic madness of the war-mongers by profession'. He organised the Forlì Socialist Party's role in the strike, for which, on 14 October, he was arrested. Certain formalities were observed: police located Mussolini sipping a coffee at his usual place, and asked him politely to accompany them to the station. He asked if he could finish his coffee first and was assured that he could. Only then did they march him off to jail. At his trial he spoke in his own defence, portraying himself emphatically as a hero, 'not an evil-doer nor a vulgar criminal, but a man of ideas and of conscience, an agitator and soldier of a faith'. Sentenced to twelve months in prison – reduced to six months on appeal – he was released on 12 March 1912, jubilant and greatly elevated in status.

Shortly afterwards, at age twenty-nine, Mussolini took over editorship of the Socialist Party organ, *Avanti!*, in Milan. He had already paid a high price for his ambitiousness and private desires, and he often now looked exhausted. But he still found time and

---

* The English version, published in 1927, was reviewed with some malice in the *New Yorker* by Dorothy Parker: 'When I am given a costume romance beginning "From the tiny churches hidden within the newly budding verdure of the valleys, the evensong of the Ave Maria floated gently forth and died upon the lake," my only wish is that I, too, might float gently forth and die, and I'm not particular whether it's upon the lake or on dry land.'

energy enough to take on a series of mistresses. To one, Leda Rafanelli, he wrote: 'With you, I feel miles from Milan, journalism, politics, Italy, the West, Europe . . . Let's read Nietzsche and the Koran together. Listen. I am free every afternoon.' (His amatory rhetoric remained banal, as transcriptions of his taped conversations, years later, with his mistress Clara Petacci reveal: 'I love you so much, so much. I don't know why I love you like this. I only love you! The perfume of your kisses stuns me, kills me. When I look into your eyes I read to the bottom of your soul! The world vanishes and I forget everybody and everything.')

When war broke out in 1914, Mussolini initially followed the Socialist Party line of 'rigid neutrality', writing thundering editorials in *Avanti!* against intervention. A year later, he switched, and was advocating intervention. Taking up Karl Marx's aphorism that social revolution usually follows war, he argued that if such unrest were harnessed to the Socialist cause, then the destruction of Italy's bourgeois system would finally be within reach. Unable to promote this heresy in the party's official organ, Mussolini resigned his editorship of *Avanti!*, and set up his own newspaper, *Il Popolo d'Italia*, whose maxim, printed beside the title, was the Napoleonic 'Revolution is an idea which has found bayonets.'

The inevitable expulsion of the traitor Mussolini from the Socialist Party quickly followed. In a turbulent meeting in Milan at the end of November, he stepped onto the platform, pale and visibly trembling, and dismissed the court of Socialist opinion as an abandoned lover: 'You hate me today because you love me still . . . Whatever happens, you won't lose me. The twelve years of my life I gave to the party are or ought to be sufficient guarantee of my Socialist faith. Socialism is in my very blood.' His words were lost in the volley of jeers, shouts, even chairs, that were hurled at him by the furious delegates.

Italy declared war against Austria on 24 May 1915. But Mussolini, who had become so keen for it, did not volunteer, busying himself instead with promoting its merits from behind his desk at *Il Popolo*. When the draft finally reached him in

September, he was assigned to a unit in the Italian Dolomites. On 17 December, after a bout of typhus earned him home leave, he formally married Rachele Guidi (who had already borne him a child) in a civil ceremony. The daughter of his father's mistress, Rachele had been Benito's second choice – he had fallen in love with her elder sister Augusta, but she, thinking him too unstable, chose a man who had regular work as a gravedigger. Mussolini returned to the front and served until that day in February 1917 when he was hit by his own mortar.

The story of Mussolini the soldier became an essential part of the Fascist construction of Il Duce. A key source for this propaganda was Mussolini's war diary, initially serialised in *Il Popolo*, then proudly released in 1923 by Imperia, the official Fascist Party publishing house, and reverently read by Italian schoolchildren and Fascist loyalists thereafter. The diary tells of how, in July 1916, its author volunteered to lead a small reconnaissance unit up to the Austrian lines in the midst of fierce fighting. For thirty-six hours, he guided his men back and forth between the two vertical lines under constant artillery, mortar, and machine-gun fire. Shrapnel riddled his helmet and he narrowly escaped death as shells burst around him. Weeks later, an Austrian shell scored a direct hit on Mussolini's dugout, burying him alive. He managed to claw his way out, his tunic torn to shreds, his face blackened but without a scratch. Day and night his unit lobbed its bombs into the Austrian lines and endured the inevitable reply of enemy fire.

My speciality was to throw hand grenades back before they could explode, a dangerous game, but if you did it quickly you could throw it in time to go off in their trenches. And then I taught my troops how to handle our own grenades. Often you had to light the fuse close to your face with a cigarette, because matches didn't burn long enough to do it, and then hold the lit grenade in your hand for a few moments. If you didn't, there would still be enough time for them to be thrown back at you. My poor little soldiers! They were all shaking, their teeth chattering, while I counted out loud, marking off the seconds from one to sixty.

Recognising the value of his wounds, Mussolini returned to his desk at *Il Popolo* in Milan in August 1917 leaning heavily on a pair of crutches, which he continued to use long after the need for them had gone.

In October 1917, two divisions of the Austrian army punched through the Italian lines at Caporetto. It was a total, panic-stricken rout, with over half a million Italian soldiers forced into surrender or retreat. Freya Stark, who was stationed as a lieutenant with the historian G. M. Trevelyan's ambulance unit near Gorizia, witnessed the troops trudging in the pouring rain along roads littered with dead horses and the wounded. Mussolini was so depressed he talked of killing himself. But he rallied, and wrote impassioned editorials calling for the nation to be fused in spirit with the army:

In this moment the Italian people is a mass of precious materials. It needs to be forged, cleaned, worked. A work of art is still possible. But a government is needed. A man. A man who, when the situation demands it, has the delicate touch of an artist and the heavy fist of a warrior. Sensitive and determined. A man who knows the people, loves the people, and can direct and bend it – with violence if necessary.

He also demanded that Italian Socialists, for the crime of opposing the war, be treated without mercy as a more dangerous enemy than the Austrians. Sir Samuel Hoare (later Foreign Secretary to Stanley Baldwin) was a senior staff officer in Italy with the British divisions sent to reinforce the Italians. Hoare was appalled at the disorder of the broken Italian army, and at the growing defeatism of the press and politicians. After being told by a member of his staff that the man most likely to stop the rot was Benito Mussolini, Hoare obtained authority from Whitehall to approach him, and government funds were soon being funnelled to *Il Popolo*. Thus, the British treasury was paying for Mussolini to establish himself as the *fabbro dello stato*, the iron-hard engineer of the new Italian soul.

In the event, it was military hardware supplied by the Allies that shored up the crumbling Italian war effort. When hostilities ended in November 1918, Italy emerged as one of the victors, but hers was a 'maimed victory' (*vittoria mutilata*) that carried the humiliation of military and parliamentary incompetence. In the midst of the 1914–15 debate about whether or not Italy should intervene in the war, a nationalist newspaper had written off parliament as 'a third-rate club, frequented by a varied collection of broken-down windbags, of letter writers who like official stationery, of old misanthropes who like to read a free newspaper, of rabid gamblers who could not live without their daily game'. The immediate post-war period saw the rise of a medley of bourgeois, intellectuals and veterans who were ready to chuck out these old windbags. Men who had once automatically viewed themselves as liberals now took to promoting the 'armed society' as the ideal political and economic model for peacetime. Mussolini coined the term *trincerocrazia* – rule by those who had experienced the trenches – to describe a generation of young, courageous and disciplined men hardened by combat, whose sacrifices gave them the moral right and the ruthlessness required to create and lead a new Italy. The country, he pronounced with menace, was dividing into two great parties, 'those who have been [in the trenches] and those who haven't; those who have fought and those who haven't; those who have worked and the parasites'. By February 1919 some twenty *Fasci di combattimento* (ex-servicemen's leagues) had sprung up in places ranging from Venice to Cagliari. The *fasci* were not Mussolini's invention, but he was quick to draw them into his world. The Fascist movement was about to be officially born.

XI

Things Snap

Mop-headed women in blue kimonos and wigs, yellow trousers, amber and emerald. Vita in breeches and a pink shirt. Virginia eating sausages in Vanessa's studio, and fainting at The Ivy. 'Violet Trefus-is who never refus-is'. Everyone 'very gay' at Charleston and talking of buggerers, 'the bursting of people's bladders, the National Gallery, incest, perhaps'. Leonard Woolf and Desmond MacCarthy looking up the word 'fuck' in the London Library. Nancy Astor doing cartwheels in the drawing room at Cliveden.

After the roaring guns of war, the Roaring Twenties. And how they roared. What a lot of parties.

Masked parties, Savage parties, Victorian parties, Greek parties, Wild West parties, Russian parties, Circus parties . . . parties at Oxford where one drank brown sherry and smoked Turkish cigarettes, dull dances in London and comic dances in Scotland and disgusting dances in Paris – all that succession and repetition and massed humanity.

These were Evelyn Waugh's 'vile bodies', publicity-seeking, fun-loving, anarchic, eager to overthrow the gloomy influence of the stiff-collared old men who had presided over the war. 'Being new at any cost' was Arnold Bennett's dim view of it.

Antonia White whizzing across to Paris in her lover's aeroplane. 'The dry glare and the intolerable noise of the "Boeuf sur le Toit" where one goes to look at the Jews and the Lesbians and the fairies.' At 20 rue Jacob, Clifford Barney, the 'Amazon of Paris-Lesbos', honouring the Sapphic muse with Gertrude Stein, Alice B. Toklas with her moustache and little black hats, baking her famous hashish brownies, Romaine Brooks, Janet Flanner, Colette with her curly, kinky hair like a wild dog, Radclyffe Hall,

Sylvia Beach, Djuna Barnes ('Are you really a lesbian?' 'I might be anything. If a horse loved me, I might be that'). These people were happy to meet the rigorous Parisian standards for scabrous and labyrinthine relationships. 'France is nothing but a big brothel' was Nancy Astor's prudish judgement.

On the fringes of this raffish intellectual Paris-Lesbos scene was Eileen Gray who, like Violet, had left Ireland in 1902. In Paris she shed her title and her beautiful ropes of hair, and thus bobbed applied herself to the Japanese art of lacquer, which made her arms blister. By the twenties she was working on the revolutionary new theories of design and architecture of the modern movement. Intensely private, Gray only rarely broke with the self-imposed monasticism of her atelier existence. Even when present she managed to remain absent, locked in a life of extreme inwardness. 'Of all the people I knew in the world, she gave the feeling of complete consecration,' an acquaintance recalled. 'One must never look for happiness,' Gray once said. 'It passes you on your way, but always in the opposite direction. Sometimes I recognised it.'

This was what Virginia Woolf described as the feeling of being 'driven by loneliness and silence from the habitable world', where the 'singing of the real world' becomes muted, distant, as the condition of pronounced withdrawal asserts itself. Such was Violet's experience. A studio photograph taken some time before the war shows her attired like a lay religious. Her pose – the distant gaze, an open book (presumably a spiritual text) resting in her hand – is studied, calculated to transmit the subdued aura of the contemplative life. According to a friend, she now 'limited her acquaintance to her own sex except in the case of priests'. At a time when the world was bursting open in a carnival of adventure (Joyce's 'extravagant excursions into forbidden territory'), Violet moved not toward it, but in the opposite direction. And perhaps she was right to, for beneath the exuberance lurked the suggestion of madness.

*

TOP Violet in a mystical mood, circa 1910
BOTTOM Virgin Annunciate, Fra Angelico

Ezra Pound dressed in 'pearl-buttoned velvet coats, fawn or pearl-gray trousers, a loose-flowing dark cape' topped with a sombrero – 'a pinwheel of affectation'. Man Ray punching a man on the nose in the front row at composer George Antheil's debut, the Surrealists punching everybody until the police arrive. T. S. Eliot's 'The Waste Land', Jaroslav Hasek's *The Good Soldier Svejk*, Virginia Woolf's *The Waves* – literary modernism's extraordinary combination of spiritualism, political extremism, sexual passion. And Joyce's *Ulysses*, anatomising the body and glorifying all its vilenesses – Bloom inhaling with satisfaction the odour of his own shit. George Bernard Shaw rejected it as 'a revolting record of a disgusting phase of civilisation'; Carl Jung hated it as 'a delirious confusion of the subjective and psychic with objective reality', containing 'nothing pleasing', an analogy for 'schizophrenia'.

Zelda and Scott Fitzgerald: their life together a dazzling exhibition of what it meant to be young and daring in the Jazz Age. But when Scott's attention wandered, Zelda's acts grew increasingly reckless, burning all her clothes in the bathtub while Scott entertained next door. She took up ballet, which restored a certain sense of self-command. Until everything slipped away from her.

In Paris, before I realised that I was sick, there was a new significance to everything: stations and streets and façades of buildings – colours were infinite, part of the air . . . And there was . . . a detachment as if I was on the other side of a black gauze – a fearless small feeling . . . I am so afraid that . . . there is nothing left but disorder and vacuum.

Inside Zelda, things snapped 'like little hooks on a dress'. She had hallucinations, heard voices. Once, she claimed to be in direct contact with 'Christ, William the conqueror, Mary Stuart, Apollo and all the stock paraphernalia of insane-asylum jokes'. Scott was, in his words, 'her great reality, often the only liaison agent who could make the world tangible to her'. Virginia Woolf, too, heard voices. After one breakdown she 'lay in bed, listening to the birds singing in Greek and imagining that King Edward VII lurked in the azaleas using the foulest possible language'. Like Zelda,

Virginia resisted the controlling hand of the doctors, refused to be turned into a 'case', was even jaunty when describing her 'madness' and her total absorption in it. 'As an experience, madness is terrific I can assure you, and not to be sniffed at,' she informed a friend. 'And in its lava I still find most of the things I write about. It shoots out of one everything shaped, final, not in mere driblets as sanity does.'

The *folies à deux* of Scott and Zelda, Virginia and Leonard. There were others. Tom and Vivien Eliot at Margate and Lausanne (the tears at the lake), he seeking respite from his nervousness, she hanging like 'a bag of ferrets' around his neck, or later stalking him across London, even appearing at one of his lectures dressed in full Fascist rig. James and Lucia Joyce: bound by a private language, baffling to others, that flared up in his work and transmitted the spark of inspiration to his daughter, kindling 'a fire in her brain'. Before it consumed her, the fire fuelled Lucia's talent for dancing. In Paris, where 'hordes of buxom young women in scanty tunics were leaping eagerly to the commands of this or that half-demented instructor', she joined the dance school of the eccentric 'unbearded Ulysses', Raymond Duncan (brother of Isadora). The style was modernist, Surrealist, anti-balletic, possessed but also self-possessed. 'I felt her tragically reaching, seeking for what could probably never be found,' remembered a friend. 'She was like the high, perishable, wishful tendril of a vine moving blindly up a wall.'

The fire in Lucia's brain: the journey into a kind of ecstasy that 'takes no account of the individual and may even destroy him'. Joyce, as if in a parody of the same idea, had followed his description of the 'radiant', 'purified' flight of Stephen Dedalus's soul with 'o, cripes, I'm drowned!'

The shipwreck of Vaslav Nijinsky. Nijinsky, who had arrived in Paris with Diaghilev in 1909, supplied all the sexual tension that the modern imagination could ask for: exoticism, androgyny, enslavement, violence. But offstage he was naïve, shy, recessive – blank, almost. At parties he would sit silently and pick his cuticles. In his 1919 diary, written in six weeks before his thirtieth birthday, he repeated endlessly the idea that he was God. In Switzerland, he began producing drawing after drawing at obsessive speed, of 'eyes peering from every corner, red and black'. He ordered people in St Moritz to go to church, he drove his sleigh into oncoming traffic, he threw his wife Romola down the stairs.

As his self disintegrated, his diary became a desperate exercise of retrieving, even vindicating, that self: 'I am not an invention. I am life.' We are in the room with him as he struggles frantically for control: 'I am weeping . . . I cannot restrain my tears, which are dropping on my left hand and my silk tie.' He is terrified of being put in a lunatic asylum. We can hear the doctors banging at his door as he writes, he records their arrival. They have been called by Romola, who is downstairs, and will take him to the asylum. '*Femmka* [little wife], you are bringing me my death warrant.' He is diagnosed as 'a confused schizophrenic with mild manic excitement'. Three months after being confined in the asylum, he is hallucinating, tearing his hair out, attacking his attendants and declaring that his limbs belong to someone else, not him. 'Why am I locked up?' he cries. 'Why are the windows closed, why am I

Vaslav Nijinsky in a Swiss clinic, 1939, reprising his famous jump
for photographers.

never left alone?' The diary gives us the end of his brief life as a dancer, the beginning of his thirty years as a madman.

When Nijinsky was photographed in the asylum, in mid-temps *levé sauté*, was he still the century's greatest ballet dancer, or was he merely a madman who could jump? Where the Victorians had been very keen to domesticate madness, to purge it of the Romantic association with poetic genius, after the First World War the line between clinical and creative madness was again blurred. The German doctor Hans Prinzhorn's work on the resources of the unconscious – 'beyond the frame, unrelated to the norm' – collated the drawings of the insane in a collection (still exhibited today) whose object was to show that inspiration and deep despair shared the same seat. And when Antonin Artaud guest-edited a special issue of *La Révolution surréaliste* in 1925, he asked Robert Desnos to write a 'Letter to the Medical Directors of Insane Asylums' calling attention to the Surrealists' belief that the insane were simply people who didn't fit into established codes of behaviour. In 1928, the Surrealists were to celebrate the fiftieth anniversary of 'hysteria' by calling it 'a supreme mode of expression'. Madness, for them, was a glamorous cultural property, a barometer of the new.

In the psychiatric wards, however, it was anything but glamorous. War, a mad enterprise, had brought forth its own special madness: male hysteria, sanctioned as shellshock, whose victims were stacking up in hospitals and asylums. This evened out the gender imbalance, at least. Now everybody could have a nervous breakdown in what Ezra Pound labelled 'the germy epoch of Freud'.

All the while, Violet was living a modest, undemonstrative life in Kensington, shorn of excitement, carefully insulated from the noisy world without by a routine of prayer and charitable acts, to which she directed much of her annual allowance. Until, on 16 January 1922, a charge detonated beneath her. That evening, newspapers carried reports that her brother Victor had been found dead the previous day in an armchair in the smoking room of the Crown Inn at Horsham, Surrey, with just three shillings in his pocket. His body had been found by the landlord, but Victor, whose signature in the visitor's book was indecipherable, wasn't identified until after his second wife Caroline's suspicions had been raised by a report in the local paper.

Though he had not fought in the war, Victor had trained a younger generation of men to become cannon fodder, a burden that had turned the once brilliant, keen and enterprising young adventurer into a confused and spent middle-aged man. He was said by a family friend to have been 'of wandering habits'; he 'occasionally went away from home without saying where he was going'; he used to 'wander about England, carrying no luggage'; recently he had been 'just knocking about with nothing to do'. His sister Constance believed that he was locked in an unhappy marriage that drove him to drink. Victor himself had told the landlord that he was a revolutionary known to the Irish police under six different monikers, and to the manager of another Horsham hotel, where he had stayed two nights before his death, he said he had always been a Loyalist but events in Ireland had turned him into a rebel. 'You may not know it,' added Victor darkly, 'but you've got a very dangerous man in your house tonight.'

Was this true, or was it the empty boast of a drunk? A friend was quoted in the *New York Times* as saying that Victor had contracted malaria when in South Africa, 'and during periodic attacks talked rather wildly of Irish affairs'. The exact nature of Victor's – and indeed Willie's – links with nationalist revolutionaries has never been determined. After Violet shot Mussolini, it was to become a significant line of enquiry for Italian police.

The inquest returned a verdict of accidental death by natural causes, there being 'no perceptible signs of poison' – a post-mortem would have settled this, but, inexplicably, none was ordered. The presence of broken glass in the fireplace, and traces of an unidentified liquid that had been spilled on the floor, added to the riddle. Constance, for one, believed he may have died by his own hand, but the matter remained unresolved. The coroner reported that Victor was 'poorly nourished and thin'.

The impact on Violet was immediate and devastating. Yet another link to her past, that fragile and tenuous domain, was gone. 'We were a large family and, as is the case in all large families, we grew up in pairs. Victor and Violet were one pair,' Constance was later quoted in the *Daily Mail*. 'He died suddenly, in tragic circumstances, and evidently, given her particular sensibility, this completely wore her mind down,' Constance added. 'The acute pain changed her completely.'

A month after Victor's death, Violet had a 'nervous crisis', but she kept it secret from her family. Only her friend Enid Dinnis knew:

I was with her two days before and saw it coming on. She told me she was going away but did not know where she was going. At that time she was so invalided [by poor health] that she always took a companion when she went out, but on Feb. 23rd, the Friday, she left her lodgings at 5 p.m. and did not return until after midnight. Next day she was both physically and mentally ill. It was ascertained that she had visited the Carmelite Fathers in their monastery at Kensington, caught hold of the brother who opened the door with both arms and then tried to make her way into what she knew to be the monastic enclosure. What happened to her after she left them she never told anyone . . . By her doctor's advice she went to a nursing home in Drayton Terrace, Kensington, for a week.

Violet would later describe this episode as being 'nothing of importance; the important thing was that for seven hours I was possessed by a good spirit, and for five hours a bad one.'

When she was strong enough, Violet travelled to France to stay with Willie and Marianne at Compiègne. Marianne de Monbrison was descended from a distinguished Huguenot family, but she too had converted to Catholicism. This was all she shared with Violet, who confided to her notebook her distrust of her sister-in-law, describing her as a 'mischief-maker'. The Australian artist Roy de Maistre, who spent much time at Compiègne during the twenties and thirties, painted several portraits of Marianne. In *Lord and Lady Ashbourne and their Poodle!* she looks rigid and geometric, an appearance accentuated by the

Willie and Marianne Ashbourne with Roy de Maistre and female companion
(centre) at Compiègne, circa 1924

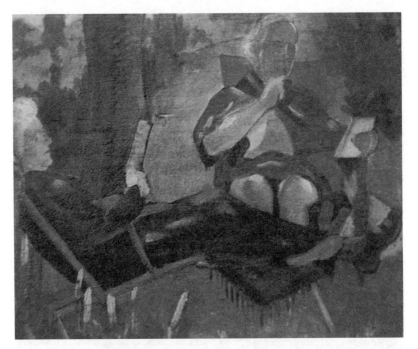

Lord and Lady Ashbourne at Compiègne, Roy de Maistre, *c.*1924

diagonal lines of her chair and the triangular shape of her hanging shawl, while Lord Ashbourne, in the background, has a much
softer, more organic form. De Maistre took part in the amateur
theatricals which were a great love of his hosts, and which were
often performed in the forest at Compiègne, famous as the site of
Joan of Arc's capture in 1430. There were also boating parties on
the river (Constance and Violet are believed to be the subjects of
his undated painting *Two Women in a Boat*). Willie joined in
when he wasn't writing articles on ecclesiastical subjects – keeping up his Modernist barrage against the Vatican – an activity
highlighted in de Maistre's work by Willie's intense concentration on his paper and pen. Marianne was fiercely jealous of Willie
and resented his attention to his sister. The only time Violet
spent alone with her adored brother was when he took her to visit
local peasant families he was supporting.

*

Two Women in a Boat, Roy de Maistre, undated

Violet's stay at Compiègne hardly provided the rest she needed, given the tension with Marianne and Willie's regular absences. Every weekend, he left Compiègne for Paris, where he put up at the Hotel International on the avenue d'Iéna. He had meetings with radical students and spent long hours at cafés with émigré

Irish nationalists. This was the 'other' Paris, the capital not of
sexual licence but of political exiles, revolutionaries, assorted
anarchists, anti-Fascists, anti-Bolsheviks, spies and agents provocateurs. 'If you went to Paris,' as the British diplomat Robert
Vansittart put it, 'you would catch some politico-venereal disease.
They would infect you with their ideas.'

It wasn't clear what exactly Willie was up to. Over the years, he
had continued to agitate for political reform in Ireland. Upon
assuming the peerage in 1913 after the death of his father, he was
asked if he would ever join the House of Lords. 'Not until we have
a parliament in Dublin!' he had replied. He broke his vow, taking
his seat on 27 June 1918 in time to join a debate on Ireland, which
was fast sliding into open warfare against British rule. '*Beidheadh
se i mo chumas gan acht gaedhlig a labhairt agus mise ag cur i g-ceil
dibh ar an g-ceist sea,*' he began. His fellow peers looked on blankly.
'I could go on and make a whole speech to your Lordships in the
language of our country,' he went on. Fortunately, he didn't, else
nobody would have understood a word he said. He spoke of the
injustice of British rule, which forced Irish school children to
recite the lines

> *Thank the goodness, and the grace that*
> *On my birth has smiled,*
> *And made me in these blessed days,*
> *A happy English child.*

The result of such indoctrination, he argued, was 'that the modern
Irishman, as we know him, is a man whose character has been sys-
tematically falsified'. Little wonder, then, that 'anarchy' prevailed
in Ireland. 'All I want to do,' Willie continued, 'is to warn any who
may think that Ireland can be dealt with by a system of repression,
even if you call it resolute government, without any attempt at
remedial legislation, that they are creating a terrible situation for
this country and for the British Empire.'

Two years later, when Willie put in another appearance,
Ireland was deep into its war of independence, a brutal exchange

of killing and reprisals that set the blueprint for Irish politics for the next seventy years. 'I myself am not in any sense a politician,' Willie told the Lords. 'If there is one subject in this wide world which annoys me it is politics. I have been so worried with politics, especially in my own country, that I have gone as far away from them as I possibly could for the last few years. I have been engaged chiefly on metaphysics and things of that sort.' He went on to describe how his dreaming had been interrupted by 'a most horrible nightmare', in which 'a big Imperial dog' and 'a small National dog' were locked in a fight, 'whirling round and round and rolling downhill towards a precipice'. His only comfort was that 'as an Irishman, I thought possibly the smallest, lightest, most compact dog, the National dog, would survive, whatever happened to the other'. At a moment when the Irish Republican Army was demonstrating that British power could be taken on with a few well-aimed shots (Michael Collins's 'Squad' decapitating British intelligence in a single morning), the narration of Willie's dream would have sent a chill through Westminster.

It was his last speech in a total of three – not a brilliant record (but three times as many as some of his fellow lords), and it revealed how irrelevant he was, worrying away at metaphysics in France while Ireland was combusting. The Troubles signalled the end of the 'picnic in a foreign land' for many Anglo-Irish families. 'In belonging to a class no longer of any substance, save now in anecdote', they became a kind of non-sequitur and passed into limbo. The time had arrived for them to decide how to deal with the problem of doubleness, whether they were to the left or the right of the hyphen, and many chose the former and moved back to England. Willie's reaction was to become ever more Irish, in his inimitable (and, to some, not very authentic) idea of what that was. But contradictorily, he chose to play out his *Gaeltacht* not in Ireland but in France – the kind of figure to send the likes of Anglo-Irish writer (Violet) Martin Ross into the deepest gloom, exasperated by 'the fluxes of temperament, the eruptions of activity, the infinities of dreaming sloth' of this brand of Irish nationalism.

Was Willie a Holy Fool, a parody Parsifal? Or was his loose-jointed, misty, suffusive appearance a front concealing another side to his character? Shortly after becoming a Catholic, he had fallen into a friendly argument with the eminent convert Cardinal Manning about the scholastic proofs of God's existence. Manning undertook to settle the question 'by argument four-squares', but first, he challenged Willie, 'you must give me my premises: do you admit that you yourself exist?' To which Willie answered, 'Not in any sense that would be of controversial advantage to your eminence.' A couple of years later, seeing Willie across a crowded room at one of his receptions, the cardinal beckoned him to approach and asked: 'Well, do you exist yet?' A lighthearted exchange, but one that infers the shadowy, elusive nature of Willie's existence.

'Moses was little good to his people until he had killed an Egyptian,' Yeats wrote, 'and for the most part a writer or public man of the upper classes is useless to this country till he has done something that separates him from his class.' Willie never quite managed this, though he did report with some pride that an American priest had once told him, 'It seems that you are the protector of the Irish race.' 'We are all doing what we can,' Willie had replied. The job of killing the Egyptian fell to his sister Violet. And she did so armed with many of Willie's arguments. It was from him that she learned the material aims of the Christian socialist mission: that the social regeneration of Europe should be promoted through the renaissance of a progressive Catholicism; that the Catholic Church should break with all royalist and absolutist regimes; that the papacy should be the guardian of liberty and the champion of democracy; and that the people, in whom was hidden the Word of God, should be sovereign. This was Willie's credo, God *and* Liberty. Before leaving Compiègne, Violet told Willie and Marianne that the Pope had betrayed the

Church, and should be eliminated. Both were shocked, and concerned for her state of mind.

Something had taken shape in Violet's brain. On her return to London, she told Enid Dinnis that the idea that 'good pious Catholics could consider it right to kill' disgusted her. Her revulsion may well have been fed by the ruthless campaign of assassination being conducted at the time by Irish revolutionaries, her support for their political objectives notwithstanding. But where her emotions revolted at the thought, her intellect drew her inexorably into the theology of murder. It was a labyrinthine subject, crammed with contradictory messages. In Exodus (20:13), the position is clear: 'Thou shalt not murder', but elsewhere in the Bible the Israelites are commanded to kill. St Michael used force to expel Adam and Eve from paradise; a Dominican friar, convinced he was doing God's work, assassinated Henry III of France; the Jesuits, who embodied the idea of the 'Church militant', boasted a long lineage of clerics who defended their beliefs with violence. More recently, in the Great War, Sergeant Alvin York had turned his trigger finger over to God and become a celebrated Christian sniper: in a single encounter, he picked off seventeen German soldiers and then shot eight more with his pistol. 'Every time I saw a head I just touched it off . . . A higher power than man guided and watched over me and told me what to do,' he explained.

Violet tussled with a whole raft of precedents that seemed to justify selective killing. One, in particular, caught her attention. Enid Dinnis wrote an account of what happened next:

[Violet] was in [a] low state of depression and dwelling on the fact that more suffering was required of her . . . She was ill and feverish. She left the house in the middle of the night in her night things and was brought back by two policemen who knew her by sight. In the morning she slipped out and the housekeeper's daughter followed to bring her back. Miss Gibson was behaving very strangely. She went down the cellar area of a house and took a knife out of her bag. It was the knife that she used for book-binding which lay on her table. The girl who had followed her screamed and the police came. The girl's hands [and face] were cut. Miss Gibson turned on her, whether as an interferer or as a 'victim' it is not known. On this occasion Miss Gibson was certified as insane and taken to the Mental Home at Virginia Water. I saw her there soon after and she told me that she had been under the impression that she was doing something great 'for God and his Church'. This was a confidence which she carefully kept from the doctors, I discovered . . . On the occasion when she went out with the knife we found by her bedside her Bible open at the chapter in Genesis containing the story of Abraham and the sacrifice of Isaac.

*

HOLLOWAY SANATORIUM, VIRGINIA WATER. COPY OF THE CASE BOOK ENTRIES, FILE NUMBER 4818, REGARDING THE HON. VIOLET GIBSON

ad. 9 Oct. 1923	Gibson, Violet Albina. 48. Single The Hon.
R.O. 9 Oct 1923	Roman Catholic
B. of C.	21, Holland Street, Kensington, W.8
10 Oct 1923	First attack.
	Age on last attack 48 years.
	Not previously under treatment.
	Duration of attack, a few days.
	Supposed cause, unknown.
	Not epileptic, not suicidal.
	Is violent. Homicidal.
	No family history of insanity.
1st Certificate	Violet Albina Gibson was sitting on the floor of the padded room, calling for people to kill, she said she had already nearly killed one, and must have some more.
Communicated	Harriet Arnold, Attendant, St Mary Abbot's Hospital, says Violet Albina Gibson is distinctly homicidal, she assaulted another patient and tried to kill her, and requires constant restraint.

2nd Certificate	Corroborates.
History	Patient says she was educated at home with governess. She says she was never strong but has always thought too much about her illnesses . . . She says she has been very thin till the last two years or so when she suddenly got fat. She got into the hands of the police for attacking a servant in the street. (The servant had to have four stitches in her face. The patient had a knife hidden in a basket).
Present Condition	Patient is of fair height, fairly well developed. In rather flabby condition – inclined to be fat. Hair grey. Looks decidedly old for her age. Eyes blue. Pupils rather large. Pulse regular – walls not hard. Heart area normal, sounds regular and of good force. No murmurs. Chest. Note fair. Movement poor. Air entry at apices of lungs at back very poor. Sounds deficient all over. No adventitious sounds. Amputation scar of breast on left side is healthy. Abdomen. Some thickening under appendix scar, which is in good condition. No upper teeth. Lower incisors require scaling. Much bruising of right foot. Knee jerks present. Urine, acid. No albumen, no sugar.
Mental	Patient is friendly and willing to talk. She has rather a vacant expression. She says she was quite well till a few days ago. She says she has always been afraid of traffic and a few days ago she made up her mind to walk backwards and forwards across Church Street, Kensington, in the middle of the vehicles. She did this for some time, till a servant from home met her

and asked her to go home. Then patient took the servant down into a cellar and tried to kill her. She is very confused at times but says she remembers being at the Kensington Infirmary. She says she is very doubtful now as to when she is speaking the truth and when she is not. She says that she tried to persuade a dentist to take out all her front teeth so that she might not have toothache if she became a nun, but she seems very doubtful as to whether she ever wanted to be a nun. She has shown no signs of violence here but says she might want to try again to kill someone. She is wet and dirty.

16 Oct   Has given no trouble. Was somewhat agitated after her return from Mass on Sunday. Is a little bit inclined to be confused sometimes. Her left terminal phalanx of the hand is injured; she says in a struggle before she came.

22 Oct   She is much better and says that she now has no desire to hurt anyone. She seems happy and contented and looks better. Is still wearing her little finger in a splint.

1 Nov   The little finger is still swollen and the bone has not made a good union yet. Patient is considerably clearer. She is up and goes for walks in the court. She says she is not worrying at all about the incidents that brought her here and that she is not wanting to hurt anyone now.

12 Nov   The little finger is now united, but the terminal joint is still swollen. The patient seems much better and is well occupied with reading, etc. Goes out in the grounds and is beginning to make friends with patients. Goes to Mass each Sunday.

26 Nov	Improvement has been well maintained. Patient is cheerful, pleasant in manner and well occupied. Has occasional abdominal discomfort in the neighbourhood of the operation scar.
8 Dec	Cheerful and friendly but is reserved and inclined to be secretive. Went on leave today, with a Nurse.
18 Mar 1924	Has improved while on leave. Discharged from leave. Relieved.

Violet went straight from Holloway Sanatorium to 5 Grosvenor Crescent, where Constance lived with the dowager Lady Ashbourne. Dinnis, who visited often, discerned a slight improvement – 'the brain was more normal' – but was troubled by Violet's repeated questions about whether or not it was right to kill. 'She asked me to give her an assurance that I did not think so, and demanded a definite denial. [Later] she asked me in a very excited state to get her an assurance in writing from some one else to the same effect.'

PART TWO

ACTS

Peter running away from persecution when he met Our Lord.
'Quo vadis Domine?'
'I am going to Rome.'
VIOLET GIBSON, NOTEBOOK

I

Theatre of Madness

Under the influence of his Jewish mistress, Margherita Sarfatti, Mussolini had drifted up-market in his patterns of behaviour. He began to cultivate a fresh image, shaving off his moustache, wearing collared shirts, generally aiming at a new elegance. In this, he was also much influenced by Gabriele d'Annunzio, the soldier-poet and dandy who for a while was considered a serious rival to Mussolini as the figure behind whom the fractious Italians might unite.

Between the death of Verdi in 1901 and Mussolini's March on Rome in 1922, d'Annunzio became the most famous Italian in the world. Modelling himself as a Nietzschean supertype, he was combative, cruel, prematurely bald and proud of it (hair, he claimed, had no useful function in modern civilisation, therefore a lack of it was a sign of higher evolutionary development). He was dedicated first and foremost to promoting himself, and thereafter to inflated and aestheticised themes of heroism, love, death and violence. Enthralled by his reputation, by his stiff collars and sharp creases and his greyhounds in livery tailored by Hermès, society ladies reserved rooms in hotels where he stayed, hoping to catch his eye. (In Italy, the fascination endures: his correspondence with his jeweller was published as a separate volume in 1989.) Less enthusiastic, the Catholic Church placed his works, rife with decadent sensuality, on the *Index of Prohibited Books*. For once, the Vatican was right, but for the wrong reason: aside from blatant plagiarism, his output is almost unreadable – love lyrics, idylls on classical themes, patriotic dramas and 'trashily plotted novels about supermen figures who are transparently the author himself'. D'Annunzio, writes one historian, 'was a spectacular case of arrested emotional development, arguably a natural Fascist'.

[103]

In a speech delivered on the first day of the Great War, d'Annunzio proclaimed: 'We have no other value but that of our blood to be shed.' Emerging in 1915 as the figurehead of the Italian intervention campaign, he went on to become the country's most publicised and decorated soldier, his daring exploits with aeroplanes and torpedo boats lifting him into a full-blown national hero. The sordid aspects of his past – adulteries, illegitimate children, trails of creditors – were obscured by the blaze of glory conferred by the press, the military and politicians. 'In truth, d'Annunzio was a propagandist more than a soldier, and propaganda is a realm where gesture is substance and words are deeds.'

After the war, he was mooted in proto-Fascist circles as a contender for national leadership. The 'stench of peace' offended his nostrils, and he was spoiling for a new melodrama to keep normality at bay. In the event, the role was contracted to Mussolini, who launched Italy onto a new path of madness, taking much of what he had learned from the *Übermensch* d'Annunzio with him. He ransacked his rival's vitalist, high-octane style; he copied his delivery, a kind of barely controlled hysteria; he borrowed his hymning of bloodlust, even the throbbing vein that appeared on his shaved temple like a subcutaneous snake; and then he neutralised him by rewarding him lavishly to stay out of politics. 'Two things can be done with a bad tooth,' Mussolini quipped. 'Pull it out or fill it with gold.' On 13 August 1922, d'Annunzio aided in his own partial eclipse: high on cocaine and apparently unbalanced in the act of fondling the sister of his mistress, he fell from a window of his villa on Lake Garda and was seriously injured.

Italy's liberal ex-premier Giovanni Giolitti was convinced that the ongoing violent struggle between Socialists and Fascists, the general political turmoil, was little more than a 'neurasthenic' postwar hangover that could, with appropriate inducements, be tamed and steered into constitutional channels. His assessment fell short on two counts: the turmoil, by 1921, was little short of civil war; and neurasthenia was not something, like an excess of alcohol, that simply went away in the manner of a morning-after headache. But though Giolitti misused the term, neurasthenia was surely the correct diagnosis for what was going on.

Mussolini's facial contortions, his eyes rolling about loosely in their sockets, projecting out like dangerous gooseberries, were strikingly similar to the photographs, much circulated at the time, of hysterical patients in the care of Jean-Martin Charcot, head of the Salpêtrière asylum in Paris. In the mid-to-late nineteenth century, Charcot had set out to classify the contents of what he called the 'museum of living pathology', establishing a photographic atelier for his new form of medical documentation. The 'objective' technology of photography could not lie: it was the perfect medium, Charcot believed, to provide a physiognomic map of the imprints left on the body by maladies of the nerves and by the deranged emotions they could produce. Trainee medics could learn the art of diagnosis from such a natural history of symptoms. Through this photographic project, the Salpêtrière amassed a vast archive of the iconography of mental illness. Charcot's hysterics, like the early silent film stars who may well have imitated their expressions (belle-époque cinema was replete with violent sensation and melodramatic incident), went through the dramatic paces of their condition for the camera.

Charcot's most famous subject was a woman known only as Augustine. Repeatedly photographed, she developed a curiously apposite hysterical symptom: she began to see everything in black and white. Like many other patients, it was as if she had learned to mimic her own symptoms, to 'perform' them for Charcot in a kind of collaborative illusion. Indeed, she was able to use to her advantage the histrionic abilities that for a time made her a star of the asylum. Disguising herself as a man, she managed to escape from the Salpêtrière. Nothing further was ever discovered about her whereabouts.

The photographs – assembled in albums, complete with case histories, descriptions of disease and methods of treatment – rehabilitated the idea of madness as dramatically exciting and earned

Charcot the sobriquet 'The Napoleon of Neuroses'. The use of hypnotism, which he pioneered (he once mesmerised a rooster and thus became the original discoverer of the 'Hysterical Cock') was quickly taken up as a theatrical device by the notorious 'magnetisers' of the late nineteenth century, of whom the Belgian 'Professor' Donato was the most famous. In his hugely popular stage shows, where he first immobilised members of the audience by hypnosis and then manoeuvred them into performing humiliating charades, Donato claimed to be investigating 'the occult motor which animates us, the mysterious forces which create life, the bonds that unite us to one another, our mutual affinities, and our connection with the supreme power, the eternal level of the world'. Doctors like Charcot objected to this vulgarisation of mesmerism, and there were calls for Donato's stage performances to be banned. But it's questionable whether Donato was more or less unscrupulous as a spellbinder than Charcot, who used mesmerism to induce the various stages of hysteria in his patients. Both gave prominent public profile to the newly emerging language and gestures of 'madness'; and entry to Charcot's sessions at the Salpêtrière was as coveted as a ticket to Donato's performances.

Is it possible that Mussolini's 'mechanisms of fascination' derived, in part, from these influences? Certainly, he developed a histrionic style of oratory that was at once pantomimic and liturgical, with wildly exaggerated poses, melodramatic hand movements, striking modulations in tone and pitch of voice. In this, there is little to set him apart from Charcot's patients. Later, Adolf Hitler took it a stage further, and, like Augustine, was photographed rehearsing the poses of his 'interminable speechifying, the epileptic behaviour with its wild gesticulations, foam at the mouth, and the alternately shifty and staring eyes'. Pass them on the street, and you would avoid asking men like these for a light. And yet they drew crowds of tens, hundreds of thousands.

There was another influence. 'The crowd loves strong men,' Mussolini once said. 'The crowd is like a woman . . . Everything turns upon one's ability to control it.' Much of his crowd theory

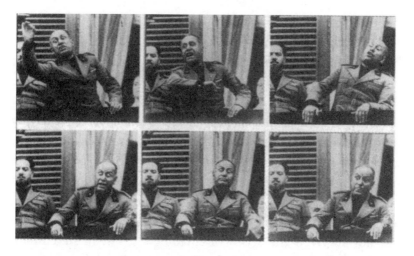

Staging madness: the controlled hysteria of Mussolini, and one of Charcot's
patients at the Salpêtrière

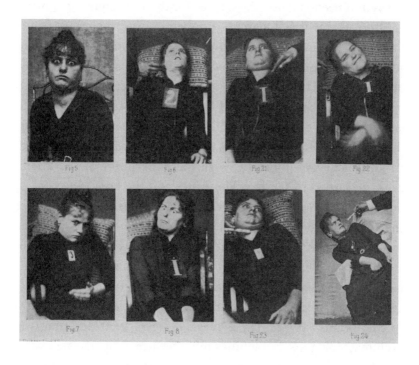

derived from the French writer Gustave Le Bon's *Psychologie des foules* (1865), which argued that crowds do not love kindly masters, but tyrants who oppress them: they trample down despots only when those despots have lost their strength and no longer inspire fear. The type of hero that attracts the crowd must always have the attributes of a Caesar: his panache must be seductive, his authority must command respect and his sabre must inspire fear. Crowds, according to Le Bon, have conservative instincts, a fetish-like respect for traditions and an unconscious horror of novelties that could change their way of life. They are not influenced by reason, and their arguments are always of an inferior order. Le Bon's theory has not survived the scorn of sociologists, but in 1921 Freud devoted several pages to it and called it a 'brilliant' description of the collective mind (*Group Psychology and Analysis of the Ego*). If Mussolini needed a pseudo-science for the techniques of control, Le Bon, as much as Charcot, supplied it. And the crowds confirmed it. 'Having lost their power of delegation, citizens do not act,' explains Umberto Eco, 'they are only called on to play the role of the People. Thus the People is only a theatrical fiction.'

Should the mechanisms of fascination not be sufficient to ensure popular compliance, Mussolini had other methods at his disposal. With Italy virtually in a state of civil war, with the spectre of Bolshevism looming, with the bankruptcy of the liberal class, he turned to the knuckle-duster and the boot. As if out of nowhere, *squadristi*, Fascist 'action squads', mushroomed all over the country. Composed typically of a dozen or so men, for the most part war veterans or students, they travelled to the scene of attack by bicycle or train, or in cars and lorries provided by sympathetic landowners and businessmen (who in turn had been targeted by socialist thugs), armed with an array of weapons: clubs (the notorious *manganello*), revolvers, daggers, grenades, rifles and even machine guns. Sometimes more bizarre weapons were used: one Mantua squad became well known for beating opponents around the head with *baccalà*, dried cod. Each squad had a sobriquet – Satan, Desperado, Dauntless, Lightning, *Me ne frego*

(I don't give a damn), or the name of some patriotic hero or event – and carried a banner with a skull and cross-bones or other macabre motif. Behind the histrionic façade was a programme of well-targeted brutality designed to break the working-class movement, led by Christian Socialists like the priest Don Luigi Sturzo whose *Partito Popolare* had trounced Mussolini in the 1919 elections. Ironically, the Fascist *squadristi* accompanied their raids with songs proclaiming the holiness of their cause, with the *manganello* – 'St Manganello' – singled out for particular veneration. The Fascists of Monteleone Calabro, for example, had a statue of Our Lady wearing a starred halo and holding the infant Christ and a Fascist club – the 'Madonna of the Manganello' – as their tutelary saint. The punishments inflicted on enemies were frequently couched in terms of Catholic penitence, as with castor oil which, as one Fascist newspaper explained, was intended 'to purge [a man] . . . of his faults, of the old sins of Bolshevism'. The powerful laxative qualities of castor oil also appealed to the scatological humour of the squads.

An estimated three thousand deaths scarred the Fascist rise to power, which culminated in the March on Rome on 28 October 1922 (adding an official death toll of three). More *coup de théâtre* than *coup d'état*, Mussolini unleashed twenty-five thousand blackshirts on the capital, waited to see how it would go, then took the overnight train from Milan, arriving in the morning wearing a black shirt, bowler hat and spats ('I come from the battlefield' was his implausible explanation for this strange outfit). He joined his volunteer army at the gates of Rome and made a solemn declaration: 'I swear to lead our country once more in the paths of our ancient greatness.' The king, Vittorio Emanuele III, having refused General Pietro Badoglio's offer to lead the army against the Fascists (he didn't think it worth the effort 'to save a cabinet of poltroons'), appointed Mussolini prime minister of Italy – at thirty-nine, the youngest in Italian parliamentary history. Less than a month later, in his first speech to the new parliament, Mussolini crowed: 'I could have transformed this grey hall into an armed camp for blackshirts, a bivouac for corpses. I could have nailed up the doors of parliament'– implying that the possibility was not to be ruled out.

The casualties of the last two years, and the ambiguous way – half coup, half manipulation – in which power had been achieved gave the new government an urgent need to justify itself. What were Mussolini's intentions? It wasn't at all clear. Here was a politician more interested in seeming to know than in knowing. 'The goal that he sedulously aims at is a constantly disturbing riddle,' ran an editorial in *The Times*, 'one of the tantalising riddles of our time.' 'The trouble with Mussolini', one of his henchmen confided privately, 'is that he wants everybody's blessing and changes his coat ten times a day to get it.'

In August 1923, Don Giovanni Minzoni, Catholic anti-Fascist priest, was beaten to death; in December, Giovanni Amendola, democrat opposition leader, was attacked by a Fascist squad; in January 1924, Gaetano Salvemini, professor at Florence University, was set upon by Fascists after putting his name to an article in the *New Statesman*, which subsequently commented, 'The Fascists are in their methods as barbarous as the Bolsheviks. For the moment at any rate foreigners cannot regard Italy as a civilised country.' On 10 June 1924, Giacomo Matteotti, leader of the *Partito Socialista Unitario* (United Socialist Party) and Mussolini's most competent opponent, was abducted while walking to parliament along the Tiber. He was savagely beaten and then stabbed to death by Fascists led by Amerigo Dumini, an old mucker of Mussolini's who had constituted a semi-official terror squad nicknamed the Ceka (after the Soviet secret police), whose function it was to intimidate government opponents. The assassins bundled Matteotti's body into the boot of their car (thus introducing the Italian custom of packing political cadavers into automobiles like so much baggage) and drove around the outskirts of Rome for several hours before stripping it, sexually assaulting it and throwing it into a shallow grave twelve miles outside the city. Matteotti's heavily decomposed body was not found until 16 August. Three days after his disappearance, the democratic and socialist Left, led by Amendola, abandoned the parliamentary chamber, branding the government unconstitutional. With that love of classical parallels they shared, ironically, with Mussolini, the anti-Fascists called themselves the 'Aventine secession', modelled on the Roman plebs who had withdrawn to the Aventine Hill in protest against the aristocracy.

For several weeks, as public outrage grew, Mussolini was in a state of anxiety verging on hysteria. His pathological indecisiveness was, excruciatingly, in full view. 'His life', Margherita Sarfatti wrote, 'seemed completely wrecked.' He denied having ordered the murder (for years afterwards he sent money to Matteotti's widow and children), but the rumour spread that he was ultimately responsible for Dumini's Ceka. Futhermore, his own party was wildly at variance on how to respond to the crisis, split between the *Legalitari* and the *Intransigenti*. The former were content to work for a strong, authoritarian Italy, freed from the threat of Marxism, but administered by the normal bureaucratic apparatus of the state (political murder, therefore, was off limits); the latter, led by Roberto Farinacci, a thuggish hierarch from the north with a fake law degree, were frustrated by what they considered an unaccomplished revolution and sought its completion in the violent destruction of the existing ruling class and the physical elimination of all opposition. They demanded a 'total' Fascist dictatorship and were openly impatient with Mussolini's vacillations.

On 17 June 1924, while the hunt for Matteoti's body was still underway, Mussolini finally made a move. He outflanked the *Legalitari* by appointing the moderate Luigi Federzoni to the post of Minister of the Interior, the guarantor of constitutional discipline in Italy. Federzoni's respectability (Mussolini once quipped that he was the sort of old man who put on a dark suit before going out to buy a roll of toilet paper) dissipated whatever doubts about Fascism and Mussolini currently lingered among members of the old elite. But the appointment did not appease the *Intransigenti*. At the end of the year, they gave Mussolini an ultimatum: either he complete the revolution his way, or they would do it their way, which he could assume would be less accommodating. On 4 January 1925, he took up the challenge in a speech later regarded as a milestone in the history of modern Europe: 'I, and I alone, assume the political, moral and historical responsibility for everything that has happened . . . When two powers clash and are irreconcilable, force is the answer.' He meant what he said. That night, Fascist militia and police, with a massive wave of arrests, began the annihilation of the opposition. This was the curtain-lifter to the 'totalitarian' state, Mussolini's six-syllabled gift to the twentieth century.

Violet, now living on her own again in Kensington, had been monitoring developments in Italy with growing horror. Mussolini's betrayal of socialism, the brutal incursions into her (idealised, surely) vision of Italy as the land of Dante, Fra Angelico, St Francis, and the silence of the Vatican – these were flagrant assaults on both God and Liberty (Mussolini's 'putrid goddess'), the principles that Violet was committed to defending. Still uncertain about her role in the Divine plan, she waited for a sign. The confusing intersection of politics and faith, the temporal and the spiritual, resolved itself on All Saints' Day, 1 November 1924, in the form of a huge Conservative majority in the general election that toppled Ramsay Macdonald's Labour government. Violet, a Labour supporter, had pledged herself to a 'sacrifice' in the event of a Conservative win. The form this sacrifice took was to renounce John O'Fallon Pope, who had been her spiritual director for nine years. 'No one will ever know the quiet inward sorrow this cost me for many a day after,' she confided to her notebook. 'He had brought me from death to life and I had a deep and reverend affection for him which permeated my whole life.'

As Enid Dinnis later recounted,

She had been talking a great deal of the martyrs. She made all kinds of haste in order to get to Rome within the octave of All Saints and achieved it. She only told me the day before and I was powerless to do anything. I could only hope that her family would take steps to keep an eye on her. Her companion was Miss McGrath who had not even been told of the exact state of her mental condition.

On 6 November 1924, the hapless Mary McGrath, a hired nurse-companion from County Meath, embarked for Rome with Violet. Violet had assembled her clothes and belongings in great haste. But she had time enough to include in her luggage a small revolver.

II

Martyrs

The moral atmosphere in Italy had changed greatly since Violet's last visit some fifteen years before. When she arrived in November 1924, the shock and grief of the Matteotti affair was palpable. The Fascist regime was still young, opposition to it even younger: in Matteotti, the anti-Fascist vocation found its first iconic martyr. His fate had become a passion narrative, his image covertly passed round like a religious object. (The Sicilian writer Leonardo Sciascia, then a child, was warned by his aunt never to say a word to anyone about the photograph of Matteotti she kept hidden in her sewing basket.) Impromptu shrines appeared overnight on street corners and city monuments, and stubborn graffiti in black enamel paint accusing Mussolini of his murder proved difficult to remove.

But public expression of this story was reduced to mere punctuation marks, hiccoughs, by Fascism's bulging arsenal of narrative instruments. A new Italy was in the making, and architects, designers, writers and artists rallied to ratify its image in bold and often crushing statements of power. It was harder – would soon be impossible – for foreigners arriving in Italy to act like so many Ruskins, privileged sightseers intolerant of and disappointed by development, restoration, anything that interfered with the picturesque. Fascism did not cut its mood to meet the demands of the pilgrim brimful with historical information and expectations derived from Grand Tour literature.

Violet, armed with her little revolver, seemed prepared for the new violent realities. In 1912, Richard Bagot had claimed in *My Italian Year* that 'the stereotyped British idea that every Italian carries a knife in his pocket which he will use on the slightest provocation is an enormously exaggerated one'. But the stereotype endured, and was reinforced by the rude cudgels of Fascism. Shortly after Violet arrived in Rome, Scott Fitzgerald, who was staying with Zelda at the Albergo Quirinale, got involved in a brawl with a plainclothes policeman, an incident he described as 'just about the rottenest thing that ever happened in my life'.

Other foreigners, too, were attacked, and it's conceivable Violet brought a pistol from England for her own protection. Still, it was a strange object to possess in the convent of Our Lady of Lourdes, near the Piazza di Spagna, where she had taken up lodgings with her companion Mary McGrath. Indeed, she seems to have hidden it amongst her belongings in her room rather than carrying it about, which suggests she wasn't that concerned for her safety, despite seeking out the poorest – and most dangerous – quarters of Rome.

Police enquiries later revealed that Violet spent much of her time in the working-class district of Trastevere, an area whose merits guidebooks struggled to assert. 'The proportion of murders . . . is larger in this than in any other part of the city,' warned Augustus Hare.

They pride themselves on being born 'Trasteverini', profess to be the direct descendants of the ancient Romans, seldom intermarry with their neighbours, and speak a dialect peculiarly their own. It is said that in their dispositions also they differ from the other Romans in that they are far more hasty, passionate, and revengeful, as they are a stronger and more vigorous race.

Trastevere, for Violet, was like Willie's Southwark in London. It was the place where her Catholic socialism could be exercised in the giving out of alms and in the selfless dedication to the *whole* person, in whatever condition of deprivation or need. This was, for her, the living significance of Catholicism, the religion of the Incarnation. Back at the convent, the nuns formed the impression that she was engaged in setting up some kind of 'charitable mission'. She told the Mother Superior that she had come across a Swedish family in miserable straits, but that she couldn't look after them as she was helping so many other poor people. Her bank statements suggest otherwise: despite organising a credit arrangement through the Westminster Bank authorising the Banca Commerciale to disburse £100 a week, she only ever withdrew a fraction of this sum. After her arrest in 1926, police found a number of envelopes in her room, each containing small denominations for distribution to the poor. Her alms-giving was not so much prodigious as symbolic of the spiritual tradition she sought to inhabit. It was in Rome, after all, that the early Christians had first acquired their reputation, begrudgingly bestowed by their pagan persecutors, for caring for the poor and the sick, and for being ready to embrace martyrdom.

If Violet was not carrying the revolver for her own protection, what was it for? To Willie and Marianne she had openly voiced the opinion that the Pope should be eliminated. She had ample motive for wishing to confront the pontiff – for his hostility to Modernism, for his autocratic detachment from the aims of Christian socialism, for his silence over Fascism's daily mugging of fundamental liberties. Was the Pope her original target? Her friend Enid Dinnis certainly thought so: 'When Miss Gibson's friends heard that she was at large again in Rome they nearly all of them expressed the same fear, that she would shoot the Holy Father. We all feared it. I never heard her speak of Signor Mussolini.'

Violet had acquired letters of introduction from priests in London, and these she presented to various eminent clerics in Rome, including Father Fedele de Stotzingen, a German Benedictine of the Collegio di San Anselmo. De Stotzingen would later tell police that he met Violet soon after she arrived in November 1924. In the first instance she asked him to arrange an audience with the Pope, a request he decided not to pursue; two or three weeks later she asked him to be her spiritual confessor, to 'take direction of her soul'. This he declined, suggesting instead that she attach herself to one of the numerous English priests in Rome. She also asked him if she should do what it was God was asking of her. He was under the impression that she meant to found a religious institution, and thought little more of the matter. Later, keen to dissociate himself from this troubling woman, he declared loftily: 'I would not have received her again after her visit, but for the fact I knew she came from a distinguished family, because I do not generally receive the same person more than once except for special reasons.'

Stotzingen's refusal to become Violet's confessor was a cruel blow. She was indeed on a mission, but it was not of the kind that he and the nuns surmised. She was struggling with her conscience. Should she kill? Was this the sacrifice God required of her? She needed help, spiritual guidance – and in Rome, of all places, she had difficulty in finding it. The disappointment, and the morbid effect of Rome on the nerves, began to tell on Violet's health. The narrow alleys and streets with their cramped dramas acted on her like bad thoughts. In *Roderick Hudson*, Henry James describes Rome's 'ponderous past, blighted with the melancholy of things that had had their day', as a constant reminder of permanent loss. His frail characters are irresistibly drawn to Rome, only to be 'morally corrupted, artistically destroyed, financially ruined, physically maimed, or flat-out killed'. As one of them says, 'If Roman life doesn't do something to make you happier, it increases tenfold your liability to moral misery.'

Could there be any place more miserable for Violet than the Colosseum, a place she visited often, taking with her a picnic lunch prepared by the nuns? Squat, overweight, the Colosseum was, for Zola, 'a world where one loses oneself amidst death-like silence and solitude'. Dickens, on his first full day in Rome in 1845, found 'its solitude, its awful beauty, and its utter desolation' striking him 'like a softened sorrow'. He wondered whether a stranger could ever be 'so moved and overcome by any sight, not immediately connected with his own affections and afflictions'. For Violet, the connection to her sensibilities was very direct. For her, every stone bled with the memory of the Christian martyrs. The black cross in the middle and the shrines erected around the circle to commemorate Christ's Passion and suffering, at which pilgrims knelt to say penitental prayers – these ponderous markers, weighted with the sorrow of the past, drove darkly across her mind. 'We have nothing good of ourselves, but only misery and nothingness,' she wrote in her notebook.

As a woman on her own, choosing to live a life apart, Violet's independence was an opportunity, giving her the freedom to create a self that was utterly remote from the self deduced by the world. 'Here we go alone and like it better so,' Virginia Woolf once hymned. 'Always to be accompanied, always to be understood, would be intolerable.' But the separateness, the pronounced withdrawal from others, was also a burden, a space filled up with doubt, brooding introspection, the anguish of self-interrogation, great intervals of nothingness. The Colosseum was a perilous place for Violet to be. In *The Marble Faun*, Nathaniel Hawthorne's heroine, Miriam, is seen under its 'dusky arches' where she has stepped aside, for an instant, 'solely to snatch the relief of a brief fit of madness'. Throwing off her self-control, she becomes 'a mad woman, concentrating the elements of a long insanity into that instant'.

On the evening of Friday 27 February 1925, Violet withdrew to her room in the convent. She read a few passages from the Bible, lit some candles on an improvised altar, knelt down, held a pistol to her chest (there where her left breast had been removed), and pulled the trigger. Hearing the noise echo through the convent, the nuns rushed to her room and banged on the door. Violet managed to get to her feet – the coppery nausea of blood in her mouth, the vertigo of self-sacrifice – and drag herself to her bed, in which position the nuns found her. According to Mary McGrath, who had also rushed to the scene, Violet was bleeding slightly from the mouth. There was no other injury immediately visible (indeed, as Violet had pulled the sheets up to her chin before allowing the nuns to enter, there was no obvious sign of what had happened). McGrath saw the revolver, and asked her what she had done. 'I wanted to die for the glory of God,' came the reply. Violet forbade her to call a doctor before calling a priest. Believing her to be close to death, the nuns complied and called an English priest, Father Charles Charola, from the nearby church of San Silvestro. Only after seeing Father Charola did Violet finally allow herself to be examined by a doctor and taken to hospital, where surgeons discovered that the bullet had entered just above the heart, bounced off a rib and lodged itself in her shoulder, leaving her, miraculously, with no serious injury. They removed the bullet and sedated her, most likely with laudanum.

The British ambassador was informed, and he called Constance, who immediately notified Willie in France. The next day, Father Stotzingen visited and found her 'very calm and repentant of her act. I reproved her for her action, asked her if she had confessed (she replied in the affirmative).' But he failed to get from her an explanation for her actions. De Stotzingen would later tell police that Violet had asked him, fifteen days before trying to take her life, to look after a small package, which he returned to her unopened when he visited her in the hospital.

Four days after she shot herself, Willie arrived by train from Paris to persuade his sister to return to London. She refused. He stayed nearly a month, walking around Rome in his tam o'-shanter, his cloak tossed over his back, a saffron kilt exposing a pair of rugged knees, in his hand a blackthorn stick of generous proportions. This attire created the impression in the British Embassy that he was 'as mad as his sister'. Meanwhile, in London, solicitors acting for the dowager Lady Ashbourne and the family asked the Board of Control of Lunacy for advice as to the steps which could and ought to be taken for Violet's care on her return to England. It was probably knowledge of her family's intention to have her committed that finally induced Violet to go to a rest home in Rome, where she could be attended to by a psychiatrist and nurses. On 8 March she was admitted as a voluntary patient at the Villa Giuseppina clinic on via Nomentana. Interviewed regularly by the director, Professor Antonio Mendicini, she refused to talk about politics (or so a nervous Mendicini maintained when, little over a year later, he was interviewed by the police). She spoke only of her desire to humble herself before God – this was why she had tried to kill herself, though she now acknowledged she had made a mistake and promised not to do it again. God had refused her sacrifice.

Writing to Dinnis while still in hospital, Violet had enlarged on this theme of sacrifice. Referring to the letter, Dinnis commented:

It made me very unhappy as I recalled that on a former occasion when she had said she was going away and did not know where, that I had laughed, and said that it was like Abraham going into the Land of Vision, and it had seemed to impress her. When she wrote to me from the hospital after the attempt on her own life, she said, 'You will understand because you know that there is a place called, "God seeth"' (which is the name Abraham gave to the place of sacrifice). This shows that her mind had fixed on that unhappy point.

Violet remained in the clinic for almost two months, and was visited daily by the faithful McGrath, who had moved to the nearby convent of Santa Brigida, in via delle Isole, to be closer to her. In April, Violet joined her companion at the convent, where she was to reside for almost a year.

Violet had refused to tell anyone (Stotzingen or McGrath or Willie or Mendicini) where she had obtained the revolver. Her reserve in this, as in other matters, was disciplined, non-negotiable. The weapon was now in the custody of the police, to whom the nervous nuns had reported the incident. McGrath would later testify that she took to searching among Violet's trunks to see if she had any arms, even a pair of scissors. Clearly, her searches were not thorough enough, for, in time, Violet would acquire another pistol, and turn it on Mussolini – apparently with God's blessing, if not that of his representatives on earth. 'How lucky it is we are to be judged by God instead of man,' Violet had written in her notebook. But does God forgive us the sins he makes us commit?

*

There is little trace of Violet for the rest of 1925. McGrath's testimony suggests that the following months were a mixture of calm –

taking tea together, doing jigsaw puzzles, reading (*Lives of the Saints*, mostly, but Violet was also a dedicated newspaper-reader), going for walks – and mysterious disappearances. Violet would send McGrath, who was by now on strict instructions from the Gibson family not to let her out of her sight, on an entirely point- less errand and then take the opportunity to slip off on her own. When one of the nuns suggested that McGrath follow Violet, 'as she was clearly unwell and could suddenly become ill in the streets', she replied that this was impossible because Violet wouldn't allow her. She added that even if she did disobey her instructions, Violet would surely notice, as 'she was extremely astute'. Often, she was out all day and would say nothing of where she had been or what she had been doing when she returned, exhausted, to the convent.

From London, Enid Dinnis kept up a regular correspondence and sent Violet her novels, mediocre confections about 'simple and devout Roman Catholics who move easily in the companion- ship of the unseen world'. In late 1925, she told Violet how glad she was that her latest book had pleased her:

History can tell awful lies – at one time it was manufactured for political purposes. I don't believe we are much better nowadays. The Locarno Pact has brought up the point that comes out in my books – King Henry VI was a dreamer of world-peace. I put the last word to the M.S. on the day the pact was signed. It was rather strange . . .

'What do you think of the Fascists?' Dinnis added, almost as an afterthought. 'They are getting quite strong over here. One of the mildest of the Farm Street ladies came into the library vibrating and told me she thought of joining them, in a very mysterious whisper.'

Dinnis's association of the Locarno Pact (initialled in October 1925 and signed two months later) with the reign of Henry VI is intriguing. Henry VI, Wordsworth's 'royal saint', was held up by the two women as a spiritual role model. Dinnis seemed to be drawing a connection between King Henry and Austen Chamberlain, who, as architect of the Locarno agreement, won acclaim for his peace- loving diplomacy. As did Mussolini. The pact marked a high point in Anglo-Italian relations, and many liberal politicians – those 'fine, decorative, worthy gentlemen in top hats and morning coats' whom Giorgio Bassani excoriated for giving Mussolini 'time to catch his breath' after the murder of Matteotti – publicly congratulated Il Duce. In general, the Italian liberal elite, instead of standing out against the tenor of Fascism, capitulated, either by just flopping along, offering no opposition, or by withdrawing into self-censorship and a gilded internal exile. Tolerance became acceptance, caution was swollen into cowardice.

Whatever historical inference Dinnis sought to draw out of the Locarno Pact, Violet was under no illusion that it would advance world peace. For her – unlike the vibrating ladies at the Jesuit church of Farm Street – any pact with Fascism was a bargain with the devil. If she had come to Rome with the intention of eliminating the Pope, this may well have been the moment when she switched her target, fixing Mussolini in her sights instead.

In this, she was not alone. At 9 a.m. on 4 November 1925, Mussolini took to the balcony of Palazzo Chigi to address a large crowd, despite the warning of Interior Minister Luigi Federzoni that an assassin was planning to shoot him from the window of the nearby Albergo Dragoni, a mere hundred yards away. Tito Zaniboni, a distinguished retired soldier and former deputy of Matteotti's *Partito Socialista Unitario* (PSU), had been part of a plot to depose Mussolini after Matteotti's murder. The failure of the plot, and the subsequent banning of the PSU, convinced him that Mussolini had to be eliminated.

Unfortunately for Zaniboni, he was ably played by an agent provocateur who was posing as an accomplice whilst he was actually setting him up (he even booked the hotel room for him). Zaniboni was arrested in his hotel room, with the rifle and its telescopic sight still hidden in a cupboard, fully two hours before Mussolini appeared on the balcony. This minor detail was not disclosed to the public, who were instead fed a story of how brilliant investigative policework had broken up an international conspiracy.

III

Gethsemane

After years of silence, Violet had begun communicating with her mother. The first steps were tentative and indirect. In early December 1925 she wrote to Constance asking her to buy Lady Ashbourne some flower bulbs on her behalf as a Christmas present. 'If you think she would like a bowl with them get it for her, so that the whole thing is very complete and full . . . No stinting about anything. I want her to have whatever she would like best.' Constance bought hyacinths, and in late January 1926 Lady Ashbourne wrote to say that they were still flowering. Addressing Violet as 'Darling Blue Baby', she sent family news, and asked of her daughter: 'I would like so much to hear how you are and what you are doing and what kind of friends you have.' Another letter, in the same vein, followed in early February. Lady Ashbourne signed off 'goodbye darling your always loving mother'. They were her last words to Violet.

On 19 March, a letter arrived from Constance: 'My dearest Vizie, Mother is very ill. She has had a stroke which has partially paralised [*sic*] her left side and she is not conscious now . . . She has been so pleased with your letters and with the flowers you sent her. I am so glad you wrote.' Two days later, on the morning of Sunday 21 March, Violet received a telegram: 'MOTHER SERIOUSLY ILL HAVE WRITTEN FULLY. CONSTANCE.'

Violet rushed to Rome's Termini station to enquire about trains to England. Carrying the telegram with her, she jotted down the times on the reverse: 'Start 11:55 a.m. Tues, arrive Wed night'. She was planning her route back to England and to a final reconciliation with her mother, even at the considerable risk of being committed by her family. But she didn't take the Tuesday train, because that afternoon a second telegram arrived: 'MOTHER DIED PEACEFULLY TODAY. CONSTANCE.'

The following letters were found in a little bundle when police later searched Violet's room at the convent of Santa Brigida:

SUNDAY 21 MARCH 1926, CONSTANCE TO VIOLET:

My dearest Vizie,

Mother passed away this morning very peacefully. I went out to early Church and when I came in I found she had had a turn for the worse. She died about half an hour afterwards . . . I have laid your little dried flowers next her heart under a night gown she is wearing which was made for her by me. She will be buried like that. Elsie is going to stay with me for a while and then I am going to let the flat and go for a long sea trip.

Very much love from

Constance

25 MARCH 1926, ELSIE TO VIOLET:

I know by now you must have got Constance's letter telling all about mother and answering your questions . . . It was a wonderfully peaceful death – she just breathed more and more gently till it stopped. Constance knelt beside her stroking her forehead – she was quite unconscious, and I stood at the foot of the bed and took Constance away when it was over. I never saw anything more beautiful than mother after she had died. I went in on the Sunday evening to see her – they had done her hair softly over her ears around her face and put a white lace thing (like Granny's black one) on her head, a white and pink night gown . . . it was the most wonderfully beautiful thing I have ever seen . . .

She was very fond of you and very anxious to do all she could for you. I think she was fond of all of us, but there were so many and she wasn't very strong. She had a happy successful life. Even these last years with their tragedies were happy in a way . . .

I hope you are well. Constance is wonderful and will be all right after a little.

Love, Elsie

27 MARCH 1926, MARIANNE TO VIOLET:

. . . Your mother went to sleep peacefully at the last, before that she had been unconscious and moaning.

The dowager Lady Ashbourne was cremated at Putney Vale Cemetery on 27 March. Marianne told Violet in a letter so clumsy as to be malicious (the reference to Lady Ashbourne's death moans) that it was 'a Christian Science Service and the weather was beautiful'. Her remains were taken to Dublin and buried with those of her husband in the family vault.

The following day, Sunday, 28 March, Violet went out. It was Fascism's seventh birthday, and Mussolini was delivering a speech to fifty thousand blackshirts and tens of thousands of otherwise-attired Italians at the Villa Glori hippodrome. It was another fighting speech, denouncing outsiders who were hostile to Fascism's triumphs, calling on Italians to rally themselves to its glorious advance. 'It is beautiful to live,' he concluded, 'but it will be still more beautiful, if it is necessary, to die.' Dr Ugo Tavani, army surgeon, would later come forward to police to state that he had observed a woman fitting Violet Gibson's description – about sixty years old (all the witness accounts have Violet at least a decade older than she is), wearing spectacles, medium height, dressed in black, and without a hat (hatlessness being a feature worth noting). She was trying to get close to Mussolini and behaving in a suspicious manner. She was carrying a bunch of flowers in her right hand, 'with which she covered a small package she was holding in her left hand'. Tavani added with disapproval that she did not join the rest of the crowd in applauding Mussolini (he doesn't seem to have considered how she was meant to do this with both hands full). Tavani pointed her out to a nearby policeman, who kept her under observation until Mussolini had moved on.

At this point, Willie, straight from burying his mother, was journeying out to Rome. Worried by the effect their mother's death might have on his sister's mental state, he was once again trying to get her back to England. On arriving, he consulted a lawyer, Antonio Ambrosini, as to the legal options. Ambrosini agreed that Violet was clearly 'an unusual person', but not legally insane. If all the strange people who came to Italy were locked up, he added, then the tourism industry would be bankrupted. Rome was a village when it came to gossip, and it didn't take long for Violet to learn of the presence of her kilted brother there. How hard he tried to find her is uncertain. There were priests of his acquaintance who knew Violet, and knew where she was living. Did he really want to find her? Regardless, she didn't want to be found, and her strategies of avoidance were by now highly refined. After a few days in Rome, Willie installed himself in a wagon-lit and returned to Paris.

At this time, Violet appeared 'as one who had lost all human sensibility, walking with her body absolutely upright, her eyes staring and her arms dangling at her sides. She neither acknowledged nor replied to greetings.' This zombie portrait was drawn by staff in the Hotel del Parco, to which she had moved, for no clear reason, on 30 December 1925, and it was later used to great effect by Violet's legal counsel to support a diagnosis of derangement. But it is also the case that Violet, in these two weeks before she shot Mussolini, became focused, determined, single-minded. For no apparent reason, she had already dispensed with the services of McGrath, who was instructed to return home to Ireland and to maintain a strict silence in the matter of her dismissal. McGrath left Rome, reluctant and disconsolate, on 17 March. To a friend, she confided her resentment and hurt, saying she didn't know why she had been sacked. She made no mention of any intention of Violet's to commit a crime. The first she heard about the shooting was from reading a newspaper report while on a train taking her on the final leg of her journey back home to County Meath.

Violet was now completely on her own. In her notebook she wrote: 'There is no pain except in the *hesitancy* to accept the cross.' She was facing her own Calvary, but she was hesitating, swaying towards a failure of the will. As her mother lay dying, Violet had decided to return to England and her family, then she abandoned that plan for its obvious futility. A week later, she had dismissed McGrath, seemingly preparing herself to act. Still she dithered, trying to repair this decision by asking Enid Dinnis to come immediately to Rome. At 10.15 a.m. on Thursday 1 April she sent her a telegram: 'COME. VIOLET.' But Dinnis's brother was ill. She could not, did not, come.

'My dear dear Violet,' Dinnis wrote by letter on 6 April,

I had a bad pain yesterday at the thought that I was not starting off for Rome . . . I *ached*. I don't like to think of you 'dead beat' and a Good Friday between you and a rest. I feel anxious and keep thinking of you. I want you to put your feet up on the couch.

Violet did not rest that day, or the next. The long and tortuous inner struggle was over. Events had dictated what she should do; the great mission was underway.

IV

What God Wants

Violet set out on the morning of 7 April 1926 to shoot Benito Mussolini at Palazzo Littorio, the Fascist Party headquarters, where he was due to appear that afternoon. This detail she had marked up in a newspaper, and written down on a scrap of envelope. Not expecting to return from her mission, she carried nothing with her except for this scrap, the Lebel revolver and the stone she had concealed in a black leather glove. Just over a week after Mussolini's speech extolling the virtues of dying for the Fascist cause, Violet shot him at point-blank range on Campidoglio. But for a fraction of an inch and an unreliable weapon, he would have had his 'beautiful' death.

Shortly after one o'clock, Violet found herself in the infirmary of the Mantellate prison, where police and magistrates struggled to establish her identity and her motive for trying to kill Il Duce. While she was being interviewed, Luigi Federzoni, Minister of the Interior (and the man who would probably have taken over had Violet's revolver not misfired), arrived at Mussolini's apartment, and together they discussed how to keep order. Foreign Secretary Dino Grandi had spread the word that the would-be assassin was a Slav acting on the orders of the Soviet Comintern, a manoeuvre designed to buy time and to ensure that any reprisals were directed against the Communists. Mussolini telephoned the King and then his wife, Rachele, who was living in the family home near Milan and who he feared might hear the news first from the radio. High-level functionaries came and went in a blur of self-importance, and Dr Bastianelli, concerned for his patient, convinced him to rest for a couple of hours, warning of the shock that could ensue after such a loss of blood.

But then the police arrived to take Mussolini's witness statement:

After coming out of the colonnade I was heading on foot towards the car and my face was turned to the right to watch a group of students who were singing 'Giovinezza', when I distinctly heard a gun shot and suddenly my nose was streaming with blood. I understood straight away that I had been hit, but that the wound wasn't at all serious. I immediately made clear that the incident should not provoke any disorder and after receiving brief medical attention in one of the offices of Campidoglio, I arrived at my residence by car.

By mid-afternoon, just as the first interview with Violet was being concluded, Mussolini was back in his Lancia, still wearing the big plaster across his nose, heading for Palazzo Littorio, her designated assassination site. As scheduled, he appeared at the presentation of the provincial secretaries to the new directorate of the National Fascist Party, where he told them that 'the Party must fascisticise the nation from top to bottom and from bottom to top'.

Fascistizzare – the clunking awfulness of the verb, the vulgarity of nouveau regime; the hissing sibilants pitched to menace. What exactly does it mean? Does meaning matter, when Mussolini's every word is set to detonate euphoria, when a mere flick of his hand is enough to redesign the whole composition of a crowd? Auden's brilliant poetic snapshot has 'Hitler and Mussolini in their wooing poses'. Wooing and winning. The applause tumbles like falling masonry. Il Duce lives, God save Il Duce! God preserve Italy's glittering destiny.

When later that evening a crowd assembles outside Mussolini's office at Palazzo Chigi, he emerges onto a balcony to address them. He wishes to show them, he says, that the ring of his voice has not changed one atom, and that the beat of his heart has not quickened. He thanks them for their spontaneous displays of enthusiasm, and calls on them to maintain strict discipline in the true Fascist style. 'No danger threatens the regime,' he bellows. Cries of 'The foreigner! The foreigner!' rise up from below. 'This danger, too, we shall face,' he replies. 'If this was the word which you wished to hear, this word I have spoken . . . I am one of your generation. That means I am the newest sort of Italian, one who is never thrown by events, but rather always proceeds straight down the road assigned by destiny.' In a dramatic peroration, soon adopted as one of the slogans of the regime, he urges the need for all to 'Live dangerously. Indeed, I say to you like an old soldier: "If I advance, follow me."' There was a second part to this lapidary sentence – 'If I retreat, kill me' – which would come to pass in due time. Then, 'If I die, avenge me.'* *'La forca, la forca!'*, 'The gallows, the gallows!' comes the answer.

'The people of the future may recall Mussolini as a kindly fat man who liked to shout from balconies,' wrote one columnist. But when Mussolini barked and bellowed from above, beneath him thronged the excited people of Italy, or of Rome, or of Fascism. 'They were what the regime dubbed an "oceanic crowd",' writes biographer Richard Bosworth, 'the indispensable extras, those who shouted "DUCE, DUCE, DUCE!" in an apparent ecstasy of faith and commitment.' For those involved – Il Duce and the people – the experience was not one of stand-up comedy, but of sacramental union.

Back at the Mantellate prison, Violet is taken to a cell, its furniture consisting of an iron bedstead, clothes-stand, chamber pot, table, aluminium plate and cup, wooden cutlery, a jug of drinking water and a wash-basin. 'It is better not to lay up possessions', she has written in her notebook, and her only request is for a crucifix, before which she prays on her knees for several hours. She then eats a meal, and falls into a deep sleep, according to the nuns who have been instructed to watch her all night.

Two lives, two parables, in degrading orbit. Mussolini is also being kept under surveillance. Telephone taps, installed a few

* The quote was borrowed from Henri de la Rochejaques, French revolutionist. In 1954, it would be recycled again by the incoming president of Vietnam, Ngo Dinh Diem.

years earlier when Mussolini was listed as a dangerous subversive, have not been removed. It is in the nature of the security state to turn in upon itself, and so it is that the private conversations of the Prime Minister of Fascist Italy were all being recorded. We learn from the transcripts of the following exchange, with his brother Arnaldo:

ARNALDO (in tears): My dearest Benito!
MUSSOLINI: Calm down. It's a mere bagatelle, there's no reason to be upset by something so insignificant. It was the briefest of episodes.
ARNALDO: But how is such a thing possible? With so many secret-service agents!
MUSSOLINI: There are certain things you simply can't foresee. That woman had a completely innocuous and innocent appearance, which made it very easy for her to slide in and . . .
ARNALDO: We must thank God. It could have been so much worse.

All over Italy, God is thanked. In churches, Te Deum ceremonies are held to celebrate Mussolini's miraculous escape. In Venice, the bells of St Mark's are rung in sign of thanksgiving. The fact that he has shed his blood on the most ancient of Roman sites does not interfere with an interpretation of the event as a contemporary Calvary. From the Vatican, Pius XI has despatched Cardinal Merry del Val (Willie Gibson's old scourge) to tell Mussolini in person that he is 'clearly protected by God'. A strange God, this, who tells Violet Gibson to shoot Mussolini, and then instructs the bullet not to kill him.

In Rome, expressions of worshipful adoration pour forth.

LETTER FROM CLARA PETACCI, AGE FOURTEEN, LUNGO TEVERE CENCI 10, ROME, 8 APRIL, 1926:

Duce, my most beloved Duce, our life, our hope, our glory – how can there be a soul so wicked to try to deprive our beautiful Italy of her glittering destiny? Oh Duce, why wasn't I there? Why wasn't I able to strangle that woman assassin who wounded our Divine being? . . . Duce, I would so love to rest my head on your chest, so that I might hear the living beats of Your great heart . . . When I heard the news, I thought I would die because I love you deeply, like a little Fascist of the first hour . . . me, a small but ardent Fascist, with my favourite motto which sums up the love that my young heart feels for you: Duce, I offer my life to You!

Unlike most schoolgirls, Clara Petacci will experience the realisation of her heart-swelling fantasy. Six years after writing this letter, when she is just twenty, she will become Il Duce's lover. A decade later, on 28 April 1943, she offers up her life for him: slammed up against a wall and shot. Her corpse is transported alongside her lover's to the Esso petrol station at Piazzale Loreto in Milan, where both cadavers are posed for the cameras – his head resting on her breast – before being strung up by the heels. Clara Petacci, the little Fascist, hanging like a prosciutto.

REPORT OF ATTILIO BAZZAN, OFFICER OF PUBLIC SECURITY, 10 APRIL 1926:

[Mussolini] was wounded and blood was spurting from his nose, and a few drops of his blood spattered onto my face (near my left eye) and on my hat.

Police on Campidoglio after the square had been closed off

After Campidoglio had been cleared and calm was restored, I went to [a nearby office] where I found my colleague, Euterpe Botti. He was explaining how the assassination attempt had unfolded, and was waving a blood-soaked handkerchief about, which he said he had used to wipe Mussolini's clothes. But when we returned to Campidoglio, Botti, forgetting what he had just said, contradicted himself, claiming that the handkerchief had become stained when he had dipped it in the blood that was on the ground. It didn't seem appropriate for me, at the time, to point out to Botti that his two versions of this event contradicted each other.

It's the passion that counts. Like all believers, Botti is transformed by his contact with this bloody representation. His handkerchief is now a devotional object; his status as its owner not subject to dispute. The truth of this cloth square as a reliquary overrides its significance as a piece of evidence.

The drama of faith. Kneel down and worship. The magdalenism of the young Petacci; the ghoulish infatuation of the excitable Botti – for fascisticised Italians, contact with the world outside their miracle cult is already abandoned.

V

Providential Escape

In the hours following the shooting, Mussolini showed impressive presence of mind. One major concern was over a possible devaluation of the lira on the world markets, and this was swiftly, and successfully, dealt with. But despite his call for no reprisals, towns and cities all over Italy were soon swollen with indignant crowds and *squadristi*. In Rome, the offices of *Il Mondo* and *La Voce Repubblicana* were sacked, their printing presses set alight. Police stood by as the mob trashed the buildings, carrying off furniture and equipment or hurling it into the fire. Rallying to the rumour that the assailant was a Comintern agent, another mob of between two and three hundred people headed for the Soviet embassy on via Gaetana and managed to smash most of the ground-floor windows and the lights outside the main entrance before the police decided to intervene.

Throughout the afternoon, groups of *squadristi* vented their wrath. They were, reported British ambassador Sir Ronald Graham, 'composed of rough-looking youths with sticks, bludgeons and occasionally revolvers [who] paraded the streets, either on foot or in motor lorries, behaving in a truculent manner, and some of them firing their weapons in the air'. A Communist was beaten up in Trastevere; a Republican was wounded in a café for refusing to shout '*Viva Mussolini*'; a bystander was hospitalised for not doffing his hat to a passing procession of Fascists. Foreigners were also targeted. A group of blackshirts marching down Corso Umberto 'became enraged at two Americans who were riding in an open carriage with their hats on. The mob smashed the Americans' hats with walking sticks.' The tyres of an American car with a British registration plate were slashed. 'It is felt in some quarters', intoned the *New York Times*, 'that the one weakness of the present regime is the conviction among Fascisti that they alone represent the real authority and are entitled to maintain discipline as they see fit.' These unseemly attacks – insults, rather – drew fire in a foreign press that was otherwise almost universally docile towards the regime. Following newspaper coverage of the burning of a straw-stuffed dummy with a bandaged nose during a massive anti-Fascist demonstration at La Louvière, the Belgian government apologised to the Italian ambassador.

One rare exception was the socialist *Freiburg Independent*, whose editorial of 8 April marvelled at the fuss over Il Duce's 'Cyrano de Bergerac' nose:

Mussolini, the disastrous Italian dictator, has lost the tip of his nose on account of the stupidity of a neurasthenic woman who couldn't aim well. Might this criminal attempt be a new comedy, the comedy of one hundred acts that is Fascism? The Fascist agencies report what they choose, above all divulging a load of nonsense, such as the following: 'A middle-aged woman fired point blank straight at Mussolini's face. The president was wounded in the nostrils.' So, the shot exploded right in his face, yet it only scratched the cartilage of his nose. What an obliging gun, what inoffensive bullets. The news of the attempt spread rapidly, and flags and standards were immediately hung out. In the narrow streets, sheets, coloured shirts, and so forth, were suspended on lines strung across balconies. Then the people went outside, in the manner of the ancient Romans, to listen to the great wounded one address the crowds. When and how does anybody in Italy find the time to work?

The business of belonging to the Fascist crowd had indeed become a time-consuming one. Soon, it was to be professionalised: one consequence of Violet's attempt was the reform of the police force, whose principal function became the protection of Mussolini. The new police chief, Arturo Bocchini, instituted a '*squadra presidenziale*' of five hundred plainclothes men. Absurdly over-the-top, the butt of many jokes, it was referred to by one historian as the 'applause squad'.

The Freiburg article was insulting, but it was also incendiary. 'A sensational event was needed to eclipse the outrage over the death of Amendola, victim of a few miserable thugs in the service of the omnipotent emperor,' it alleged. 'Nonetheless, the event has surprised even the head of Fascism, who has acquired a new popularity by losing the tip of his nose.' Giovanni Amendola, leader of the Aventine Secession and vocal critic of Mussolini's reign – he accused it of despoiling the Italian people of its fundamental rights – had been set upon by Fascists in a carefully staged attack near Montecatini in July 1925. This attack followed that of Boxing Day 1923, when he had been clubbed insensible by five *squadristi* in the centre of Rome. His compounded injuries were so severe (three of his ribs had to be removed, one of them having caused a haemorrhage of the lungs) that friends arranged for him to be taken to a hospital in Cannes, where he died, aged forty-four, at 7 a.m. on the day of Violet's attempt.

Amendola was the director of *Il Mondo*, which he founded in January 1922 as an anti-Fascist review. Hence the attack on *Il Mondo*'s offices – to stop it publishing news of his death. Perfunctory notice of his funeral was published in some Italian newspapers on 9 April, but the news was completely swamped by coverage of the assassination attempt. In the wake of Matteotti's murder, and with his cadaver still hovering like Thomas à Becket, Mussolini could ill afford a reprise of the public indignation and outrage this had provoked. Better to focus on the missing tip of his nose than on the mounting pile of political corpses. As the Freiburg article presciently warned, events on Campidoglio were to offer a turning point, an opportunity, cynically exploited, of restoring Mussolini to public sympathy and admiration, and enabling him, finally, to bury his opponents.

This connection was lost on the British ambassador, Sir Ronald Graham. As soon as he heard the news, he telegrammed to London:

TELEGRAM. SIR R. GRAHAM. SENT 5.20 P.M. 7 APRIL. RECEIVED 7.45 P.M. 7 APRIL.

When Signor Mussolini went this morning to open the International Medical Congress an attempt was made upon his life. Happily the bullet only scratched his nose. The shot is believed to have been fired by a Russian woman but no details yet available.

Graham then rushed to the Ministry of Foreign Affairs to offer his personal and official congratulations on Mussolini's narrow escape. When he returned to the embassy, he found it surrounded by police. Only once he got inside did he learn the shocking news that the perpetrator was a British subject (Ireland having acquired the status, in 1922, of a British Dominion). This prompted another telegram:

TELEGRAM. SIR R. GRAHAM. SENT 8.15 P.M. 7 APRIL. RECEIVED 9.30 P.M. 7 APRIL.

I regret to report that the Prime Minister's assailant turns out to be Miss Violet Gibson, sister of the present Lord Ashbourne. This lady was in Rome two years ago and in February of last year attempted to commit suicide by shooting herself . . . She is said to have been twice in a lunatic asylum . . . Italian authorities would be grateful if our police could furnish any information regarding Miss Gibson's antecedent relations etc., with a view to establish whether her attempt was an isolated act or result of a plot. She seems to be just the sort of fanatic and exalted person who could be worked up to an attempt of this kind.

Later that evening, Graham was able to supply a fuller report:

Prime Minister had narrow escape. As he was entering his motor car on leaving capitol a little white haired old lady who had wormed her way through the crowd fired at him at point blank range with a small revolver. His Excellency happened to turn and draw back his head slightly at the moment in response to greeting from the crowd and bullet passed through the gristle of the nose grazing both nostrils. Wound is painful but presents no danger. Signor Mussolini treats the matter lightly and says that it will not interfere with his departure for Tripoli tomorrow but I fancy this must be delayed. Town is beflagged and there are large crowds in the streets but only disorderly incident has been attack on office of *Mondo* newspaper. I called at once at Ministry of Foreign Affairs and expressed in suitable terms regret at attempt and congratulations on its failure.

Despite the reference to the attack on *Il Mondo*, Graham made no mention of its owner's fate.

In London, details of the attack were immediately circulated to the cabinet. This was now an affair of state. It was agreed that the prime minister, the foreign secretary and the king should instantly communicate their regret at the incident.

TELEGRAM. 7 APRIL 1926, 9 P.M. SIR AUSTEN CHAMBERLAIN TO MUSSOLINI:

I am horrified to learn of the abominable attempt on your life. My wife joins me in congratulating you on your escape. We trust the wound is not serious.

From King George (who thirty years earlier, during the visit to Howth Castle, had been photographed with Mussolini's would-be assassin), a telegram to Sir Ronald Graham: 'Please express to the Prime Minister my horror at the dastardly attack made on his life. I rejoice to hear that the wound has not proved serious and deeply regret the assailant is a British subject. I hope that his recovery will be rapid.'

From the United States, President Calvin Coolidge sent word of his relief, as did the presidents of France and Germany and many European monarchs. From Mr Cosgrave, President of the Executive Council of the Irish Free State, came the following: 'I have the honour to congratulate Your Excellency and the Italian people on the providential escape of Your Excellency from the odious attempt on your person. I send you my most earnest wishes for your speedy recovery. The infamous attempt has caused much indignation here.'

At the Interior Ministry, Luigi Federzoni issued instructions for regional and municipal prefects 'to take all necessary measures to secure public order, in accordance with the express wishes of Mussolini and the General Secretariat of the Fascist Party'. Particular attention was to be paid to providing protection to all foreign consulates and businesses. From across the country, telegrams poured in to the ministry and police headquarters with updates on the situation.

Trieste, 13.50 – Fascist squads led by a notoriously violent and self-important man have attacked the local Masonic lodge, carrying away Masonic paraphernalia (swords, masks, candelabra) as trophies; attacks also on the offices of several lawyers, two local newspapers, and a shop selling Slav food. Lorries and trams full of Fascists are rushing about the city terrorising people.

Genova, 16.20 – Despite severe measures to maintain order, news of the attempt has spread rapidly and created great agitation. Large groups of Fascists gathering and spreading throughout the city. All attempts to calm the situation being made, but mood is very alarming.

Turin, 16.50 – News of attempt met by profound consternation. Special editions of local newspapers being prepared, including information on official rallies in support of the Duce. No repercussions so far, but mood in the city increasingly tense.

Bari, 18.15 – Local Fascists have been warned not to take any reprisals. Army is on standby to deal with any eventual disorder.

Ravenna, 20.30 – Congratulations on Mussolini's miraculous escape, celebration of which will take place in organised demonstration this evening.

Cosenza, 20.50 – Energetic measures taken in co-ordination with army and local Fascist organisations, for preserving the peace. Entire province is in shock at the news. Flags are flying all over the city and public buildings have been illuminated.

Rome, 17.10 – In protest against the attempt on Mussolini's life, all criminal and civil courts, including Court of Cassation, Appeal, Tribunal and Assize, have been suspended.

The message telegraphed back was clear: order must be maintained at all costs: 'Il Duce commands that there shall be no act of violence. You must obey. Fascism will inflict upon itself the painful discipline of restraint, being sure that nothing can arrest the march of history.' But all over Italy it was a restless night. In Milan and Rome, the houses of prominent opposition figures were attacked, including that of the dead Amendola, which was looted by blackshirts. The *New York Times* described Mussolini's call for no reprisals as having 'something of the saintly' in it. It was not a very penetrating political analysis. If Mussolini's instructions were sincere, then why could he not rein in his own footsoldiers, those *compagnons de guerre* who had marched on Rome? The brutishness – the knuckledusters and boots – was key to Mussolini's rise to power. Violence was there at the birth of Fascism and it could never be written out of its heart. The temper of Fascism was as extreme as that of its leader, a man whose character was described by his own adoring brother as being underpinned by 'something which borders on the criminal'. And so it was.

Violet, in her cell at the Mantellate, slept through the night's disturbances. So, it was reported in the papers the next day, did Mussolini. But he was woken early, at 'the first flush of dawn', by the crowd that had collected outside his residence on via Rasella, eager for news of his condition (and ignorant that his bed was shared with Sarfatti). Shortly after 6.30, Dr Bastianelli arrived to inspect Mussolini's nose. He found him pale, his eyes heavily rimmed with red – caused by powder burns from the point-blank shot. Worried about delayed shock, he tried to persuade Mussolini to postpone his trip to Libya. 'I'm going, even with a plaster on my nose,' Mussolini retorted. Shortly after, he appeared on the pavement, 'smiled and nodded at the crowd, which lustily cheered him, and waved his hand with easy familiarity', before getting into his waiting car.

Mussolini was bound for Ciampino Airport, then a shabby compound of hangars in fields east of Rome, to give his blessing to Colonel Umberto Nobile's mission to the polar north on board the airship *Norge*. (The expedition was vaunted as an Italian enterprise, though Nobile was under the command of the Norwegian Roald Amundsen, who was also competing for national glory. They loathed each other.) The security order for 8 April, circulated the previous day, had been rescinded and superseded by another, far more detailed, protocol. Mussolini's entourage and VIPs at the Ciampino event were to be carefully separated from the crowds, to which end colour-coded tickets had been issued. The number of military and police and secret service agents present was to be massively beefed up, with motorised squads now added to the detail of agents mounted on horseback and bicycles assigned to Mussolini's route. There were to be security checks at all railway stations and terminals, with special attention to any foreigners behaving suspiciously. Surveillance was to be carried out on 'the mentally disturbed and known political dissidents'. All officials of the security forces were to be extra vigilant and to 'remember their patriotic sense of duty and rally their subordinates to the same'. The call to patriotism was a calculated one: the chief of police was painfully aware that the resources at his command were inadequate to the task, and that his forces were stretched to the 'very limit of human capability'.

Mussolini's appearance at Ciampino was brisk. After twenty minutes he was on his way to the port of Fiumicino, where the battleship *Conte di Cavour* was waiting to carry him to Libya. Thousands of onlookers packed onto the quay and Mussolini mingled with the crowd 'as if he were the safest man in the world'. After inspecting a platoon of Fascist militia, he got into a motor launch and, standing to attention in the stern with his arm raised in the Fascist salute, sped to the waiting dreadnought. He was greeted with the firing of thirteen guns, followed by the bugle-call to attention as he boarded the ship. From the deck, his nose still bandaged, he called down to the journalists who were bobbing about in little boats below: 'Tell England I am not dead yet!'

And then Scipio sailed to Africa, followed by the *Julius Caesar* and several units of the Italian fleet. On one of the ships was Liliam Gibson, an American journalist whose assignment for the *New York Herald* had turned into something of a queasy adventure when police appeared at her hotel the previous evening to question her. She was temporarily detained, then released once it was established she was not related to the Miss Gibson who was already in custody. Liliam was so enchanted by Mussolini that she later accepted his invitation to give him English lessons. She reported his fondness for idioms: 'It never rains but it pours' was a particular favourite.

*

Three days later, astride an Arab mount, his nose still bandaged, Mussolini addressed the people of Tripoli: 'My visit . . . is intended as an affirmation of the power of the Italian people. Nothing is able to impede the destiny which is represented by the extraordinary will of Italy.' Owing to a misadventure, his under-secretaries of War and Air were unable to join the parade: the Italian seaplane convey-ing them to Libya had belly-flopped into the sea. Its passengers were plucked from the waves by a passing merchantman, and brought to Malta, where the warship *Tigre* was sent to collect them.

Press coverage of the tour was uniformly adulatory, describing the enormous and joyous crowds that turned out to greet Mussolini wherever he went. Only an intrepid reporter for the *New York Times* paused to enquire of the local Arab population what they thought: 'The few who know [of his visit] seem not to care whether the great Fascist leader is coming or not.' The Fascist governor of Tripoli was happy to confirm this finding: 'Italian Africa is peopled with an untutored and comparatively passive group of Arabs, the majority of whom are too ignorant to bother about political matters and too indifferent to take any initiative unless stirred up.' The governor went on to boast about the Italian policy of 'making revolt impotent by cutting off its head' – mean-ing the arbitrary round-up of tribal leaders who were then brought before a military tribunal and summarily sentenced to death.

Mussolini had vehemently denounced Italy's 1911 incursion into Libya as 'mock-heroic madness', and been imprisoned for his troubles. But in this, as in so many other things, he had changed his mind. His strategy for conquering the region explicitly reca-pitulated the ancient Roman campaign, as described in Tacitus, using the same bases and following the same routes. But there was little to show for it. Though a great part of ancient Libya was desert waste, it had been highly productive in Roman times, due to irrigation and scientific farming. When Horace designated a man as enormously wealthy, he said that he had granaries in Libya. The single city of Leptis Magna once paid to Rome an annual tribute of one million pounds of olive oil. Libya had another resource as well, far more valuable to a modern coloniser: fuel oil. But the Italian occupation failed to uncover or exploit it. 'We thought,' wrote one Italian soldier, '"Why should so many people be killed to come and get some sand, four palms and a few lemons?" . . . There was nothing, nothing, only sand blowing around and filling in the holes.' A dusty imperium.

'Mussolini leaves for North Africa. Libya awaits him just as two thousand years ago Africa awaited Pompey,' an editorial in *Il Cittadino* pompously intoned on the day of his departure. 'Let us leave the old Irish woman in the silence of her cell.' And indeed, while Mussolini was sailing for his North African sandpit, that was where Violet remained, calm and composed.

Built around the convent complex of the Mantellate sisters, an order founded in the fourteenth century, the women's section of the prison was known as the Regina Coeli, after the prayer recited at regular intervals by the nuns. The convent bell, the Campana della Mantellate, rang out the daily routine: wake up, breakfast, lunch, supper, work, prayer, sleep. McGrath would testify that, during her stay at the Santa Brigida convent, Violet had sought to imitate the life of a cloistered nun. Now she adapted with ease to her carceral seclusion. The nun-jailers observed that she seemed relaxed, happy even. Like a woman who continues to sip her tea in the midst of an earthquake, hers was a kind of 'indecent forgetful serenity', the atmosphere that Charles Lamb described as enveloping his sister Mary in the days following her unprovoked murder of their mother in 1796.

VI

Questions

From the moment of the shooting, Chief Superintendent Epifanio Pennetta knew that he only had a few precious hours to gather evidence. Competent, tenacious, sceptical, Pennetta was a good old-fashioned plod with twenty years' experience and a solid reputation for solving cases and keeping out of politics. It was his investigation that had led to the arrest of Dumini and the Ceka squad that had murdered Giacomo Matteotti, and he had testified at their trial just a month earlier, in March 1926. Unbeknownst to him, Violet had also taken a keen interest in the trial, travelling to the remote hill town of Chieti in the Abruzzo where it was held. An onlooker to the proceedings would tell police that Violet was 'an assiduous spectator', and had expressed the desire for proper justice to be served on those who had murdered Matteotti, a 'poor martyr'. The trial, predictably, was a whitewash, a platform for Roberto Farinacci, the thuggish boss of the *Intransigenti*, who assumed Dumini's defence, and it culminated in the accused receiving derisory sentences. If Violet was looking for evidence of Fascism's immersion in vulgar, corrupt demagoguery, it was here on shameless display; if she was wavering in her intention to eliminate Mussolini, here she was galvanised.

Pennetta had acted fast to assemble the evidence in Violet's case, despatching two squads by car to addresses supplied by her when she had first been questioned in the infirmary, while he interviewed some of the numerous eye-witnesses who came forward to help with the investigation. Three, 'all respectable citizens', gave the same account: they had seen a well-built man with a beard standing next to Violet moments before the attempt. Struck by the consistency of their descriptions, Pennetta had the bearded man traced and called in for questioning. He was a Romanian professor, accompanying his students to Rome, and had never set eyes on Violet until the moment she approached him and asked who was present at the ceremony. He was released without charge. Pennetta next searched Violet's room at the Hotel del Parco – she had been staying here in the weeks leading up to the attack, but had left suddenly and returned to the convent. Staff who were interviewed gave a picture of a solitary woman who conversed little with other guests and took her meals mostly in her room. When she left, she said she would be returning in a week, and asked a chambermaid to look after her vase of violets (one of the few pleasures Violet permitted herself).

Pennetta returned to his office, and sent for Professor Antonio Mendicini, director of the Villa Giuseppina clinic where Violet had recovered after her suicide attempt. Violet had given this as one of her addresses, but Pennetta's squad had returned a report that nobody there had ever heard of her. In Pennetta's office, Mendicini was hauled over the coals for this denial, and for his failure to register with the authorities Violet's sojourn at his establishment, as required by law (he countered that the law only required him to register the names of lunatics, and that Violet had, on the contrary, been suffering from a nervous illness). Mendicini left much chastened, followed by a surveillance team who kept a round-the-clock watch on him and his staff, who were listed as being 'of anti-Fascist sentiment'.

The other address supplied by Violet was of the Santa Brigida convent on via delle Isole. It was midnight by the time Pennetta arrived there with a squad, and the formidable Mother Superior Elizabeth Hesselblad had to be called from her bed. She agreed to allow her nuns to be interviewed, but only in her presence. Sisters Caterina (Catherine Flanagan, Irish) and Riccarda (Katherine Beauchamp Hambrough, English) were both produced. They said that Violet had been a quiet, discreet guest, obviously engaged in an important project, a charitable mission perhaps, that she didn't want anyone to know about. There had been no reason, in the six months she had stayed there, to doubt her mental state. Hesselblad concurred, before adding, somewhat contradictorily, that she was under the impression that Violet was engaged in a 'mysterious undertaking' and that she was not acting alone. She clearly remembered Violet telling her that four people were in favour of her plan, and one was against. Violet had said:

In asking for your advice I will be able to give you an idea of what worries me, but I won't be able to name the people involved, because I do not have permission to do so or to tell you any details. I have been called to undertake a great, a very great mission, upon whose outcome depends the destiny of many tortured souls. I am doubtful that God wishes it so, but they want me to do it, though I feel that I am not strong enough . . . They want me to be too big for my shoes.

Hesselblad advised her that God was content with humble and not grandiose works. They prayed a triduum together, after which Violet thanked her, and said, 'Perhaps, Mother, you are right.' The following day, however, Violet appeared more withdrawn than usual. She was by nature 'very guarded, but on this occasion she was cold' and did not refer to their earlier conversation. Every day Violet left the convent to go and meet 'friends' and every evening she returned exhausted. If she had co-conspirators, then they certainly never came to the convent. No one, Hesselblad emphasised, could possibly imagine that Violet was capable of attacking anybody. Though there had been concerns about her health, her solitary excursions, her taciturn, reserved nature, the dominant impression she gave was one of meekness, of 'a gentle and refined manner'.

There followed a visit to Violet's room, where Pennetta found several anti-Fascist newspapers, carefully marked up to indicate Mussolini's public appearances. There was a sheet from the London *Observer* of 13 December 1925 that contained an article on 'Fascism and Labour', and another captioned 'Muzzling of Italian Press'. An article from *Il Piccolo* of 10 March 1926 concerning Austen Chamberlain and the Locarno Pact had also been saved. In the drawer of a desk he found bundles of letters, several devotional objects, her passport and a box of bullets. He had already

Banknote found in the police search of Violet's belongings at
the convent of Santa Brigida

examined the revolver, which had been brought to him that afternoon, and was now tagged as evidence. Interestingly, the bullets
Violet had used were not Lebel manufacture, but 'STAHLSTECK-
NADELN CENTAUR 50, gramm. N.4' – this may explain the misfire
(or, simply, the cartridges were old and the powder may have been
corrupted). Two bullets recovered from the pistol had been sent to
the Office of Hygiene where tests were being conducted to ascertain whether they might have been poisoned. They weren't, but
the idea that they might have been was inspired by a rumour,
unfounded, that a small phial containing a mysterious liquid had
been knocked out of Violet's hand in the ruckus on Campidoglio.
The story enlarged the malign dimensions of her dastardly deed.

In the early hours of Thursday, 8 April, Pennetta returned to his
office to write his first report. He emphasised the possibility that
Gibson was an intelligent and sly fanatic, eccentric and neurotic
maybe, but not mad; and that she had not acted alone, but more
probably she was 'part of a group of unidentified conspirators who
had devised a careful plan to assassinate Mussolini'. Pennetta
would doggedly pursue this line of enquiry until his political
superiors determined that it didn't suit them and relieved him of
the case.

Pennetta's report was on the desk of interior minister Luigi Federzoni first thing in the morning. Alongside it was a report by chief of police Francesco Crispo Moncada stating that order had been restored in Rome (bar a few *Intransigenti* who were still roaming around looking for 'subversives' to beat up). Federzoni, a moderate, had a problem: if Violet was part of a conspiracy, and no conspirators were found, then that would generate huge embarrassment, and encourage the extremists in their belief that Mussolini's government was soft. Moreover, any political complexion in the case could jeopardise relations with Britain, which brought Mussolini an important measure of legitimacy. For Federzoni, the best route was to stick to the insanity line, which he duly fed to the *Corriere della Sera*.

In contrast to Violet, who slept soundly through her first night in prison, Pennetta hadn't slept at all by the time he arrived at the Mantellate, at 8 a.m., to escort her to the School of Scientific Police, where his old tutor, Professor Samuele Ottolenghi, a famed specialist in criminal medicine, was waiting to examine her. An hour or so earlier, Violet had been talkative with her nun-guards, but as she sat before Ottolenghi, she was rigid and silent. He tried to get her to talk about her mental history, she refused any co-operation, and when he listened to her heart she looked straight at the wall, and 'made no attempt to help with her own undressing'. Ottolenghi noticed the criss-cross of stitch-marks and scars across her body – one by her appendix, another to the right of her umbilicus, another where her left breast had been removed – and the entry hole of the bullet from her suicide attempt. The encounter lasted two hours, after which Ottolenghi reported to Pennetta that it was impossible to establish what Violet's mental condition was, given her refusal to co-operate. She could either be feigning madness, or she could indeed be mad.

Violet was taken back to her cell, where she now met Crown Prosecutor Judge Xarra and examining magistrate Rosario Marciano, whose job it was to prepare for the courts the preliminary investigation into her case. She received them courteously, 'as if in her own drawing room'. At first, their questions yielded nothing. Violet was mute, her features carefully locked, her tired and austere face relieved occasionally by a secret smile. They persisted. 'Are you, or have you ever been, mentally ill?' She stared past them, then, after a long silence, repeated what she had told them in her first interview: something about having tried to commit suicide the previous year, that her family had tried to have her returned to England, that she didn't want to go because she knew they wanted to put her in a lunatic asylum. 'Why did you shoot Mussolini?' Silence. Then, as if stirred by her own thoughts, she spoke. Yes, she now remembered why she shot Mussolini: it was to glorify God, because God's message in such matters was clear, and in addition he had sent an angel to steady her as she took aim. Who were her accomplices? She had been counselled by the wisest men who ever lived, but they were now dead. She had a special ability to communicate with the dead; her room in the convent had become 'a meeting place of the spiritual elect and famous men' (the echoes of Madame Blavatsky's Great White Brotherhood of Masters), and they were all her accomplices.

Where had she got the gun? The answer to this was more mundane: a friend had left it to her on his death, and she had brought it with her from England. After an hour of this, the magistrates concluded that, owing to her mental infirmity, it would be difficult to try her. But the prosecutor nominated a defence counsel for Violet, as required by law.

*

The Ashbourne family paid a heavy price for Willie's failure to remove Violet from Rome. The morning after the shooting, he was approached by a journalist in the lobby of a hotel in Dublin, where he was attending the annual congress of the Gaelic League. Did he know that Mussolini had been shot, and that the assailant was his sister? Willie understood on the instant that his reaction to this devastating news could impinge deeply on Violet's fate. 'The poor dear has been ill all her life,' he told the journalist, 'and at times she is much depressed and very nervous.' He immediately sent a telegram to the Italian government: 'The Gibson family regrets the incident and expresses warm sympathy.' He then took the next mail packet for England, to discuss with the family what to do.

In London, Constance, who was preparing to go on the 'long sea trip' she had promised herself after her mother's death, was told the news in a telephone call from a junior diplomat at the Foreign Office. She too sent a telegram: 'Sincere congratulations on Signor Mussolini's escape.' Violet's nephew, David Gibson, then a child, later recalled how the telephone at the house in Grosvenor Crescent rang all night, as journalists from across the world sought a comment from the family. Constance had initially tried to play down Violet's state of mind, telling a reporter that her recent letters had all been 'of a quite ordinary nature. She gave no indication that there was anything upsetting her mentally.' But she was now diligent in sticking to the line set out by the Foreign Office: Violet had had a nervous breakdown after the sudden death of her brother Victor, and had never fully recovered. 'She gave way to paroxysms of grief which finally unhinged her mind,' Constance was reported as saying.

There has been nothing in her letters to indicate she intended to murder Premier Mussolini or anybody else, and I have no idea why she should seek to do it. These paroxysms come without warning, and may last an hour, a day or weeks. When she recovers she is the same Violet as before.

In Compiègne, and without her husband to restrain her, Marianne spoke to a journalist from *Le Petit Parisien*. Her comments – published with a photograph showing her at the gates of the Ashbourne villa, holding back an enormous dog – conveyed little warmth towards her sister-in-law:

[Her] extreme act does not surprise me. For some time now she has not been in full possession of her mental faculties and she is subject to periodical mental crises which are both dangerous and extravagant. She has tried on more than one occasion to take her own life. We tried to have her interned in a rest home, but Italian law, we have been informed, does not allow one to commit individuals who are only affected by such problems intermittently . . . I'm only surprised that she shot Signor Mussolini, given the fact that she repeatedly declared her desire to assassinate the pope.

Marianne also fired off a telegraph to Mussolini, which was altogether more fulsome in tone than the one her husband had sent: 'I am deeply stricken with sorrow over the attack on you, a person so precious to the entire world. Permit me to express my embarrassment, my indignation and my disgrace. I offer all my wishes for the preservation of your life.'

Violet had always been wary of Marianne. In her notebook, she wrote of 'the jaundiced eye of jealousy' and resolved to 'get at Marianne when she is *not* under this influence'. Also:

Tell Marianne that kindness in spirit and in truth must come not only from herself but from those who pass through her hands. For her to be kind to my face while making mischief behind my back won't do. When I see that happening that will put certain time to pass between each meeting.

The ill-will was reciprocated. Marianne's comments to the press seemed calculated to do more harm than good. There were to be no more interviews. The question of Violet Gibson – the existence, even, of Violet Gibson – would no longer be subject to public acknowledgement by any of her family.

In private, however, there was much to be discussed. It was clear that a member of the family must proceed immediately to Rome. The obvious choice was paterfamilias Willie, and he set out immediately, stopping in Paris to collect Marianne. When the Foreign Office communicated this news to Sir Ronald Graham, he was vigorously opposed: 'Lord Ashbourne insists on wearing a kilt on all occasions, and as this particularity has been signalised in the press, he would run serious risk of being assaulted in the street.' The jocular retort of a Foreign Office official, that Lord Ashbourne's appearance in a kilt would be most useful to Violet's defence counsel 'with probable event of his wishing to plead hereditary insanity on behalf of his client', was ignored. 'He is a crank,' noted another official. (Willie would have been undisturbed by the remark. 'The "silly kilt" question is not absorbing my mighty intellect,' he once told a friend.) It was agreed instead that Constance would go. Willie and Marianne, according to Italian secret-service agents, got as far as Genoa before turning back. It was a wise decision: publication in Italy of Lord Ashbourne's telegram regretting 'the incident' had provoked outrage. 'It seems that the Gibson family has a monopoly on mental illness,' one newspaper ranted. 'If the sister is an old madwoman, then the brother is an ageing idiot if he believes that "incident" is an appropriate description of attempted murder.' Mussolini, the article continued, had shown extraordinary and admirable 'sangfroid' at the scene, but William Gibson's 'British phlegm' was grotesque.

The Gibson family and the Foreign Office were all proceeding along the line of Violet's insanity, and presuming that she would be released into their custody within a very short period of time. (King George was of the same opinion, privately informing the Italian ambassador in London that 'the would-be assassin comes from a notoriously unbalanced family'.) All the early signals from the ministries in Rome supported this hope, as did most of the press coverage (it was natural, commented one newspaper, to believe that the would-be assassin was mad, as no sane person could want to eliminate Il Duce). But on 9 April, two days after the shooting, Ronald Graham received a telephone call from Police Chief Crispo Moncada: Chief Superintendent Pennetta believed there was evidence pointing to a conspiracy and that Violet was feigning madness in order to escape punishment for her criminal (and political) act. Even the *Corriere della Sera* was leaning towards this view, suspicious of the official version put out by Federzoni that Violet was insane. Worse, the *Intransigenti* extremists were manoeuvring to play Violet as a card in their game against moderates like Federzoni. Crispo Moncada concluded that it wasn't going to be a simple matter of handing Violet over into British custody, and advised that her defence lawyer be chosen with great care.

Constance arrived in Rome by night train from Paris on 11 April. She was met by Andrea Serrao, legal counsel for the British Embassy, and a dozen plainclothes policemen, provided for her own safety. They proceeded directly to the embassy, where the news wasn't encouraging: state prosecutors were preparing the grounds for a trial, Violet might indeed be tried regardless of her mental state, nobody would be granted access to her until the preliminary investigation was completed, and who knew when that would be. The family, Serrao insisted, needed to hire the best lawyer, at whatever price. Graham had further bad news: there wasn't a single hotel in Rome that would accept a booking in the name Gibson.

The most highly regarded criminologist in Rome at the time was Enrico Ferri ('the Italian Clarence Darrow', as *Time* magazine helpfully described him to its readers), and Serrao accompanied Constance to his offices. Tall, patriarchal, sporting a spectacular moustache and a neatly trimmed pharaoh's beard, Ferri was professor of criminology at the University of Rome and author of legal tomes that were required reading for Italian policemen. A former leader of the progressive wing of the Socialist Party, he knew Mussolini when he was similarly aligned. When Mussolini became prime minister, Ferri had distanced himself from politics, a shrewd move that enabled him to maintain good relations with Il Duce. Mussolini, according to an aide, liked meeting with Ferri, as the association conferred on him a certain intellectual élan ('Forgive my learned references' was a phrase that fell often from Mussolini's lips). Ferri told Constance his price for defending Violet would be £1,000 (*circa* £41,000 today), a huge sum, but Constance immediately acquiesced.

Constance was told to write up all the facts relevant to a defence of Violet as insane. This she did on the evening of 11 April at the Hotel dei Principi, where a room had finally been obtained for her under an assumed name. Had she desired to visit

Reconstruction of the crime scene on Campidoglio, showing the entrance to Palazzo dei Conservatori, the position of Violet (d), Mussolini (c), the students whom Mussolini turned to acknowledge (e), and the location of the spent bullet (f).

Campidoglio the following morning, she would have found it roped off while police (including Pennetta and several of the officers who had been there and were key eye-witnesses) reconstructed the crime scene with a photographer. But Constance was in no mood to linger. She paid off Violet's outstanding bills and left Rome thirty-six hours after arriving, on the 10.45 pm train, tailed by undercover police officers as far as the border at Como-Chiasso. 'Miss Constance Gibson was having such an awkward time here . . . that she has left again for Switzerland,' Ronald Graham explained in a despatch that evening to the Foreign Office. She booked into the Park Hotel in Lausanne, and waited. Serrao wrote to her there several times, promising that 'everything in my power will be done to help you and your family in such a tragic matter'. He was convinced that Violet 'was not conscious of what her tragic destiny has brought her to do' and that, Italian

The scene reconstructed from a different angle, facing the statue of Marcus Aurelius. Violet is represented by the policeman standing in the position marked *d*, the students by *e*, and Mussolini's car by *g*.

justice being trustworthy, they could be optimistic of a speedy outcome.

There was nothing for Constance to do now but sit it out by the lake. She stayed in Lausanne from April to the end of July – an expensive sojourn – and hardly speedy. The wait gave the family plenty of time to ponder what to do with Violet when she was returned to their care. 'Violet is quite as much afraid of us as of the authorities. Perhaps more so,' Willie wrote to Constance.

One thing we have to be ready for is: to find out what to do if Violet is given over to us without our having sufficient authority to get her interned for the rest of her life. Perhaps the two governments should come to an agreement, otherwise there's the risk that Violet could be released after a few days in the belief that she is cured: she seems so calm when the crisis is not on that it makes the position of the doctors very difficult.

The Gibson plan was internment for life. Violet was to resist it with every sinew, every resource she could command. But this amounted to very little.

VII

Secrets

The Honourable Violet Gibson, prisoner number 14967, requests the services of her dressmaker.

TO MADAME OLY, VIA GREGORIANA.

Dear Madam, Can you come here!! to try on the dress and coat I ordered? Come any time that suits you.
    Yours faithfully, Violet Gibson.

More than a week after her arrest, Violet was still wearing the same clothes in which she had set out from the convent to shoot Mussolini. On Thursday, 15 April, she asked to be allowed to write a letter. She was given a pencil and a sheet of lined paper, on which she wrote, in a very faint hand with hardly any pressure behind it, to Madame Oly. The dressmaker, perhaps reluctant to attend her now infamous client, did not reply. A week later, Violet wrote again to explain that her dress 'was greatly torn the day I came in here', that all her clothes were 'in rags', hence her need for the new dress she had already ordered. 'I would also like two black hats to be sent, only on approval so that if they do not suit I may return them to you.'

    A more realistic plan was devised. Violet was to be allowed to request some of her own clothes, along with other belongings, from her room at the convent. To Mother Superior Hesselblad, she wrote asking for the following:

2 night gowns
3 chemises
4 prs stockings
1 light summer vest
Black hat (please take care to send the right hat, as the others are worn out)

Black marabou boa
Black chiffon dress
Black jersey
2 boxes of jigsaw puzzles
crucifix and rosary
soap & sponge & new tooth brush & powder
scissors, needles, bk & white cotton
pencils, pens, nibs
cheque book
brush & comb
The Imitation of Christ
All the hairpins you can find
Hand mirror
Little metal holy water stoop
Clock
Cascara pills
The smallest mantilla
The little bottle of aspirins
Spectacles

The investigating magistrate, Rosario Marciano, who saw Violet almost daily and was consulted on every detail of her custody, consented to all these items – ascetic, black, frayed, religious (but for the jigsaws) – bar one: the cheque book. According to the British consul, who visited Violet on Saturday, 10 April, the nuns were ordering in food for her from a local restaurant. Prison food was of very poor quality, provided by outside contractors who competed to provide the cheapest possible service. It was not – is not – uncommon for inmates of Italian prisons to make such arrangements, but the food needed to be paid for. Marciano's refusal of the cheque book (an important piece of evidence) was to have serious consequences. Within a few weeks, she was hardly eating.

Marciano had also issued instructions that Violet be subjected to 'diligent and rigorous' scrutiny by her jailers, and forbidden to communicate with other prisoners, 'especially foreigners', or to receive 'clandestine' letters. All of Violet's incoming correspondence was intercepted by the police (the confusion with the journalist Liliam Gibson persisted, and her letters were also seized) and forwarded to Marciano, who also read her outgoing correspondence. On 9 April, Enid Dinnis had written (she sent the letter care of Mary McGrath at the convent, ignorant that she had been despatched back to Ireland):

My dear Violet,

You have been dreadfully ill, but we are all calm and keeping our ends up. You will be seeing us all soon so come home as quick as you can and see how we have kept our ends up. I for one am indecently proud of myself. You remember how I kept smiling when you had the Big Operation [a reference to the 1916 surgery for peritonitis]. This has been a much worse illness . . . Much love from Enid.

It was a lifeline at a time Violet later described as terribly lonely and confusing. She didn't know if she had been abandoned by her friends and family, dismissed from their affections because of what she had done. She hadn't been told that Constance had journeyed to Rome and had not been allowed to see her, or of Willie's willingness to come.

After his aborted trip Willie was back in Paris, where he was requested to present himself at the Italian consulate to give an account of his sister. He was received by the consul on 19 April, who noted the meeting:

Lord Ashbourne, an imposing red-faced old man with a head of abundant, snow-white hair, entered my office in his habitual traditional costume and, with lips trembling, said 'Quelle horreur!' He continued, expressing his family's deep regret and sense of desperation regarding the atrocious assassination attempt . . . He added that he believed his sister to be mentally unbalanced and at times insane, affected by a mystic, religious mania with periods of violent elation . . . The family has taken steps to have her permanently interned but doctors have vigorously resisted the idea.

The Italian government had demanded written evidence of the Ashbourne family's political affiliations, and when the consul pursued the matter, Willie was at pains to point out 'the delicacy of his personal situation, particularly in relation to the British

Government because, as a political man, he had taken part in the revolutionary movement which had led to the founding of the Irish Free State'. He was able to affirm to the Consul 'his principles and sentiments as a conservative, an imperialist and a patriotic revolutionary, but also as an enemy of all internationalists [Bolsheviks] and an admirer of His Excellency Mussolini – the only man, he said, who was capable of bringing due respect to his Country'.

The indignities suffered by the Gibson family accumulated, adding to the overload of resentment at the embarrassment caused by the errant Violet. Elsie's husband Lord Bolton, a Conservative member of parliament, had to undergo the humiliation of attesting in writing to the Italian authorities that he was not, nor had he ever been, a Communist. Sir John Ross, ex-Lord Chancellor of Ireland, Baronet, wrote in support of Bolton, stressing his conservative credentials and his membership of the Carlton Club and the Kildare Street Club, Dublin. Sir Dunbar Plunket Barton bestirred himself at the Carlton Club to pen a similar anti-Communist reference for Violet's brother Edward (of Haslemere, Surrey).

At exactly the time Willie was being interviewed at the consulate, two undercover police officers posing as Italian journalists were making discreet enquiries in the village of Compiègne. Taking up position in an antiques shop, they watched Willie's 'mysterious' villa at 17 rue des Domelieres, but saw nothing – the place seemed 'semi-abandoned'. After softening up the owner of the shop by purchasing a small object, they were told that Willie had bought the villa in 1920 and was married to a woman descended from ancient Breton nobility. He lived a 'strange life', associating with a crowd of rowdy students who occasionally descended on his home, or with aristocratic families in the area, though he did much charity work with the local poor and was held in great esteem by everybody. On 22 April, the agents were in Paris, making enquiries at the Hotel International, where

Willie stayed most weekends, always returning to Compiègne on Monday. There, he received few visitors, mostly French clerics. But he was, they ascertained, well known in the Latin Quarter and the Sorbonne as an eccentric academic who loved beer, literature and radical students. Guido Leto, the senior of the two agents, later became head of OVRA, Mussolini's secret police.

While Epifanio Pennetta waited on the intelligence from Paris, he concentrated his enquiries in Rome on Trastevere, following reports that Violet had often been seen there. At the British Embassy, Sir Ronald Graham was in receipt of similar intelligence, reporting to the Foreign Office that 'It seems that she has been spending most of her time praying in churches or visiting the poorer quarters of the town, where she distributed alms.' Graham had a direct line into the enquiry, taking regular – and confidential – briefings from the chief of police. From the outset, Crispo Moncada was designated to work with the British ambassador to find a painless solution to the Violet Gibson problem, one that would not interfere with the good diplomatic relations between the two governments.

The police were deeply suspicious of the *Trasteverini*. If Violet had accomplices – in Pennetta's mind, she was made-to-measure for a conspiracy – this was most likely where she met them. Did they furnish her with the revolver? Extensive enquiries turned up nothing. Not surprisingly, given that the Lebel had been acquired without a licence and used against Mussolini, none of the arms dealers interviewed by Pennetta's officers was able to identify the weapon or bullets.

Pennetta had another reason for his interest in Trastevere: it was the gathering place of a group of Catholic dissidents and followers of Father Ernesto Buonaiuti, a key figure in the Italian Modernist movement and a vocal opponent of Mussolini, and Pennetta suspected Violet of associating with them. Buonaiuti was closely linked to George Tyrrell, Willie Gibson's mentor and friend, and, like Tyrrell, Buonaiuti was an annoyance to the Jesuits and the Roman Curia. The Vatican had excommunicated him in January 1925, declaring him '*vitandus*' – an individual whom Catholics should avoid at all costs. The timing was significant. The Church was about to enter into secret negotiations with Mussolini, which would lead ultimately to the Lateran Treaty of 1929, recognising the Vatican as an independent state, and it was not about to risk any obstacle. Bringing the Vatican over was a shrewd move on Mussolini's part; given his former rants against the Church, the pact was welcomed throughout the Catholic world (Cardinal Bourne's paper, *The Tablet*, surpassed the *Morning Post* in its admiration for Mussolini). Buonaiuti belonged to that minority of Catholics who intuited early on that the pope was embarking on an odious compromise by which Fascism would make an *instrumentum regni* of the Church. Buonaiuti's feelings of profound anguish when negotiations were first mooted may have matured into desperate measures. Violet, tutored by Willie in the Vatican's perfidy – hence her statement to him and Marianne at Compiègne that the pope should be eliminated – was working from the same script.

Pennetta's instincts were rewarded with a report from one of his detectives confirming the link between the heretical priest and Violet.

Every evening, especially after 8 o'clock, Buonaiuti receives [...] so many followers that his house is full to bursting. Buonaiuti also paid visits, as a priest, to Gibson. Gibson went to his house on at least one occasion, where she was received as a senior English lady worthy of regard. Buonaiuti is vigorously anti-Mussolini . . . He has often expressed himself very passionately on this subject, and called for someone to kill Mussolini. The house where he resides belongs to [a] Communist. On the evening of the attempt against Mussolini, somebody said that it was astonishing that anybody could have missed from such a short distance, but Buonaiuti appeared to disagree.

Pennetta was now convinced that there had been a plot to murder Mussolini, and that Violet was as a child in the hands of skilled intriguers who had simply melted away after the crime. But his interviews with Violet were fruitless. In his presence, she either kept an 'occult silence' or 'talked with evident pleasure of angels and apparitions'. This, Pennetta believed, was part of her strategy to convince him she was mad.

Conspiracy theories breed conspiracy theories, and many bizarre leads were now accumulating on Pennetta's desk. One, provided by the Italian military secret service, claimed that Violet was an active member of the Independent Theosophical League in Rome, 'founded mainly by Zionist Jews'. Long before Mussolini introduced anti-Semitic legislation, Jews, along with Freemasons, were demonised by Fascists as being part of a world-wide plot to destabilise Italy. The Roman branch of the Independent Theosophical League was at 5 via Gregoriana, a few doors away from Violet's first lodging in Rome at the convent of Our Lady of Lourdes. She could hardly have failed to notice it. But police enquiries drew a blank: unsurprisingly, the League claimed to have no record of any visits from Violet.

Another lead came from a respected White Russian secret agent who materialised at the Italian Legation in Bucharest to allege that Violet had been sent by Stalin and the Comintern to deliver a hit on Mussolini. The agent could produce no proof, and Pennetta did not linger on his report. From another source, Pennetta learned that the Prince of Greece, currently in Rome, was putting it about that Violet belonged to the Irish Secret Society, the aims of which were described in the book *Secret Societies* by the British journalist Nesta Webster. Webster, later a member of the British Union of Fascists, was a walking bile-pot who peddled scare stories about a web of occultists, Jews and Freemasons committed to Communist world domination. She presented herself to the Italian Ambassador in London and told him she believed Violet had been a witting instrument of the society, and that her attempt was linked to that of Tito Zaniboni (via the Third International and Irish radicalism). Pennetta, to his credit, observed that Webster could provide absolutely no evidence for her theory and was merely repeating what she had already rehearsed in her book, which he had perused with cool contempt.

Secret this, secret that. There are what Henry James called 'secrets for privacy and silence' – if they're to function effectively, they stay secreted. Pennetta rightly deduced that what was landing on his desk was a form of excreta. He had nothing that could be presented as evidence of a conspiracy, no credible witnesses. Until, that is, Antonio Radoani surfaced.

Radoani was a Dublin-based businessman who was temporarily living in Florence's Murate prison awaiting trial for fraud. Claiming to be 'a foreign agent of the Fascist Party', for which his job as a representative in Ireland of Fiat, Lancia and other automobile companies was a cover, he had much to say on the subject of Violet Gibson. On 8 April, the day after the attempt, he requested to speak to a prison warder. He alleged that Violet belonged to the executive committee of Cumhama-na-Bahnea (presumably a mangling of Cumann na mBan, the Irish Republican Army's subaltern women's wing), and that her brother William was 'president of the Irish Gaelic Society, a republican nationalist organisation'. Lord Ashbourne and Violet Gibson, Radoani continued, both lived abroad because they were active members of the revolutionary League of Oppressed Peoples, of which the Irish national branch was the most committed.

When news of this exchange reached Pennetta, he immediately despatched an officer to the Murate prison to take a full deposition. Formally interviewed on 9 April, Radoani enlarged on his previous statement: Willie, he claimed, was 'one of the most active leaders of the Irish republican movement, appointed by [Eamon] de Valera'. Living 'on foreign soil', he was able to 'conduct the kind of activity that would be forbidden in Ireland', and was using his great wealth to maintain 'a headquarters of the Irish republicans in Paris'. Willie had also 'attacked Fascism and Mussolini on several occasions' and was a friend of noted anti-Fascists. As to his sister, Radoani was certain that she 'could not have acted independently of her brother, given that she is recognised in Ireland to be an intelligent, courageous and fanatical woman, utterly devoted to him'. Furthermore, 'in keeping with an ancient Irish strategem, she has faked a verbal dysfunction', wearing a 'veil of mental ill-ness to disguise a rare cunning' and to distract attention from the fact that she was following the orders of her secret political masters, who had armed her with the gun.

Radoani had some of his facts wrong – Willie was not hugely wealthy, he was not president of the Gaelic Society, and neither he nor Violet was a member of the League for Oppressed Peoples – but he knew more than Pennetta did at this stage about the Ashbournes. Pennetta asked for background on Radoani. The results were not encouraging. He was, wrote the interviewing officer, 'a cunning man with a fervid imagination and politically suspect'; he claimed to have participated in de Valera's revolutionary movement and to have been a member of the Dublin Fascist community, which explained 'his superficial knowledge of Irish politics', but all the while he was actually defrauding people, and 'tarnishing the good name of Italy there'.

Radoani was clearly untrustworthy. In a discussion of the activities of Italian Fascist spies operating abroad, historian Franco Fucci depicts a milieu in which people like Radoani thrived. It was an environment full of

> . . . dubious Fascists, ex-Fascists persecuted by the regime, emissaries of Mussolini with the false identities of refugees, suspect characters and paid provocateurs all thronging into France, Switzerland and Belgium creating a confusion in which it was difficult to identify the real anti-Fascists. Among these 'spurious exiles' there was neither unity of intent nor co-ordinated action; they consequently embroiled themselves in a frenetic crossfire of reciprocal accusations having no other common aim than to act against the anti-Fascists, many of whom fell easily into their traps.

It is curious, however, that all these people were coming forward with tales of Violet's and Willie's nefarious activities. Was this simply because the more eccentric and unknowable people are, the greater the speculation? Or was there some truth to the allegations? Willie had certainly lied to the Italian consul: he was not a conservative, or an imperialist, or an admirer of Mussolini. And while he claimed (to the House of Lords) to have removed himself from Irish politics because they sickened him, his role in the Gaelic League suggested otherwise. Dismissed by its critics as an 'ingenuous programme of jig dancing and warbling passé treason', 'senile and slobbering', the League had in fact sharpened its claws and set itself to more effective issues. Though remaining a grass-roots cultural movement, distinct and separate from Sinn Fein, it had embraced the rhetoric of a liberation army (speeches as 'bullets to fire at the enemy', in the words of its founder, Douglas Hyde). A key element of the Fenian philosophy – that it was useless for an Irishman to confront an Englishman without a gun in his hand – defined a new kind of Irishness. And even though Willie's idealism had not been translated into action, he, Victor, and Violet were all implicated, by one account or another, in Irish revolutionary politics.

Another mystery. Violet's bank records indicated that she 'had a good deal more funds at her disposal than could be accounted for by allowances made to her by her family'. Two weeks before the attempt, she had changed her credit arrangement with the Westminster Bank, which duly authorised the Banca Commerciale Italiana in Rome to disburse up to £100 a week on her account. What, Pennetta mused, could she be intending to do with such funds, and where did they come from? Her annual income, derived from the trust fund set up by her father, came to no more than £400. Both the police and the British Embassy were much exercised by this riddle. Violet offered a perfectly rational answer – the credit arrangement was for emergencies – and the modest withdrawals from her account (£16 on 30 March being the most recent) supported her explanation. Pennetta was not persuaded, so Violet wrote to the Kensington branch manager of the Westminster Bank asking him to supply a statement, translated into Italian, clarifying that the facility to cash £100 a week 'does not mean, as they think it does, that I have £5,200 per year, which of course is far from the truth! If I were to draw a cheque of £100 for four consecutive weeks I would have drawn out my entire income.'

This seemed to settle the matter, though not in Violet's favour. For Pennetta, Violet's madness clearly did not encompass her ability to arrange her financial affairs. On the contrary, her letter, unlike her statements in interview (she continued to 'mumble disjointedly'), showed her to be perfectly lucid.

VIII

The New Augustus

The notion that Benito Mussolini might be more dangerous than Violet Gibson never managed to engage the imagination of the British establishment. Indeed, by the time he had become an enemy and the subject of concentrated opprobrium, Violet had been completely forgotten. From the days during the First World War when treasury money lubricated his editorial rants, to the moment he invaded Ethiopia in October 1935, Mussolini basked in the approval of the British. His first foreign visit as premier had been to England where, in December 1922, he was received by the prime minister and the king, and laid a wreath at the Cenotaph. Large crowds gathered wherever he went, including British blackshirts who sang 'Giovinezza' gustily and with terrible pronunciation. Mussolini, who liked to boast that he slept in his underclothes like a real working man and didn't own a pair of pyjamas, put up at Claridges and missed a press conference because he was in bed with a prostitute, but the overall impression he left was that he was 'a man with whom one could do business'. The visit of George V to Rome in May 1923 added a further gloss of respectability to the new regime. The king was so impressed that he decorated Mussolini with the Order of the Bath and suggested Britain might cast a generous eye on Italy's colonial claims. Mussolini, who once complained that foreigners viewed all Italians as 'strolling musicians, sellers of statuettes, Calabrian bandits', now confidently declared that the world would be made to bow to the 'new, great, Italy'. England was the first 'great nation' to treat Italy with the respect it craved.

In the year of King George's visit, Sir Ronald Graham was reporting in his despatches that Mussolini was 'a statesman of exceptional ability and enterprise . . . if inclined to be hasty and violent'. There were days when he fell into 'fits of ungovernable rage', and to some extent Il Duce was 'a strange man and has lately caused some comment by driving about through Rome in his two-seater with a well-grown lion cub sitting beside him'. But 'the Italians seem to like this sort of thing' and, 'after his moment of acting up, Mussolini was soon calmed and was then open to sweet reason like any other gentleman'.

On 24 April 1924 British journalist John St Loe Strachey visited Mussolini in his office at Palazzo Chigi (the pretentious move to the Palazzo Venezia was still a few years off). Strachey found him

> . . . hunched up behind his desk, and making no attempt at a conventional welcome to a foreigner beyond a rather awkward nod. Imagine Vulcan interrupted at his forge. Mussolini is the Vulcan who is hammering out the new Italy on his anvil day by day. You can feel the heat of the furnace, the strain on his body, in the set of the muscles of his face, in his heavy shoulders, and in his regard.

And yet, Strachey concluded, 'I can imagine Mussolini in action anxious in a high degree as to his choice between the two roads – left, or right.' This was a weakness, the journalist forecast, which could 'turn his noble Chronicle play into a tragedy'.

Mussolini dithering at the crossroads: this was Strachey's key insight. The choices he made, including the vehement exercise of power and the crushing of the opposition, were always reactive, 'an opportunist exercise in the value of negatives', and the significance of his ideas was usually identifiable only by their consequences. Fascism was a one-dimensional object posing as a three-dimensional reality. Part of this *trompe l'œil* effect was to give the impression of incessant action, of constant revolution, but this masked a lack of depth or meaning. If Mussolini was the *fabbro dello stato* (an appropriate metaphor for a man who as a child had worked the bellows in his father's smithy), then what was Italy going to look like once Vulcan had finished hammering it out? There was never any iron in the ideological soul of Fascism, the writer Ignazio Silone commented, just the fraudulent substitute of 'political and mental margarine'.

Strachey did not publish his notes, but sent them for comment to Ronald Graham, who responded in a private letter on 8 May 1924:

I entirely agree with you as to the impression he makes of a smouldering force, and to see him 'white hot', as I have on one or two occasions, is not an altogether agreeable experience. You have appreciated his good points; his weakness, though perhaps it has certain advantages in this country, is that he is essentially a violent man. Underneath the statesman, acute, quick in decision and yet ready to learn and to profit by experience, there lies something of the prize-fighter. He is, as you say, intolerant of opposition and I fear that he does not really, in his heart, disapprove of the violence used towards his political opponents. Otherwise more effective steps would be taken to stop them. Still, he has already accomplished a wonderful change in the life of Italy and, given five or six more years of power, which only some accident can prevent, I think British opinion will be surprised to see the position to which he will raise his country. In many respects he is a great man and a friend worth having, while he would certainly make an extremely unpleasant enemy.

Strachey, as confirmed by Graham (whose private conscience examined Mussolini more critically than his official one), was more perceptive in his observations than most. When the Catholic writer Hilaire Belloc visited Il Duce in the same year, 1924, he could barely contain his excitement: 'What a contrast with the sly and shifty talk of your parliamentarian! What a sense of decision, of sincerity, of serving the nation.' G. K. Chesterton, also a Catholic, followed a few years later and was flattered to discover that Mussolini was a fan of his novel *The Man Who Was Thursday*. Chesterton came away less enthusiastic than Belloc, though he was pleased to discover that Mussolini shared his loathing of capitalism, usury (meaning Jews) and Communism.

Austen Chamberlain, Foreign Secretary from 1924 to 1929, shared with his half-brother Neville the congenital flaw of believing in the good nature of bad men. Following his meeting with

Mussolini in Locarno in October 1925, he wrote an account, full of wistful *longueurs*, to Ronald Graham:

All my pleasant impressions of him [...] were renewed and confirmed ... If I ever had to choose in my own country between anarchy and dictatorship, I expect I should be on the side of the dictator. In any case I thought Mussolini a strong man of singular charm and I suspected of not a little tenderness and loneliness of heart.

It was as if Chamberlain had seen into Il Duce's soul. Finding there a deep well of solitariness, he developed what can only be described as a crush, thinly concealed in his billet-doux-by-proxy.

Meeting me but seldom and quite alone and finding me sympathetic I expect that he shows me a side of his character which the public is never allowed to see, and even his most intimate friends but seldom if ever. I believe him to be accused of crimes in which he had no share [a reference to the murder of Matteotti], and I suspect him to have connived unwillingly at other outrages which he would have prevented if he could. But I am confident that he is a patriot and a sincere man; I trust his word when given and I think we might easily go far before finding an Italian with whom it would be as easy for the British government to work.

Suspicious of the relationship between the two statesmen, a British parliamentarian asked the House of Commons in July 1927 what was being achieved by their 'peculiarly close intimacy'. Chamberlain preferred to describe it as a 'coincidence of purpose'. The sentiment was mutual. After one meeting with Chamberlain, Mussolini made particular note of Lady Chamberlain's Fascist badge and the Roman salute which the British party gave him on his departure. He concluded that 'Chamberlain is, in his heart, rather a sympathiser of Fascism'. Gaetano Salvemini commented bitterly that Chamberlain's 'handshake was worth an empire to Mussolini'. Certainly, his show of support in the wake of the Matteotti murder created a reserve of gratitude that was drawn on when the question arose of what to do with Violet Gibson.

The British political establishment and press remained pervious to Mussolini's charms, impervious to his lack of scruples. It was even possible to acknowledge his criminal tendencies without

disrupting a positive view of his function. One way was to understand Fascism as the product of Italian conditions and designed
for Italy alone. Harold Nicolson noted complacently in 1925 that

... obviously it is a mistake to view the problem from the angle of our own
traditions and prejudices: a system which would be quite intolerable for us,
is intolerable only to the small number of Italian intellectuals. The great
mass of the Italian people is either acquiescent or cowed. The reaction
which, in this country, would be rapid and inevitable, may well be turned
into other channels: for the only stable element in the Italian character is
their opportunism.

Austen Chamberlain held a similar view on the national relevance of Fascism. When, in November 1926, Ronald Graham
reported the series of severe measures which included suspension
of the whole opposition press and dissolution of all associations
carrying on activities opposed to the Fascist regime, a junior
Foreign Office official minuted his report with the sentence, 'The
analogy with the Soviet regime at once suggests itself, so alike are
the measures by which tyrannies maintain themselves in power.'
This provoked an angry retort from Chamberlain, Mussolini's
gaslighter:

It is easy to denounce 'tyrannies' and I have no love for them, but are these
generalities very helpful? Was life safer in Italy before the March on Rome?
Was law better observed? Was the average Italian as free even as he is today?
There is no greater mistake than to apply British standards to un-British
conditions. Mussolini would not be a Fascist if he were an Englishman in
England.

'British standards' – this was Chamberlain's moral range, and it
contained all the narrowness and smugness of an imperial conceit.
    Winston Churchill went even further in making the case for
Italian exceptionalism. As Chancellor of the Exchequer, he
would tell Italian journalists in 1927: 'If I had been an Italian, I am
sure that I should have been whole-heartedly with you from
start to finish in your triumphal struggle against the bestial
appetites and passions of Leninism.' Mussolini, he added, was

the personification of Roman genius, 'the greatest living legislator'. Churchill and Mussolini, not alone in the twentieth century,
could turn this rhetorical trope on and off at will – the anti-
Bolshevism of both leaders would not prevent them, in time,
from creating alliances with Soviet Russia. As long as it suited,
Mussolini the dictator was regarded as a recuperative leech for an
Italian body politic long corrupted by (failed) liberalism and
threatened by Bolshevism.

This was *the* great miscalculation: a political philosophy or
movement cannot be founded solely on an antithetical relationship to another ideology. What exactly *was* Mussolini's political
philosophy? It was non-existent, totally made up on the spot,
propped up by a panoply of theatrical devices. 'The colossal
emptiness and lack of meaning of these never-ending events was
by no means unintentional,' wrote one critic. 'The population
should become used to cheering and jubilation, even when there
was no visible reason for it'. There was no serious interrogation in
the British Embassy or the Foreign Office of the utter preten-
tiousness – the emptiness, even the madness, the *folies de grandeur*
and megalomania and collective de Clerambault syndrome – of
Mussolini's regime. The symptoms were not incipient, they were
on full display in the shop window of Fascism, but British policy
was *Stato forte*, stability in Italy at any cost.

Certainly, the favourable view of Mussolini taken by the
Foreign Office and the conservative press was tested by the
Matteotti murder – and by Mussolini's abandonment of any pre-
tence of coalition government by January 1925. And yet *The Times*
warned its readers against exaggerating the episode. 'Murder is
more common [in Italy] than in most of the civilised states.' The
Morning Post and the *Daily Mail*, too, were unimpressed by the
charges against Mussolini, arguing with obscure logic that his
assumption of dictatorial powers demonstrated that he was too
intelligent to rely simply on brute force. Even sections of the
Fascist press did better than this. In *Critica Fascista*, Giuseppe
Bottai, a future minister, wrote that the murder was 'the most

cruel, inhuman and stupid' of crimes, amounting to a 'criminal degeneration of political behaviour'.

Matteotti's murderers, let it be remembered, were Fascists close to Mussolini, and most likely acting on his orders. However puny their sentences, they were in jail, a symptom of the deep crisis the affair produced for Mussolini. Of course, *The Times* did not formally condone murder, and it had harsh words for the 'village ruffians' and 'hooligans in the towns who committed crimes on the pretext that they were serving the Fascist cause'. It even acknowledged that Mussolini might have 'provoked Nemesis himself'. But then and later, *The Times* believed in his ultimate good faith, applauded his struggle against Bolshevism and agreed that his fall was 'too horrible to contemplate'. (The same *Times* that would, in 1933, advise its readers not to put 'too sinister an interpretation' on Nazi electoral gains.) Mussolini could get away with murder – that was the message.*

Through the rest of the 1920s, conservative opinion maintained the line adopted by 1925, ignoring powerful indictments by those who had seen Fascism close up, such as Gaetano Salvemini, whose critique *The Fascist Dictatorship in Italy* was published in 1927. Against the backdrop of the 1926 General Strike in Britain, the *Morning Post* rejoiced that Bolshevism had been routed in Italy by 'trim handsome black shirted lads'. The same lads who had just assaulted anti-Fascist intellectual Piero Gobetti to the point that his ribs punctured a lung, sending him, like Matteotti and Amendola, to an early death. Rothermere's *Daily Mail* saw Mussolini as the Napoleon of modern times. There may have been doubts in the Foreign Office about Mussolini's temper, but his use as a strategic factor secured him invaluable defenders. Before 1935, there was an almost total absence of comment in the British parliament on the Italian regime.

*

* Indeed, few were the voices raised anywhere against this fact. When, in 1936, the French premier Léon Blum stated, 'I shall refuse to have any dealings with Matteotti's murderer', Mussolini responded by mocking Blum in *Il Popolo d'Italia* as 'one Jew who did not possess the gift of prophecy'.

Mussolini returned from Libya on 17 April, sailing home 'in a blaze of glory', the heavy dressing that had covered half his face on his departure replaced by small strips of adhesive plaster on the bridge of his nose. The *New York Times* described Il Duce's welcome: 'Guns boomed, church bells pealed and airplanes circled overhead . . . Scores of thousands of citizens greeted him with enthusiastic acclaim, such as in olden times they accorded only to commanders of Roman armies returning to the Eternal City after inflicting defeat upon Rome's enemies.' (It would be several decades before the *New York Times* dug a bit deeper for journalistic insight: for Libya, Italian occupation meant mass rapes, mass starvation, concentration camps, and over one hundred thousand civilians killed in a 'pacification' programme.)

As a young man, Mussolini had loathed Rome as 'the parasitic city of cheap low-grade hotel-keepers, shoe-shine boys, prostitutes, priests and bureaucrats'. Just outside the city gates, he lamented, families in the Agro Pontino still eked out their survival in straw huts. These people, like the malarial marshes, were a piece of slum-land in need of reclamation. As the new Roman emperor, on 21 April, Mussolini stood proud in the shadow of the arch built to Constantine, a stone's throw from where Violet had shot him two weeks earlier, to review a parade of Fascists and launch his programme to restore Rome to the splendour attained under Augustus. Four ceremonies at four different points (Teatro Marcello, Scipio's Tomb, Trajan's Forum, Villa Celimontanus) marked the beginning of work to clear away the clusters of squalid medieval dwellings that surrounded these ancient relics.

Rome had been great and powerful in the time of Augustus. Now it was returning to prominence thanks to Mussolini, who claimed to be his heir, if not his actual reincarnation. At twenty, Augustus, then still called Octavian, without any official position, had organised an army 'at his own expense and at his own initiative' (in his own words) and used it to help the Senate to crush Mark Antony's forces before Mutina in 43 BC. When the ungrateful Senate slighted its youthful benefactor, a March on Rome took place; hemmed in by the swords of his veterans Octavian dictated terms to a cowed and helpless city. He was elected consul, head of government, without more ado. He was soon deporting political enemies and criminals to the islands, a precedent for Mussolini's similar action.

Romanità was an idea Mussolini borrowed, like so much else, from d'Annunzio, who had once intoned:

We do not want to be a museum, an inn, a holiday destination, a horizon touched up with Prussian blue for international honeymoons, a delightful marketplace for buying and selling, for swindling and bartering. Our Genius calls us to put our stamp on the confused material of the new world.

When inaugurating a motorway, Il Duce (from the Latin *dux*, 'leader') recalled that Rome had been a great builder of roads; when opening a woman's congress he declared that it was necessary to march 'in the Roman fashion'; Fascists held out their arms in the Roman salute, and their militia was subdivided into legions, cohorts, *centurie* and maniples like the ancient army of Rome; soldiers marched with the 'Roman step' (though King Vittorio Emanuele couldn't do the *passo romano* – he had abnormally short legs – and was mortified).

The gravitational pull towards the archaic, the 'retrojection of ideas, desire, or fantasies into the past', seduced many observers. The British historian Kenneth Scott, for example, wrote enthusiastically in 1932,

Symbols of the past and its significance for modern Italy are everywhere in Italian life today – even on postage stamps, where we find Julius Caesar, Augustus, and the wolf of the Capitoline. Perhaps Fascist theory is correct, and the Roman Empire never really died but goes on in the New Italy and its premier.

But a more recent and sceptical commentator argues that the regime's lack of consistent ideas gave rise to a fake *romanità* and 'an aesthetic overproduction – a surfeit of Fascist signs, images, slogans, books, and buildings – to compensate for, fill in, and cover up its forever unstable ideological core'.

'There's no such thing as a Latin. That is "Latin" thinking,' says Rinaldi in Hemingway's *A Farewell to Arms*. The joke was lost on Fascism. Patrimony was destiny.

IX

Hidden Hands

Cesare Rossi,* who ran Mussolini's press office between 1922 and 1924, made the point that any government that wasn't gripped by suspicion and fear would have dismissed Violet's attempt within forty-eight hours as the act of a madwoman and had her confined in a lunatic asylum. This didn't happen, Rossi argued, because the Fascist Party needed to give momentum to the theory that Violet was part of a vast international plot. And indeed, rumours of a conspiracy were now well afoot in Italy: Luigi Federzoni was behind it (mooted as a dauphin, he had motive); Don Luigi Sturzo, former leader of the *Partito Popolare*, was behind it – wasn't it suspicious that on the day of the attempt, the Sicilian priest was giving a conference in Dublin, where Willie Gibson (whose peripatetic lifestyle was now rendered in the press as 'mysterious') was attending the congress of the Gaelic League? What of the fact that one of the nuns at the Santa Brigida convent, a certain Sister Giuseppina Segatini, was from Badia Polesine, where Matteotti was also from? Or that another nun, Sister Teresa Ursella, was linked by her birthplace to an alleged accomplice of Mussolini's would-be assassin, Tito Zaniboni? In the cramped minds of the conspiracy theorists there was no room for mere topographical coincidence.

The most attractive theory was that Violet was part of a widely spun international web dedicated to the elimination of Il Duce and his regime. As Umberto Eco puts it in 'Eternal Fascism: Fourteen Ways of Looking at a Blackshirt':

* Rossi, a Fascist moderate, had openly accused Mussolini of the murder of Matteotti in 1924, and was forced to flee to France. Arrested in Switzerland in 1928, he was returned to Italy and sentenced to thirty years' imprisonment. He spent fifteen years in a Fascist jail.

The first appeal of a Fascist [...] movement is an appeal against the intruders ... Thus at the root of the Ur-Fascist psychology there is the obsession with a plot, possibly an international one. The followers must feel besieged. The easiest way to solve the plot is the appeal to xenophobia. But the plot must also come from the inside: Jews are usually the best target because they have the advantage of being at the same time inside and outside ... However, the followers of Ur-Fascism must also be convinced that they can overwhelm the enemies. Thus, by a continuous shifting of rhetorical focus, the enemies are at the same time too strong and too weak.

The enemy within, the enemy without. On 9 April, *Il Popolo d'Italia* published a cartoon by Mario Sironi depicting Violet Gibson, armed with her revolver, as a wicked old witch riding not on a broomstick but on a clawed foreign hand. Sironi, who took part in the March on Rome, was one of the regime's key image-makers, perfecting a distinctive form of vocabulary composed of daggers, bayonets, artillery shells, eagles, stars, wings, columns, Roman numerals, stone-chiselled images of Mussolini's head. His cartoon of Violet acted as a lightning rod for anti-foreign sentiment. Speculations as to her links with political defectors abroad increased with the identification of the revolver as a Lebel, a French weapon. (Violet claimed she had brought it with her from England. But she had already used one revolver – on herself – in 1924, and this had been confiscated by the police at the time. Did anyone seriously believe that she had travelled to Rome with *two* guns? There is no record in the police files or the preliminary investigation of anybody putting this question to her.)

The link to France, however tenuous, provided the regime with the opportunity to persuade Italians that, being threatened by 'external' enemies, their interests were now synonymous with those of Fascism. 'The infamous, the nation's traitors, the exiles and the vile, have seen from Mussolini's joyous calm, once and for all, that the time of assassination attempts is passed,' a journalist snarled. 'Il Duce is ours; heaven help those who wish him harm!' In this climate, the priority for the Foreign Office and the Gibson family was to disentangle Violet's case from any possible association with a conspiracy. Anything that gave 'a political complexion to Miss Gibson's deed' would be 'undesirable', Ronald Graham stressed. It must, at all costs, be presented as 'simply the act of a demented woman'.

Mussolini's own view, as expressed to Graham on his return from Libya, was that Violet was mad, and he was bored with the whole affair (notwithstanding, he had ordered that all developments in the case be communicated to him directly). Graham reported the meeting in detail to Austen Chamberlain:

I [said] that I was glad to see from the excellent health and spirits in which His Excellency appeared to be that the attempt had produced no evil results. Signor Mussolini replied that there had never been the slightest resentment against Great Britain owing to Miss Gibson's attempt and even less against the Embassy. I asked His Excellency whether anything further had transpired regarding Miss Gibson. He replied that from the outset the whole affair had been of scant interest to him and he had not been following its developments. It appeared evident that Miss Gibson was stark, staring mad and he hoped that before long she would be sent back to her native Ireland where, according to his information regarding the inhabitants, she would find plenty of congenial company!

Il Duce's ennui was on ostentatious display at the re-opening of parliament on 29 April. The house pullulated with indignation (only Fascist members were present, as the opposition was still withdrawn in its Aventine protest). Mussolini entered to tumultuous applause, lasting five minutes, after which the Speaker delivered the ritual panegyric:

For the second time in just a year, an assassin's hand has attempted to take the life of the Head of Government, with the profane intention of depriving the nation of its great and providential leader [*condottiere*] and of stopping in a pool of blood the magnificent rise of the new Italy. This second attempt is the work of foolish fanaticism and it increases the repulsion felt by all of us that this was the hand of a woman, whose nature is intended for beautiful and gentle things. Fortunately, this is a case of foreign madness, because Italian woman is already a long way from such savage feelings . . . God gave Mussolini to us, beware who dares to touch him!

Mussolini eventually replied to this and further lengthy encomia by saying he was 'irritated and bored' by the whole business. He added: 'Mussolini has his own unmistakable style, and loves his share of risk. Consequently, he has no intention of removing himself from contact with the people.' But he already had, by referring to himself in the third person.

Il Duce may have been bored, but there was due process to be followed. On 3 May he was interviewed, as the principal witness in the Gibson case, by the investigating magistrates. Enrico Ferri, as Violet's counsel, was also permitted to attend. Afterwards, Ferri held an impromptu press conference, and announced his satisfaction at finding Il Duce in rude health, calm, 'smiling as I have seen him do in his best moments, with that depth of intimate and profound, almost mystical, gravity which is the chief characteristic of his personality'. The meeting, he added, was very short, given Mussolini's complete recovery and the healing of his 'little stitch'. In answer to a reporter's question, Ferri said he was in no doubt that his client was completely psychotic, and threw out some colourful (and entirely invented) facts from her life in support of this opinion. Asked if he had actually met his client, Ferri admitted he hadn't, but said he would do so once the preliminary investigation was completed. He threw a bone to the extremists by conceding that Violet may have been part of a plot, but insisted that this didn't alter the fact of her mental infirmity.

According to the minutes of a Home Office meeting of 26 June 1926, 'Miss Gibson's relatives are no doubt perfectly willing to pay for her in a private asylum, and will be only too delighted if she could be kept there for life.' The problem for all concerned, however, was how to lock Violet up indefinitely when she clearly 'has lucid intervals in which no doctor would certify her, and there would be nothing to prevent a visitor getting her released after a year or two'. Violet's sister Frances had spoken vaguely of threats against the royal family, and Ronald Graham had speculated that Violet, if let loose, might 'have another shot at the Duce – or for that matter, at any other foreign potentate'. This anxiety had spread to the Home Office, which took the view that 'Miss Gibson seems to be just the sort of person likely to turn her attention from Mussolini to prominent people nearer home'. The trouble was, Violet had made no such threat. Though this seemed of no interest to anybody, her particular identification of political evil was not accidental. If she had just wanted to kill someone, why not choose the British prime minister, or some other, unguarded, politician? (In 1922, the Irish Republican Army had killed the ex-chief of the Imperial General Staff simply by waiting for him outside his house in London's Eaton Place and shooting him as he stepped from a cab.) Regardless, it was recognised that 'it would be extraordinarily difficult to keep her confined on such grounds if she, by and by, had the appearance of being sane'.

Attached to the minutes is the following memorandum: 'It is necessary to add that Violet Gibson is a Catholic but Mrs Porter [her sister Frances] and some others of the family are not: Mrs Porter and the other Protestants seem determined to get Violet shut up for life: the Catholics may have different views.' They did not, but if history were to repeat itself as reliably as the cliché, the family schism might have played out in Violet's favour. One of her father's roles as Lord Chancellor had been the oversight of lunatics, and in this paternal-legal capacity he often visited asylums. In 1892, following a visit to the Retreat Asylum in Armagh, he took up the case of Mrs Martha Godfrey. Finding that she was sane, he 'directed that she be allowed to choose where she wanted to go, as there was some friction between herself (a Catholic convert) and her family (who were Protestant)'.

X

Lives of the Saints

In time, Epifanio Pennetta would concede that Violet Gibson was mad: but only partly mad – Hamlet's 'north-north-west' – and not to the extent that she had lost her faculty of reason at the time she shot Mussolini. There was too much method – premeditated, calculated – alongside the madness. The mystery as to why she wanted to kill him, and under whose influence she was operating, remained.

Pennetta plodded on, following every lead, however improbable. But in doing so, did he neglect the internal evidence, the material he had gathered in his searches of Violet's rooms at the convent and the hotel? How much attention did he give to the bundle of papers and the little black notebook that were now sitting on his desk? The contents provide vital clues to Violet's state of mind in the weeks leading up to the attempt. But their relevance, and their tragic dimensions, were inevitably lost on Pennetta, who didn't speak a word of English, and had to rely on a colleague for rough translations.

Violet had started the notebook at Father O'Fallon Pope's retreat in July 1916. The early entries show her grappling with the stringent requirements of the Exercises of Saint Ignatius – 'We cannot always control our feelings but we can always control our will', 'Delight in self contempt', 'Never allow your peace to depend on any object outside yourself' – and reaching for the rewards of a life dedicated to 'the Sacred Heart of Our Lord'. The theme of sacrifice, which first became explicit in late 1924, when she gave up O'Fallon Pope for the general election and set out precipitously for Rome, becomes a growing obsession. 'It is for God to inspire us one by one with the sacrifices he expects of us,' she wrote, 'and to give us the courage to make them.' She herself 'must rise above every human consideration' and 'suffer all the trials he chooses to send without thinking either of what use they can be or what will be the end of them'. (The echo of Nijinsky's diary: 'I did not know for sure what his commands signified, but I carried out his orders.') The 'more weak and miserable' she was, the more fitting 'for the operation of divine love'. It was this uncompromising imitation of what Violet called the 'heroic detachment' of the saints that Enid Dinnis found alarming: 'She adopted a religious form of life and practised very severe self-discipline. I considered her mind unbalanced (whilst admiring her heroism) as there was exaggeration in many things she did.' Dinnis supplied an example of how Violet's 'peculiarities' had intensified: 'I came up against the first direct evidence of her mind being unsound when in the place of a Christmas invitation and a little carefully prepared pleasure I got a letter telling me I would not see her for three years as I interfered with her prayers.'

In happier days, Enid and Violet had walked together in the woods near Buckfast Abbey, to all appearances like the heroines in one of Dinnis's novels, open to 'the divine possibilities in lives and events which "ordinary people don't notice"'. But Violet had moved on from this perambulatory mysticism, leaving Dinnis trailing as she sought out the more demanding regimen of the hermits and desert saints and anchorites who had fled the vices and treacheries of the world to wear out their lives in penance.

The first hermits shunned each other as they shunned the image of evil; every human relation was a snare (hence Violet's banishment of Dinnis, and her belief that friends were 'possessions' which should not be laid up), and they sought each other out only in moments of moral or physical extremity, when flesh or spirit quailed before the hallucinations of solitude (as when Violet had submitted to her emotional pain in March 1926, after the death of her mother, and asked Dinnis to come to Rome). The frescoes and paintings on the walls of the churches Violet visited in Rome were crammed with idealised images of these solitary saints communing with God from caves (St Francis) or huts or even the cramped hollow of a chestnut tree (San Vivaldo). They were shown finding Christ, as well as the devil, in their lonely exile, and mitigating the grimness of their isolation 'by acts of friendly ministry and innocent childlike intercourse' (Violet in Trastevere, giving out alms).

Violet built on and embellished her own experiences of separation with mystical tropes, the suprarational, the doctrine of revealed truth. 'There are among us spirits called to a like grace,' she wrote in her notebook, 'as far as it is possible for man to resemble the angels; they are those who, by the cessation of all intellectual operation, enter into the ineffable light.' Alongside the practice of self-mortification came this possibility – of following Fra Angelico's bright, gilded angels towards heavenly peace, what Yeats called the 'white light of piety'.

Maybe, in moments of inner peace or repose, Violet did encounter God. But, on the brink of her own dissolution, her escape into this mystical space became more and more disorienting. Where previously a kind of equilibrium had obtained, with everything arranged, systematised, to make her faith credible and concrete, suddenly everything began to fall apart as the fragments shored up against her ruin were hit by the running tide of mental and physical exhaustion. Violet's handwriting, usually neat and precise, begins to show the sheer labour of trying to keep it together. It's as if she is witnessing her own derailment and trying in vain to bring herself back on track. Her sentences become more and more disjointed. There is a loosening of associations, repetition, elision, odd juxtapositions – the verbal disarray evoked in T. S. Eliot's 'Burnt Norton':

> *Words strain,*
> *Crack and sometimes break, under the burden,*
> *Under the tension, slip, slide, perish,*
> *Decay with imprecision, will not stay in place,*
> *Will not stay still.*

Violet's notebook should have been the key site to any sensitive forensic search for her motive. Pennetta examined it, but with the wrong lens: instead of using a magnifying glass, he peered down

July 24th/16. Retreat given by... To John O'Fallon Pope S.J.
A Saint is a man who ... his conscience perfectly.

They excel in possessing a well balanced judgment.

Spirituality is an edifice. Its foundation is [the end of ...] first principle.

Don't build yr structure on sand.

We must be like the oak trees in our English parks which stand when the storms & winds ...

...

SANCTITY cosists in the mortification of self will.

We must renounce without exception everything that is not god alone. It is then for God Himself to lead us by degees to a perfect death to ourselves; it is for Him to inspire us one by one with the sacrifices He expects of us, and to give us the courage to make them. She must rise above every human consideration: To suffer all the trials He chooses to send her without thinking either of what use they can be or what will be the end of them, yet the same time never to on her own initiative, to give up any of her exercises or practices

...LIEF OF OUR HEART. THE REPROACH OF MAN + THE OUTCAST OF THE PEOPLE. YET THIS DEEP SENSE OF ONE'S OWN NOTHINGNESS BRINGS NO DISCOURAGEMENT; ON THE CONTRARY, WHILST PRODUCING A GREAT MISTRUST OF ONE'S SELF, IT FILLS THE SOUL WITH CONFIDENCE IN GOD.

WHEN I AM WEAK THEN AM I STRONG IN THY STRENGTH I CAN DO ALL THINGS

IF WE DO THE LEAST LITTLE THING IN OUR OWN STRENGTH IT IS NOT SUCCESSFUL

HE WHO LOVES GOD SEEKS NOT TO BE ... A SAINT BUT TO ATTAIN

THE MORE WEAK + MISERABLE YOU ARE, THE MORE FITTING ARE YOU FOR THE OPERATION OF DIVINE LOVE. BUT YOU MUST CONSENT TO REMAIN ALWAYS POOR + WITHOUT STRENGTH.

DELIGHT IN SELF CONTEMPT.

WE MUST ENDURE OUR OWN WANT OF PERFECTION, IF WE WD ATTAIN PERFECTION IT IS BY THE ENDURENCE OF THIS SUFFER, THAT HUMILITY IS NOURISHED.

THE SUPERIORITY OF NEGATIVE CONTEMPLATION OVER THAT WH. IS AFFIRMATIVE. NEGATION IS SAFER + WORTHER OF THE DIVINE BEING. IN NEGATI from the wrong end of a telescope. He sought a pattern to link up the bits of her life, and he found only the weird, the irreconcilable, the troubling, the difficulty in making sense of someone who was trying to make sense of herself. But there *was* a pattern – a pattern not of incident, but of meaning. The notebook reveals Violet's true self, a self not fixed by the eyes of others, full of internal contradictions, existential incoherence, but no less authentic for that. It is not possible to understand Violet's story without acknowledging the need to embrace contradictory evidence. Thus, by any definition, Violet must be considered mad, at least some of the time, but this does not mean that the whole of her life should be rewritten to fit this conclusion. She was attached to the idea of sacrifice and martyrdom, but this cannot be solely ascribed to religious mania. In the political world around her (to which she paid deep attention) this notion acquired elevated status in the passion narratives of Giacomo Matteotti, the priests George Tyrrell and Ernesto Buonaiuti, the Irish republicans who took part and died in the 1916 Easter Rising. Their stories were all underpinned by the Catholic symbolism and traditions of martyrology.

One entry in Violet's notebook reads: 'As Beatrice Ansi was about to be executed she turned round and looked with loving pity on the crowd who were about to do away with her.' And another: 'The Catholics told St. Ignatius he was to come to be publicly whipped. St. Ignatius was delighted. He said, "Now I am getting Our Lord's lot."' Writing to Enid Dinnis some months after the attack, Violet reflected on her own experience at Campidoglio, describing 'the battle between the police and the people':

. . . the latter had set on me, pulled out my hair and rained blows on me . . . the bravery of the police saved my life. My clothes were torn to pieces and my [holy] medals ripped from me. But inside I was transported to another place that had nothing to do with politics and, without any effort on my part, my heart was filled with sweetness and a great love. I just shut my eyes and made no resistance.

Like Teresa of Avila, one of her favourite saints, Violet had felt 'the sweetness caused by this intense pain', a pain 'so extreme that one cannot possibly wish it to cease, nor is one's soul then content with anything but God'. When the Huguenot Christian martyr Blanche Gamond was tied to a beam and whipped by a bunch of highly excitable women, she rejoiced.

I had the greatest happiness of my whole life, for I had the honour of being whipped for the name of Christ and of being crowned with his mercy and consolation. I can't describe the peace and consolation I felt inwardly. I was ravished . . . The women cried, 'We must strike twice as hard. She feels nothing and neither speaks nor cries.' How should I have cried, when I was swooning with happiness within?

A person who welcomes being set upon by a murderous mob might be considered insane, or so despairing of life that she collaborates in her own extinction. The study of martyrdom confers a different meaning: what the persecuted experience is called *afflatus*, the inspiration (literally: breathing into) of the Holy Spirit whose miraculous presence brings uplift and separation from ordinary prosaic life and illuminates the hidden dimensions of the world. Nietzsche called it 'ecstatic reality', and warned of its consequences.

How was it that Violet found exaltation in her failure? Had not her mission to kill Mussolini, and in the process sacrifice herself, remained unaccomplished? Yet, in her letter to Dinnis, she recaptures a feeling of complete and luminous sanity, as if the universe had opened up to her like a burst casket of jewels. Violet had her ideas about the 'beautiful death', just as Mussolini had his. For one brief moment, she sang with the angels. It was a great success, the high point – the apotheosis – of her life.

*

Several weeks into her detention, Violet's physical condition deteriorated rapidly. Tina Pizzardo, a petty criminal, later claimed that Violet paid to have her meals brought to her on silver plates directly from the Hotel de Russie, by a chauffeur dressed in white. Pizzardo's account could only have been based on hearsay, as she did not begin her sentence till October 1927, fully five months after Violet had left the Regina Coeli. In fact, according to a prison memo of 5 May 1926, Violet's state of health was 'disastrous'; she was extremely weak and needed money urgently to buy food. The rations provided were 'only sufficient to prevent her dying from hunger', and if measures were not taken to improve her situation she would not be fit to respond to further questioning. Alarmed by her condition, Rosario Marciano finally relented on his earlier decision to withhold Violet's cheque book. A letter from the Banca Commerciale Italiana to Marciano, dated 25 May, confirms that 4,901.15 lire had been paid to the Mother Superior of the prison, in respect of a cheque presented by Violet.*

Meanwhile, Guido Leto, the undercover agent who had been sent to France to make enquiries about Willie Gibson, had arrived in London, where he seems to have learned nothing beyond what was already available in the *Evening Standard*. Pennetta put him to better use by instructing him to co-ordinate efforts with the Italian consul in Dublin to persuade Mary McGrath to return to Rome to be interviewed. McGrath was vital to the enquiry: if anybody knew who Violet's accomplices were, it was she. Indeed, in an interview with the consul on 19 May, she let slip that Violet had been visited at the convent by various people, but it had been made clear to McGrath 'that they did not want to be recognised or approached in public'. This information was eagerly seized upon by the consul, who pressed McGrath to proceed to Rome and give a formal statement. She demurred, fearful that she had already compromised Violet. Moreover, she had no money. The consul promised her a first-class return ticket to Rome, and £20 to cover two weeks' expenses. Still she refused.

The Gibson family, on the advice of the Foreign Office, turned up the pressure. McGrath should proceed immediately to Rome

---

* Roughly £35, or £1,500 today, this represented a sizeable portion of Violet's annual income.

and tell the police that Violet was mad. A terrified McGrath was summoned to Frances Porter's house in Dublin, where she said that she was frightened not only of betraying Violet, but of incriminating herself. 'I told her', Frances wrote to Constance, who was still in Lausanne, 'to get a priest or someone to write her a character [reference] to say she was not messed up in politics.' The suggestion scared the hapless McGrath more than ever, put her 'in a terrible fright and fuss'. So Frances turned to Enid Dinnis (a woman of whom she strongly disapproved, believing her to be a negative influence on Violet) and asked her to work on McGrath. Dinnis, who herself had just been interviewed by the Italian consul in London, urged McGrath to compose a written statement. 'What [the police] want to prove', she explained to her, 'is that [Violet] has not been made a tool of by Socialists. I suppose you were always with her and can vouch for the fact that she had no interests or friends unknown to you. That is what they want.' McGrath's words, she continued, could save 'our poor darling' and 'get her home to us very soon'.

This was enough. Frances wrote again to Constance with the news that McGrath had submitted.

She seems to realise that only by offering solid evidence of V's mental condition can she be of any use to her, and I think that she is now willing to give up all selfish motives and really help. I do feel sorry for the poor thing, she loves V. so and it is upsetting her that her evidence will do just what V. has been trying to avoid – locking her up – however she sees it is a choice of prison or an asylum.

As an afterthought, Frances added: 'I have been wondering about writing to V. Would it be kind? The last time I saw her was when she came to see Mother and would not speak to me, we have not corresponded since.'

While arrangements were being made for McGrath's trip to Rome, the Gibson family collated all the evidence that could be found to support the case for Violet's madness. Into the dossier went Violet's psychiatric notes from Holloway Sanatorium. The

notes, showing that 'Miss Gibson had at one time shown homicidal tendencies and been certified as insane', had been sent by the
Home Secretary to the Foreign Secretary, Austen Chamberlain,
who had read them to the cabinet at its meeting of Thursday, 15
April 1926. The Gibsons also asked Dinnis to write a full account
of her friend, emphasising her religious mania and stressing that
she was acting alone. Dinnis was happy to comply.

16 MAY 1926, ENID DINNIS TO THE ITALIAN CONSUL:

Dear Sir,

This is the account which I am very thankful to be allowed to give of my
friend, the Hon Violet Gibson.

I have not seen Miss Gibson since she left England for Rome on the 6th
of November 1924 but we have corresponded regularly. Latterly her letters
showed some depression and mental unrest. After her mother's death,
which occurred on March 21st she wrote that she had had a mental shock
and 'must go quietly'. She expressed a great desire to have me with her. On
the Monday in Holy Week she wrote and asked me to be prepared to go to
her if I got a wire. The wire came two hours after the letter. I was not able
to go, owing to illness in my family. I greatly feared the effect of the disappointment. She had said in her letter that she was 'dead-beat' and intended
to take a complete rest after Good Friday. We, her friends, always dreaded
Holy Week for her on account of her physical and mental ill-health as she is
very strenuous in her religious exercises. I was filled with anxiety and apprehensions.

On the following Wednesday the newspapers contained the tragedy. Next
day I got the letter she had written on the Monday after hearing that I could
not come. It was written in a state of *elation*. She expressed pleasure that she
could make a *sacrifice*. The depression and physical fatigue were suspended.
I wrote directly after hearing of the tragedy to Miss Mary McGrath, Miss
Gibson's nurse-companion, who I never doubted was still with her. On the
contrary Miss Gibson had sent her home to Ireland saying that someone
was coming in her place. Miss McGrath left Miss Gibson on the Monday
in Holy Week. This means that Miss Gibson was alone from then up to the
time of the tragedy. I don't doubt that sending her companion away was a
sign of the clouding of the brain.

Whilst Miss McGrath was with her it was impossible that she could have
got into association with any people outside her own circle of religious folk.
She always had Miss McGrath with her . . . It is unthinkable that anyone of

the unscrupulous kind who would advocate assassination would have got access to Miss Gibson as such a type would have been most repugnant to her . . .

I never heard her speak of Signor Mussolini, but I should say that she would have been full of admiration for him and his ideal. She admired the Imperial spirit and was always keen on the betterment of the people, and I should think would have considered him the ideal combination. She would have chosen him in the same condition of mind as that which would have chosen the Pope, as the central figure. Hers was not a weak or defective brain, but a diseased one. She had immense strength of will and character and a particularly *independent* outlook. It is inconceivable that she could have got into touch with socialists during those nine days, and moreover, homicidal mania, I imagine, returns at its own times and seasons and could not be induced by suggestion? I believe this form of sacrificing another is not an uncommon form when very religious people go insane. In that case the other is someone of whom they have a high opinion . . .

I sincerely hope that I may have been able to present her in a true light in these notes and to allay any fear as to her having been made a tool of by others.

On 29 May, McGrath arrived in Rome to give her statement. Over the next few days, she was questioned repeatedly by Pennetta and Marciano. Frightened and confused, she told a friend she was worried that the interpreter had not properly understood what she was trying to say. She was allowed to visit Violet soon after she arrived, and again on Wednesday, 2 June, when she was kept waiting at the prison for two hours, on her feet, and was finally given just five minutes with her. Marciano was present at both visits, and communicated with Violet in a mixture of French and Italian, neither of which McGrath understood.

McGrath was the first (and, as it turned out, the last) friend Violet was allowed to receive for the duration of her imprisonment. Bringing cherries and a bunch of roses with wild flowers she had picked, McGrath was shocked to discover Violet's loss of weight and parchment-yellow skin. She promised to bring her some pastries ('like the ones you used to buy for me'), and to find out why she was being so poorly fed, despite the recent payment to the Mother Superior (McGrath was later assured that Violet could have whatever she wanted to eat, she only had to ask). She urged her to go outside for fresh air at every opportunity, which suggests that she was declining to do so of her own will. Violet also told her she was sleeping badly.

Following her first visit, Marciano set out to McGrath what it was he wanted to know. From the letter McGrath subsequently wrote to Violet, it appears he had given her a script to follow. She asked,

> Do you remember that you once asked me if I loved Rome more than you? You must know that at this moment nothing interests me beyond helping you, if I am able. I am taking this opportunity to ask you, in the name of God, that when you next see the magistrate you are perfectly frank and answer all the questions he puts to you. This is in your interests, and for your own good. For example: he wishes to know why you attacked Mussolini. Were you impelled to do this by a ritual motive or were you perhaps influenced by a bad person? . . . Forgive me if I take the liberty to make these suggestions. I do so only because I love you and want to help you and God helps those who help themselves.

McGrath ended the letter with an account of her visit to the four great basilicas of Rome, and her ascent, on her knees and in prayer for Violet, of the Santa Scala, the Holy Stairs at San Giovanni in Laterano. A few days later, she returned to County Meath, to her family home and a cherished little Roman teapot and two cups that Violet had once given her. She would never see Violet again.

Everybody, including the loyal McGrath, wanted Violet to give a full account of herself. The pressure was immense. A week after McGrath's departure, Violet requested to see the Crown Prosecutor. She was ready to confess.

XI

Mea Culpa

Violet began her confession in a room at the Regina Coeli on Saturday, 12 June 1926, in the unattenuated heat of the Roman summer. Present were the lead Crown Prosecutor Marinangeli, investigating magistrate Marciano, Violet's defence lawyer Enrico Ferri and his sidekick Bruno Cassinelli, and Andrea Serrao, the British Embassy's legal adviser, who acted as interpreter. They listened in startled silence as Violet began to unravel the story of why she had shot Il Duce.

She had done it, she said, for love. Before the war, she had been introduced to Giovanni Colonna, Duke di Cesarò. He had invited her to go Germany to study philosophy and theosophy at the Anthroposophical Society of Munich. After having visited the Society on several occasions (this much was verifiable, as the Scotland Yard file could attest) she had abandoned her studies. She had, however, seen the duke several times after the war. When she arrived in Rome in 1924 she learnt that he had married. The news had given her great sadness but, not wanting to harbour rancour, she resolved to undertake something to impress him. Knowing that he had become one of the most bitter opponents of the Fascist regime, she decided to kill Mussolini. She maintained that the duke knew nothing of her plan and, in fact, had never even talked of Mussolini. For now, this was all she was prepared to say on the matter. She was tired, and requested to be taken back to her cell.

Five days later, on 17 June, Violet volunteered further information. She said that about a month before the attempt she had seen the duke at the Villa Borghese. They did not exchange words, but he was carrying a newspaper featuring a photograph of Mussolini.

A short while after, she saw the duke a second time, carrying a newspaper on which she noticed a vignette representing, on the one side, a man and a woman engaged in confidential discussion, and, on the other, some men with a smoking gun. She became convinced the duke had displayed these images in order to convey to her that he desired the assassination of Mussolini. There was a third encounter, this time on the Terrazza del Pincio, at which they had finally spoken. 'How big is your heart?' the duke asked her. 'You will see,' she replied. Upon which the duke had handed her the revolver and the bullets, saying, 'You know what you must do with these?' 'Yes,' she answered, and left immediately.

There was more, but Violet kept her audience in suspense for a further two days before she was ready to bring her story to its climax. On 19 June, they gathered for a third time in the same torrid room, nothing to cool themselves with but the sheaves of notepaper on which they were transcribing Violet's words. On the day before the attempt, Violet told them, she had again met with the duke (she couldn't remember at what hour), this time in Piazza di Spagna. He approached her and whispered, 'Great things tomorrow. Go to Piazza Venezia in the morning.' On 7 April, she met him at the appointed time and place. He set off towards nearby Campidoglio, she following discreetly behind. When they arrived, he took up position at a certain distance from her. When the moment came for her to carry out the deed, he signalled to her by lowering his head and raising his hand slightly.

Giovanni Colonna, Duke di Cesarò, descended from ancient Roman nobility, was forty-eight and happily married with two children. He was of slight build, with a pale complexion, and wore a small, white goatee beard. He was lame in the right leg and walked with a limp. Nobody fitting this description had so far been identified as being at Campidoglio on 7 April. Di Cesarò had served in Mussolini's cabinet as Minister of Post and Telegraphs in 1922, but after the murder of Matteotti he had played a prominent part in the Aventine protest, and together with Giovanni Amendola had solicited the king to dismiss

Mussolini. For this, he had earned himself a round-the-clock police surveillance team.

Marciano asked Pennetta – who was by now very much second fiddle to the investigating magistrate – to produce the relevant surveillance records. These showed that the duke had travelled to Palermo on 25 March, returning to Rome by train at 13.20 on 6 April. He had gone directly home from the station, on foot, followed by an undercover agent on a bicycle. Later that day, he left his house, but, inexplicably, none of the three police agents posted outside his house stirred. The next morning, 7 April, he was observed leaving his house after ten o'clock. Again, he was not followed. It was possible, therefore, that the duke had reached Campidoglio before 10.58 a.m., the time of the shooting.

Di Cesarò first learned that Mussolini's would-be assassin was in love with him when Marciano called him in for interview on 5 July. Marciano, who harboured several suspicions about Violet's confession, opted for a strategy of discretion, and the interrogation was brief. The duke confirmed that he had met Violet at a meeting of the Bavarian Theosophical Society in 1911 or 1912, that he had seen her again in Rome during the same period, but had not set eyes on her since. He had realised that Violet was obviously affected by a form of religious mania, though he had no idea she held particular sentiments of affection or love towards him. Marciano concluded the interview, and the duke, in his own words, 'thought no more of the matter'.

Marciano had not disclosed Violet's allegation that the duke was the hidden hand behind her attempt, but somehow this detail reached di Cesarò. Observing that his surveillance team had been bulked up, and that his every move was now being closely monitored, he had cause to think more on the matter. Too frightened to go to the British Embassy, he arranged to meet a British official at an undisclosed location. He was, the official reported to the ambassador, deeply shaken by the turn of events:

The Duke had been informed that the strongest moral pressure had been exerted upon Miss Gibson to make her confess that she had accomplices. According to this story she had been told that the authorities were quite convinced that she was mad, and were prepared to let her go if she would confess who had prompted her and helped her. Her answer had been at first that if she were mad then her evidence had no value – a perfectly logical argument, and one she would stick to. The Duke thought, therefore, that her inculpation of himself must have been extorted by violence. This was simply a deduction, and he had no evidence, or even rumour, to support his supposition.

Ronald Graham dismissed di Cesarò's apprehensions as unjustified. He told Austen Chamberlain in a despatch:

He is not one of those Opposition leaders who have incurred special Fascist resentment, and the idea of connecting him with Miss Gibson's attempt seems too ridiculous to merit serious consideration. I may say that the Duke di Cesarò is of a highly strung temperament [and] in a nervous and depressed state of mind regarding his own position. I should add that while the Italian authorities have made every effort to obtain from Miss Gibson revelations as to possible instigators or accomplices, I have no reason to believe, from the information at my disposal, that she has suffered any ill-treatment during her detention.

When Graham's report reached the Foreign Office, one of the civil servants following the Gibson case penned these comments:

The Duke di Cesarò opens up a ghastly picture of torture and forced confessions, horrible to contemplate. But Sir R Graham evidently disbelieves the story and the Duke is well-known as an excitable and unbalanced person. Italian judicial procedure is unlike ours and far less considerate to the prisoner and the treatment of criminal lunatics is benighted to a degree: we must take it that Miss Gibson is not being treated with the consideration she would have received in similar circumstances in England. But this is a long way from saying that she is being deliberately ill-treated with a view to extorting confessions. On the whole I think it is best to leave things alone – at any rate for the time being. Q. No action.

Another note added to the report reads:

We could not possibly found any action on this story. For the present we can only pray that the Italians are not ill treating Miss Gibson. I cannot believe that they are. In the first place there is little doubt that she is a lunatic, and secondly what would they gain by such treatment? Mussolini is far too big a man to countenance anything of the kind, so zeal on the part of subordinates can I think be discounted.

Notwithstanding their breezy dismissal of the idea that Fascist officials might use violence, Ronald Graham and the Foreign Office were probably right: if Violet's incriminating confession was a complete or partial fabrication by the Fascists, extorted under pressure, then surely her defence lawyers and the embassy's legal representative – all present for the confession-in-three-acts – would have raised the alarm. Violet was not being tortured. As Marciano had suspected, it was she who was fabricating, and she was taking great pleasure in the process. 'The good God knew what he was about when he gave me an Irish tongue to get me out of tight places,' she confided in a letter to Dinnis which, like all her letters, was read by Marciano.

I cannot now understand how anyone minds losing their reputation. To me it is sheer joy, and I take a mischievous joy in piling it on. I draw a herring across the path and we all look down gravely at it. Then the others look gravely at me and I look up with the most innocent face you can imagine. Then we all look down again at the herring, and the herring always gains the day. The reputation is getting blacker and blacker every day. It is like putting on a new dress and I thoroughly enjoy it.

'How sick one gets of being "good",' wrote Alice James in her diary. 'How much I should respect myself if I could burst out and make everyone wretched for 24 hours.'

A feeling of wretchedness descended on the Gibson family. Violet's confession played right into the hands of the extremists who hungered for a conspiracy and a full trial. There was now a real possibility of her facing lengthy imprisonment in a Fascist jail. There was no longer any point in Constance lingering in Switzerland, so she returned to London, where she would be better placed to press Violet's case with the Foreign Office. To this end, she appealed to an old family friend, Viscount William Bridgeman, First Lord of the Admiralty. Bridgeman, an archetypal conservative of the old school, had difficulty understanding why a titled lady was holed up in Italy for the not altogether incomprehensible act of trying to kill a detestable foreigner – a point he made with seadog bluntness in a meeting at the Foreign Office. The Foreign Office stood firm: Italian law had to take its course, and any British representation on Violet's behalf had to tread carefully around the fact of Italian national pride and a growing mood of xenophobia. To this end, Austen Chamberlain himself was making all the right noises, praising Mussolini at the end of June 1926 as the saviour of Italy. He was also scheduled to visit Mussolini in September, at which point he would speak on Violet's behalf (the meeting took place at Livorno on 30 September, Lady Chamberlain sporting her Fascist brooch). In Rome, Ronald Graham kept up his twice-monthly audiences with Mussolini, an honour not granted to any other ambassador, and on each occasion he brought up the Gibson affair.

*

On 26 June, a fellow inmate at the Regina Coeli scribbled '*Viva Mussolini!*' on a scrap of paper and waved it under Violet's nose. Not having shown any signs in prison of being violent, Violet had been allowed to take part in recreational activities such as flower pressing, which, for some unfathomable reason, involved the use of a small hammer. This she now applied vigorously to the inmate's head until guards intervened and wrestled her to the ground. When she calmed down, Violet declared that 'it was against the will of God that Mussolini should continue to exist.' Her victim, Ida Ciccolini, was taken to the infirmary suffering from concussion, and a report of the incident was sent to the Crown Prosecutor. Violet's madness had acquired a new and much-needed lustre.

Why had Violet tried to kill Mussolini? This was the burning question, put to her repeatedly by the police and the magistrates. Here was her answer, expressed literally as a hammer blow. She had already disclosed her motive in her first interrogation on the day of the attack, and it was writ large in her notebook: she was following God's orders. It was as if her questioners had positioned themselves behind a high wall – when she gave her answer, they were unable to hear her.

Soon after this incident, Rosario Marciano ordered that Violet be moved to the San Onofrio lunatic asylum to undergo 'an extensive somatic and psychiatric examination'. She was transferred on 5 July, accompanied by two doctors and Chief Superintendent Pennetta. His investigation was now being seriously undermined by the madness defence. The conspiracy theory and the conspirators, if they existed, were slipping from his hands.

XII

Examination

<hr>

Robert Musil's description of a visit in 1913 to Rome's Santa Maria della Pietà asylum satisfies every grotesque requirement of the narrative of institutionalised lunacy. In his account, we hear the clang and thump of heavy doors being opened and closed, the cries and gibbering of patients, the whining of a young man who pleads, 'I want to get out, when will you let me out?' and then his voice taking on 'an urgent, threatening tone, something whirring, fluttering, some unconscious expression of danger' as the wardens force him down onto the bench. In the women's ward, Musil encounters an old inmate who gives the accompanying doctor a letter for her husband. The doctor shows it to Musil: 'Ernesto, beloved! When are you coming? Have you forgotten me?' The doctor promises the woman the letter will be delivered. As soon as the matron has closed the gate behind them, he tears it up.

Musil advances into a men's ward.

Idiots, the most horrific sight there is. They sit in bed, their whole posture lopsided, lower jaw protrudes and hangs down, violent, chewing movements with it whenever they struggle for words. One old man – dementia senilis – like a thin leather sack stretched over a small skeleton. Little, sunken red eyes.

Then on to the section for disturbed cases, where

. . . the patients sit in the beds, crying out and gesticulating. Some of them have their hands tied to the bed in slings that leave them only a limited freedom because of the danger of suicide. Paralysis, paranoia, dementia praecox . . . A courtyard, locked, surrounded by a gallery. At the entrance, idiotic boys, smeared with snot.

Shortly after Musil's tour, this human aviary was shut down and its patients transferred to the recently constructed asylum on Rome's highest hill, Monte Mario, to the northwest of the city. A showcase of the latest principles of custodial psychiatry, the new Santa Maria della Pietà (soon renamed San Onofrio) was a vast and self-sustaining complex set in 150 hectares of parkland. Chosen for its elevated height and gentle breeze drifting in from the nearby Mediterranean, the area was zoned into central buildings (with the church at its core) and outlying 'pavilions' in which the patients were housed, surrounded by generously proportioned lawns and avenues planted out with a rich variety of native and exotic trees – umbrella pines, oaks, cypresses, palms, eucalyptus, sequoia. The iron fencing around the individual pavilions and the outer perimeter of the site was artfully concealed within hawthorn hedges.

The surroundings and the facilities were a huge improvement on the old asylum, and a long mile from the spartan, cramped conditions of the Regina Coeli prison. Moreover, patients were looked after by nuns of the Order of the Poor Sisters of Saint Catherine of Siena, a martyr greatly esteemed by Violet. Thus, despite her dread of being locked up in an asylum, she was initially enthusiastic about her new accommodation. The day after her arrival, she wrote, in passable Italian, to an inmate she had befriended at the Regina Coeli:

Everything is now well. Tomorrow the Director is giving me a nice bedroom all to myself, and I have a special menu for eating. It is all good for one's health. The air is perfect and everybody is very kind to me . . . How God is good, is that not the truth? I am reading a little from a book of the life of Saint Francis.

Violet was to be allowed to go to Mass three times a week, and to order in some jigsaw puzzles. There were also to be no restrictions on the number of letters she could write or receive. She immediately wrote to Dinnis asking for a new notebook and two pencils, and some books, including an anthology of medieval mystic poetry and Dinnis's own *More Mystics*. What she desired, Violet stressed, was literature 'which expressed the truth in perfect form'. She also had some books in store in a warehouse in Kensington, including an edition of Dante given to her some years ago by a dear friend, and she asked Dinnis to go through them and send her a selection – Petrarch, perhaps, and Tasso, and anything written by 'a good Catholic novelist'.

Violet ended the letter with a jaunty reference to the scrutiny to which she was still subject: 'You can now write to me as often as you want. All your letters will be read by others, but write fully in any case.' Violet herself did not write a single word without the act being observed. Her letters, outgoing and incoming, were forwarded in the first instance to Marciano, who had typed translations made for the file. Even letters Violet had started but abandoned, tearing them up into tiny pieces and throwing them into the bin, were diligently retrieved, sent to Marciano and added to the file. They are still there, in the Italian state archive, falling out of little stapled pouches like so many fragments of a life.

These strictures notwithstanding, some effective correspondence was taking place. Violet's letters are lucid, intelligently written, coherent, and reflect Dinnis's comment, in her affidavit to the Italian consul, that her nature was meek. 'Those who have given their impressions of Miss Gibson in her early days agree that she was hot-tempered and egotistical,' Dinnis had written, 'whereas I myself and others who have known her in the later years found her gentle, patient and, although tireless in listening to other people, particularly reluctant to talk about herself.' Violet's letter to Willie – her first since her arrest in April – was very much in this spirit.

My dear Willie,

It was remiss not to write till now, and, as you have always been a good brother to me I knew you would be doing everything possible to help me. I can guess what the extent of that help must have been . . . Thank you my dear brother.

Cassinelli said you had written to ask if I would like to see you. Yes. But I only live from day to day, and if you come the day you receive this you will find Rome very hot, so I leave it to you to decide when to come. If Marianne comes she must take great care not to get ill again. When you write will you let me know the attitude of 'the family'. I expect Elsie is much cast down and I am anxious for you to see her and cheer her up. Will you let me know her feelings before I write to her. Where is Constance? I wrote to you at the time of our darling mother's death, but the letter was probably swept away with all the others into the magistrate's possession after I was put in prison.

I have never been able to tell whether you came to Rome when I was first in prison. I was told you had come but the stories told at that time were so tall it was difficult to know what to believe . . .

Violet's transfer to an asylum had not been effected so that she might write letters or do jigsaw puzzles. Marciano seemed well-disposed towards her, despite his frustration with her aristocratic ways ('I don't feel up to talking to you today, so come back in a few days when I'm feeling stronger,' she once told him), and the feeling was mutual: she referred to him as 'a most remarkable man'. But he could not afford to appear lenient in her regard. Whatever his personal views, he had the negative merit of being a magistrate under Fascism – magistrates were included among those public servants who, by a law of December 1925, could be dismissed from their post for 'making themselves incompatible with the general political aims of the Government'. Opinions within the government in the matter of Violet Gibson being ever more sharply divided – Luigi Federzoni confided to his diary that the wranglings were like 'the screeching quarrels of washerwomen' – Marciano urgently sought answers. Specifically: could Violet, at the time of the shooting, be considered to have acted consciously and with free will, or was she insane? And if she was insane, could credence be attached to the declarations made by her during interrogations to date? On Thursday, 8 July, the comprehensive examination he had ordered began.

Charged with the far from simple task of penetrating Violet's secret were Professor Augusto Giannelli, director of San Onofrio, and Sante De Sanctis, professor of psychology at Rome University and the *éminence grise* of Italian clinical psychiatry. They started with a full medical examination, noting every detail of her physiological condition, including her skin, musculature, blood, urine, inner organs, mobility, balance, optical, aural and olfactory performance, and psycho-cardiac and vasomotor reflexes. Although the subject was of a delicate constitution and slight of stature, weighing just forty-two kilos (six and a half stone) and standing a mere 1.57 metres (five feet one inch), no significant somatic abnormalities were identified. After two days, Violet's clinical history and condition had been fully noted. On 10 July, the doctors moved on to their in-depth psychiatric investigation. It was to last for an exhausting twenty days.

Their analysis of Violet's intellectual capacities indicated she was 'a woman of well-developed general intelligence', 'an astute woman of spirit'. Despite a 'modest' education, she was well read in philosophy, and her replies to questions often appeared 'astute and sometimes even profound'. But her critical faculties they judged to be 'fairly poor' and 'always unilateral'; her discourse was consistently lucid, ordered and precise, but lacked spontaneity; her powers of calculation were 'weak', and her approach towards practical affairs was 'no different from those observable in foreigners who travel alone and spend their lives in hotels'.

The doctors also examined Violet's madness file – a bulging folder that included the dossier compiled by her family and the Foreign Office – and found it to be consonant with their own observations: the subject was 'a closed character, taciturn, mistrusting, meek but suspicious and touchy, jealous of her liberty and independence, intolerant of any control, a lover of isolation and having a propensity to disregard the counsel of others, including friends'. She harboured a persecution complex, consistently blaming her family for being the cause of her illness and of wanting to deprive her of her freedom. There were also symptoms of megalomania: she talked repeatedly of having to carry out 'great things'. On one occasion, she asked Giannelli and De Sanctis if it were true that the entire Italian nation had telegraphed Mussolini to ask for her pardon and liberty; on another, she declared, 'I gave my life for Italy, but is Italy grateful?' Other 'salient characteristics' were her absolute suspicion of others and lack of compassion or generosity towards the victims of her actions. She expressed 'neither regret, nor remorse' for the 'insane act' of shooting Mussolini – indeed, at no time did she make an appropriate evaluation of this act. Similarly, whilst she had declared her love for the Duke di Cesarò, she never reflected on the fact that her accusations could seriously damage him, arguing instead that he had no cause to complain about her allegations as 'what I say can't be believed because I'm mad'. And though she had offered five hundred lire to Ida Ciccolini in reparation for the injury she suffered in the hammer attack, she never showed any remorse or even curiosity as to the physical damage she had caused.

Despite finding her 'almost always in an elevated psychological state', Giannelli and De Sanctis discovered no signs of psychic dissociation, hallucinations or delirious ideas. On the contrary, the fundamental characteristic of her mental structure and behaviour was 'without a doubt, dissimulation'. For every one of her actions, she gave different and artificial explanations. For example, she had explained her motivation for trying to commit suicide as being 'for the glory of God', but in a letter to Enid Dinnis, she claimed to have done it 'to appear insane', and to the psychiatrists she maintained it was 'so that they would say I was mad. In truth, I didn't want to die.' She insisted, 'as usual', on being regarded as insane, attributing her condition to chronic physical illness and surgical interventions. Because of her 'stubborn dissimulation', every attempt to penetrate her veil was problematic. The doctors gave an example of their difficulty, transcribing directly the following exchange, which took place on 22 July:

VIOLET: I hope you are persuaded that I am mad.
DE SANCTIS: Absolutely, but your defence mechanisms could also undermine our diagnosis of insanity and confirm instead one of criminality.
VIOLET: This is very serious [reddening in the face]. What would you do?

DE SANCTIS: I would tell the truth.

VIOLET: But that's not necessary if you believe I'm mad . . . You could say that the charges against me are invalid because I am insane.

'This argument,' noted the doctors, 'went on for a good half hour.'

Can a person who pretends to be mad claim to be sane? There is no mention in the psychiatrists' report of Violet's notebook. Had they read it, they would have found a reference to an episode from the *Lives of the Saints* that had caught her attention:

Blessed John Avila and his penitent who could not bear being thought a fool or lunatic. So Fr. John allowed him to pretend he *was* a lunatic. And he was put in an asylum and Father John paid him visits. That was the way he *chose* [underlined three times] to kill his self love.

Violet's truncated version of the story was not quite accurate. John of Avila's penitent, John (later St John of God, also known as the Waif, died 1550), did indeed pretend to be mad in order to glorify Christ. But when news of this reached John of Avila, he visited his penitent in the lunatic asylum and scolded him out of his manoeuvre. According to the account of Jesuit Alban Goodier,

He pointed out to John that he was untruthful, he was pretending to be mad whereas he was quite sane. He was unjust; he was living on the alms intended for lunatics, while he was quite able to look after himself. He was wanting in charity; for he was giving endless trouble to everyone about him, though he had resolved to spend himself in their service. All this made John see his folly in a new light. He became immediately sane, and Blessed John of Avila was soon able to secure him his release; possibly some may have thought that he had worked a miracle.

But Violet was sticking to her interpretation of the story. 'Some time ago,' she wrote to Dinnis,

I thought the bravest thing that anyone could do would be to allow themselves to be certified as mad in a foreign country and I said to myself that I could never never achieve *that*, whatever else I might have to go through.

But when it came to the point I accepted it easily and joyfully for the simple reason that I never gave a thought to myself.

Reason is an unstable raft. Unreason can be a sign of mental illness, but it may also be a purposeful strategy of representation. The degree of Violet's mental infirmity is debatable, but the cost of her ploy to be seen to be insane would, in the last degree, be powerlessness and silence. In the hands of the psychiatrists she had already become an object of study, rather than a credible expressive subject.

Day in, day out, Giannelli and De Sanctis persisted. 'Each of her discourses contained a programme,' they recorded. 'Every reply was thought out. In total, her behaviour was consciously organised towards defence.' She insisted that her secret was 'between her soul and God', declaring it was not necessary to bare her soul to anyone: 'To tell or not to tell the truth is not important. What is important is not to say what one cannot say. Certain secrets one can never reveal.' Asked to elaborate, she replied that she could not, 'her face reddening and her pulse quickening as she spoke'. Despite prolonged questioning in this area, she steadfastly refused to discuss religious matters. 'We are not convinced that Gibson possesses a real religious conscience,' the psychiatrists concluded.

Giannelli and De Sanctis were impressed that Violet was 'calm and resigned' throughout the period of examination and showed no hostility towards anyone, and only occasionally presented signs of being depressed or worried. But Violet's powers of concealment were considerable – what she showed and what she felt were sometimes wildly at odds. In her letters, she confessed to terrible loneliness, to feeling 'very very small'. The mischievous pleasure in blackening her own reputation was wearing off: 'One remembers that – what seems long long ago – people spoke well of one and loved one, whereas in these days one is held in such derision that it requires a strong act of faith to believe that anyone ever did love one.' And the constant scrutiny was becoming unbearable. 'It is the being watched and guarded which is the trial,' she explained, 'and the feeling of never being alone. You can imagine how trying this is to my sort of life.' 'The difficulty here is that one must show neither joy nor sorrow,' she told Dinnis.

I am so very much guarded and watched I can do nothing without being seen. The other day I wanted to weep for my dead mother, but felt I must not do so because the tears would be seen. Yet when one's heart is full of love (as mine is) one longs to express it.

There was another aspect to the lunatic asylum that was playing on Violet's nerves: it was full of mad people. 'The ill people are dears,' she wrote to a friend, 'all excepting two called Fortuna and Gadzano who have red eyes and moan out loud.' The woman Fortuna, in particular, was 'a great trial to us all . . . She has a par-alising [*sic*] effect.' Grimly determined that 'every day spent here should be a penance', Violet described with some humour how 'In an asylum it requires a supernatural strength to keep one's spirits from going into one's boots (or rather shoes, which is all one is allowed to wear here!). "Out of the depths . . ." Sursum Corda!' She did not want 'to spoil everything by grumbling, my only anx-iety is to make certain of success in this part of my life. So patience. The greatest enemy is self. The greatest battle is against self. The greatest victory – its conquest.'

Ma guerre à moi. Violet's project of self-conquest meant she had to hold onto her thoughts amid the sway of events, and so hold out against conquest by others. It was less an act of self-cancellation than self-possession: the right to own her soul in silence. Where her brother Willie bought into a romantic ideal of sincerity, she answered to the 'darker imperative of authenticity', where there can be no cordon sanitaire, no escape, or nostalgia, to soften the blows. 'No one will know my judgement except myself,' she told her 'darling' Dinnis. 'I will be silent. I love the Italians and hope they will allow me to stay with them, and I hope everyone will be patient with me.'

Violet's secret was not negotiable, in any currency. She cared little for the court of world opinion, or the opinion of policemen or judges or magistrates or psychiatrists, because her own implacable tribunal was herself.

On 3 August 1926, Giannelli and De Sanctis delivered the sixty-one-page report of their examination to the investigating magistrate. They proposed that Violet's symptoms of intransigence, poor sociability, excessive pride, fanaticism and megalomania all corresponded to a diagnosis of 'chronic paranoia'. They drew attention to two facts: firstly, the paranoiac was not imputable under law; secondly, the paranoiac had no capacity to witness, thus rendering the subject's declarations legally inadmissible. In conclusion, they warned that 'If given her liberty, Violet Gibson could certainly present a danger to herself and to others.' Their recommendation was that she should be detained in a lunatic asylum.

Details of the psychiatrists' findings were published in the next day's press. Despite the blistering embarrassment this caused her family – it was now publicly stated that 'the psychological abnormality of the Ashbourne family could not be excluded' – it gave impetus to hopes that Violet would not be sent for trial. Her release – if not her liberty – seemed imminent.

XIII

Stigmata

'Women have served all these centuries as looking-glasses possessing the magic and delicious power of reflecting the figure of man at twice its natural size,' wrote Virginia Woolf in *A Room of One's Own*.

Whatever may be their use in civilised societies, mirrors are essential to all violent and heroic action. That is why Napoleon and Mussolini both insist so emphatically upon the inferiority of women, for if they were not inferior, they would cease to enlarge ... How is he to go on giving judgement, civilising natives, making laws, dressing up and speechifying at banquets, unless he can see himself at breakfast and at dinner at least twice the size he really is?

One woman who failed to enlarge Mussolini was Ida Dalser, his former mistress, who was consigned to a lunatic asylum in June 1926. Dalser claimed to be Mussolini's legal wife (she had a son by him, Benito, whom he initially recognised, and some evidence exists that they had a form of religious marriage in late 1914), and publicly denounced him for throwing her over. He set a surveillance team on her and ordered that all documentary evidence of their relationship be traced and destroyed. Her fate was sealed after she approached a Fascist minister about her cause. She was forcibly taken to a mental hospital, despite the protestations of friends that she was perfectly sane, and from there she was transferred to an asylum on the island of San Clemente in Venice, where she died in 1937. The son, Benito, fared no better. He died in 1942, aged twenty-seven, in a lunatic asylum in Milan, after being repeatedly dosed with coma-inducing injections.

Mussolini's wife, the sturdily built Donna Rachele – memorably described as 'a doughtily Fascist Red Queen from the

provinces'– did a far better job of enlarging him. Where his mistresses rarely conformed to the Fascist ideal of the 'authentic
woman' – fertile, rosy-cheeked, stocky, broad-hipped and ample-
bosomed – Rachele organised her life around breeding seasons
and made no secret of her dislike of feminism, declaring publicly
that women had a duty to obey their husbands and should focus
on 'their natural and fundamental mission in life' of child-rearing.

Fascist propaganda worked hard to promote this positive
stereotype. (It was also enthusiastically taken up by the British
Girl's Own Annual, which advanced Rachele as a role model in a
gushing profile published in 1929). Youth organisations trained
men to be warriors, women to be mothers of warriors. Part of the
training for future maternity consisted of a military-style drill, in
which girls were passed in review carrying dolls 'in the correct
manner of a mother holding a baby'. Fascist nuptial politics
rewarded women who bore large families and censured those who
didn't – women who practised birth control were threatened with
all sorts of dire consequences from problems with the uterus to
outcrops of facial hair. The Party made repeated attempts to regu-
late female sexuality, issuing guidelines about the length of skirts
and the shape of bathing suits, and ordering newspapers not to
publish pictures of unusually thin women (dieting promoted
infertility) or women with dogs (child substitutes). All this to
counter what it saw as decadent 'foreign' models of femininity: the
so-called 'crisis woman' who was neurotically obsessed with her
appearance, wasp-waisted and in all likelihood barren.

Violet Gibson, unmarried and 'sexless', was perceived as living
at an impossible angle to the proper order of things. According to
several reports of the incident on Campidoglio, Mussolini's first
words after being shot were 'A woman! Fancy, a woman!' On 9
April 1926, the Fascist rag *L'Assalto*, with specific reference to
Violet, railed:

We have always had a fierce hatred of these women of the third sex. Old,
ugly repulsive women who come from abroad in groups, caravans, regiments
to pollute the beauty of our skies, the fertility of our land. From abroad we

get only ugly women, suffragettes who are no longer (and perhaps never were) able to unburden themselves physiologically, feeling the imperious need to become nihilists or 'Sinn-Feiners'. But while God allows the nihilists to engage in their activities in Russia or in Ireland, we don't want them coming here to murder our men-folk and our fathers.

The idea that Violet had ever 'unburdened' herself physiologically seemed both unnatural and repugnant. When she had claimed, in an interview with Giannelli and De Sanctis, that she had 'enjoyed sexual relations with several men', their judgement was that none of those relationships had drawn on her 'capacity to love' (a view supported by Constance, who once dismissed her 'many flirtations' with the comment, 'I don't think she ever cared'). In the opinion of the psychiatrists, the fact that she had never held aspirations towards maternity or the creation of a family 'completed the pallid psychosexual portrait of Gibson'.

But there was something about Violet's sexual history – or her account of it – that troubled the investigating magistate. Did Marciano not believe that she had been capable of physical intimacy? Did he think she was lying – again? Why, in mid-August, well after the comprehensive examination was completed, did he order that she be subjected to a gynaecological visit? On 13 August, Professor Giannelli wrote to Marciano with the results of

... the examination of the genital organs conducted on the patient: I proceeded to undertake the gynaecological examination, to which Gibson submitted without protest. The hymen is not intact: it permits with ease the introduction of two exploratory fingers; the uterus is retroverted; the ovaries are normal; there is no pathological secretion from the urethra, even after it is squeezed.

Why was Violet submitted to this physical degradation? What possible interest could Marciano have in her uterus? Most likely, he and the psychiatrists were influenced by the prevailing belief – expounded at length by Aristotle, and little improved on since – that a woman's state of mind was a function of biology, and that the seat of her madness could well reside in the womb (hence *hysteria*). According to this theory, as explained by the *Encyclopaedia Britannica* in 1788,

The *furor uterinus* is in most instances either a species of madness or a high degree of hysterics. Its immediate cause is a preternatural irritability of the womb and pudenda of women (to whom the disorder is proper), or an unusual acrimony of the fluids in these parts. Its presence is known by the wanton behaviour of the patient . . . In the beginning a cure may be hoped for; but if it continue, it degenerates into a mania . . . When the delirium is at the height, give opiates to compose. Injections of barley-water, with a small quantity of hemlock-juice, may be frequently thrown up into the uterus; but matrimony, if possible, should be preferred.

The theories that guided the doctors' practice from the late nineteenth century to the early twentieth century held that woman's normal state was to be sick. Women were 'more vulnerable to insanity than men because the instability of their reproductive systems interfered with their sexual, emotional, and rational control'. This idea was not advanced as an empirical observation, but as a physiological fact: medicine had 'discovered' that female functions were inherently pathological. Dr Isaac Baker Brown advocated surgical removal of the clitoris (clitoridectomy) and even the labia as a cure for female insanity, performing the surgery in his private clinic in London in the 1860s. He operated on patients as young as ten, on idiots, epileptics, paralytics, even on women with eye problems. He operated five times on women whose madness consisted of a wish to take advantage of the new Divorce Act 1857, and found in each case that the patient 'returned humbly to her husband'.

The examination of Violet's uterus revealed no abnormalities, but in other respects she was seen to conform to the common distinguishing features of female hysteria: 'exceeding selfishness, delight in annoying others, groundless suspicion, unprovoked quarrelsomeness, instances of self-mutilation [and] the "unnatural" desire for privacy and independence'. This model of female hysteria was enthusiastically embraced by Darwinian psychiatry, which revolved around the idea that insanity derived from

evolutionary imperfection, a kind of backsliding from the biological standard of excellence. Visual proofs – 'the stigmata of degeneration' – existed to support the theory. The psychiatrist Henry
Maudsley urged men to examine potential wives for any physical
signs that might betray degeneracy, arguing that 'outward defects
and deformities are the visible signs of inward and invisible faults
which will have their influence in breeding'. He advised fellow
psychiatrists to pay special attention to 'malformations of the
external ear' and 'peculiarities of the eyes'. In April 1926, the *Daily
Mail* had published a close-up photograph of Violet's eyes by way
of supplying graphic evidence of her derangement.

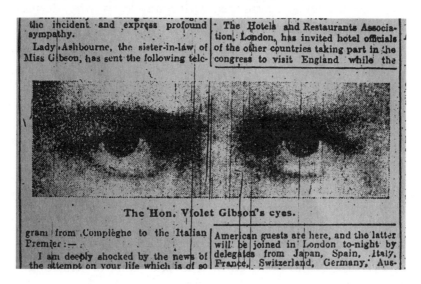

the incident and express profound sympathy.
Lady Ashbourne, the sister-in-law of Miss Gibson, has sent the following tele-

The Hotels and Restaurants Associa-
tion, London, has invited hotel officials of the other countries taking part in the congress to visit England while the

The Hon. Violet Gibson's eyes.

gram from Compiègne to the Italian Premier : —
I am deeply shocked by the news of the attempt on your life which is of so

American guests are here, and the latter will be joined in London to-night by delegates from Japan, Spain, Italy, France, Switzerland, Germany, Aus-

XIV

Heretics

From the very beginning of his regime, Mussolini was consistent in at least one thing: no fear of assassination attempts. For him, they were of 'no importance', they were part of the 'living dangerously' that he had chosen; his was the 'impassiveness of the national donkey . . . burdened with many loads' who, despite everything, continues to draw the cart in the interests of the nation. Hence his 'gesture of disdainful courage' when, on 4 November 1925, he took to the balcony of Palazzo Chigi to address a large crowd, ignoring Federzoni's warning that an assassin (the hapless Zaniboni) was planning to shoot him from the window of a nearby hotel. Hence also his reaction to the events that unfolded on 11 September 1926, when another attempt was made on his life.

At ten o'clock that morning, Gino Lucetti, an anarchist marble-cutter recently returned from a period of clandestine emigration in France, threw a hand grenade at Mussolini as he was driven through the Porta Pia towards his office. According to official reports, the bomb bounced off the side panel of Mussolini's Lancia and landed in the street, where it exploded, leaving eight bystanders wounded amid acrid smoke and fumes. Speeding away from the scene, Mussolini arrived minutes later at Palazzo Chigi where, with great showiness, he told a group of party officials how the bomb had landed at his feet in the car and that he, the 'old *bersagliere*' who had perfected the art of lobbing grenades during the Great War, had very calmly picked it up and thrown it back at the assassin.

As with the Zaniboni attempt, there is another, less heroic version of the facts. Both Mussolini's driver and his personal valet

[218]

Quinto Navarra, who was travelling with him, later maintained that the windows of the car were closed, that he was reading a newspaper at the time and was caught completely unaware, and that the car was already thirty feet away when the grenade actually detonated. Moreover, when Il Duce arrived at Palazzo Chigi he was observed visibly shaken and consulting nervously with his security escort.

He did, however, recompose himself in time to address the huge crowd that thronged into the great square outside Palazzo Chigi after news of the attempt spread. There, according to *Time* magazine, Il Duce appeared on a balcony above a sea of a hundred thousand supporters and, 'jaw set, eyes luminous', shouted,

> This kind of thing must end! . . . I say this not on account of myself, because I truly love to live in danger, but on account of the Italian people, who work and produce and have a right not to be disturbed by such recurrent happenings . . . I shall make it increasingly difficult for a handful of madmen and criminals to disturb the life of the nation.

Mussolini was no longer in the mood to spare the lives of those who sought his. As he was speaking, police were breaking down doors and making arrests, a round-up which included Lucetti's entire family and circle of friends in his hometown of Avenza. In Rome, between three hundred and four hundred 'anarchists, pseudo-anarchists, and ex-anarchists' were taken into custody; six hundred houses were searched overnight, with a further 355 arrests.

At San Onofrio, Violet now made a huge tactical mistake. She confided to a nurse her disappointment at Lucetti's failed attempt, said that she had great sympathy for him but he had been 'clumsy and compromised other people'. She even boasted that she was 'clearly the most intelligent of all the would-be assassins' (there was some truth to this: nobody, except her, had actually drawn blood). Violet's remarks were passed on in a report to Marciano. It followed that of a few weeks earlier in which she was quoted by the same nurse as having said that 'she had accomplices but would never reveal their names because they were relying on her silence'. Marciano reacted angrily: Violet was no longer to be allowed to go to Mass, or to walk in the gardens. If she wanted air, she was to take it in a small internal yard. 'One's heart sinks each time one enters it,' she wrote in a mournful letter. 'The ill people are pathetic.'

Realising that the nuns had informed on her, Violet felt utterly betrayed, and turned in desperation to Dinnis:

As something has just happened to make me feel very lonely here, I am writing to you, to make me feel that at any rate there is someone in the world who is true . . . San Onofrio is a stronghold of Fascisti, beginning with the head . . . so now I must use prudence and beware of traps . . . I am determined to run no risks which may end in failure. I am out to run a race which ends with Victory.

Violet knew that she had lost ground. A week later, the same nurse-informant reported:

She has cried all day, repeatedly washing her face to conceal the fact. Two things are making her sad: one, that she can't go to Mass, the other is a very important thing that she can't reveal to anybody. She has heard about the latest attempt on Mussolini and is stunned to find that they think she was in some way involved. She knows nothing about it. She now believes that she will be implicated in all other attempts . . . In the evening she said she had a headache from crying so much and she added that she had much crying to do tomorrow.

If Violet feared the consequences of the Lucetti episode, she was right. A political furore erupted, with the extremist *Intransigenti* claiming that the assassination attempts were all linked, and that the leniency shown to Violet (whom they believed to be languishing in idle luxury) was encouraging others to take up their evil part in the plot.

Barely a month earlier, Ronald Graham had sent an enthusiastic update on the Fascist regime to the Foreign Office. 'Things are being attempted here today with confidence, energy and already some measure of success, that were never thought of before or never undertaken with any heart owing to the inevitable presupposition of failure.' Sounding much like Miss Jean Brodie, the ambassador continued, 'There are dragons still in the way, old weaknesses and old scandals persist, but I do not believe it possible for any experienced and unprejudiced observer to deny that there is a new spirit working strongly in the country, a new faith and a new determination.'

Graham was right about the new determination, but he had not anticipated the direction this steeliness would take. The *Intransigenti* were about to get their way. On 21 October, Crown Prosecutor Marinangeli, a highly competent magistrate but an enthusiastic supporter of the regime, submitted the case of Violet Gibson for prosecution. Epifanio Pennetta, who continued to write reports stressing the possibility of a hidden hand behind her attempt, could finally look forward to a trial. A week later, on 29 October, two police cars carrying uniformed officers arrived at San Onofrio. One car would have sufficed, but a certain show of force was now expedient. The order was for Violet to be taken back immediately to the Mantellate prison. She barely had the time to collect her belongings and say goodbye to the nurses.

On the same day, Ronald Graham informed Austen Chamberlain that he had just learned, 'on good authority, that some of the most highly placed Fascist leaders have declined to accept the medical evidence, and have brought all their influence to bear to secure that the trial shall proceed [despite the fact that Miss Gibson] is now, from all accounts, mentally quite unfit to appear'.

Graham's fear – that 'the extreme Fascists in Italy will not be induced to believe that she is really insane, but think that the whole incident of her attempt on Signor Mussolini's life was part of a deep-laid plot' – was confirmed by publication of Marinangeli's lengthy submission for the prosecution. The case against her, he argued, was compelling, and needed to be answered by the defendant. Challenging the findings of the psychiatrists,

Marinangeli argued that 'sectarian or political factionalism, involving the direct or indirect complicity of other persons, associations, organisations or groups hostile to Fascism and resolved to get rid of the head of the Italian government, would appear to be the most probable motive'. He had arrived at the conviction that Violet had fired her weapon with 'premeditated, firm and decisive intent to kill; and that the crime was not consummated because of sheer accidental factors which were extraneous to her will'. In support of this, he noted the perfect suitability and deadliness of the weapon; the point-blank range from which it was fired; forensic evidence of a second bullet which was fired but failed to explode; the part of the body aimed at and hit; the shrewd choice of place and occasion for carrying out the crime; the cunning which must have been employed to escape the vigilance of the police; the recovery of a newspaper dated 6 April 1926 from the accused's lodgings which carried a portrait of Mussolini and an announcement of a ceremony due to take place on the 7th; the piece of paper on which she had written 'Palazzo del Littorio'; and the stone which she was carrying at the time of her arrest, which she admitted would have been used to break the window of Mussolini's car if he had managed to enter it.

The charge of unaccomplished premeditated murder could not be in doubt. Violet Gibson had matured her criminal project over a long period of time. During questioning she had admitted that her dismissal of Mary McGrath was done in order not to compromise her. This was but one example of how she 'demonstrated both cunning and patience and therefore a firm capacity of will, rather than lunacy'. Moreover, the accused had, from the start, maintained an evasive attitude, screening herself, with 'manifest cleverness' and 'a certain ostentation', behind reiterated protests of not remembering anything, instead promoting her defence of insanity and asking to defer her interrogations in order to be able to speak at a more opportune time. When she did begin to talk, it was to incriminate other people, but her statements were riven with contradictions. The psychiatric defence was unreliable because of the scarcity of information relating to the accused's previous life, and the fact that the psychiatrists had been forced to elicit that information from the accused's own mouth. Marinangeli also dismissed the notion that Violet's 'secret' was 'a manifestation of some paranoid or delirious system of metaphysical-mystical-political content from whence the crime had derived'. It was, rather, part of her 'habitual tendency to dissimulation and artifice'.

This was the case for the prosecution of Violet's 'execrable misdeed'. The prosecutor therefore requested that the accused should be referred 'in the same state of custody' before the court to answer the following charges:

– first, of having, in Rome on 7 April 1926, with premeditated intent to murder, fired two shots from a revolver (only one of which exploded) at His Excellency Benito Mussolini, the Head of Government, on account of his office; of accomplishing all that was necessary for the consummation of the murder, without achieving her purpose because of circumstances independent of her own will; and causing Mussolini an injury which had required fifteen days to heal, but which had not, thanks to the hand of Providence, stopped him from carrying on his marvellous and incessant activity;
– second, of having, in the same circumstances of time and place, carried a revolver outside of her place of habitation without licence from the proper authorities;
– third, of not having paid the appropriate tax for the possession of the revolver;
– and fourth, of having omitted to inform the police authorities of the possession of the said weapon.

Not since those vital seconds on Campidoglio when her life was threatened by mob justice did Violet's fate look so precarious. The prosecutor was not interested in the sophistry of shrinks, but in the enactment of justice: Gibson must face the full authority of Fascist law. Constance, who had been so convinced of Violet's imminent release that she had put herself in readiness to leave London and come to Rome at any moment, was told to stand down by the British Embassy. 'Things being as they are, I don't think it would be of any use for you to come,' wrote the embassy's legal adviser, Andrea Serrao.

Rest assured that everything possible has been done, and will continue to be done, for your sister. She is well although depressed after having heard that the public prosecutor intends to send her to trial. She is only asking to be allowed to go to Mass often and to have money put freely at her disposal for charitable purposes.

*

There were now three would-be assassins at the Mantellate pending trial – Zaniboni, Lucetti and Gibson – and no sooner had Violet settled into her cell than news broke of a fourth attempt.

31 October, 5.40 p.m. Mussolini had just finished addressing a huge crowd at a newly opened sports stadium in Bologna. It was another fighting speech, ending with a call to arms: 'Blackshirts! Raise high your rifles, so that the entire world can see the forest of bayonets and feel the beating of your determined and invincible hearts.' As he was leaving the stadium in an open-topped car, a pale-faced teenager whipped out an automatic revolver and took aim. 'The shot rang out beside me,' Foreign Secretary Dino Grandi recalled. 'The bullet seemed to strike Mussolini full on the breast. It even scorched the Order of Saint Maurice silk sash he was wearing, then tore through the mayor's coat, until finally driving into one of the panels of the car.' The boy-shooter, Anteo Zamboni (aged fifteen),* was immediately engulfed by the crowd and lynched on the spot – kicked, strangled, stabbed, and then finally despatched by the commander of the Fascist militia and Minister of Economy Italo Balbo, who, with total lack of economy, shot every chamber of his pistol into the mangled but still writhing form where

---

* Zamboni was known to have been an enthusiastic member of the Fascist Youth. Why he should want to kill Il Duce – or whether indeed the shot was fired by him – has never been clarified. Rumours of a plot, organised by Roberto Farinacci, leader of the *Intransigenti*, who wanted to push Mussolini aside and lead a far more violent revolution, have never been settled.

it lay in the gutter. 'Doo-chay, Doo-oo-chay', came the scream-ing chorus from the crowd. 'Be calm!' Mussolini bellowed, still upright in his car. 'Nothing can hurt me!' He then sped past the bloody, naked corpse of Zamboni towards the station and his private train.

Once again, Mussolini assumed his pose of 'maximum indiffer-ence', referring with Olympian serenity to the 'tenacious ballistic attention' to which he had been subjected in recent months. The pope, on being informed of the attack, said that God had once again intervened to protect Il Duce. Actually, he was protected by a 'corselet of fine Ansaldo steel which covered his stocky torso from neck to hips, between his shirt and undervest', though no mention was made of this publicly.

Mussolini was not indifferent to the threats that faced him – he was scared for his life. But in a very important sense the four attempts that took place between November 1925 and October 1926 were of enormous advantage to him. Exploited to maximum advantage by the regime, the attempts, according to Mussolini's former press officer, Cesare Rossi, became 'the cornerstone upon which a strategy of the totalitarian conquest of Italian life' was built; they were 'the lubricants that set the cranky, rusty political gears moving, the psychological fortifiers for the creation of the myth of Mussolini'.

This myth relied on a paradox: Mussolini's invincibility was inseparable from his vulnerability; his power was predicated on the awful possibility that he might lose it. Thus, the intervention of God himself, of the Divine hand, was necessary to save both Il Duce and the Italian *patria* from the menace of human affairs, an intervention for which the Vatican itself offered public thanks after every attempt. There was some logic in this, as clearly every-body else had failed in the task. And yet the regime was able to benefit from and amplify claims that its leader's escape was miraculous.

This claim was advanced in a series of Fascist propaganda exercises that construed Mussolini's story as a passion narrative.

A text produced for use in elementary schools, 'The "Yes" of the Deaf-Mute', describes how a little boy, while listening to a speech by Mussolini, is miraculously cured of his affliction and able to shout out enthusiastically: 'Yes! Du-ce! Du-ce!' in answer to his leader's questions. Mussolini's simple origins were an important element in the cult, and their emotional resonance was reinforced by explicit parallels with the life of Jesus. Il Duce's blacksmith father became the carpenter Joseph, while his patient and long-suffering mother, the schoolteacher Rosa, took the part of Mary: 'They are but Mary and Joseph in relation to Christ, instruments of God and history ordained to look after one of the greatest of national messiahs – indeed, the greatest of them all,' wrote Edgardo Sulis in *Imitation of Mussolini*, a tract that ludicrously stole from the 'Imitation of Christ' genre. Pupils in some schools were even required to learn the following alternative version of the Creed:

I believe in the high Duce – maker of the blackshirts – And in Jesus Christ his only protector – Our Saviour was conceived by a good teacher and an industrious blacksmith – He was a valiant soldier, he had some enemies – He came down to Rome; on the third day – he re-established the state. He ascended into high office – He is seated at the right hand of our sovereign – From there he has to come and judge Bolshevism – I believe in the wise laws – The communion of citizens – The forgiveness of sins – The resurrection of Italy – The eternal force. Amen.

As Mussolini once said, 'The crowd does not have to know; it must believe.' Referring to the Fascist *ecclesia* of believers and militants, he explained that 'It is faith which moves mountains because it gives the illusion that the mountains move. Illusion is, perhaps, the only reality in life.' What united Fascists was not a doctrine but an attitude, an experience of faith, which was concretised with the myth of a new 'religion of the nation'. Faith, then, was the illusionist's conjuring trick, of the kind the infamous Professor Donato used in his stage shows. Should it fail, Fascism availed itself of other methods to impose the fact of Mussolini's sacred status – its familiar instruments of violence, intimidation and repression, which were now applied with new vigour. Mussolini usefully outlined the tactic, whose aim was to 'sudden-ly take the initiative and strike my adversaries at the time of their greatest disorder and panic'. Whatever the would-be assassins hoped for, their efforts acted as catalysts, hastening and hardening a dictatorship bent on the cancellation of what remained of dem-ocratic life in Italy.

The security measures instituted after Violet's attempt were manifestly inadequate. How could Lucetti, a known anti-Fascist, have re-entered Italy unnoticed? How could Zamboni have got close enough to take a shot? The consequences had already made themselves felt. Police chief Crispo Moncada was dismissed on the very day of the Lucetti attempt. Soon after, Federzoni, the moderate Interior Minister, became the target of accusations, and Arnaldo Mussolini considered him '*cotto*', fin-ished. He was. Mussolini stripped him of his ministry, which he took into his own hands. It was just the beginning – the effects of the attempts were to be felt by far more than a few sacked officials.

Official British opinion was slow to apprehend the significance of the unfolding situation. Lord Lloyd, the British High Commissioner to Egypt, who happened to be in Rome, wrote enthusiastically to a Foreign Office mandarin of an audience with Mussolini on 5 November 1926:

I had an absorbingly interesting hour with Mussolini. He has a *very* remark-able personality. Whatever he is or is not he is a very great man. No one could talk to him and be in any doubt about that . . . he argues that it is bet-ter that the Government should themselves take in hand and control the measures necessary to prevent the recurrence of these [assassination attempts] than to let the Fascists embark on reprisals of their own. He has therefore once again a very difficult corner to turn and one prays that he may succeed.

On the same day, the *New York Times* reported in more omi-nous tones that 'Within twenty-four hours the machinery of the Fascist regime will be set in motion to destroy every trace of organised opposition against Mussolini and to proscribe every individual suspected of antagonism to him.' This, Cesare Rossi claimed, was the flare signalling Fascism's 'real *coup d'état* ' – the moment when Italy became a totalitarian state.

XV

Lockdown

Mussolini unveiled his new machinery of repression on 6 November 1926, driving the Act for the Enforcement of Public Security through a parliament now stripped of opposition. The Aventine secessionists, who had been left in limbo since January 1925, were finally deprived of their seats; opposition parties, unions and associations were formally banned; and clandestine emigration was blocked with greater energy – the days when dissidents like Gaetano Salvemini could be smuggled over the Little Saint Bernard Pass while the border guards ate a long lunch were over, theoretically at least. Italy was to be converted into a Fascist fortress. The legislation, a juggernaut of unconstitutional decrees, also laid down severe penalties for:

> ... all those who have committed, or manifested the deliberate intention of committing, acts subversive of the social, economic or national order, or capable of diminishing the security of the State or opposing or hindering the action of the State authorities in a way capable of prejudicing national interests according to the internal or international situation of the moment.

The *Washington Post* correspondent reported, somewhat credulously, that 'Publication of the new laws and decrees in the Fascist press this morning revealed how strong and extensive are the underground efforts against the government.' Perhaps the correspondent had reflected on Article 5 of the law, which threatened foreign journalists with jail sentences of five to fifteen years 'for spreading abroad false, exaggerated or malicious reports' concerning internal conditions in Italy. All foreigners in Italy were now under suspicion. Lord Lloyd, who had lingered in Rome to discover how Mussolini might turn his 'difficult corner', found an answer of sorts when he was arrested by a police constable whose suspicion was aroused when Lloyd asked him where Il Duce's private villa was. Lloyd, dressed impeccably in cravat and morning clothes, was marched off to the nearest police station. There, he protested furiously, and only after an hour was he allowed to use the telephone and call the British Embassy. A scandalised Sir Ronald Graham sped in person to the police station, identified Lloyd, swore that he was no potential assassin and secured his release from a reluctant Fascist captain. Lloyd's enthusiasm for Mussolini was undiminished by the experience. He remained a passionate supporter of Anglo-Italian co-operation, happily pointing out that 'the Italian genius has developed, in characteristic Fascist institutions, a highly authoritarian regime which, however, threatens neither religious nor economic freedom, or the security of other European nations'. But foreigners in Italy less potent than Lloyd redoubled their care to salute smartly the Fascist banner wherever displayed, on pain of arrest.

The public security law was a mere muscle-flexing exercise, the warm-up for the knockout blow of 25 November, which Mussolini delivered in the form of the Emergency Law for the Defence of the State, a package that included the power to confiscate passports, close down newspapers and opposition parties indefinitely, and exile political dissidents without trial. Membership of the Communist Party (declared illegal in the first Bill) was now punishable by law. Further, the death penalty, abolished in 1889, was reinstated for attempts on the life of the prime minister and members of the royal family, and for a total of fifteen political crimes, such cases to be tried by a Special Tribunal for the Defence of the State. This tribunal was effectively a wartime court martial – the extremists, who believed that in true Fascism life is permanent warfare, warmly embraced it. Crimes under its jurisdiction included engaging, while in foreign countries, in 'any activity whatsoever capable of prejudicing national interests' (five to fifteen years' imprisonment); 'carrying out propaganda concerned with the doctrines or the programme of any opposition party'; and all acts which 'tend' to incite the citizens of the country to armed insurrection against the power of the State (maximum penalty, the death sentence). Under this clause, Mussolini's March on Rome could not be repeated, and if it were, its leaders would hang for it.

Other crimes were so vaguely defined that the most innocuous activity, even academic discussion, could be, and was, construed as seditious in character. The Special Tribunal was a flagrant breach of Article 7 of the Italian constitution, which declared that 'No exceptional tribunals or committees to administer justice may be set up'. Fascist to its core, it was presided over by an official appointed directly by Mussolini from among the generals of the army, navy, air force or Fascist militia; no legal degree was required for the appointment, and the tribunal's first president, a general of the regular army, had no legal training whatsoever. The president and the five assisting judges were each bound by the Party oath 'to obey the orders of Il Duce without discussing them and to serve the cause of the Fascist revolution with all my power and if necessary with my blood'. The time of trial could be announced to the accused and his counsel as late as twenty-four hours before the proceedings, and at the discretion of the president even that period could be reduced. Naturally, under these conditions, there were few lawyers keen to accept the role of defence. When, in September 1930, the tribunal appointed counsel for a group of Slavs charged with having thrown a bomb at the premises of a Fascist journal in Trieste, the lawyer declared in camera that his clients found themselves 'in a terrible situation' and 'that a death sentence would be the proper thing'. He then charged the father of one of his clients thirty thousand lire (equivalent today to £9,000) for his efforts.

The laws of November 1926 were the work of Mussolini himself, but their ideological thrust owed much to the newly appointed chief of police, Arturo Bocchini, who replaced the disgraced Crispo Moncada. Bocchini, whom many believed was, until his death in 1940, 'the occult and extremely powerful dictator of the dictator', was also given control of the new Division of Political

Police, which commenced a merciless war against the enemies of Fascism, spying on clandestine opposition groups and infiltrating agents into their cells.

Looking for assassination plots, Bocchini's police found them everywhere – an inevitable truism of the restless paranoia of the security state. At the Italian state archive the relevant folders, pretty scant until the end of 1926, begin to expand and multiply with details of suspicious activities. Undercover agents abroad report on a rash of plots being prepared in Los Angeles (involving the Sicilian mafia), France, Switzerland, Montenegro, Belgium, Austria, Albania, Rio de Janeiro. Somebody is to throw a bomb at Mussolini while he is motoring down the Tevere; a man dressed as a policeman is to kill him in Perugia; one woman claims that her husband, a barber in Milan, has told her of his intention to kill Mussolini – the man, Rodolfo Passardi, is arrested and sent to internal exile for five years. Another file reveals that one Farina Orlandok, a sous-chef at the Hotel del Quirinale, arrested in Viterbo for suspicious political activity, has alleged that a Russian by the name of Grasso Vincenzo Oscar is planning to assassinate Mussolini by detonating dynamite on the horse-racing track at Villa Borghese (investigations are suspended when Orlandok is charged with 'calumny and fraud'). Another folder contains intelligence received in late 1926 on a meeting held in Marseilles where it has been decided that an attempt will be made using poison gas, hydrocyanic acid, which a woman, courtesy of her sexual charms, is to smuggle into Il Duce's residence.

As the files multiplied, so did the arrests. Internment for certain types of offence, including vagrancy and habitual drunkenness, pre-dated Fascism, and usually took the form of enforced residence under police jurisdiction. But Mussolini's laws of November 1926 added a new class of political offender to that group. Bocchini, a zealous enforcer, instructed police in every city to compile a list of all suspects and forward their details to provincial commissions with the legal power to issue deportation orders. Often, the accused was condemned without ever having been interrogated and first learned of the charge after having arrived at the place of internment. Between 1926 and 1943, fifteen thousand Italians were deported to internment colonies on the islands of Ustica, Ponza, Lampedusa and Lipari. Scraggy, undeveloped outposts of extreme poverty, these sites were invisible to the million tourists who in 1926 rolled along the mainland's new metalled roads, and therefore ideal dumping grounds for Fascism's undesirables.

Prison was even worse. 'The Fascist regime can boast of having renewed the exploits of the Bourbon prisons,' wrote one political exile. It ignored all codes and penal laws providing for the special treatment of political prisoners, who were treated much more severely than common criminals. Beating was common, as were other forms of torture – tying the prisoner to a chair and repeatedly striking him over the heart with a rubber-covered hammer; beating the soles of feet with steel strips or forcing them into boiling water; searing the body with an alcohol flame; tearing out fingernails; squeezing testicles. The use of *reclusione* or *segregazione cellulare*, solitary confinement, was commonplace, lasting from six months to three years. Many political prisoners died in custody, among them the co-founder of the Italian Communist Party, Antonio Gramsci, whose slow assassination took eleven years.

*

On 8 November, two days after Mussolini's first raft of legislation was introduced, *The Times* ran an article headlined 'The Defence of Fascismo'. It was an acerbic piece whose author was clearly irked by laws restricting freedom of expression. It attacked the newspaper *L'Impero* for its 'savage satisfaction at the final discomfiture of its enemies' (the former Prime Minister Francesco Nitti had been stripped of his citizenship, but *L'Impero* called for him to be declared an enemy of the country and condemned to death, 'the sentence to be executed by any Italian citizen who can succeed in catching him'). There was also a lament for the disgraced Luigi Federzoni. With the departure of this moderate 'blue-shirt', Italy, to its detriment, faced a future 'in which neither the ideas nor the men of the old order will have any part'.

The criticisms – a rare departure for *The Times* – caused real irritation at the Foreign Office: 'It is a pity that at a moment when Italian nerves are somewhat on edge the *Times* correspondent in Rome should have sent home such an alarmist account of the effect of the new legislation,' an internal memorandum reads.

It does no good and may do a lot of harm. The *Times* correspondent is not fit for his post. He belongs to that narrow, insider class of intellectuals who has passed judgement on Mussolini long ago. He will leave no stone unturned to prove to us that his estimate is right and his Editor does not control him. His name is Mr [Victor] Cunard and he is a nominee of Lady Astor. I am sure that if Mr John Astor, one of the proprietors of the *Times*, knew how pernicious his influence is both here and in Italy, he would change him.

The Fascist sympathiser Ezra Pound typically exaggerated when he told Wyndham Lewis that 'certainly HERE in Italy is more freedom to print than under the shitten arse of the *Times* in London' – but he had a point.

Victor Cunard had touched a very sensitive nerve. British foreign policy had invested so heavily in Mussolini's success that it could not afford now to withdraw its support. 'Fine manners . . . will butter more parsnips in Italy than anywhere else,' Austen Chamberlain advised. 'It is essential that we should keep Italy, a growing power, in sympathy with our policy and cooperation with us.' Misgivings about Mussolini's methods may exist, but they were not to be publicly aired, lest they give comfort to his enemies. Again, the spectre of Bolshevism was invoked, but it was an armchair tic. The real fear was that, if Mussolini were eliminated, a power vacuum would be created into which a 'village ruffian' like Roberto Farinacci, leader of the extremist wing of the Fascist party, might step.

The question of Mussolini's succession had first surfaced after Violet's attempt. Then, Federzoni had warned Il Duce: 'It's useless to fool ourselves: in us, the men of the government or the party, Fascism offers you the spare parts for the engine which you have to drive; but there is no other driver.' Ronald Graham shared this concern: Fascism was too much of a 'one-man show', this was its Achilles heel. Mussolini's hold on power, which had kept Italy from the brink of civil war, could, if he gave way, lead to it, precisely because the forces he controlled would become uncontrollable. 'There is no doubt that had Mussolini been killed or gravely injured there would have been a massacre and indiscriminate fighting in the streets,' Graham had reported the day after Violet's attempt. The fact that he hadn't been killed was therefore 'cause for celebration'. Part of the 'anguish and profound consternation' felt by the Vatican was down to a similar concern over who might succeed Mussolini. For the Pope, just as for the British, he was the man to do business with.

As far as Mussolini was concerned, no man of the regime was to put him in the shade, no one should appear as his possible successor. In 1934, Leone Ginzburg, an opponent of the regime who died ten years later in a Fascist prison, claimed that Mussolini was certain of the fact that his creation would not survive him. For this reason, Ginzburg explained, he was 'completely indifferent to the rise of a political class, indeed he was hostile to anyone who attracted popular sympathies to himself: the problem of the succession was perhaps becoming more disquieting for the Fascists than for the enemies of the regime'. In light of Mussolini's overthrow by the Grand Council of Fascism in 1943, it was a prescient observation.

With regard to Violet Gibson, the events of November 1926 left Ronald Graham treading a very thin line. It was still his determined task to secure her release, but this he had to achieve without undermining Mussolini's political authority. Privately, Mussolini never wanted a Violet Gibson trial, but if he was to avoid it he would now have to circumvent the very legislation he had just introduced. *L'état, c'est moi*: this is what dictators do. But his officials had yet to appreciate the fact. Indeed, on the very day that Mussolini's first public security bill was passed, 6 November

1926, the Crown Prosecutor confirmed that the Gibson case would be sent for trial.

Ardent Fascists gave a very clear signal of the kind of justice they sought: in Bologna, a contingent of blackshirts pushed a handcart through the streets bearing the dummy of a hanged man and placards daubed with the names of Zaniboni, Gibson and Lucetti. 'The extreme section of the Fascist press has recently become very violent in its comments on Miss Gibson's case and demands for the infliction of the death penalty upon her have been made by several newspapers,' Ronald Graham told the Foreign Office. 'The "Resto del Carlino", for instance, after pressing for the execution of Zaniboni and Lucetti, continues, "and Gibson as well. The scientists have declared her irresponsible? That does not matter . . . Mad dogs are killed, although no blame can attach to them for their ferocious madness."'

Once again, the British ambassador's influence on Mussolini prevailed. Having established that, under the new laws, Violet could not receive the death penalty because 'such offences are not retroactive and it is authoritatively stated that the special tribunal can, in the infliction of penalties, only apply the previously existing law', Graham was the bearer of further encouraging news. On 16 November he reported to Austen Chamberlain on a meeting with Mussolini, in which Graham had taken

. . . the opportunity of putting in a word for Miss Gibson. I said that his Excellency's reply reassured me. This misguided but unfortunate lady was, in spite of the unanimous opinion of the medical experts in the case as to the state of her mind, to be deferred before the tribunal. But I now felt sure that there would be no danger of political feelings in the tribunal bringing about any miscarriage of justice. Signor Mussolini replied that I could feel perfectly safe on this score.

XVI

Special Justice

Across Italy, police cells and prisons were soon receiving the new population of criminals created by Mussolini's public security laws. The Mantellate quickly swelled with new intakes, and Violet, stripped of the relative comfort and privileges of life at San Onofrio, now found herself sharing a cell. As a woman who found nothing but unhappiness and discomfort when close-quartered with anyone, she was singularly ill-adapted to cope. In this, her class as well as her temperament was a determining factor. She was not accustomed, as was now required, to urinate in a chamberpot in full view of other people. At 7.20 a.m. on 3 December 1926, after asking a guard to turn around while she relieved herself, Violet dashed the full chamberpot to the floor and, taking up a jug of cold water by the washstand, advanced on the guard and bashed her over the head with it. Her victim stumbled amid the broken shards of pottery, clutching her bloody crown, whereupon another orderly intervened and ordered Violet, who was still in her nightgown, to get back into her bed. When asked to explain herself, Violet said she was terribly sorry if she had hurt the guard (who formally complained of receiving a mild head wound), but she had simply been overtaken by an impulse to attack her.

Two weeks later, Violet's inability to cope had become even more dramatically apparent. Since being returned to prison at the end of October, she had been spending hardly any money on food, and since the attack on the guard she had consumed nothing but milk. The Mother Superior of the Regina Coeli was so alarmed by her condition that she contacted Violet's junior defence counsel, Bruno Cassinelli, to tell him that she feared his client might not survive much longer. Violet, she said, had lost two stone (if this calculation was correct, then Violet now weighed a mere five stone), her throat was inflamed, and she had developed 'a persistent and incurable fever'. Cassinelli immediately visited Violet, and found that reports of her condition had not been exaggerated: she appeared to be dying.

Refusal to eat is one of the few gestures of protest left to a prisoner whose every other action is subject to control. Was Violet's self-starvation a symptom of her failing mental capacities, or an act of defiance more typically associated with political prisoners? According to a prison memorandum of 20 December, it appeared to be the latter: word had it that Violet was on hunger strike.

For her defence team, this was the moment to strike. In a letter to the examining magistrates, Enrico Ferri warned that her deteriorating condition could result in the highly embarrassing outcome of her dying in custody; that the medical facilities in the Mantellate were not adequate to her urgent needs; that she should therefore be transferred instantly to an institution, agreed on by all parties, that could assist in her recovery. Ferri's manoeuvre worked. The Special Tribunal issued a medical certificate authorising her removal to the Villa Giuseppina, the clinic where she had stayed following her suicide attempt two years earlier.

On 15 January 1927, the sack of bones that was Violet Gibson was escorted to the clinic under armed guard. There, she was given a private room with a little sitting room and bathroom, central heating and carpets. After her first meal, chicken, she said that she hadn't eaten so well in months. These details were communicated to her sister Frances in a curiously elliptical letter from Ferri, who did not refer to Violet by name, but only as 'the person in whom you are interested'. To date, Ferri's correspondence had been conducted with Constance, who had initially hired him. But suspecting that his letters were being intercepted and read, he hoped that a letter addressed to Lady Bolton would escape detection. Nevertheless, he took care to conceal both Violet's identity and the business to which he was referring. 'Despite the problems of previous months,' the letter ended cryptically, 'I now have every reason to believe that the matter will be concluded within a short time.'

Ronald Graham seemed to be possessed of the same information, reporting on 25 January that 'Signor Mussolini is anxious to finish with the Gibson case as soon as possible.' The comments of Chancellor Winston Churchill, who had two meetings with Mussolini in Rome on 14 January, further oiled the diplomatic wheels. 'I could not help being charmed, like so many other people have been, by his gentle and simple bearing and by his calm, detached poise in spite of so many burdens and dangers,' Churchill had told reporters. In his struggle to wrest Italy free from the Leninist threat, Mussolini could count on his support.

Mussolini's struggle had little to do with Bolsheviks, more to do with his own Fascist party. It is a measure of how deep the divisions were within his powerbase that he had such protracted problems in exercising his will in the matter of Violet Gibson.

Superficially, the documents relating to this stage of the case appear riven with contradiction, confusion, irreconcileable shifts in direction. Had Violet herself been aware of what was going on, she would have been justifiably perplexed. But her physical health had deteriorated to such a degree that she was by now virtually catatonic. All that Professor Mendicini and his staff at the Villa Giuseppina clinic could do was to try to feed her up to a viable weight. In any event, she was the last person to be privy to the truth of what was going on.

The truth is, Ronald Graham and Mussolini were pursuing what can only be described as a parallax diplomacy – publicly, officially, the case was speeding towards the judge's bench at the Special Tribunal; privately, unofficially, it was going in the opposite direction. A deal had been brokered: Graham had asked that Violet be treated as insane, not as a political criminal, and Mussolini had agreed. On 1 February, fully three months after Marinangeli's pronouncement that Violet was to be tried, the Foreign Office informed Constance that Violet's release was imminent. Nine days later, Ronald Graham confirmed in a confidential despatch that Violet will 'not be brought before the special tribunal but will be conducted to the frontier by Italian police in the near future'. Graham added that 'Signor Mussolini has made no allusion in conversation to any conditions attaching to [Violet's] release'. There would be no trial. Violet was to be released and expelled from Italian territory.

Mussolini, Cesare Rossi claimed, wanted to close 'the bulky file for foreign policy reasons'. (He clearly expected something in return, and held onto the file up until his death. According to the Preliminary Catalogue of Mussolini's Private Files, a batch of documents confiscated by the Allies after the war from Mussolini's residence, Bag 16 contained 'The Case of Mussolini versus Violet Gibson'.) The police investigation, and Chief Superintendent Pennetta's conspiracy theory, were to go nowhere because 'Dictator Mussolini' (as *Time* magazine, a fan, now jauntily called him), in concert with the British government, had decided that it was better to have her mad than bad.

Responsibility for his would-be assassin was to be transferred entirely to the British authorities and her family. Graham advised:

Before or after Miss Gibson's release to this country, it will be desirable to impound her passport, and to make certain that she cannot slip back into Italy and have another shot at the Duce – or for that matter, at any other foreign potentate . . . What will happen to Miss Gibson on arrival in England? Presumably the relatives will take their own steps to secure her certification as a dangerous lunatic without delay. Although she is a dangerous homicidal lunatic, I take it that His Majesty's Government can do nothing in the matter as hitherto she has committed no crime in this country.

The family had indeed taken steps to secure Violet's confinement, arranging for her to be placed in St Andrew's Hospital for Mental Diseases in Northampton, as Constance explained to the Foreign Office on 16 February: 'I had considerable trouble in finding a private asylum which would take Violet. They all said that it was a dangerous case and that she should go to Broadmoor. Ultimately St Andrew's agreed to take her if [the chief medical superintendent] was not responsible for the certificates [for her committal].' Constance added that 'It will be an immense relief if we can get Violet home, though I can't say I am looking forward to the return journey or to the responsibility which will devolve on me when she lands.' It was always, constantly, Constance who assumed the burden of responsibility. From Willie, or younger brother Edward, or sisters Frances and Elsie, there was seldom any sign of comparable exertion on Violet's behalf. For Constance, the second trip to Rome in a year was a frightening prospect, but she screwed her courage to the sticking place, telling the Foreign Office with some flourish, 'My Expeditionary Force can start in 24 hours notice.'

After almost a year in which the Violet Gibson case had been bounced between the equally dim borderlands of psychiatry and politics, the pace now quickened towards Mussolini's promised solution. On 3 March, he informed Graham that Violet's defence would, after all, have to present their case before the Special Tribunal. Public opinion would not be satisfied with anything less. But he assured Graham that the hearing would take place in camera, and that full proceedings against her would not be pursued. This would happen after Tito Zaniboni had been tried by the tribunal – presumably, the thinking was that the extremists, given the bones of Zaniboni to chew on, would be too distracted to notice. Zaniboni's trial had been scheduled for the end of March, but Mussolini had undertaken to give the British Embassy ten days' notice of Violet's deportation.

The practical difficulties of how to get Violet back to England needed to be thrashed out. On 8 March, Constance wrote to the Foreign Office with details of her plan:

I shall be quite ready to start with my cortege whenever you notify me it is advisable for me to do so. If the Italian Government show the slightest desire to hand Violet over to me at the frontier please let them do so. I will of course go to Rome if it is necessary, but Italy is not the spot any of Violet's family would select for a joy-ride.

Contance's 'cortege' consisted of three nurses, all from St Andrew's Hospital, and a Thomas Cook courier. Thomas Cook had offered the first conducted excursion of Italy in 1864, taking fifty people from London to Naples and back for a fixed sum. The experiment was a great success, a rebuke to critics who had carped that 'the characteristic independence of Englishmen would revolt against a plan that reduces the traveller to the level of his trunk and obliterates every trace and trait of the individual'. In the task of retrieving Violet from Rome and delivering her back to England, this is exactly what the Thomas Cook courier hired by Constance would be required to do.

In the third week of March, the Foreign Office gave Constance the news she had so long awaited: Mussolini had signalled that she was free to set off for Rome, travelling by any route she chose. To this end, police chief Arturo Bocchini had telegrammed instructions to the border authorities that her passage should not be impeded. 'It really looks as if the horrible nightmare will be ended before very long,' a Foreign Office diplomat commented hopefully.

It was to be a long and costly wait, adding to the extraordinary expenses incurred so far in defence and medical fees – an estimated £3,000 (£130,000 today). To Constance's extreme frustration, news arrived of a delay: the president of the Special Tribunal had been taken sick, and Zaniboni's trial had been postponed until 12 April. Again, Mussolini had reassured Graham that 'as soon as it was over Miss Gibson . . . would be allowed to leave Italy'.

*

The Special Tribunal had got off to a resolute start on 2 February 1927, imposing nine-month prison sentences for *apologia di reato*, 'illegal defence of a crime', on two Roman labourers who had been overheard lamenting the failure of Lucetti's assassination attempt ('They still haven't managed to kill him!' one was alleged to have exclaimed). Evidence in both cases was brought by Chief Superintendent Epifanio Pennetta – small pickings for a man whose main quarry continued to elude him. More than 160 people were brought before the tribunal in 1927 to answer similar charges. 'Approval' of Violet Gibson's action led to the indictment of, among others, a Roman vineyard worker, a peasant from Alessandrino, a road-mender from Padua, a decorator from Turin and a seaman from Pesaro. An English woman, Mrs Winifred Slater, wife of Major Algernon Slater, narrowly escaped a similar fate. Arrested and imprisoned on 3 October 1926 at Volosca, in Istria (now in Croatia), on a charge of having spoken against Mussolini's policy and having expressed regret at the failure of Lucetti's attempt, she had been bailed pending trial after the British Embassy intervened. When Ronald Graham brought the case to Mussolini's attention, he ordered all further proceedings to be quashed, 'a very graceful act' for which the Foreign Office expressed its gratitude.

The tribunal was located within the vast ugliness of the Palazzo della Giustizia, a carbunculous nineteenth-century building on the Tiber just a few hundred yards from the Mantellate (prompting the joke that it was like 'living above the shop'). The main chamber, bedecked with police and soldiers in full dress uniform, was overlooked by a series of galleries crammed with party functionaries, Fascist sympathisers, secret police, accredited reporters and, if they dared to, relatives of the accused. In keeping with the gravitas of the court, no women were allowed to attend – unless they were defendants, in which case they were held, like the men, in a cage to the left of the judges' presidium.

On 12 April 1927, the court rose for the stiffly braided presiding generals. There followed the reading out of the procedural rules, the nod to justice and the ubiquitous emphatic homage to Il Duce, 'the man sent to us by God'. In the cage, rattling the bars and shouting out 'Mussolini is an impostor!' was Tito Zaniboni. The case against him was a hodgepodge of concocted links to world Freemasonry and secret political cabals. Zaniboni strenuously denied he had acted in concert with others, but freely confessed his intention to eliminate Mussolini, who was 'the illegal head of the government' and was 'trampling on freedom and the Constitution'. On 19 April, the tribunal handed down its sentence: thirty years' imprisonment. Two months later, Gino Lucetti met the same fate.

If sent for a full trial, this was most likely the sentence Violet, too, could have expected. On Friday 6 May 1927, the Investigating Commission of the Special Tribunal finally assembled, in camera, to consider her case. She was spared the full spectacle of open court – and the cage. At Enrico Ferri's instructions, she was not present at all. The last thing her defence lawyer wanted was for her to compromise his arguments by appearing normal.

XVII

Lucid Insanity

Enrico Ferri's 'Defensive Memorial, A Character Study and Life History of Violet Gibson' was a masterful concoction of advocacy, casuistry and fraud. Its effect was to lock Violet into a tragic paradox, whereby her freedom was sought in exchange for her liberty. It entered into the balance sheet the debt of her decision to take up a strategic position of insanity, and proposed exorbitant terms of repayment that the fund of her unused life would never be sufficient to meet.

Opening with all the requisite noises about 'the great sense of horror' aroused by the attempt on Mussolini's life, Ferri immediately addressed the theory that his client had been influenced by a putative third party who, 'with cruel ferocity, worthy of his vile nature, thought to avail himself of a mad woman as his agent'. The inflated language is straight out of a gothic novel, and the borrowing was deliberate, a linguistic inflation deployed to make the deflation that followed all the more dramatic. The hypothesis that Gibson was 'the blind instrument of some base criminal' was, Ferri next declared, totally irrelevant, 'beyond our actual sphere of interest'. The question, he advanced, was not how to solve a genre mystery, but to establish, as required by law, whether the accused was in 'a condition of mental infirmity' when she shot Mussolini.

The proper instruments for pursuing this enquiry were to be found in the 'science of psycho-pathology', and Ferri's task was to explain this science to those who had no 'special knowledge [or] practical acquaintance' with it. Thus, he was able to offer with confidence his professional opinion that Gibson was 'conscious' of her deed – it was not accomplished in the 'unconscious frenzy of delirium, or terror, or hallucination' typical of many acts of homicidal lunacy. It was, rather, a premeditated act, made openly and in the presence of witnesses, but one that derived from 'a slow invasion of the mind of the homicidal idea'. This placed her in a class of criminals – those who were simultaneously 'insane and sane' – which Ferri had made it his special business to study.

The issue, therefore, was not whether Gibson had been deprived of her perception of right and wrong, 'but of her freedom of will to act'. Quoting from the Crown Prosecutor's submission, Ferri argued that Gibson's 'watchful intelligence' and 'shrewdness', her 'dissimulation' and her disciplined silence about the 'secret' motive for the attempt, were evidence less that she had will power, more that hers was a 'sick will power'. These were proofs not of her ability to reason, but of 'her mental state of paranoia', and perfectly fitted a diagnosis of 'lucid insanity'. To the uninitiated, Gibson might indeed appear as a person of 'normal intellect', but, stated Ferri grandly, to one of his expert knowledge it was 'an easy matter to bring to light certain shady and irregular regions of her mind'. These included her religious mania, her tenacious dissimulation and her stubborn refusal to acknowledge Mussolini's great achievements – his 'idealistic mysticism', 'high motives' and 'heroic love of his country' that were illumined by 'the magnificent daily visible results of his ruling'. Gibson's 'expression of frigidity or dislike for Mussolini's achievements' was, at the very least, overwhelming proof of her abnormality. Here, Ferri struck a fatal blow at the Crown Prosecutor's case, and made it virtually impossible for the Special Tribunal to reject a simple conclusion: nobody in their right mind could want to stop Mussolini in his historic tracks.

Ferri next placed Mussolini's personal assessment of his assailant before the judges, telling them that Il Duce had confirmed, at a meeting with Ferri during the preliminary investigation, that he believed Gibson to be 'of insane mind', and that Ferri's defence of her was 'a good thing: thus Miss Gibson will be defended with all the serene calm that science can afford her'. This, Ferri noted, was typical of Il Duce's grandiloquence and nobility of spirit: 'History and contemporary chronicles show us that a like attitude of calmness in similar cases of attempted homicide is very rare, especially when it concerns governments who have arisen after a revolution and are still passing through a more or less critical period of their political existence.' With brilliant sleight of hand, Ferri managed to turn the focus away from the question of Violet's mental health to that of the tribunal itself. To continue in 'the great progress in her civil evolution', Italy and its institutions needed to remain 'sane and unbiased' in dealing with the accused; to do anything else would be to devolve from the current exemplary position of Fascist moral excellence.

Ferri had rehearsed this theme of Mussolini as a Darwinian supertype in a widely publicised lecture in Rome on 9 March 1927. The timing of the lecture – two months before presenting his 'Defensive Memorial' to the Special Tribunal – was not accidental. Rather, it was a key element of his strategy for defending Violet. In his 'anthropological profile' of Il Duce (subsequently published as 'The Statesman Mussolini'), Ferri had argued that Mussolini's distinguished political career was due to his 'exceptional temperament', which was associated with a particular anthropological 'type': he was a man of action, similar in physical stature to Julius Caesar, Napoleon, Cavour, Garibaldi and Lenin; he even possessed the 'Napoleonic face', characterised by a 'broad prominent forehead' and 'square lower jaw'. This was a particular kind of jaw, no longer solely connected with its assigned biological function but signifying 'the supremacy of the will'. Mussolini also boasted an 'excellent thyroid' which, in individuals whose physical development had reached its peak, acted as a sort of 'psychic lubricant'. With this 'biological structure', he was destined, as exemplar of the 'new man', to represent 'the superior expression of political thought and action'.

Ferri went on to propose that Mussolini had survived Violet's attempt because at the moment she fired he had affected the 'mystic gesture' of lifting his head towards the sky at the sound of the Fascist hymn 'Giovinezza'. This was consonant with the 'man of genius' who acted like an 'electric accumulator', gathering the diffuse electricity present in an atmosphere which would otherwise remain 'sterile, vague and elusive'. The transformed energy would then 'fly off in a spark of light in a shock of locomotive force'. It was as if Mussolini possessed the power to turn back the bullet.

Ferri had publicly stated that he was not a Fascist, a career manoeuvre designed to ensure that the regime could accept his opinions as being based on 'objective' scientific analysis. They were nothing of the sort, of course. His profile of Mussolini was balderdash laced with tawdry sweet-nothings. *Il Becco Giallo*, a satirical journal (suppressed, and published out of Paris), lampooned Ferri's claim that Mussolini was over-evolved in a cartoon that showed him actually *devolving* into an ape. But Ferri knew exactly what he was doing. 'The Statesman Mussolini' was an intervention calculated to promote a narrative in which Violet could later be positioned, as the transgressor, in a comparative relationship with Mussolini, the drama's hero.

Stripped of its mythologies and textual curlicues, Ferri's narrative implies a far more startling possibility: that the diagnosis conferred on Violet Gibson could just as well apply to Benito Mussolini. Violet's psychiatric profile underscored her well-developed intelligence, intransigence, solitariness, dissimulation, fanaticism, suspiciousness and intolerance; it stressed her refusal to listen to the advice of others, her capacity to hurt people without showing remorse, and her megalomania, the belief that she was carrying out a divinely ordained mission – all proof, the psychiatrists claimed, of 'a serious form of mental alienation'. What, then, of Mussolini's solitary nature, which Austen Chamberlain had taken to be the bleak quality of a serious, contemplative man? Mussolini disliked familiarity, didn't enjoy social life, preferring to live in seclusion and even eat alone, retaining only one or two personal attendants who were chosen for their unobtrusiveness and discretion. 'One must accept solitude,' he once told an admirer. 'A chief cannot have equals. Nor friends. The humble solace gained from exchanging confidences is denied him. He cannot open his heart. Never.' Was this evidence of a virtuous detachment or a symptom of paranoia, indeed of megalomania, of the belief in his own infallibility and the divinely sanctioned nature of his mission? Unfortunately, no one was on hand to pass down a diagnosis. (When the Russian psychiatrist Vladimir Bechterev was called upon by Stalin's entourage to determine if their leader was paranoid, he concluded that he was, and was immediately executed for his troubles.)

According to biographer Denis Mack Smith, Mussolini kept himself apart because he was 'a misanthrope with an abysmal view of human nature that discounted altruism and idealism. He assumed that everyone was utterly selfish and nearly everyone incompetent and untrustworthy' (which may explain why, in 1929, he held a portfolio of no fewer than eight ministries to himself). The key to his personality was that he was 'an actor, a dissimulator, an exhibitionist who changed his role from hour to hour to suit the occasion'; he was without moral scruples and made 'little distinction between good and bad or justice and injustice', though his enemies and many of whose acquainted with him recognised him as a criminal and a murderer.

Mack Smith, like the majority of historians and biographers, has warned against treating Mussolini as a lunatic or a raving maniac: why, they ask, would a complex society be prepared to follow someone who was mentally deranged, a 'pathological' case, into the abyss? Yet millions did follow, goose-stepping in a fever of adulation, shouting '*Eia! Eia! Alalà*', the atavisitic, meaningless ululation brought on by Fascism's 'mystical vision' and the incantations of Mussolini, its prophet. It is with this in mind that Violet's religious mania, her 'ecstatic reality', should be viewed. If this was a manifestation of her madness, then she wasn't alone in that borderland of insanity.

At the Special Tribunal, Enrico Ferri concluded his presentation with an outright deception. The accused, he acknowledged, 'must be considered as a dangerous subject and in consequence should be deprived of her personal liberty'. He went on to state that 'Miss Gibson herself is quite persuaded as to the correctness of the above deductions . . . she acknowledges that she should be confined permanently in an asylum . . . (i.e. for an absolutely unlimited period)', and that she 'has agreed that such a decision would meet her case perfectly'. Ferri had not told his client of this decision, nor had she acquiesced to her permanent internment in a madhouse.

After hearing Ferri's submission, the judges retired to 'deliberate' – it was a farce, of course, as the outcome had been determined long beforehand – emerging after a short while to issue their decision. Filed as 'Sentence Number 41', the tribunal's judgement was that the findings of the psychiatrists

> . . . leave no doubt that, because of the chronic paranoia with which she was affected, the accused was not responsible for her actions at the time she committed the crime. Although conscious of the act which she was committing (a characteristic of these forms of mental illness) she did not have freedom of will because of the morbid, delirious impulse to which she was subject.

The judicial function of the tribunal should not be involved with such cases of mental infirmity (in other words, it did not want to preside over a court of lunacy), but acknowledging that Violet was a danger to herself and others, the tribunal's president called for the application of Article 46 of the Penal Code providing for the protection of society, 'which cannot remain undefended against dangerous psychopaths who make attempts on human life and can even turn on that which is most sacred and dear, the Nation'. He ordered Violet be handed over to the police authorities and then confined in an asylum.

The quality of justice dispensed by the tribunal was rarely short of scandalous. But if Violet had been sent to a full trial and subjected to its particular form of due process, would the conspiracy theory – that she was the tool of politically motivated accomplices (the assumption always being that she was not capable of her own, independent political motivation) – have been proved? Probably not. Violet was too good at covering her tracks. We shall never know. In any case, the deal agreed between Mussolini and the British was a fait accompli. The Crown Prosecutor, Chief Superintendent Epifanio Pennetta and the extremist *Intransigenti* had finally been thwarted. All that remained was to get rid of Violet.

*

Violet was at the Villa Giuseppina during the hearing, and there she stayed, despite the tribunal's order that she be returned to the San Onofrio asylum, in order that she could be 'shown' to be handed over to her family from there. Two days later, she was told she had a visitor. It was Constance, come to her sister directly from the train that carried her and her expeditionary force from London.

There is no account of their reunion, nothing by which to know what emotions both experienced. Ironically, Violet probably looked in better health than when Constance had last seen her, more than two years ago. The staff at the clinic had worked a miracle, bringing Violet back to health. She was now, according to a doctor's report, 'well fed'. What did Constance tell her, beyond the fact that she was free to leave Italy, that the arrangements were being made and they would travel in a matter of days? The meeting was brief, as Constance's cortège was already booked into the Hotel dei Principi in Piazza di Spagna (Mussolini's temporary residence just after he had taken power, where he had privately enjoyed a series of whores), and she needed to join them to make the necessary preparations.

The next day, a Monday, the police confirmed that they would accompany the Gibson party to the frontier, where they would then rescind Violet's residence permit. Much sifting of the files followed, before the realisation dawned that she had never applied for or received this permit, as required by law. Expert frowns all round. The wheels of bureaucracy required a permit even if for the sole purpose of withdrawing it, so one was issued the following day. The search for Violet's passport now ensued. Enquiries revealed that it was still in the custody of the judicial police as part of the dossier on the case and was, therefore, already withdrawn from the holder. Most likely it was on Pennetta's desk, and most likely, given the fact that it never reappeared, he stubbornly held on to it. Constance, at her wit's end, appealed to Ronald Graham, who immediately arranged for the British Consulate to issue an emergency certificate valid for the single journey to England.

After further, unexplained delays, a police official called at the British Embassy on Wednesday, 11 May to confirm that Violet's expulsion from Italian territory had been authorised, and that she should be removed forthwith. An inventory had been drawn up of her confiscated possessions (little envelopes containing small denominations of money for distribution to the poor, her cheque-book, some letters, and 'a large quantity of religious material'), and most of these were now restored to her at the Villa Giuseppina in large brown envelopes closed with the wax seal of the Special Tribunal.*

Violet reacted calmly to the news of her release, still ignorant of Ferri's lie that she had acquiesced in his diagnosis and agreed to her own indefinite internment in an asylum. To her, it seemed simply that justice had finally been done. Her mood was serene when, together with Constance, she gathered and packed her personal effects. Constance, fraught with anxiety about any last-minute hitches, and noticing that her sister showed no particular curiosity about what plans had been made for her arrival in England, told her nothing.

Late in the morning of Thursday, 12 May, Professor Mendicini signed the necessary forms, and Violet was ready to set out with Constance and her party. Outside the clinic, a plainclothes police escort was waiting to accompany them to the station in an

---

* The Lebel revolver and the bullets were held in the safe at the Special Tribunal's offices, and were still there in 1933. The black glove and the stone Violet was carrying at Campidoglio were 'destroyed' in June 1929.

unmarked car. Shortly before departing, Violet asked to be allowed to write a letter. It was addressed to the Mother Superior of the Mantellate prison:

Dear Mother Superior, I feel obliged to write you these lines to thank you for the kind consideration you showed towards me while I was in prison. You were so careful in the choice of the guards assigned to watch over me, and in allowing me on occasion to take some air and go to Mass. Please be so kind as to offer my thanks also to the Director. Remember me to all the nuns.

The Honourable Violet Gibson had not forgotten her manners.

XVIII

Exodus

A highly professional smuggling operation is under way. Nobody at Rome's shabby Termini station (the Fascist face-lift is still to come) notices that the woman who shot Mussolini is in their midst. The dimunitive Violet, completely ringed by a cordon sanitaire of undercover police officers, Constance, the Thomas Cook courier and the nurses (none of whom is in uniform), is conveyed invisibly through the thronging terminus and onto the Paris-bound *treno lusso*, where she is settled into a first-class two-berth sleeper compartment, shared with Constance. The rest of the party is divided into adjoining compartments. Two police officers also board the train, positioning themselves in the corridor. Minutes later, the train leaves punctually at midday. In his office, His Excellency the Prime Minister Benito Mussolini, Il Duce, is sitting behind his desk, receiving his proconsuls and listening to their petitions. A normal Fascist morning.

Rome, Florence, Pisa, then on up the Ligurian coast – Violet's beloved Italy flicks past, and people wave to her, or at least she will later claim that this is what they do. Does Violet, the exalted heroine, imagine this? Or do people actually wave? Probably, though not at her, for her presence on the train is a secret. (And who, recognising her, would dare to?) Does she wave back? Why not? The people of Italy are indebted to her, their 'Violetta', for trying to save them from Mussolini. Her mood is light: she has been released from prison, she has not been sent for trial, she is, as far as she has been told, a free woman. When she is better – all she needs is some rest, time to reflect without the constant and intrusive presence of prison guards and doctors – what is to stop her from returning? Italy rushes by, the rich springtime palette of greens tinged intermittently by the deep pink blossom of the Judas tree.

When the train arrives at the border station of Modane it is 2.50 a.m., and Violet is asleep. With the two police officers in attendance, the border formalities are executed. Violet's temporary travel document is stamped with an exit visa, and her newly-minted residence permit is withdrawn. With that, the policemen leave the train. For a brief interlude, Violet is indeed a free woman. The Italians have relinquished custody, and the French authorities have no jurisdiction over her. This detail has been worrying Constance, who in February had written to the Foreign Office for advice:

Legally she will not be a lunatic from the time she leaves Italy till she is certified in England. Can you get the French authorities to forbid her staying in France? She is very cunning and may very cleverly sham illness or give trouble going on to the boat [across the Channel]. We cannot give her a sleeping-draught or she would not be certified on landing.

Nothing doing, comes the reply, Violet has committed no crime on French soil, or indeed on British soil. Arrangements for her custody now rest solely with her family. To this end, the Ashbournes have hired a French private detective, and he is waiting on the platform at Modane to take up position outside the door of Violet's compartment. This is of comfort not only to Constance, but to the Thomas Cook courier, whose terms of engagement have been drawn up with Violet's homicidal tendencies at the forefront. The contract reads,

We beg to make it quite clear that we should not be prepared to arrange for our courier to travel with Miss Violet Gibson unless that lady was accompanied by yourself [Constance], or someone appointed by you to act on your behalf, in addition to a male or female attendant . . . until the lady was accommodated in any institution in England.

Violet awakes in the morning to discover that Italy is behind her. She is impassive, staring out of the window as France speeds by. Although it does no such thing, of course – landscapes don't move because of trains passing through them; they only heave and buck when men set out their wars on them. Violet is still, makes no attempt to get off. Does she move only when God or the angels or the wise men tell her to? Constance sits opposite her, a bundle of nerves, strung out by the lies she has woven around her sister, by the long-prepared betrayal whose consequences are imminent, but to Violet, unthinkable.

When the train reaches Paris at 2.35 pm on Friday, 13 May, Violet is eating lunch. This would be the ideal opportunity for Willie to join the party from his home in nearby Compiègne and continue with them to England. Violet would surely be thrilled to see him, the adored brother, the revered mentor. But Willie has a habit, as he once confessed to the House of Lords, of removing himself from troubling atmospheres, tasking himself instead with thinking about things in a metaphysical way. In Paris, there is no sign of him. He will never see Violet again.

Violet's train leaves Paris behind – Willie and his clerics and Sorbonne radicals, the political émigrés and agents provocateurs, the Revue Nègre, Josephine Baker, Action Française, Surrealism's chance encounters with umbrellas and sewing-machines and sex on tables, Lucia Joyce, a young girl with a cast in her eye, dancing, dancing, while her father James looks on with what is left of his sight.

After the crossing from Boulogne to Folkestone, at 10.50 p.m. the train arrives at London's Victoria Station. 'I won't be staying here long,' Violet tells one of the nurses, Gertrude May Jones. 'I will be returning to Italy as soon as possible.'

'Why?' asks Jones.

'To shoot Mussolini,' comes the reply.

The family house at Grosvenor Crescent is just a short drive from Victoria Station, and Violet might reasonably assume that this is her final destination. It was here she had recovered after the knife attack that had led to her first taste of the lunatic asylum. But the hansom cab sweeps right past Grosvenor Crescent, around Hyde

Park Corner, and continues up Park Lane. Only when Violet sees that it has turned into Harley Street can she begin to understand that this is not the end, but the beginning of something. For a person afraid of psychiatry and its enormous powers of control, this is the antechamber to Hades.

The cab draws up outside number 87. Constance instructs the driver to wait and, together with Violet and the nurses, mounts the steps and rings the bell. The visit is expected, despite the hour, and the response is speedy. Seconds later, barely enough time to remove her coat, Violet is seated before Dr Maurice Craig in his consulting room.

Maurice Craig: Cambridge graduate, highly regarded medical psychologist, former assistant physician at the Bethlem asylum, leading expert on shellshock, pet shrink of the Bloomsbury Group. When Virginia Woolf consulted him between 1913 and 1915, during a prolonged bout of madness which brought with it violence, hallucinations and a refusal of food, he dosed her with foul-smelling and sedating paraldehyde and prescribed quiet inactivity and no writing (the Weir Mitchell regime, named after the doctor who diagnosed Charlotte Perkins Gilman's 'nervous prostration', and warned her to 'have but two hours intellectual life a day. And never touch pen, brush, or pencil as long as you live'). When Leonard and Virginia discussed the possibility of having children, it was Craig who advised them not to.

In his textbook *Psychological Medicine* (1905), Craig acknowledged that 'it is impossible to define insanity', but insisted it 'is nevertheless necessary for educational purposes to be dogmatic even at the risk of being wrong'. Describing insanity as behaviour that 'interferes with society', he explained that 'the healthy-minded man is gregarious, the insane is solitary. Some of the insane only believe their own opinion to be correct, not withstanding that it is unsupported by evidence and contrary to the ideas of everyone else.' Insanity, therefore, could be classified as

... such derangement ... as disables the person from thinking the thoughts, feeling the feelings, and doing the duties of the social body in, for, and by which he lives. Insanity means essentially then such a want of harmony between the individual and his social medium ... as prevents him from living and working among his kind in the social organisation. Completely out of tune there, he is a social discord of which nothing can be made.

In *Mrs Dalloway*, Woolf's smug Harley Street psychiatrist Sir William Bradshaw, an amalgamated portrait of Maurice Craig and the famous Sir George Savage, is presented in scathing terms. The novel suggests a conspiracy between social engineering, the restraint of the mentally ill and the patriarchal self-protection of the Establishment. Bradshaw shuts up his lunatics in 'nice' homes in the interests of the 'goddess of Proportion' and his ever-growing bank balance: 'To his patients he gave three-quarters of an hour,' writes Woolf. As for Sir William, he 'not only prospered himself but made England prosper, secluded her lunatics, forbade childbirth, penalised despair, made it impossible for the unfit to propagate their views until they, too, shared his sense of proportion.'

Violet doesn't even get three-quarters of an hour. Within minutes, Craig has reached a diagnosis of 'delusional insanity with paranoia'. The acoustic of her thinking is all wrong, she is out of tune; she seems to believe that 'killing and injuring persons were proper acts'; she talks 'in a childish and mentally enfeebled way'; she shows 'abnormal self satisfaction, a distortion and weakness of judgement'. He pens a certificate of committal and hands it discreetly to Constance. It is nearly midnight. The party then leaves number 87, and proceeds down Harley Street to number 77.

There, surrounded by leather-bound volumes and all the accoutrements of a respectable practice, a second 'examination' of Violet is conducted by Dr Bernard Hart, physician in psychological medicine to University College Hospital. Again, it is a matter of minutes before the good doctor determines that her nature is 'hysterical and suspicious; unbalanced and unreliable'. When Violet explains that 'all acts of violence were done merely with a view to preparing a defence of insanity when she attacked Mussolini',

Hart is disinclined to believe her. He signs the second certificate, and gives it to Constance. Armed with this paperwork – sheets that remove from Violet all rights to self-determination – Constance loads her sister back into the cab and, together with her bleary-eyed expeditionary force, heads to nearby Euston Station in time for the last train to Northampton.

The exhaustion of everyone on this final, dark leg of the journey is total. After arriving at Northampton, Violet is again in a cab, travelling through the empty streets before passing through a set of high gates and up the drive of what appears, in the gloom, to be a country estate. The monochrome shapes of trees and lawns shoulder the drive, which terminates in front of the porticoed entrance to an enormous building. The only sound at this hour is the crunch of gravel under their feet as the party walks towards the front door.

Inside, Violet and Constance are separated. Constance is taken to an office to complete the necessary formalities: the order for Violet's reception (prepared earlier by a judicial authority under the Lunacy Acts on the petition of Constance, and dependent only on the psychiatrists' certificates) is waiting to be signed. There are other documents to be filled in, questions to be answered about Violet's medical history, her private life, questions to which Violet is no longer required or entitled to supply the answers.

Violet is taken to the study of St Andrew's chief superintendent, Dr Rambaut, a kindly gentleman not much older than her, and a brief interview is conducted. From here, she is escorted to a comfortably furnished room on the second floor. After washing, she is given a sleeping draught. A nurse then wishes her good night, closes the door, and locks it. Violet's life sentence has begun.

PART THREE

LAMENTATIONS

Somewhere, some time, I made a choice in freedom
and lost my freedom.
SAMMY MOUNTJOY, William Golding's *Free Fall*

I

Mansion of Despair

Violet was in the lunatic asylum she so dreaded before either she or the press had time to catch up with events. On 23 May 1927, *Time* magazine reported her departure from Italy, but appeared not to know her whereabouts once in England – the 'destination kept rigidly secret'. Despite their expansive coverage of the Gibson affair, other newspapers were either ignorant of, or uninterested in, the final outcome.

Violet had lost everything, bar a few possessions and her 'secret', the secret that all those doctors and policemen and magistrates had tried in vain to crack. On her History Sheet (one of the forms completed by Constance on the night of her admission), Question 7 asked: 'Was there any cause for the attack [of insanity], such as illness, family trouble, poverty, drink, or immoral habits, love affair, religious excitement, sunstroke, fright or injury?' In reply to which Constance had written: 'Religious excitement fostered by hysterical friends was probably the chief cause.' Violet may have been following God's orders when she set out to kill Mussolini, but her political conscience was squared to the task: she believed that Mussolini was a totalitarian dictator who used violence and intimidation to acquire and hold on to power; she resented his (and the pope's) betrayal of Christian socialism; she cherished the Italy of Fra Angelico and St Francis, and loathed the Italy that was in thrall to Matteotti's murderers. The possibility that she might have been both mentally unstable *and* highly motivated to act on deeply-held convictions was beyond consideration.

Was Violet mad, or was she pretending to be mad in order to execute a political agenda? Try as they might, those charged with deciphering her could not break her code. This was her secret. Her family, too, now had a secret. Certificates of committal are *lettres de cachet*, instruments of concealment. Violet, who had caused them so much embarrassment, so much distress, was now hidden away: out of mind, possibly; out of sight, certainly.

There was, however, one last piece of etiquette to be observed before Violet was dropped down the oubliette of history. Noting that her 'release practically without trial was really the personal work of Signor Mussolini, since there was very strong feeling in Rome in favour of punishment being inflicted upon her', the Foreign Office advised that a favourable mention of his generosity should be made in the British press (the *Telegraph* was suggested as the appropriate carrier-pigeon for this message) and that the family send a letter of thanks to Il Duce. This was forthcoming:

The family of Violet Gibson feel they cannot let the conclusion of her trial pass without writing a few lines of deep and heartfelt thanks to his Excellency Signor Mussolini for his intervention on their sister's behalf. The family fully shared the storm of indignation which was aroused in Italy by Violet's attempt on Signor Mussolini's life. They can never be thankful enough that the attempt failed and the Duce has been spared to complete the great work which he is doing . . . That Violet's mental condition should have led to such a terrible crime will always be to the family a memory filled with horror, only relieved by the great generosity and consideration shown to them by His Excellency Signor Mussolini which gives to the world one more proof of his great eminence and distinction.

If it gave proof of anything, it was that Mussolini wanted done with Violet Gibson, and he had sidestepped his own, unconstitutional laws in order to do so.

The letter was signed 'Ashbourne, Elizabeth Bolton, Edward Gibson, Frances Horsburgh-Porter, Constance Gibson.' At their request, no further public mention was ever made of Mussolini's shooter. At the Foreign Office, Violet Gibson's file was closed.

In the absence of any material information as to her whereabouts, *Time* supplied its readers with the following elucidation of her diagnosis:

She is afflicted . . . with chronic hallucinatory paranoia. This is a disease which develops very slowly, coming to maturity in middle life, and characterised by delusions of persecution or grandeur. To the persecution type belong persons such as Miss Gibson who are driven by fear and hate to attack their imaginary persecutors. The grandeur type develops, in rare instances, into such 'supermen' of genius, energy, and egotism as Napoleon (now generally considered a paranoiac). This opinion is not shocking if it be recalled that science no longer conceives of two classes of persons: the 'sane' and the 'insane'. The 'sane' are simply that large, vague mass of humanity which neither rises sufficiently above the normal to attain 'genius' or sinks sufficiently below it to become the object of restraint. The action of so-called 'mental diseases' may either benefit or harm humanity, may bring the 'diseased' power and wealth or lead to the madhouse.

The article borrowed from the swaggering claims of experts like Enrico Ferri, who used the language of science to arrive at totally unscientific conclusions about madness. But it went further, implying that Mussolini (as the paranoiac Napoleon-type) was in theory just as mad as Violet, only he put it to good use as a 'superman' whereas she belonged in the nuthouse. Bizarrely, given the bottomless ignorance that informed it, the article arrived at a kind of wisdom: that sanity is not in one place and insanity in another. Sadly for Violet, a lunatic asylum was not a congenial setting for such a discovery to thrive.

*

When she awoke on Saturday, 14 May 1927, Violet might have mistaken her new lodgings for one of the stately homes she had graced in her youth. Her room was generously appointed with fine Victorian furniture and Aubusson carpets, and a large sash window gave onto a panorama of over a thousand acres of beautiful pastoral scenery. Where the fictional asylum of the Romantic imagination often teetered atop a sublime precipice on the edge of an abyss, the Victorians had placed their asylums in a middle ground that literary critic George Levine called 'the realist's landscape', a kind of *paysage moralisé* in the style of Constable or Wordsworth. Crowning this setpiece at St Andrew's was the chapel, a High Gothic

Nurses in a parlour in the women's section of St Andrew's Hospital

confection designed by George Gilbert Scott (his more famous works include St Pancras Station Hotel and the Albert Memorial), and prominently positioned on the lawn opposite the front entrance. Here, 'the weary and the heavy laden' could be led from their 'temporal to their spiritual physician, and through this means bring their souls to God'. The porticoed arch inside the chapel was the favourite spot of poet John Clare, an inmate of St Andrew's for twenty-two years until his death there in 1864.

The main building itself, with its neo-classical façade and elegantly proportioned interiors, was the pre-eminent expression of the principles underlying a vast programme of asylum-building in the second half of the nineteenth century, sanctioned by a series of parliamentary acts which licensed and regulated madhouses. This reform movement envisaged asylums that would be 'fitting receptacles' for Victorian domestic values, and introduced the concept of moral architecture: reproducing structures of class and gender that were moral – 'normal' – by their own standards. These buildings imitated the architecture of the English country house, with its carefully demarcated spaces for men and women (some even had separate kitchens and mortuaries), masters and servants. By controlling the lunatic's environment down to the last detail, doctors and administrators hoped to make the new public asylums instruments as well as places of therapy; the building itself was a 'special apparatus for the cure of lunacy'. As the cultural historian Elaine Showalter writes, 'In the façades they created for the houses of madness, the Victorians defined their façades of sanity as well.'

Founded in 1838 on the site of a Cluniac priory, Northampton General Lunatic Asylum initially provided accommodation for 'pauper idiots'. By the 1870s, most of these inmates had been moved to a county asylum, and the name was changed to St Andrew's Hospital for Mental Diseases. The new clientele were fee-paying 'chronic ladies and gentlemen' – the well-heeled in need of healing, afflicted by 'moral' disorders such as 'anxiety, trouble, disappointment in love, fright, jealousy, pecuniary difficulties, religion, novel-reading and spiritualism'. 'Physical' causes of insanity included 'apoplexy, brain disease, change of life, drink, fall from horse, heart disease, hereditary, injury to head, masturbation, old age, over-study, overwork, self-indulgence, sunstroke, syphilis and unknown'.

The widening gaze of the medical profession was part of a process whereby private lives were increasingly 'engineered' to comply with institutional norms, and to this end no detail was overlooked. In 1858, the Commissioners in Lunacy suggested to the management committee at St Andrew's that

. . . objects of interest and amusement be supplied to every ward, regard being had to the classes of patients occupying them. We would suggest cheerful Illustrated Publications (as the *Leisure Hour*), prints, maps, statuettes, chimney ornaments, flowering plants, singing birds and domestic animals. We also suggest the introduction, for the amusement and instruction of the Inmates, of Stereoscopes, a Magic Lantern, Cheap Microscopes and Kaleidoscopes. The patients would also, we think, much enjoy many games, as Les Craces, Carpet bowls, Ninepins etc. We suggest, among other occupations, mat making, straw plaiting, hat and bonnet making, basket making, netting and spinning.

The St Andrew's Asylum Amateur Dramatic Company, consisting chiefly of nurses and attendants, flourished (carefully avoiding the misjudgement made by Fisherton Asylum for the criminally insane, where an actor's recitation of the murder scene from *Hamlet* upset the inmates, 'especially one who had cut off his doctor's head and kicked it about the garden'). There was a Patients' Annual Ball, an outdoor fête, concerts, cricket and football matches, even archery, though this activity was carefully restricted. There was an eighteen-hole golf course, tennis courts and croquet lawns, carriages to take patients for drives (replaced in the 1930s with several cars, including a Daimler and a Rolls-Royce), a pack of beagles, even 'hunting parties' where a few patients were allowed to ride to hounds. In 1879 selected inmates were invited to dine regularly with the Hospital Officers. For the coronation of Edward VII in August 1902, 'first-class patients' received a glass of champagne, 'second-class' a glass of port. No wonder Maud Vernon, the heroine of Sheridan LeFanu's *The Rose and the Key* (1871), thinks she is at a party at a country house when she is actually an inmate in Dr Antomarchi's lunatic asylum. She doesn't realise where she is until a patient she has taken for a duchess is put into a straitjacket, and she herself has been subjected to a cold shower.

The archives of St Andrew's record a July 1862 cricket match between members of the staff and a team drawn from local clubs. Patients assembled on the nearby bowling green, and 'regaled themselves ad libitum with tea, plumcake, etc., their appetites being sharpened by the strains of the Asylum brass band'. After tea, a programme of entertainments was energetically entered into:

Dance: Hands Across
A hurdle race for men
A Comic Scene by two black men
Dance: Polka
A flat race for old women
A song and chorus by the Asylum Glee Club
Dance: Quadrille
Bobbing for tobacco and buns dipped in treacle

Game: drop handkerchief
A comic song by two old female itinerants
A wheelbarrow race blindfold
Dance: Scottische
Jumping in sacks
A flat race for women under forty
Dance: Triumph

Much of the official record of St Andrew's is really an advertorial, a triumph of positive gloss. In the treatment of 'nervous diseases and mental cases' it was hailed, in the year Violet arrived, as 'not only the largest of the 13 registered private hospitals in England but the most up to date'. In October 1927, a large new reception hospital, complete with 'hydrotherapy centre and Turkish baths modelled on the famous spas at Aix-les-Bains and Harrogate', was opened by the Lord Chancellor. 'The most modern equipment for intestinal lavage on the Plombieres system is also installed, as this is now considered especially valuable in the treatment of mental cases.' But Violet was amongst those patients who were kept firmly at a distance from the opening ceremony. 'By means of the handsome new building all patients who are recoverable are spared the distressing experience of being brought into contact with chronic cases, thereby lessening the danger of becoming permanently deranged.'

These last words spoke, if inadvertently, to the less cosy reality of the asylum, labelled the 'mansion of despair' by Mary Wollstonecraft. A major extension onto the Billing Road in 1885 was completed despite the objections of the Mayor and Town Council of Northampton, who spoke on behalf of the good burghers of the town who did not want to live cheek by jowl with permanent derangement:

Such a step will in our opinion be very prejudicial to the comfort of a large class of respectable people now living in that neighbourhood. The Hospital is nearer to the Road than it should have been as the cries and noises from the Patients are occasionally most distressing and indeed occasionally alarming to passengers using the Billing Road, which we need scarcely say is fast becoming the most desirable locality for residents in the town of Northampton . . .

Samuel Beckett (who visited Lucia Joyce after she arrived at St Andrew's in the early 1950s) favoured a picture of peaceful domesticity to the messy canvas of distress. As literary critic Hugh Kenner writes,

[He] would one day hint that mental patients were escaped into a system of benefits out of the howling fiasco called civic life. It is the padded cells in Beckett's *Murphy* that are bowers of bliss, and his lunatic Mr. Endon (Greek for 'in one's own country') is busied with a chess game: a queer sort of game in which he takes no offence in any sense of that phrase, but simply plods his pieces out and then back again.

Dominique Maroger, another of Lucia Joyce's visitors, formed an altogether different impression. She thought of St Andrew's halls as the portals to the Heart of Darkness. She noticed guarded doors, knitting women, unspoken horrors. The centre of her reverie became the lift, which she saw as

. . . the gate to the prison that separates one from liberty. In its vicinity one is always under surveillance. There is a reason the exterior grills are wide open, for the patients must never be allowed to feel deprived of liberty . . . One woman knits; the others are mute, staring forward, the gaze blank . . . At a sign, all the women get up and are swallowed up in the open mouth . . . They return in concerted silence to the first floor . . . In that 'medicalised' milieu, every effort of the spirit appears dangerous. One kills time, one doesn't live, and undoubtedly all the patients must be imbued with a spiritual numbness favourable to maintaining them in an institution. All creative ardour is banished.

When Clara, in Antonia White's *Beyond the Glass*, emerges from a bout of insanity that has virtually knocked her unconscious for months, she discovers she is in an asylum. The beginning of her recovery is rewarded by Sister Ware's offer: '"How would you like to have something to do? Some knitting, for example?" "I don't know how to knit." Sister Ware looked very disapproving.'

A lunatic asylum is a world, or a non-world, where every tomorrow is the same as every yesterday. A place to drive you mad.

II

The Absence of God

The first superintendent of St Andrew's, Thomas Octavius Prichard, forbade all forms of mechanical restraint, a pioneering contribution to the development of psychiatry that had hitherto considered it indispensable. But, just as the Victorians freed their lunatics from the Bedlamite hell of muzzles and manacles, they fixed them instead in the paper chains of the new state apparatus with its growing medical bureaucracy. Violet's files are held in the archive room at St Andrew's, one of numerous case-history folders jammed into grey metal filing cabinets – an image of custodial psychiatry under which all patients are equal as deviants. The space is limited, and periodically the part-time archivist employed to maintain order sifts the folders, ripping up those deemed to be of no special interest. The torn documents are dumped in the loony bin's bin, a final psychiatric burial.

When Ezra Pound was admitted to Washington's St Elizabeth's Hospital in 1946, he told a psychiatrist: 'If this is a hospital, you have got to cure me.'

'Cure you of what?' the shrink asked.

'Whatever the hell is the matter with me,' came the reply.

Despite regularly claiming to be hospitals, lunatic asylums were never really about cure, so much as homes for incurables. St Andrew's, for all its lavish equipment and therapies, was a grandly appointed warehouse for the useless, the intolerable and the troublesome.

What was the matter with Violet? The trouble with Violet, as far as the doctors could ascertain in initial interviews conducted in May and June 1927, was that she was suffering from 'expansive

[271]

delusion'. She was 'exalted in her ideas' and 'perverted' in her judgement. One note reads,

Abnormally self satisfied, she considers herself a heroine, and imagines herself the darling of the [Italian] people. In next breath she admitted that she only just escaped being lynched by the infuriated crowd. Believes herself to be peculiarly gifted and says she can read people's thoughts . . . Has great work to perform. Italian nation 'my people', and she believes they regard her as their saviour and their friend. She is their 'Violetta', and though they do not openly acclaim her, it is only because tactful policy dictates silence. She has read their feelings and their hearts in their faces.

Far from regretting her actions, she displayed 'no regrets', only 'glories and boasts', and resented being brought back to England, whose legal system was far inferior to that of Italy. This was debatable, but Violet was entitled to a poor opinion of British law, which offered few if any means by which to contest the frighteningly brisk method of her admission to and long-term detention at St Andrew's.

There are letters in Violet's file: letters written by Constance to the medical superintendent and his staff, letters written to Violet by friends, and letters written by Violet herself. Disturbingly – and in contravention of the 1890 Lunacy Act – the presence in the file of the originals suggests that many of these were never sent. The terms of Violet's letter-writing privileges are unclear. She certainly had access to pen and paper, but that all her correspondence was regularly forwarded to its intended recipient is doubtful. When Helen McTaggart visited Lucia Joyce at St Andrew's in the 1970s, Lucia asked her to send her writing materials – pen, paper and envelopes. McTaggart complied, only to receive a tart letter from a senior nursing sister rebuking her for doing so. McTaggart was left with the impression that the package she had sent Lucia had been confiscated.

In June 1927, a month after her arrival, Violet wrote to a friend:

So, let's talk realistically for a moment: I am sure that I can live an active life as long as it is clear that I have extremely delicate health and I need to eat and rest regularly . . . I really do feel as though I have arrived at enough distance to make an assessment of my situation . . . A delicate person can do many things, just as much as a strong person, if not more; but one's friends must take into account one's fragility.

Her thoughts were of an active life, not of spending the rest of her years at St Andrew's, knitting, killing time. The question was, how could she get out?

Initially, Violet seems to have remained calm and reflective. On 1 July 1927 a medical officer noted that she 'devotes time to reading, draughts and chess. Composed, self possessed and an extremely pleasant person to talk to.' However, 'her appearance and attitude become dangerous when she discusses religion'. Just as in Italy, Violet loathed the probings of doctors who wanted to tune into 'the silenced world beyond', to peer into her soul. She wrote of her soul in her notebook as 'that little heaven'. She wanted to shut herself in there, 'and look at nothing outside it . . . my life is hidden in this abyss'.

Violet's self-composure, her pleasant demeanour, even her devotion to the chessboard may have been a ploy, a demonstration of civility and decorum intended to undermine the notion that she was delusional. It didn't work. In September, her mood turned suddenly. For a week or so, she was observed 'acting as a strange woman'. On the 18th, she had an 'attack of acute excitement in the night'; she was 'noisy, disturbed', and had to be moved from her bedroom to another ward.

Violet's agitation was viewed as evidence of the storms going on inside her turbulent mind. This was reasonable enough, but nobody paused to enquire whether she might be internalising external struggles. And indeed it does appear that the wider political world was once again at the heart of her distress. Violet had access to newspapers which, as always, she read hungrily. The middle of September 1927 was dominated by news of a general election in the Irish Free State, following the collapse of the current government. The political arithmetic of this election, held on 15 September, broke down into minute fractions (only three votes separated the largest parties, Cumann na nGaedhael and Fianna

Fáil), and Violet's own calculation of the outcome is not known. But, just as with the British general election of November 1924 (following which she had rushed off to Rome), there is no doubt that she was intellectually and emotionally heavily invested in a particular result.

This is confirmed by a letter dated 5 December 1927 to the medical superintendent of St Andrew's from Violet's sister, Frances, who had just visited her.

The conversation drifted towards Irish politics and it was as if a fuse had been lit. She told me: 'We have to free everybody from the British . . . We have to see to it that important positions are given to Irish nationalists who care about the country and enjoy the trust of the people.' She said that, even though she was a socialist, she knew that the Irish loved the aristocracy and that this could be exploited in order to liberate Ireland from England. I must confess, she knew much more about the principal actors in Irish affairs than I do, and seemed completely up-to-date on . . . the present situation.

It was an acknowledgement, however grudging, that Violet's political brain was still sharply engaged. But Violet was a mad woman in a lunatic asylum, and everything was now organised to ratify the stereotype. Her ideas were so wrong-headed, Frances commented, that they merely confirmed the diagnosis of insanity – 'despite not shouting out her hallucinations like the other old ladies around, she is clearly completely crazy'. Frances even accused Violet of 'hatching some Irish plot with her papist friends', and warned that she might pretend to be Frances – whom she physically resembled, and 'could easily overwhelm' – and, so disguised, simply walk out of the gates to freedom.

Frances was right about one thing: her sister was determined to get out of St Andrew's. She still had things to do in the world outside, and spoke often of her deep regret that her attempt on Mussolini had not succeeded. This was considered of a piece with her 'impaired judgement' and 'exalted state', her refusal to 'accept ordinary social convention'. Deemed 'dangerous and highly escapable', she was kept 'under close observation'.

'I cannot keep my mind right.' John Clare. 'It is getting to be a great effort for me to think straight.' Charlotte Perkins Gilman. 'I it is im possible im possible im possible.' Vaslav Nijinsky. 'The world feels less and less like a home.' Violet Gibson. These are the instructive, unbearable, mournful intonations that invite us to bear painful witness to the slippage, the crooked thinking, the beginning of the descent into madness. On the night of 4 April 1928, Violet started to shriek that 'the devil was in her room'. Like John Clare, whose head at night 'was a full of the terribles', she was seized by panic, and had to be calmed with a sedative. Several days later, she became 'wildly excited, seized a broom, and used it freely on those about her'. After a violent struggle, she was overpowered, and the broom was removed. She was injected with morphine sulphate and removed to a 'silent' (padded) 'room' (cell). She had hurt Mrs Lee, a depressive, who was confined to bed, and who suffered bruising to the forehead. 'Why', a doctor later asked, 'did you hit Mrs Lee about the head?' The questioner was punished for his pedantry. Violet's reply (which was by no means an answer), was unassailably logical: 'I am like a gentleman, I cannot hit below the belt.'

Other episodes followed. A month later, she called out to nurses in the night and told them she had 'actually seen the devil in her room. When she sees him she jumps out of bed and thumps the walls and door.' She refused to return to her bed 'while the devil was in it', and was again removed to a padded cell. Staff could find 'no apparent reason' for these attacks, despite the fact they had started two years, almost exactly to the day, after her attempt on Mussolini's life. How many times did those seconds on Campidoglio flash across Violet's retina? There he is, standing less than a foot away. Her arm is raised, her finger presses the trigger, the shot rings out as the revolver recoils in her hand. Yet he is still there. He does not fall. April crises – expressions, one suspects, of the frustration and anger and disappointment at her failed mission – were to become a regular occurrence over the years of Violet's confinement, but not once did the psychiatrists charged with her care make this connection.

Perhaps the devil was the scalding memory of this failure, a memory so powerful and so disturbing that it projected out of the dark night of Violet's soul like a living malignant force. For her, the only prophylactic against the devil was the Catholic rite, and this she was denied at St Andrew's. In September 1928, she wrote to Enid Dinnis that she had just learned that her 'protestant' sisters had taken charge of her affairs from Willie, and had sent her 'to an asylum where there is no chapel, not even for Sunday Mass, and where obviously I cannot receive Communion'. *Immuration* is a term referring to the ancient practice of closing up the door of the cell of a religious, who continued to receive food, light and air through a window and followed the ceremonies of the Church through an opening or 'squint' in the chapel wall. It was a voluntary act of enclosure, described by Dinnis in her novel *The Anchorhold*, and Violet had at various intervals in her life sought a metaphorical enactment of it. But at St Andrew's, a Protestant establishment of restraint, she was now immured against her will and without the spiritual benefit of the squint, the view into the ineffable light of piety beyond. Her family had left her 'to fall into wicked hands', she told Dinnis. 'I feel that I have no friends. I don't know if there is still anybody who loves me. Help me to understand my situation.'

It is a desperate account of abandonment, loneliness, confusion. Dinnis did not reply, because she never received the letter. It is still in Violet's file. Identified by the family as one of Violet's 'hysterical' Catholic friends, Dinnis was not encouraged to visit her – and there is no record that she ever did.

By October 1928, Violet's formidable powers of resistance seemed to be waning. In a letter to Constance, she wrote:

Once again I have seen the Devil, and was so mad last night they had to put me in the padded cell. All this shows that it was madness which has made me act as I have done in the past. Will you forgive me and come and take care of me as I should have let you do in the beginning? Please be very forgiving and come as soon as you can. With love from Violet Gibson.

It wasn't a question any longer of forgiveness. Constance, the unwilling gatekeeper of Violet's life, held fast to her post, unable or unwilling to conceive of any other options. Too late, Violet, too late.

*

For the next two years, Violet's life at St Andrew's followed the same pattern. For long periods, she was calm, self-possessed, lucid. Then, always around April, her ability to control herself vanished in a flurry of unprovoked attacks on fellow patients (Mrs Lund and Mrs Knight were added to her list of victims, both taking blows to the head), and exhausting struggles with the devil.

Enough. Violet wanted out. In her notebook, she had written extracts from the story of St John of the Cross, the sixteenth-century mystical theologian and poet to whom she was devoted. Born into a wealthy Spanish family, at fourteen John took a job caring for hospital patients who suffered from incurable diseases and madness. He then joined the Carmelites, but his reformist tendencies earned him the disapproval of many fellow friars, a group of whom kidnapped him, locked him in a tiny cell and beat him three times a week. There was only one tiny window high up near the ceiling, 'yet in that unbearable dark, cold, and desolation, his love and faith were like fire and light. He had nothing left but God.' After nine months, John escaped by unscrewing the lock on his door and creeping past the guard. Taking only the mystical poetry he had written in his cell, he climbed out of a window using a rope made of strips of blankets. With no idea where he was, he followed a dog to civilisation. He hid from his pursuers in a convent infirmary where he read his poetry to the nuns.

For several months, beginning in early 1930, Violet secretly collected scraps of cloth that, 'strengthened with tapes sewn in', she slowly and carefully fashioned into a rope. But the rope was not for escaping. It was a ligature for killing herself. At 9.18 pm on 2 April 1930, she was found in her room with a noose tightened around her neck. The nurse immediately released the rope and called for a doctor. Violet, all the while, was conscious. In her medical notes, dated 7 April, is the following entry: 'Red mark around neck but no further injuries. Determined attempt or carefully staged to create a distraction and sympathy?'

'Nullity had charms', reflects Clara in *Beyond the Glass*. 'It was sober and decent. There would be no more struggles, no more of those ludicrous or tragic catastrophes which result from trying to do things. Above all, there would be no more violent feelings, either of pleasure or pain. Null and void. Null and void.'

III

Buried Alive

It was Mussolini's view that Violet Gibson, being mad, would find congenial company amongst her fellow Irish. Hugh Kenner, commenting on 'melancholy degeneration' in the Irish, picks up an alarming statistic: Ireland's incidence of insanity, measured by admissions to mental hospitals, was twenty-seven per thousand in the first decade of the twentieth century, 'the highest figure on earth'. It was as if 'everyone [was] taking his friends to the asylum or bringing them back from it'. But what the figures mean gets controverted.

Are they inflated [Kenner asks] by counting readmissions as separate cases, some depressive drawing the statistical strength of ten from sidling in and out of custody every five weeks? Or do they not reflect the great charity with which God's most blessed people look after one another? Or is it that the figures from the rest of the world cannot be trusted, whereas in Ireland, as readers of Beckett know, to count and calculate accurately is a mania?

The debate, Kenner concludes, 'is as melancholy as the withdrawal and derangement it would minimise', and in no way alters society's unwillingness to recognise itself in the suffering individuals it rejects or locks up.

The answer to what *The Times* claimed in 1927 was a 'worldwide increase in lunacy' may lie in the asylum itself. No sooner had madness been institutionalised in the grand Victorian programme of asylum-building than it reached pandemic proportions. Historians have written of the 'Napoleonic march of the asylum': the irresistible logic, once established, was to expand. A commissioned history of St Andrew's, published in 1989, airily states that 'The devoted attention given by the Management Committee to making St Andrew's as comfortable as possible was rewarded by the increasing number of patients entrusted to their care.' But bulging madhouses witnessed to the failure (hence 'bin'), rather than success, of rehabilitation of the insane. Attics were emptied of 'mad' relatives and dependents who were given – whether they liked it or not – new and often permanent domicile in the asylum. Once in, it was almost impossible (*pace* Kenner and his commuting depressives) to get out.

In June 1922, Lilian Jane Gaul, a middle-aged unmarried woman of Kensington, claimed for damages for false imprisonment in St Andrew's. As reported in *The Times*, Gaul, who held a first-class degree from Cambridge, conducted her own defence before the High Court. Against her were arrayed Earl Spencer and a phalanx of the great and the good, who, as members of the committee and management of St Andrew's, appeared as defendants. Gaul had been admitted in 1917 as a voluntary patient for a 'rest cure', but was then certified insane and 'closely confined without legal authority'. She was 'deprived of her clothes and other possessions' and subjected to 'gross indignity and misery, to noise, obscenity, and terror'. St Andrew's defence was that she had declared her intention to commit suicide if Germany occupied Britain, as she would rather be dead than a captive subject (in 1940, Leonard Woolf was to store petrol in the garage 'for suicide should Hitler win'). Ironically, this statement of intent had led to her becoming a captive subject of the asylum for three months (at six guineas a week, she pointedly informed the court). Gaul, as plaintiff, spoke for seven hours before going into the witness box for cross-examination:

DEFENCE COUNSEL: Do you deeply resent being certified as a lunatic?
PLAINTIFF: Yes.
HIS LORDSHIP: Who do you think, in a general way, is the best judge of insanity – a person who has devoted himself to the study of insanity or the patient?
PLAINTIFF: I think the expert is very often the worst person to decide a question of that kind.

Dr Haydn Brown was next up, called as a witness for the plaintiff. A psychologist with thirty years' experience, he was one of those rare experts who held a different view. While he was on the stand, his Lordship read from the certificate of lunacy as follows:

HIS LORDSHIP: 'Talks volubly, but is rather rambling and incoherent. Very emotional and bursts into tears, but suddenly quickly recovers. Harps continually on the subject of suicide [and] quotes from the Bible . . . Gives a long description of her own attempt to poison herself with laudanum. States that her mother degenerated into a vile and degraded woman.' You say that that is not evidence of insanity?
DR HAYDN BROWN: None whatever.
HIS LORDSHIP: If any prisoner ever wants to set up a plea of insanity, I should advise him not to call Dr Brown. (*Laughter*)

Cross-examined by defence counsel, Dr Brown said that he did not think that attempted suicide constituted in itself evidence of insanity. If the plaintiff had attempted suicide, and he saw her the next day, he would not ask her not to repeat the attempt. He would give her humane, kind treatment, and place her in a proper environment. He thought the plaintiff was ill at the time. People were 'frightened to death of cases like hers because they did not understand them'.

Summing up her case, Gaul said: 'I have been suffering for five years from the law laid down by Harley Street, and I come to the Court to have the law laid down by the King's Bench.' To which the judge replied, to laughter in the court, 'Harley Street is not outside the law. Harley Street is not Alsatia.' Gaul lost the case, and was ordered to pay costs.

Questioning the claim that psychiatry made positive advances in the period of late-Victorian reform, cultural historian Roy Porter argues instead that 'Moral therapists were no more interested in entering into the witness of the mad, in negotiating with their testimony, even in exploring and decoding its meanings, than the advocates of mechanical and medical treatment had been'. This lack of negotiation, of engagement, applies in Violet's case.

Despite being kept 'very closely supervised' during the early years of her confinement, the psychiatric assessment to which she was subjected yielded no insight. She was formally assessed twice a year, in March or April and in September. The overall – and unchanging – conclusion was that she was incongruent, unable to reconcile the rational, 'sane' features of her personality with the delusional, exalted dimensions of her self-perception, though much the same could be said of those charged with her care. For 'exaltation', one need look no further than the self-aggrandising and unfounded claims that custodial psychiatry made for itself. (Dr Rambaut, the chief medical superintendent who had admitted Violet, advanced as fact, rather than opinion, that 'the rain, needle douche, sitz and hot air or Turkish baths are invaluable in the treatment of the different varieties of insanity'.)

Further, Violet's psychiatric notes do not seem to have been compiled or studied in tandem with her medical notes. Hence, possible organic or physical causes of her episodic attacks are overlooked, and the possibility that her mental and emotional distress – the pain, the sheer desolation – might be environmental, related to the place in which she was being held, against her will, was never interrogated. Often, one gets the impression that neither set of records was read at all, beyond the last entry – a dissociation bordering on neglect. Violet may have had difficulty in discerning the real from the false, but so did her doctors. It would come to the point where one of them dismissed her claim that she had shot Mussolini as a symptom of chronic delusion. This, at the time when Violet had acquired a kind of immortality in the hugely popular song 'Underneath the Arches', first recorded in 1932 by Bud Flanagan and Chesney Allen. Violet had a little radio, given to her by Constance. She may well have heard the song, which was introduced with this spoken exchange:

CHESNEY ALLEN: Lovely melody, Bud. Do you remember when we first sang it?

BUD FLANAGAN: Yes, Ches. We used to sit on a seat with the Thames Embankment behind us. You had a newspaper and read the headlines.

ALLEN: That's quite right, Bud. I've still got that paper. Do you remember the date? Nineteen hundred and twenty-six.

FLANAGAN: Ches, read those headlines again.

ALLEN: Ah, here's one. Gertrude Ederle, eighteen-year-old American. First woman to swim the Channel.

FLANAGAN: Listen to this. Cricket. Ashes for England after fourteen years.

ALLEN: Irish woman, Violet Gibson, shoots Mussolini in the nose.

Violet once railed against Constance for being 'fond of reading history, whereas I have made history'. But at St Andrew's, history was reduced to an endlessly repeated act of stenography, to pages of black ink smeared with unrevised opinions and foregone conclusions:

17 September 1930. Still under close observation. Has made attempts at concealing cords made of dress material. Refuses to talk with doctors.

15 April 1931. Still delusional. Actively suicidal. Very closely supervised.

22 September 1931. Morbidly suspicious.

22 March 1932. No insight, therefore thinks she is victim of persecution because she is detained in a mental hospital.

20 September 1932. Still regarded as dangerous and suicidal. Suicide and escape. Sullen and morose.

17 March 1933. Refuses to speak with anyone in authority or to see her visitors.

17 September 1934. As above. Offhand with most of her relations.

Seven long years after the train had carried her away from Rome, Violet was more alone than at any time in her life. When nobody is listening, it's a perfectly sane reaction to stop talking, to cut free from 'the choking knotweed of miscommunication'. Her refusal to speak to 'anyone in authority' or to see her visitors (Constance, chiefly) was a deliberate act of withdrawal. Apart from suicide – and Violet's skills in this department were demonstrably poor – it was one of the few gestures of defiance left to her.

If asylums are places that dismantle the self rather than rebuilding it, Violet showed a fierce determination to hold on to those parts of herself she had long been true to. Denied the spiritual comfort of the Catholic liturgy, she focused once more on the mystical, contemplative traditions of the Church. She spent more and more time outside, cornering an area of the grounds just in front of the main building where she waited patiently for little birds to feed from her hands. 'I hope Violet continues her interest in the birds,' Constance wrote to the medical superintendent in October 1934. 'It seems to me the most human contact she has had since the cloud fell on her.'

It took time, patience, stillness, discipline, faith – by February 1935, the staff at St Andrew's were so impressed by Violet's relationship with the birds that they suggested she be photographed feeding them. She consented, and was pleased enough with the results to sign the prints with her name (and her title). The photographs show her reclining on a deckchair surrounded by breadcrumbs on which the birds, sparrows, feed busily; or standing with her arm extended, the birds settled on her upturned palm. She never faces the lens – we cannot see her face.

Violet's saint-like deportment (was she consciously imitating St Francis, as depicted by Giotto, in his sermon to the birds?) precipitated a discussion over the future of her care. For a brief interval, it seemed as if her own suggestion, that she be cared for by a community of nursing nuns at a convent in Bexhill, might be seriously considered. A Harley Street psychiatrist, Dr Henry Yellowlees, was brought in to examine her and provide a second opinion. On 4 September 1935 he submitted his report to Constance:

I have no doubt that she is suffering from a chronic form of mental disturbance and that many delusional fancies still persist. Her condition now, however, is a more general maladaptation to life and an inability to settle down harmoniously as a member of any kind of community than an acute delusional state.

Was Violet's condition no more, no less, than this: a problem in living, an unsuccessful reaction to the public world, to the conflicts and anxieties it contained? Violet's 'technique for living', as the sociologist Georg Simmel once called it, was deemed to be irreparably maladapted. Her request to be moved to the convent was refused.

Contrary to appearances, she had not eschewed all human communication. Rather, she had resolved on a campaign to reach people in the real world, the one that lay beyond the gates of St Andrew's. In November 1933 she had written to Sir Mervyn Manningham-Buller, member of parliament for Northampton (and a veteran, like her brother Victor, of the Boer War), setting out the case for her release. She received no reply (again, the original is in her file). Suspecting her letters were not being sent, she adopted a clandestine strategy, asking friends to smuggle them out for her. The opportunities were rare, as she had so few visitors – unsurprisingly, since hardly anybody knew where she was. She had to wait three more years until, in June 1936, a friend agreed to post a letter addressed to her sister-in-law, Marianne.

Marianne? Surely she was the last person to take up Violet's cause? Why didn't Violet write to Willie? Had he so thoroughly washed his hands of her that she didn't think it was worth the effort? Or did she fear, quite reasonably, that Willie would share any confidence with his wife? Perhaps Violet hoped that Marianne had mellowed in her attitude towards her. She had not. True to form, she immediately forwarded the letter to Constance, who noted acidly that Violet's accomplice was a Catholic. It was, Constance reported back to the medical superintendent, 'a very clever letter to be laid before the Home Secretary asking for her release'. Violet had included in the letter copies of the photographs showing her feeding the birds. The intent was clear: she wanted to demonstrate that she was not a danger to anybody, that if her arm was now raised, it was not to fire a gun, but to feed an innocent creature; that in communing with nature, she was also communing with herself, a self given over to acts not of violence, but of passive contemplation. Once again, her pleas were ignored. And with the discovery of her letter to the Home Secretary, Violet's smuggling career was over.

*

Prolonged captivity can breed a vast indifference to one's fate – people cease to be curious about the future when they feel they haven't got one. Not so Violet. She had made history – she had shot Mussolini, and though she hadn't killed him, she had come closer than anybody else. The job still needed to be finished, and though she may have relinquished that particular role, she might yet have a part to play in his downfall. By the summer of 1935, the tone of reports on Mussolini issuing from her little radio began to change. His unprovoked threats against Ethiopia in that year introduced a new dimension to his imperial ambitions – it was no longer a matter of mere rhetoric, gesture, *romanità* expressed as architecture or mise-en-scène. Il Duce had said he wanted an empire, and now he set out to get one.

When the world wants rid of its dictators, it applauds resistance, even armed resistance, as a virtue, as conscience that won't be tempted. In 1926, there had been no appetite for Violet's act – it stuck like gristle in the political throat, just wouldn't go down. A decade later, Mussolini's behaviour was such to strain the goodwill of many of his foreign admirers. The official position began, slowly and reluctantly, to change from advocacy and support to suspicion and censure.

Predictably, in the myopic world of St Andrew's this wider picture was not even glimpsed as a possible context for Violet's behaviour. It shouldn't have been that hard: in her psychiatric interviews at this time, she referred repeatedly to Italy, to its need to be rescued. On 2 September 1935 she was assessed as being 'still in a state of exaltation', believing she was 'chosen by God [with] some divine mission to perform'. Violet had detected the waning attraction to Mussolini, and read it as a confirmation of her opinions about him. Her invocation of God as the ultimate authority for her beliefs, as the emissary for her mission, can be – and was – dismissed as a sorry delusion, a symptom of what Constance called her 'religious mania'. (James Joyce was only half-joking when, on learning that Lucia had developed religious longings and had even gone to Mass, he had said, 'Now I know she is mad.') Given that every other authority had failed Violet in her political, as well as her personal convictions, a less censorious view might be appropriate. A delusion is usually defined as a false belief arising without stimulation or validation by others and which is impervious to reason. Violet's belief in God had widespread external validation and was held by many others, so it can't of itself be called delusional in the generally accepted sense of the word. Whose God was He, anyway? The time was not far off when statesmen would enlist Him in their mission to destroy Mussolini and all that he stood for.

'You're the top! You're the great Houdini! You're the top! You are Mussolini!' By the time P. G. Wodehouse reworked Cole Porter's famous lyric, in a 1935 London production of *Anything Goes*, such flattery was already out of tune. In May 1936, Mussolini defied the will of the world (imperial) powers and annexed Ethiopia, thus enlarging the modern Roman empire of Libya and Somalia. Two years later, he launched claims for Djibouti, Tunis, Corsica and Nice. The new-forged Italian race, asserted the Vulcan Mussolini, was entitled to a repristined role on the world stage.

Pursuing this task of re-engineering the Italian soul, in October 1938 Il Duce – once hailed by Winston Churchill as 'the greatest lawgiver among men' – introduced as law 'The Declaration on Race'. Jews were no longer allowed to teach in state schools, marry or employ Aryans, own more than a hundred hectares of property, serve in the military, insert death notices in the newspapers or possess telephones (when one Mario Fornari, of Ancona, installed a telephone line by registering it in the name of his maid, he was deported to Auschwitz, where he died in 1944). These provisions for 'the defence of race' were signed by the King 'for the grace of God and for the benefit of the nation'. The Nazis were surprised by the swift Italian adoption of racial ideas, and secretly astonished that so racially corrupt a people could be so bold. To his son-in-law Count Ciano, Mussolini suggested that the Jews might be despatched to a concession in Somalia, where they could enjoy the natural resources, 'Among the rest, a shark-fishing industry which would be especially good because a lot of Jews could be eaten up.' By the end of the war, 7,500 Jews had been rounded up from Italy (mainly by Italians) and fed into the Nazi death camps. Six hundred and ten survived.

An immediate consequence of the race laws was Mussolini's attempt to eradicate all traces of his liaison with his former mistress, the Jewish Margherita Sarfatti, despite the affair being well known to the public. Ciano was instructed to 'tell the Italian press to ignore Margherita completely. Her public appearances were not to be reported and her name was not to appear in any Fascist publication.' In November 1938 she fled to Switzerland, fearful of her fate if she remained in Italy. The ranks of Mussolini's former lovers had already been thinned by the death the previous year of Ida Dalser in a Venice lunatic asylum. Only Clara Petacci remained, though Mussolini continued his habit of brisk sexual mountings with other women, too numerous to count, in the offices and corridors of Palazzo Venezia.

This was the 'rough beast, its hour come round at last', that was slouching 'towards Bethlehem to be born'. Yeats, who died in the south of France in January 1939, had seen the coming of chaos with Mussolini, Hitler and Stalin, telling a friend the year before his death to read his poem, 'The Second Coming', as a description of the current scene:

> *Things fall apart; the centre cannot hold;*
> *Mere anarchy is loosed upon the world . . .*

In August 1939, having first secured a Pact of Steel with Mussolini, Hitler swept one million troops into Poland. In September, Britain and France declared war on Germany. The following May, Germany invaded France and the Low Countries. Before the month was out, Norway, Holland and Belgium had fallen. The Wehrmacht's advance into France was so rapid that, as the French front line crumbled, the British beachhead at Dunkirk was collapsing in a bloody sandpit of failure.

At St Andrew's nothing changes. All is the same. The pieces on the chessboard are plodded out. The knitting women knit.

IV

Cometh the Hour

Mussolini 'wanted war as a child wants the moon', and he chose an extraordinary date to pitch Italy into the conflict on Hitler's side. The announcement came on 10 June 1940, the sixteenth anniversary of the murder of Giacomo Matteotti. It was a telling omen: 'Mussolini had chosen to enter a perilous conflict with the incarnadine stain of that notorious crime still unwashed from his hands. Blood was destined to call for blood.'

From the balcony of Palazzo Venezia, his headquarters since 1929, Mussolini delivered his speech declaring war on France and England to an enormous crowd. It was a wild performance, an inimitable piece of Balcony Empire. His voice issued like a machine gun, hammering, clamorous, peremptorily insistent. He rolled his eyes, puffed out his cheeks, pummelled his chest. This was a war sanctioned by destiny, a war 'against the plutocratic and reactionary democracies of the West, who have repeatedly blocked the march, and even threatened the existence of the Italian people'. Thanks to him, Italy now had an empire to defend, a real Augustan legacy. Let those who wished to 'starve' Italy 'with their retention of all the riches and gold of the earth' be vanquished in the field. This was 'a struggle of the fecund and young peoples against barren peoples slipping to their sunset'.

Violet Gibson, long ago dismissed by the Fascists as a barren old hag, left to slip to her sunset in a lunatic asylum, was once again ready to pitch herself into the fray. Her opportunities for doing so were limited, on account of her domicile, but she had some suggestions, and these she set forth in writing – lucidly, in a steady hand – to Mussolini's erstwhile admirer Winston Churchill, now prime minister. Her ideas were not grandiose or fantastical or delusional, but pragmatic points to explore 'in case they have been overlooked'. She stressed the need for good mapping of the British Isles, especially remote areas like the Scottish and Yorkshire Moors that might be chosen by the enemy for airborne landings. She had done her maths. 'Each enemy plane brings fifty parachutists. In one hour twenty planes could land 1,000 enemy in the country. Are you prepared for them to try and land ten thousand men in one night in different parts of England, Wales, and Scotland??' She continued:

It is good to collect local people in each place, and rifles will suffice in small spaces, yet for the big spaces machine guns, tanks and planes will be necessary. The planes should be waiting separately on the ground, so that if the enemy tried to bomb them they could only hit one at a time.

Owners of large estates should be equipped with the means to 'protect their own big spaces, as far as possible themselves, till troops arrive'. Rocket signals should 'be arranged for *everywhere* telling just where the enemy have landed. Though you will have watchers everywhere yet you cannot place a full force everywhere, but a rocket should bring them on the scene in ten minutes.'

These were the material points that Churchill was invited to consider. But Violet also had concerns about 'the internal side of the country's needs', about public morale and declining standards of integrity. 'I myself am a victim of this state of things,' she wrote. 'In 1926 I tried to assassinate Mussolini. One year internment would have been ample for that, but because . . . for every two years I can be kept here £1,000 clear profit is made . . . I have not been set free.'

With regard to assassination, Violet gave the following assurance:

I never intend to do it again, because it is not my talent, and all the precious years wasted in this place must be made up for by using my real gift for my fellow men, which, if I had been allowed to use before would probably have prevented this war.

Mindful of how busy Churchill must be, she asked him to get his secretary

... to write a line to the superintendant [*sic*] of this place saying that something *genuine* and *practical* must be done to facilitate my release. It is a mockery to go to war and to sacrifice all those lives for the freedom and justice of the individual and, at the same time do nothing towards a case like mine. You have reached your eleventh hour. The enemy is just on you. Free me and it will be a gesture signifying that if you gain the victory you will, in future, do everything to bring about a state of things in which integrity and sincerity is practised between man and man. I will keep silent, but prophesy that if not free the blessing of God will not be on this country, no matter what material defences you use. Yours sincerely, Violet Gibson.

The letter, together with its unstamped envelope, remains in the file.

At sixty-four, and in delicate health, Violet was unlikely to sally forth again with a loaded revolver. She was committed to a different kind of campaign, one waged 'with pen rather than the sword', as she described it. Doctors at St Andrew's noted with their usual wan familiarity that she still believed in her 'mission', and that 'her special knowledge might be profitably used to deal with international affairs . . . She remains grandiose.' (When Dr Wendell Muncie was being cross-examined in Ezra Pound's insanity hearing after the war, he conceded that Pound's ideas – that he and a handful of others could have prevented the war, that he had no peer in the intellectual field, that he had the key to the peace of the world through the writings of Confucius – were not by themselves necessarily delusional or evidence of insanity. When asked how Pound's schemes for saving the world differed from those of European leaders who wanted to conquer the world, Muncie sensibly replied that he had not examined the other European leaders and therefore couldn't comment.)

The progress of the war most likely confirmed Violet in her view that she had the power of prophecy. In early June 1940, Hitler pushed the British off the beaches of Dunkirk; in August he launched the Luftwaffe into the skies above Britain, and in September the remorseless bombing of London began. On 15 January 1941, St Andrew's received a direct hit. Amazingly, there were no casualties. Soon after, another bomb landed on the front lawn, creating a huge crater. Extensive alterations were undertaken to convert underground rooms and passages into well-ventilated air-raid shelters, and staff were trained in anti-gas measures and in dealing with incendiary bombs. As the war began to bite, fuel shortages put the Russian and Turkish baths out of commission and X-ray films could only be used in essential cases. In 1942, the Air Training Corps was allowed to use the cricket field on condition they provided petrol to enable the grass to be cut. Otherwise, life continued pretty much as normal.

*

Mussolini's war was something of a fiasco from the outset. Its first significant casualty was the one-time Minister for Aviation, Italo Balbo, the killer of Zamboni, who was mistakenly shot down by his own nervous men on 28 June 1940 as he flew above Tobruk. Italian troops invaded North Africa, British Somaliland, then Greece, but the advertised blitzkriegs were never delivered. In September 1940 the Ministry of War still closed at lunchtime for the siesta; in November, its fleet of warships was crippled by an RAF attack with ageing biplanes on the navy's main base at Taranto. Mussolini's speech on board the *Cavour* the day after Violet had shot him had rendered homage to the 'glorious navy' on which 'the brightest hopes for the future' rested, enabling Italy once more to rule the seas – but not one shot fired by an Italian battleship hit its target in the war. Six weeks into what was meant to be a stroll to victory, Italy had been revealed as a power weaker than little Greece and Mussolini's dictatorship could not match the ramshackle government of General Metaxas. The rout in Greece was followed by others in Eritrea and Ethiopia. In May 1941, Haile Selassie entered Addis Ababa, exactly five years after he had been forced to flee, and Italy's new Augustan era effectively came to an end. Only part of Libya remained – together with its undiscovered oil reserves it fell to the British in February 1941.

The crater left by a bomb on the front lawn of St Andrew's, January 1941

Mussolini himself seemed to be cracking up. Colleagues noticed his pallor and insomnia, his ageing physique that seemed to be collapsing under the weight of office and the evidence of failure. In January 1941, the *Picture Post* ran an article asking 'Why Mussolini Failed', and concluded that the cause was 'a progressive unbalancing in [his] personality'. Frequently impossible to contact, he was rumoured to be 'Petaccified', spending every afternoon with Clara. Mussolini attempted to quell the rumours by demonstrating he was in superhuman form. He staged a sporting event at Villa Torlonia, his private residence, and appeared before twenty-three foreign correspondents in a white singlet, leaping over jumps on his horse before striding onto the tennis court where, according to one reporter, 'he violated every tennis rule and tradition', smashed at lobs 'that a lame man with a broken arm could have hit', and delivered 'soap bubble serves'. All this to show that Mussolini and his vitalist regime were still pitched at the point of maximum energy, could no sooner be defeated than that iconic emblem of Fascist superiority, Primo Carnera, the champion heavyweight boxer known as 'The Ambling Alp'. But Carnera's invincibility was another forgery pulled from Fascism's bag of tricks: all images of this human mountain lying knocked out on the canvas were censored.

Such antics could not distract from the catastrophes unfolding at the front. All was dominated by 'a failure of preparation' and by 'improvisation', according to high-ranking Fascist Giuseppe Bottai. The truth was that Mussolini, unable to work out a system of military and economic priorities, was spending time instead on language lessons, settling down to do a translation of Manzoni's *I promessi sposi* into German, and carrying on his affair with Petacci. Since 1936 she had enjoyed an apartment in Palazzo Venezia and had become a sort of *maîtresse en titre*. She would arrive at 2 p.m., have a quick smoke (hiding her habit from her disapproving lover) and then make ready to greet him. It wasn't a very comforting relationship by this stage. She would moan about her body, her teeth, her health and the size of her breasts, and stay in bed all day eating chocolate if given the chance.

On 7 February 1941, Benghazi, the last Fascist stronghold in eastern Libya, was encircled, trapped in a British pincer movement. It fell two days later, effectively ending Italy's new Augustan era. From London Churchill broadcast a speech confidently predicting victory against the Axis and pouring scorn on Mussolini as a 'crafty, cold-blooded, black-hearted Italian'. The next morning Constance wrote to Dr Tennent, the deputy medical superintendent at St Andrew's: 'As things are today one feels it would have been kinder to Mussolini if [Violet's] effort had succeeded.' Dr Tennent agreed.

Mussolini may have been losing his war, but Violet was also losing hers. When she requested to be moved to a ground-floor room, it was assumed that this was part of a plan to take advantage of the blackout restrictions and seize 'the opportunity of escape'. But Violet was in no state to go leaping out of windows, ground-floor or otherwise. Her gripe was that she had been moved to a room on an upper floor where the window shutters were kept locked at night. 'I feel the lack of air very much,' she protested, 'and, as both sides of my family have TB, and two of my brothers died of it, and as I have contracted it here through closed shutters in the beginning, they [subsequently] were opened and remained open – till I came up here.' Her health, she went on, was rather important, and her request was being made 'with a view to getting out of this place without any further damage, so that I may be as useful as possible. *Please* [underlined twice] do something practical to get me out.' She added that she would be resigned to bars being installed on the window if that was the price of having fresh air. Hardly the ruse of a woman planning her escape. When the request was denied, she informed her keepers that the 'conditions under which she is expected to live amount to attempted murder on our part'.

Violet had indeed had tuberculosis in adolescence, but examinations at St Andrew's revealed no recurrence. She took exception to this diagnosis – or lack of – and was reported as being 'in bed and taking Ol' Monk and Malt. Also salicylates which she believes prevent "lung trouble".' Throughout the 1930s, she had complained of 'breathlessness, attacks of pain in the region of the heart'. Though 'not dangerous', doctors acknowledged that such attacks served 'to frighten her and make her apprehensive'. Her 'cardiac insufficiency' was treated as 'hypochondriacal'. At times she would call out, claiming she was having the 'worst heart attack'. Her pulse was found to be 'rapid but feeble', but she was 'otherwise in excellent condition'. She disagreed, in a manner that was described as 'rude and overbearing at times. Sarcastic, complaining.'

A note in her medical file, dated 12 March 1938, reveals a great deal about Violet's attitude towards doctors. 'Studies physical condition meticulously,' it reads.

Has her own ideas about herself which do not conform in any way with that of doctors. Subject to recurrent 'heart attacks.' Before doctor is called she places a list of instructions for him to observe when he arrives and at the top of this list is written 'To the young and inexperienced Doctor.' Ideas about how to be examined – only pulse of left wrist is to be taken.

During an examination in 1939 she announced: 'I am suffering from phthisis, glaucoma, myocarditis, and chronic peritonitis.' No definite signs of these could be found, but Violet was undeterred. In April 1940 she informed a doctor that she was 'the wonder of the medical profession' and told him that he should 'marvel at the fact she is still alive after all she has been through'.

It was as if Violet was examining her doctors, and not the other way around; she patronised them with her diagnosis, delighted in confounding and discomforting them ('Her pulse and circulation are, she says, quite separate'; 'she claims to have been "practically dead" as result of bad circulation'). She was right to be distrustful of their care. When she felt a lump in her throat 'which alters the nature of her voice', she feared cancer or tubercular disease. Her larynx was examined, and neither was found to be present. The discomfort persisted, and so did her complaints. Finally, another doctor was brought in for a second opinion. He found the larynx to be healthy, but 'the mecti of both ears were full of extremely hard plugs of wax, which he removed, and which he thinks may have been the cause of her throat irritation'. It was not a serious condition, but it was a serious oversight.

More worryingly, for years Violet's complaint that she suffered from regular heart pains had been dismissed. Then, in March 1941, following a visit from Constance that upset her, she claimed to have suffered a 'heart attack'. An electrocardiogram was ordered, and showed 'definite evidence of recent coronary thrombosis'. This followed an ECG of 2 August 1939 that had also shown her to have coronary disease. So why had they continued to disbelieve her for almost two years?

The discovery, while vindicating Violet in her self-diagnosis, was used against her. In late November 1941, when the German army was within thirty miles of Moscow, Violet once again attempted to lift her personal siege. She formally requested that the Board of Control (the statutory body charged with overseeing the Lunacy Act) consider her eligibility for discharge: 'I am seriously ill with heart disease and want to spend the little left to me of life in a religious enclosure or Catholic nursing home kept by nuns.' The Board asked St Andrew's to furnish

. . . a report on her complaint of heart disease and [to inform] in addition whether she is well enough to be discharged to a religious community or alternatively, if this is not practicable, whether she is likely to feel happier and more contented if she could be removed to such an institution as St George's Retreat, Burgess Hill, Sussex, or St Peter's Convent, Plympton House, Devon, which it is understood pay special consideration to believers in the Roman Catholic Faith.

The medical superintendent swiftly complied, writing to the Board less than a week later:

As you know, she suffers from delusional insanity. She believes that she is predestined to rule the Italian people and she invariably refers to them as her people. She considers also that by virtue of her supply of intellect she should be consulted regarding the International Affairs of this country. In the past she has been actively homicidal, quite apart from her attempted assassination of Mussolini, and she is known to have made sly, dangerous attacks on defenceless patients in this Hospital. She is also intensely hypochondriacal and is much concerned about her physical state. She has stated that other human beings could not have withstood the physical diseases which have befallen her and she wants this statement to support her belief that she is no ordinary person. She suffers from time to time from various heart attacks, which appear to be entirely functional, and generally arise as a result of some difference of opinion with some member of her family or of the Hospital staff.

Electrocardiographic examinations have been carried out several times without giving any conclusive evidence to support her suggestion that she is suffering from heart disease. Nevertheless, since Miss Gibson will not accept any statement which suggests that her heart is not diseased we allow her to assume that this is so, and energetic measures of treatment are invariably taken following these attacks.

Miss Gibson is frequently visited by a Roman Catholic priest who, I understand, deals adequately with all her religious needs. I am of the opinion that her suggestion that she should be allowed to live in a Catholic nursing home kept by nuns is in the hope that the degree of observation would be less strict and that she would be afforded a greater opportunity to escape. I understand that she refuses to discuss this suggestion with members of her family because of delusional ideas. She is visited from time to time by one sister [Constance], but not infrequently she refuses to accept her and orders her to leave the room. These visits are invariably followed by another heart attack.

Whether Violet's heart attacks were functional or hypochondriacal was surely not the point. Electrocardiograms confirmed that they were taking place, and that she also had heart disease. St Andrew's report to the Board, a manoeuvre designed to foil her attempts to be moved, lied on this point. But the Board was easily convinced, as was Constance, who weighed in with the following objections:

Violet was resident in a Convent all the time she was in Rome. A Convent to her, therefore, is a centre of intrigue from which she can sally forth in 'God's Service.' We know that her homicidal instincts though dormant are not extinct. When I saw her a few days ago she walked with a firm, strong step. I believe an access of strength would come if she saw the most distant opportunity of indulging her instincts. I believe that in a Convent she would create a situation in which such an opportunity would occur. I cannot therefore agree to her being moved.

Violet was kept at St Andrew's not because the law required it, but because her custodians – her doctors and her family – refused to countenance any alternative.

*

Willie Ashbourne lived long enough to see the rout of France. On 22 June 1940, the French government signed an armistice with Germany in a railway carriage in the woods near Compiègne where he and Marianne used to stage their amateur theatricals. Within a few weeks, nearly a quarter of the French population had left their homes. In central Paris, less than a third of three million residents remained to see the German army arrive. Willie did not move. He died in Nazi-occupied France on 21 January 1942. Despite his tireless perambulations in pursuit of the Gaelic cause – travels that took him on an increasingly broad circuit, both in Ireland and the length and breadth of England, though he did not once stop at Northampton to see Violet – he ended up like a souvenir of Olde Ireland, a figure on a tea-towel. The Gaelic League had modernised, pushed an increasingly radical agenda that offered the rain-battered peasantry of Ireland more than just a potato or sweet words of Gaelic. But somehow Willie had never managed the transition from the romantic to the political sphere of action. On the back of a letter to Marianne, dated 1937, was the scrawled draft of a poem:

> *I turned away, my soul was rich with sadness,*
> *And wandered thence in brooding reverie . . .*

A suitable epitaph.

Willie had no issue. The only remaining Gibson brother, Edward, had died in 1928, aged fifty-five, so the baronetcy passed to his son Edward Russell Gibson, who was serving in the navy in the Mediterranean. The new paterfamilias was quick to affix the

Ashbourne coronet to his stationery, but less enthusiastic about assuming the burden of the mad aunt that came with it. On 21 May 1942, he received his first briefing from the medical superintendent of St Andrew's:

I need not recapitulate a history which must be well known to you, from which you will realise that adequate supervision is an essential feature of The Hon. Violet Gibson's care; and for this purpose a special day, and a special night nurse are constantly provided. She also occupies a private room, and is given special attention in regard to diet. For this accommodation and the associated services a fee of 12 guineas a week [£470 today] is charged. It is very difficult to estimate how long these expenses which you have assumed are likely to exist. Her recovery from the mental point of view is extremely unlikely.

As to Violet's general physical health, it was described as 'poor'. The heart problems that had so recently been dismissed as insignificant were now given an altogether different emphasis. She had

... at some time in the past few years suffered a coronary thrombosis, the existence of which was recently revealed by an electrocardiographic examination. This defect of the heart is a condition which is likely to recur, sometimes with great suddenness, and almost always without much previous warning, and from the nature of it, it is possible that a recurrence may arise at any time. Added to this, Miss Gibson has a functional cardiac condition, which manifests itself in times of stress or annoyance. On these occasions she suffers syncopal attacks in which she becomes pulseless and assumes that she is about to die. Such attacks have followed visits from her sister, The Hon. Constance Gibson, whom she professes to dislike intensely. This dislike is of course assumed on delusional grounds. It is very difficult to assess accurately your aunt's expectation of life; nevertheless if one excludes another attack of coronary thrombosis as an immediate possibility she should still enjoy some years of life. You may be interested to note that your aunt still takes a lively interest in current events, and is now convinced that the incident which led to her admission to hospital was entirely justifiable, and she is satisfied that events have proved it so.

The new Lord Ashbourne had no intention of moving Violet. He wanted her kept at St Andrew's, but at reduced cost. Violet took up her cause, writing on 5 July 1942 to Dr Tennent, the deputy medical superintendent:

I hear that my nephew says that I am to have only one nurse, and that *you* say I am to be in the dormitory during whichever time I have no nurse. I suggest that for a week I experiment spending the night in the dormitory, and at the end of that time I will tell you which nurse it is best to discard. For this week I will do without the night nurse. In any event it is essential I should be in the quiet of my room in the day time, as I lead a kind of nun's life, and regard my room as a cell.

The experiment lasted not a week, but several months, at the end of which an exasperated Violet again wrote to Dr Tennent to say that it had 'led to nothing except the complete breaking of my sleep which has affected my heart and, on September 13th it took a bad turn which increased till now it is very serious. As every one who knows anything about heart trouble knows that rest and quiet are essential for it, I write this to ask you to let me remain in my private room night *and* day.'

She asked only that a night nurse from the dormitory check in on her occasionally, and that she keep her day nurse, 'but will let her join in the general work in the ward most of the time. Also I find that I don't need nursing these days. I can manage things better myself.'

When Dr Tennent put this suggestion to Constance, she was in no mood to yield.

We have suggested that Violet should sleep with other people to save the family £200 a year. The suggestion was not made to allow us to live in luxury. All the young people are living in cottages, doing their own house work – their own cooking, and looking after their own children without any help whatever. The taxation (as you know!) is half our income . . . Violet is one of our family responsibilities. She is not our only duty. I do not believe it would harm her to be made to realise that it is a fact which she must face. I therefore consider she should continue to sleep in a ward with others.

The money for Violet's care was increasingly a matter for concern. As the war began to erode inherited capital and privilege, her family was no longer disposed to ignore the significant financial burden of St Andrew's fees. These had been covered by the income from Violet's own capital (built on the legacy left to her by her father, and a further trust fund of £2,500 set aside by her mother) until April 1940, at which time the deflationary impact of the war hit her fund, and the capital itself was being spent. Violet had thanked her father, in 1911, for 'the little fortune' he had given her, as it enabled her to be 'completely independent'. She had used her money frugally, only for it to be exhausted on her long-term confinement.

The cost of her care would have been considerably reduced had she been transferred to a convent nursing home, a request she continued to put forward, despite being refused at every turn. On 18 November 1944 she wrote another supplicant letter. She was now nearly seventy, and her handwriting had become shaky, spidery, but her tone was still firm. The letter was addressed to Her Royal Highness, The Princess Elizabeth, who had recently turned eighteen:

Your Royal Highness,

In the happiest period of your life, I make this request – that you write to the Home Secretary saying you will be glad if he will release me from this Mental Hospital so that I can go into a Convent. Your grandfather and grandmother – their Majesties King George V and Queen Mary visited us when they came to Ireland, and we were often at Buckingham Palace at parties as well as Courts . . . None of these worldly things matter. I am quite simply hoping that you have a *heart*. In 1926 I shot at Mussolini and was shut up in this Hospital 'for the course of his Majesty's pleasure.' I feel sure that your kind hearted grandfather would not take any pleasure in keeping me here any longer – 20 weary years and six months. [Here, Violet's maths failed her: she had been interned for eighteen years and six months. Unsurprisingly, given the monotony of her life, she had 'gained' two years of captivity.] I am now old, bedridden with very bad heart disease and other illnesses, and . . . very neglected and lonely. So I want to be sent to an RC Convent nursing Home where I can practice my religion, and also be nursed, as in a Convent there is never a shortage of nursing nuns and I will be cared for in my last days, and be perfectly happy and content, so you will not need to fear that I will ever shoot anyone again, as I am old and ill, and occupied in very quiet matters, mostly prayers.

Violet Gibson's name can now be added to those of the women in Princess Elizabeth's own family who were living out life sentences in obscurity, cut adrift from their family, disappeared.

Nerissa and Katherine Bowes Lyon were first cousins of Princess Elizabeth, nieces of her mother Elizabeth Bowes Lyon, King George VI's consort. The sisters were both 'born mentally impaired', though the impairment has always been ill-defined. At the time of Violet's (unsent) letter, they were twenty-two and fifteen years old respectively, and had just been removed from their family home and placed in the Royal Earlswood Hospital in Surrey, an imposing, grim, red-brick Victorian pile. On the same day, they were joined by three of their first cousins, also nieces of the queen – Idonea, Etheldreda and Rosemary Fane. A dramatic cull, within a single family, of those possessing what has been vaguely referred to as 'the fragile gene'.

The Bowes Lyon family informed *Burke's Peerage* in 1940 that Nerissa was dead. She actually died in Royal Earlswood forty-six years later, and was interred in what amounted to a pauper's grave, marked with a plastic tag bearing just a serial number and her name. Rosemary died in 1972 and Etheldreda in 1996, both while still institutionalised. Katherine, who at the time of writing is still living in a home in Surrey, remained a non-person for the British monarchy and aristocracy, listed as dead in the 1961 edition of *Burke's Peerage*. In 1996 she and Idonea were moved from Royal Earlswood to a care home nearby, their weekly fee of £771.49 paid for by the National Health Service. In 2001 the home, Ketwin House, was shut down following allegations that male members of staff had been washing female residents and that patients had been found wandering on dangerous country roads. When it closed, the two, who had been companions for nearly sixty years, were finally and painfully separated.

When Katherine's existence came to light in 2002, Harold Brooks-Baker of *Burke's Peerage* said he could find no listing of her in any lineage records. 'She appears to have just vanished into obscurity,' he said. No one at Glamis Castle, her ancestral home, claimed to know of her either: 'Her name doesn't ring any bells here. We can't throw any light on who she is at all.' A care worker who knew her told a journalist: 'She's a lovely person. She loves to watch TV, especially Royal weddings, although she was never told that a relative was getting married. She laughed all the way through Charles and Diana's wedding. She really could have prospered but instead she's been left to vegetate.'

The story of Nerissa and Katherine Bowes Lyon and the Fane girls has grim echoes in the myths surrounding the late Queen Mother's family seat at Glamis Castle, just outside Inverness. The castle is famed for the legend of the Monster of Glamis, the much-embellished tale of a deformed male heir whose existence was allegedly covered up by an entry in *Debrett's* in 1841 claiming he had died at birth. The story has it that he lived on for anything up to a century, severely mentally disabled and stunted and locked in a hidden room.

In the attics of family memory, there was no corner for the Bowes Lyon or the Fane girls. Violet, at least, knew who she was. And, at the last, after her death, she escaped being similarly obliterated. Against her entry in the current edition of *Burke's Peerage*, her legend is clearly writ: 'Went to Rome in 1926 and tried to assassinate Mussolini by shooting.'

V

By the Heels at Milano

'Fascism is not only a party: it is a regime. It is not only a regime: it is a faith. It is not only a faith, it is a religion . . . Are you ready to follow it?'

(Unanimous cry): 'Yes!'

'Follow it to the point of sacrifice?'

'Yes! Yes!'

'I will take your cries, then, as an oath . . . Long live Fascism! Long live Italy!'

This amatory duet took place between Mussolini (on the balcony) and the crowd (below) at Pesaro in August 1926. When push came to shove, Italians chose, quite sensibly, to reject the compact, to be Italians rather than Fascists, to spurn the Fascist nostrum of 'companions dead at my side, hopes consecrated with blood'. So it was that the masses, when their leader was arrested on King Vittorio Emanuele's orders on 25 July 1943, did nothing. Nowhere in the country did any serious gesture of protest occur at the overthrow of the man whom millions had supported passionately for decades. The attention of the crowd, concentrated breathlessly on Mussolini for twenty years, was suddenly released. Like Icarus falling out of the sky in Auden's poem, everything was turned away

> Quite leisurely from the disaster; the ploughman may
> Have heard the splash, the forsaken cry,
> But for him it was not an important failure . . .

In the end, it was an important failure, a comet's tail of defeat for which Italy paid a very high price.

Mussolini's arrest followed an all-night meeting of the Grand Council of Fascism at Palazzo Venezia on 24 July that culminated in a vote of no confidence. In the morning, he was back at his desk in Palazzo Venezia's enormous Sala del Mappamundo ('You virtually need a pair of binoculars to see him', quipped one journalist) as if nothing had happened. He then kept his bi-weekly appointment with the king at 5 p.m., arriving at the Villa Savoia in the same crumpled suit he had been wearing the night before. The king told him he had decided General Badoglio (the man who had offered to oppose Mussolini at the gates of Rome in 1922) should take over as head of government. A dazed Mussolini walked back to his car, but was politely intercepted by a captain of the *carabiniere* police (which had remained under royal control) and whisked off to imprisonment in a military hospital. Two days later he was escorted to the tiny island of Ponza, still wearing the same 'baggy, unpressed, shabby, blue-serge suit'. There, Tito Zaniboni, who was serving out his thirty-year sentence, observed Mussolini's white face as the boat drew into harbour. 'I shan't go for a walk again,' Zaniboni said. 'I don't want to risk a quarrel with a ruined man.' It was a noble sentiment, but he needn't have worried – Mussolini was put in a dilapidated house some distance from the main settlement.

Allied forces had landed in Sicily a few weeks earlier, having bombed and then seized the 'impregnable' islands of Pantelleria and Lampedusa, the latter at the cost to the invaders of one man bitten by a donkey. A vast armada of ships covering a thousand square miles of ocean off the Italian coast was fast disgorging troops and materiél for the land assault. Ponza was now militarily insecure, so on 7 August Mussolini was moved to a naval base off Sardinia. This, he was told by the officer guarding him, was for his own safety. 'Nonsense', Mussolini retorted angrily. 'It isn't nonsense,' came the reply. 'The Fascists [seem] to have disappeared. There are signs of reaction against them and against you everywhere. The offices of *Il popolo d'Italia* have been attacked in Milan. I myself saw a bust of you on the floor of a public lavatory in Ancona.' Mussolini ridiculed, murdered in effigy. It was an ill omen. A few weeks later, he was moved to Campo Imperatore, a ski resort at the Gran Sasso, 6,500 feet up in the Abruzzo Apennines – 'the highest prison in the world', Mussolini declared with some pride.

Meantime, General Badoglio and the king were fumbling to get out of what they now called the 'Fascist war'. On 8 September 1943 the surrender to the Allies was made official, but early the following morning the king and his government, taking fright at the advancing German line, lifted their skirts and fled Rome. As did Ezra Pound, who for two years had been broadcasting his support of Mussolini from the studio of Rome Radio. The exercise – a compost heap of hate – was to cost him thirteen years in a lunatic asylum after the war, and a reputation as the worst kind of Fascist, the intellectual Fascist, a 'filthy apologist and mouther of slogans which serve men of power'. Pound, who was now wanted for treason in the US, made his way back to his home in Rapallo, on the Ligurian coast, by train and on foot, and waited for the American military police to knock on his door.

As the Germans pushed southwards, the Allies were preparing to move northwards. On 12 September, amidst all the chaos, Mussolini was dramatically plucked from his mountain prison by an SS glider team and flown to Munich for a reunion with his family, who had made their way to Nazi sanctuary via diverse routes. A week later, Mussolini broadcast from Munich: 'Only blood can cancel so humiliating a page from the history of the *patria*.' Hitler, listening to the radio in his office, intoned '*Duce! Duce! Duce!*' with malicious pleasure. 'In the last analysis, he is nothing but an Italian, and he can't get away from that heritage.' Mussolini, who had repeatedly demanded that 'Italy be treated by the great nations of the world like a sister and not like a waitress', was now chained to a dictator who would never treat Italians as partners, 'but always as slaves'.

On 4 June 1944 Rome fell to the Allies. Two days later, D-Day, they landed at Normandy and began the relentless push into Europe. By 25 August they had entered Paris, and a month later they reached the German border. On the eastern front the Soviets slowly clawed back their own territory and by late 1944 had pushed the Germans out of the Baltic States, Finland, Romania, Bulgaria, and much of Poland, Hungary, Czechoslovakia and Yugoslavia. Mussolini, installed by Hitler in the Republic of Salò, headquartered in the eponymous town on Lake Garda – the puppet regime famously portrayed by film-maker Pier Paolo Pasolini as a sadistic pantomime of sodomy and shit-eating – spent the rest of the war, as he put it, trying to 'stand erect in quicksand'. The conjuring trick, at the last, had failed the conjuror – 'Hitler and I have surrendered ourselves to our illusions like a couple of lunatics,' Mussolini groaned.

'The bullets pass. Mussolini remains.' So Mussolini once bragged to a journalist. 'I'm convinced I shall die in my bed when my work for the Greater Italy is done.' His powers of prophecy were woefully lacking. On 28 April 1945 (a fateful almost-anniversary: the same month that Violet Gibson had shot him twenty years earlier), the bullets finally reached Mussolini. According to the accepted version, he and Clara Petacci died at 4.10 p.m. at the gates of a villa overlooking Lake Como. Petacci was said to have stumbled on the wet grass in her high-heeled black suede shoes. Pushed against a wall with Mussolini, she threw her arms around him. A partisan shouted to her to let go, then pulled the trigger of his sub-machine gun, but it jammed and he had to borrow a French sub-machine gun with a tricolour ribbon tied round the end of the barrel. At this point, Mussolini apparently cried, 'Aim at my heart!' His autopsy report suggests a less heroic final gesture: two entry–exit perforations of the right arm indicated attempted bullet deflection by the victim. The autopsy, carried out on 30 April at Milan's Institute of Legal Medicine, revealed that four bullets had struck his descending aorta with a bursting rupture, an instantaneous lethal injury. Other bullets were lodged in the clavicle, neck, thyroid gland and thigh.

The bodies were brought to Milan's Piazzale Loreto the following morning, Sunday 29 April, and posed on the ground, Mussolini holding a Fascist *gagliardetto*, or sceptre, now a hollow symbol of power, his head resting on Clara's breast. Crowds spat at their corpses, kicked and hit out at them with sticks and bare hands. 'Make a speech now! Make a speech now!' somebody jeered. 'The breathless, bloody scene had an air of inevitability,' wrote *New Yorker* correspondent Philip Hamburger. 'You had the feeling, as you have at the final curtain of a good play, that events could not have been otherwise.'

This slice of hell – thousands of partisans firing their machine guns into the air, the cadavers swelling beneath the hot sun, the pressing, taunting crowd – received its final embellishment when the bodies were hoisted up onto the rusty gantry of a disused Esso gas station, there to hang by the ankles. Brain matter seeped out from the right side of Mussolini's head, which, after its assault by the crowd, was 'misshapen because of destruction of the cranium'. Other injuries inflicted after death included a lacerated eyeball, 'crushed due to escape of vitreous matter'; a fractured upper jaw 'with multiple lacerations of the palate'; crushed cerebellum, pons, midbrain and part of the occipital lobes; a 'massive fracture at the base of the cranium with bone slivers forced into the sinus cavities'.

When Achille Starace – a fanatical killer and former Secretary of the Fascist Party – was brought into the square in an open truck several hours later, he almost fainted at the sight. Starace was shot in the back and winched up onto the beam, from where a partisan turned toward the crowd and made a broad gesture of finality. 'There were no roars or bloodcurdling yells,' reported Philip Hamburger. 'There was only silence, and then, suddenly, a sigh – a deep, moaning sound, seemingly expressive of release from something dark and fetid. "Look at them now," an old man beside me kept saying. "Just look at them now."'

*

'There is too much future, and nobody but me and Muss and half a dozen others to attend to it,' Ezra Pound once declaimed. Mussolini had been Pound's idol for twenty years. He kept a scrapbook of his life and work, wrote to him frequently and published a book comparing him to Thomas Jefferson. He met Il Duce only once, and had been so pleased that he hung the official notice granting the interview on the wall of his apartment in Rapallo. But what was 'Brother Benito' now, if not a parcel of oozing matter dangling upside-down at a petrol station? And what of Il Duce's companions, those 'jovial comrades' remembered in Pound's translation of Villon's 'Testament', who once 'sang so well, talked so well / And so excelled in word and deed'? They, too, had been shot, to be mourned in Pound's 'Canto 84', which had a place for more or less any minor Axis celebrity who came to grief.

And where was Pound himself, if not a prized exhibit on display in a reinforced steel-mesh cage at a US army detention centre near Pisa, a camp built to hold 'the slime and filth of the whole Mediterranean Theater of Operations'? There, on a writing table built for him out of a packing crate by a black American soldier (a 'coon', in Pound's lexicon), 'Uncle Ez' bashed out his Fascist martyrology on a typewriter. Fellow poet Norman Rosten urged the case for him to be repatriated to the States and tried as a traitor, for which the maximum penalty was the death sentence. 'It is unfortunate indeed that Mr Pound considered his poisonous mouthings akin to the innocence of poetry,' Rosten warned. 'It was not. And Mr Pound shall find death no clever metaphor.'*

And what of the future Mussolini had promised to arrange for Italy, the 'arms for ten million men, and fighting airplanes to obscure the sun!', the army that would 'vomit death at all who block our way to greatness'? It never materialised. The best Mussolini could do was to sick up a cruel joke on his nation. Reprisals continued for months after the end of the war, exacting a death toll estimated at twelve thousand. The war itself, so blithely entered by Mussolini in June 1940, had cost Italy more than four hundred thousand lives, not counting those whom the Italians had killed and maimed. Adding the body count from the imperial campaigns in Libya, Somalia and Ethiopia (where mustard gas and arsine were used with murderous abandon†), Mussolini's dictatorship must have sent early to the grave at least a million people, possibly more. A cruel record, and one that should not be obscured, as it routinely is, by the dogmatic propaganda of lesser-evilism that invites us to consider the outrages of Nazism and Stalinism as morally more repugnant because they were numerically greater.

* After being flown back to Washington in November 1945, Pound became a full and voluntary partner in the use of insanity to escape trial, stating 'categorically that he is not of sound mind and could not participate effectively in his own defense'. He was sent to St Elizabeths Hospital, where he spent the next thirteen years holding court, surrounded by acolytes who could visit whenever they liked. He was so happy in the 'bughouse', as he called it, that he lingered for weeks after he was told he could leave. He eventually sailed back to Italy and upon arriving at the port of Naples he gave a Fascist salute from the deck of the ship.
† Only in 1996 did the Italian Ministry of Defence finally concede that these chemical agents and arsine had been used in Africa.

Nor should history be allowed to dismiss Fascism as the plaything of a buffoon or a madman, though Mussolini may indeed have been both. 'Fascism is not insanity,' said Nancy Cunard, 'unless evil itself, all evil, be insanity.' Six months after Italy's entry into the war, Winston Churchill had declared that the responsibility for the Italian choice was borne by 'one man and one man alone' (the man he had long endorsed as Italy's saviour). There being every reason to single out Mussolini for blame, it was easy to overlook the embarrassing and cynical *sauve qui peut* of the old ruling elite which, having bungled the attempt to change sides in September 1943, deserted the country. (Notwithstanding, the management of Madame Tussaud's moved Vittorio Emanuele out of a group of Axis leaders including Mussolini, Hitler, Göring, Goebbels and Ribbentrop and repositioned him among the American presidents, right between Hoover and Franklin Roosevelt.) Piero Gobetti, who recognised very early the tyrannical orientation of Fascism (his reward was to receive a bludgeoning by *squadristi* in 1924, from which he died), argued that it represented the 'autobiography of the nation', an accretion of all the ills of Italian society. In particular, he claimed, Fascism continued a political tradition of compromise and opportunism.

'Fascism only regiments those who can't do anything without it,' Ezra Pound said, and though his judgements were often wildly distorted, in this he was right. For all its high-octane, vitalist rhetoric, its new roads and high-speed trains, Fascism actually profited from inertia. Politically, the regime was daring in words but conservative and prudent in deeds; it was a revolution which, lacking a central ideological core, only ever revolved around itself – a vortex of narcissism. The contradiction was lost on the cowlike crowds who stopped thinking for themselves, preferring to chew the cud of more than two decades of stupefaction.

There were exceptions. Many Italians remained quietly non-Fascist (by definition, their numbers are hard to calculate); many sheltered Jews from deportation; many others grasped the opportunity to wrest Italy free from the regime by joining the resistance (including the boxer and Fascist idol Primo Carnera, who became a partisan as early as 1937). The early torchbearers for resistance, the political prisoners and would-be assassins who had rotted for years in Fascist prisons or on the islands, were now liberated and embraced as heroes. Tito Zaniboni was freed by the Allies on 8 September 1943 (he resumed his political career, dying in 1960); Gino Lucetti made a daring escape from prison in 1943, but was killed shortly afterwards during a bombing raid on Ischia.

Only Violet Gibson remained captive, forgotten by all but a few. Those who did remember her, like Chief Superintendent Epifanio Pennetta, knew nothing of her fate once she had been spirited out of Italy. Pennetta himself was retired, but in 1946 he was called to give evidence at the retrial of Giacomo Matteotti's killers, who finally received the long sentences they were due for a political assassination that has never been fully exorcised from Italian memory. For Pennetta, it was satisfaction of a kind. In the case of Violet Gibson, he would have to live with the enduring frustration of being denied the chance to prove his theory that she was part of a conspiracy.

VI

Casting Off

In November 1946, a friend from Violet's youth, Countess Winterton, wrote to the medical superintendent of St Andrew's to ask if she was still a patient there. The Countess explained that

... during a recent illness I had a nurse who was her nurse for two and a half years and she cannot understand why Miss Gibson was not let out when we went to war with Italy. Naturally, at the time she shot Mussolini, to say she was mad was the only way to get out of an awkward situation, but she cannot have been certified now for that.

From Budapest came a similar enquiry from Fanny Esterházy, who said she had once been 'a great friend' of Violet's. Was she still at St Andrew's? If so, that was 'very sad'. The medical superintendent confirmed that she was, and explained,

With advancing years she is now more or less constantly confined to bed but she is mentally still alert and takes a full interest in current affairs and events. After so many years residence here she is now more or less resigned to her position and naturally we do everything possible to make her as comfortable and contented as we can. The ideas which originally led to her admission to hospital still persist but are now possibly held with less conviction.

Violet, after two decades in a lunatic asylum, and now seventy years old, was in no way resigned to her position. She insisted that it was 'not too late to put the wrongs of the world to right by releasing her', and that her survival amongst people determined to ignore her health was 'a miracle'. In March 1947 she announced that current severe weather conditions were 'the result of the treatment she has received from fellow beings and she predicts even worse to come'. In July 1948 she told the medical superintendent that she had agreed to be moved from her room to a ward only on condition 'there would always be a nurse in it capable of under-standing my difficult and rare pulse – a good Catholic who would realise when the moment came to send for the Last Sacraments', and that this promise having been neglected, she wanted him to 'return some of the money you have been taking for my "care" . . . Though not a Scotch man I do not like paying through the nose and getting nothing for it.'

Violet fought on, but Constance, three years her junior, was exhausted. Far back in 1927, Constance had rightly feared the responsibility that would devolve on her once Violet had been retrieved from Rome, but she had discharged her legal duties as official petitioner (the person legally responsible for her commit-tal and bi-annual visits), and gone far beyond that, travelling fre-quently to Northampton on the train from London to visit Violet, who on more than one occasion treated her with contempt or even refused to see her. If Constance's good nature was often strained, it was hardly surprising; if she was unresponsive to Violet's request to be moved to a convent, it was most likely because she, Constance, could expect little or no real assistance from the rest of the family should something go wrong. For all these years, Constance, the designated nanny-in-chief, had been left to man-age the intractable Violet on her own. Indeed, when she told St Andrew's in November 1946 that she wanted to 'retire' as Violet's petitioner – 'I am not strong enough for the continued strain' – she was forced to acknowledge that 'There is no one in the family to replace me.' The obvious candidate was Violet's nephew, Edward, Lord Ashbourne, who had already reluctantly assumed oversight of her financial affairs (the practicalities of which were still left to Constance, however). But Edward refused the role for a further six years, during which time the care-frayed Constance, by now afflicted with heart problems herself, was obliged to continue the dreary, disheartening visits to St Andrew's.

While this unhappy arrangement prevailed, Violet continued her campaign for release, writing in the spring of 1950 to the Official Solicitor, who was charged with oversight of lunatics' legal rights. Amazingly, the medical superintendent of St Andrew's seemed finally disposed to back the plan, informing the Official Solicitor on 29 April 1950 that

Miss Gibson is now more or less constantly confined to bed but from the physical point of view she could, I think, travel by ambulance to George's Retreat, particularly in view of the fact that her confinement to bed is largely the outcome of her hypochondriasis. I do not know whether the Home Office still retains an interest in this lady's location but I am informed that when she arrived here they desired to be informed of any change from this hospital.

The Home Office retained no interest in Violet. Her file had long been closed. So there was nothing now to stop her being transferred – except Constance, who considered that 'To start in new surroundings in the care of those who do not know [Violet] would indeed make life difficult for her.' Beyond overriding Violet's wishes, Constance had a practical motive for refusing the move: she had applied to the recently created National Health Service to accept financial responsibility for Violet's maintenance at St Andrew's. In support of this application, the deputy medical superintendent, Dr Tennent, informed the NHS that Violet was

... a very distinguished lady who might have altered the whole course of history if she had been a little more accurate when deciding to dispose of Mussolini in the early 1920's ... During the past six months her physical health has declined and she is at present confined to bed more or less constantly. Nevertheless she is still fully in touch with her surroundings and is in my opinion the type of patient who on medical grounds requires the special amenities of this hospital.

Once again, St. Andrew's was inconsistent in its presentation of Violet's needs, on the one hand conceding that her move to a convent nursing home was appropriate, and on the other claiming that it was in her interests that she stay where she was. Shortly after, the NHS confirmed that it would pay for Violet's basic care. The stocks of her remaining capital were sold out, leaving her dwindling annual income insufficient to pay for a private room, which meant she had to be moved 'to less expensive quarters'.

For the Honourable Violet Gibson, the downgrading of her status, or what was left of it, came as a severe blow. In January 1951 she contracted a high temperature that persisted for four months. In early February, Constance was informed that her sister was 'suffering from influenza and her condition is now giving rise to some anxiety. She is still running a temperature and is mentally more confused and restless than we have previously known her . . . I shall keep you informed of any further change, but I feel that you would be wise to pay an early visit.' Violet remained in bed in a dormitory in the cheaper quarters, under constant observation. At the end of April, it was reported that her 'general physical health has been deteriorating during the past month, during which time has become increasingly weaker and has lost much flesh'. She now weighed less than six stone. Again, Constance was advised to 'pay an early visit', although her sister was not thought to be in 'immediate danger of death'.

Violet did not die, but she was so feeble after the long illness that doctors considered it 'doubtful if she will be able to leave her bed again'. Thoughts of a final reckoning pressed in on her, one outcome of which was a reconciliation of sorts between her and Constance. In May 1951, Constance reported the softening of mood in a letter to Dr Tennent:

I think Violet enjoyed my visit today as much as I did. We had a very pleasant chat. I will visit her again next Friday and continue to visit her on Fridays unless I hear from you to the contrary. I am sending her a child's story my mother gave her many years ago. It has Violet's name in it from Mother.

'I am sure she will appreciate the story book,' replied Dr Tennent, 'because she is still very much in touch with the past.' He added that, following Constance's visit, Violet appeared to be 'a little better', and was making 'ardent appeals' to be allowed to leave her bed and go outside to feed the birds.

By the autumn, Violet was still extremely frail, but twice a week she was taken in a wheelchair to Mass in a small Catholic chapel

that had been installed in the main building, to which she had
donated a pair of candlesticks and a crucifix. Constance continued
her weekly visits – 'as they break the monotony for her' – and in
December Violet entrusted her with the details of her last will and
testament. She said that she wanted to be buried in the Catholic
part of the cemetery of St Andrew's with all the rites of the
Catholic Church (had her wish been granted, her final resting
place would have been in ground that had supported a Cluniac
foundation, the original St Andrew's Priory of 1100). She desired
that the remainder of the money settled on her after her father's
death be withdrawn from the settlement and held in trust for various bequests, including to the Reverend Father Foley of the
Cathedral of Northampton to celebrate a requiem Mass and
Masses for her soul; and to Mrs Emily Corner of 29 Upper Moor
End Road, Cheltenham (as Violet explained in her will, 'Mrs
Corner nursed me for many years after a serious operation and
took no money for her devotion and by so doing saved me many
hundreds of pounds which I would have had to pay for nurses').
There was to be £100 for the erection of a tombstone over her
grave, and the rest of her estate, after funeral and testamentary
expenses, was left in trust for her sister-in-law the Honourable
Mrs Caroline Gibson (Victor's second wife). There was one final
wish, which Constance communicated to Dr Tennent in a letter
dated 3 December 1951: 'Violet and I have agreed that as she wants
only Catholics near her when she is dying I would rather not be
present so when you notify the end is near I will not go to her.'

In this way, Violet dispensed with the remaining members of
her immediate family, including Constance. Marianne, as a
Catholic (if not as a sympathetic witness), would have qualified
for the deathbed scene, but she was to die before Violet. The
Protestant Elsie had died in 1943, a year after Willie. That left
Frances, who had not seen Violet since the visit to St Andrew's in
1927 when she had imagined herself into a scene worthy of Wilkie
Collins's *The Woman in White*, whereby Violet would overpower
her and, stealing her identity, make good her escape from the

asylum. Frances, who loathed Catholicism, had remained a staunch Christian Scientist and in 1952, after realising that Violet's membership of that church had never been formally relinquished, could not restrain herself from communicating her discovery to Violet. It was a shockingly insensitive gesture, one that smacked of revenge, and Violet reacted with predictable revulsion:

Dear Frances,

Your letter merely reminded me of a so called religion principly [*sic*] regarded as a group of totally unprincipled *liars*. Your letter proves this to be true. I feel quite shocked by your utterly unprincipled letter. For something like *fifty years* I have been a devout Roman Catholic. You have known this, and it is most dishonourable of you to pretend you did not know. It proves what people say of C.S. [Christian Science]. It is a small body of *utterly unscrupulous liars*.

Certainly take my name off any membership with a Christian Science Church. And – if I ever give a thought – it is that they be swept off the face of the earth.

Violet Gibson

'Keep this letter so that you cannot say you have not received it', Violet scribbled on the back of the envelope after sealing it. The envelope was opened not by Frances, but by staff at St Andrew's, who placed it, together with its contents, in Violet's file – and there it remains, unstamped and unsent.

*

At the time Violet was casting off her family, Lucia Joyce arrived at St Andrew's with a few possessions and a carton of Lucky Strikes, having been cast off by hers. She was committed on 15 March 1951, aged forty-three, in what must have been a condition of total disorientation. For the past twenty years she had been shuttled between clinics and asylums, probed by psychiatrists (including Carl Jung), treated with barbiturates and injections of seawater and animal serum, and wrestled into straitjackets by men in white jackets. Diagnoses ranged from hebephrenic psychosis to schizophrenia to nothing much wrong.

Born in 1907 in the pauper's ward of a hospital in Trieste, Lucia grew up in cheap hotels or rented rooms where her parents James and Nora survived on handouts. By the age of thirteen, she had lived in three different countries. After the First World War, the family moved to Paris, where she took up dancing – the new, anti-balletic dance of modernist and Surrealist groups – with some success (in 1928 she appeared in Jean Renoir's film *The Little Match Girl*). Her father adored her and treated her, much like his writing, as a kind of intellectual and psychic cryptogram (she once described herself as 'a crossword puzzle'), but her mother and brother Giorgio were less enamoured. When she was twenty, she fell in love with her father's assistant, Samuel Beckett, who treated her like 'hors d'oeuvre' and stated that he was more interested in James than in her. Thereafter her behaviour became increasingly erratic, her dance career slipping away as the 'sinister choreography of her unconscious' began to envelop her. In 1932, at a party to celebrate James's fiftieth birthday, she threw a chair at her mother. Amid the ensuing dismay, Giorgio alone responded to her action without hesitation: he took her immediately to a *maison de santé*. He thereby changed her fate. She was twenty-five, and except for a brief exile in Ireland, would spend the next fifty years – the rest of her life – in institutions.

The outbreak of the Second World War magnified the displacement of the ever-peripatetic Joyces, who found themselves in Zurich while Lucia, in a clinic in Ivry, was stuck in occupied France. The already dislocated Lucia was now permanently split off from her family. Despite moving heaven and earth to get her out, James died suddenly of peritonitis in January 1941. Nora and Giorgio abandoned her at Ivry, and there she remained until 1951, when a friend intervened and arranged for her to be moved to St Andrew's.

'The poor child is not a raving lunatic, just a poor child who tried to do too much, to understand too much,' James Joyce once pleaded in his daughter's behalf. Lucia's biographer, Carol Loeb Shloss, has argued passionately that 'Lucia's self-understanding deserves a place in the historical record', but access to her records has been checked by Giorgio's son Stephen, the keeper of the Joyce flame. At St Andrew's, her files are stored in a filing cabinet next to Violet's, but permission to read them is denied. Lucia, who for long stretches would refuse to speak, remains a silent – and silenced – riddle.

Lucia Joyce in her room at St Andrew's, 1977

VII

Death in Exile

For Violet, and now for Lucia, the drag of half-dead days stretched endlessly ahead. Constance was finally relieved of her role of petitioner in October 1952, when Edward, Vice-Admiral Lord Ashbourne, CB, DSO (as he styled himself), begrudgingly assumed the position. Writing to Dr Tennent, he gave it as understood that he would be expected to take on the two annual visits to Violet. Was this, he enquired, a statutory requirement? 'It is a statutory requirement that a responsible person must visit your aunt once every six months during her residence in hospital under certificate,' Dr Tennent replied. Ashbourne duly fixed a date for his first visit, but was at pains to give notice that he would only be staying for 'a quarter of an hour or so'.

To his relief, there were few visits left to undertake. By late 1954, Violet, now seventy-eight, was dangerously weak. Her mordant wit was still in play, however. 'I am at once alive and not alive – a unique state,' she told a doctor in December. He noted that she believed she had no pulse and was therefore a living corpse; she 'regards herself as a medical curiosity and would like to go to an international centre for cardiac research'.

On 11 September 1955, Ashbourne was warned, prior to one of his visits, that he would find that

... she has become much more frail during recent months and mentally she is also more confused. Over the weekend she was very perturbed and for a time, at any rate, believed that she was on board a ship and at sea. Today, however, she is more lucid but in general she is failing both mentally and physically.

A few months later, she suffered 'a small cerebral thrombosis during the night', and the following morning was 'somnolent and confused. Not easy to rouse.'

The slide continued for several more months, and in March 1956 Ashbourne was advised that she was 'now very frail and is looking pale and weak'. Though she was 'still bright and her attention can be easily obtained', he was advised to 'visit her at your early convenience if you so desire'. 'I would be grateful if you could let me know if she has indicated any wish to see any of her relations,' Ashbourne wrote by return. 'If she has, I will certainly do my best to pay her a visit in the near future. If she has not, I will leave it for a month or so, when it will be more convenient.'

Constance responded differently to the bulletins on Violet's failing health. Despite having just come out of a nursing home 'where she went because of the condition of her heart' which her doctor had said 'could never be cured and she would always have to be very careful in future', Constance was begging a friend to organise a taxi to take her to Northampton. The friend, worried for Constance (who was not strong enough even to write a letter), resisted, and wrote to St Andrew's asking that they no longer inform Constance of Violet's condition as it was too distressing for her 'to think there is nothing she can do for her sister'. There was nothing she could do. She would not see Violet again.

A few days later, as Violet's life was leaking away, Ashbourne wrote again to St Andrew's:

In the event of the death of my aunt, The Hon Violet Gibson, I would be grateful if, so far as the press and publicity in general is concerned, you could let the matter pass unnoticed. I appreciate of course that certain normal formalities must be observed, but if press publicity can be avoided, so much the better.

On Wednesday, 2 May 1956, at 12.45 a.m., Violet Gibson, the woman who shot Mussolini, died.

Epilogue

I am – yet what I am, none cares or knows;
My friends forsake me like a memory lost:
I am the self-consumer of my woes –
. . . And yet I am and love – like vapours tossed

Into the nothingness of scorn and noise
Into the living sea of waking dreams
Where there is neither sense of life or joys
But the vast shipwreck of my life's esteems . . .

JOHN CLARE, 'I Am'

For the last thirty years of her life, Violet was compelled to live at odds with her conscience and her desires. Even in death, her wishes – as to the disposal of her estate, her body, and her memory – were denied. Violet left money for a requiem Mass at the Catholic cathedral of Northampton. The Mass was given not in the cathedral, but in the far humbler surroundings of St Gregory's, a local Catholic church. She requested to be buried in the Catholic part of St Andrew's cemetery 'with all the rights of the Catholic Mass'. She was in fact interred at Kingsthorpe Cemetery, a dreary expanse of flatland butting up against a noisy through-road of Northampton. (Lucia Joyce, who died in 1982, three decades after she was committed to St Andrew's, is also buried here, just feet away from Violet.)

As per Lord Ashbourne's request, there was no public announcement of Violet's death. There was no friend, no member of the family present at the burial, not even Constance, who was too frail to make the last journey to Northampton (she died three years later). Ashbourne himself declined to attend, settling the question of his aunt's remains and the closing of her affairs by correspondence. On 4 June 1956, fully a month after her death, Dr Tennent wrote to tell him that 'Fortunately, she did not have much suffering and her passing was a peaceful one.' There were, he added, 'no matters outstanding with the accounting department'.

Graveyards are crammed with narratives, all of which end in death. Gravestones are the permanent marks we leave to give notice to future generations that we were once in the world – the sign made, just as we leave, that we were here. They are laid out in neat rows, a grid to impose order on the enormous tangle of human existence. In her will, Violet had set aside £100 for the erection of a gravestone. In this, as in everything else, she was short-changed. Above her grave, plot number 12411, is a bland cross in cheap grey quarry stone. Its inscription – 'Violet Gibson, 1876–1956.' – is equally parsimonious. The punctuation is highly unusual, the result of the stone-cutter following Ashbourne's text, which was communicated by telegram.

The comma: it suggests something to follow – a sentiment perhaps, a memento mori, or words that supply a brief record of the life. A comma is a breathing space, a tiny pause, before a further thought. Here, it is merely an awkward hiccough. 'What is life?' asked John Clare in his poem of the same title. 'Its length? A minute's pause, a moment's thought.' Nothing follows the comma on Violet's gravestone, except the dates of her birth and death. Full stop. Set in stone. Her extraordinary story lies hidden between the comma and the full stop.

The Honourable Violet Gibson deserved better.

Acknowledgements

Each historical archive is a world within a world, governed by its own apparently unfathomable laws. I am indebted to those many custodians of the past who unravelled the mysteries of their collections to me, in particular Dottoressa Maria Pina di Simone and the staff at the Archivio Centrale dello Stato, Rome; Federica Onelli at the Ministero degli Affari Esteri, Rome; Ted Jackson at Georgetown University Library, Washington; Liz Ridley and Bobbie Judd at St Andrew's Healthcare archives, Northampton; the archivists and librarians at the National Library of Ireland, Dublin; and in London, at the Public Records Office, the House of Lords Record Office, the British Library and the London Library.

The current Lord Ashbourne kindly allowed me to explore the contents of an old leather travelling case belonging to Violet, his great-aunt. I am very grateful for access to this rich cache of documents and photographs, and for permission to quote from Ashbourne family papers from various sources. Thanks also to Helen McTaggart for sharing her recollections of a 1977 visit to Lucia Joyce at St Andrew's, and for lending me the photograph of Lucia in the asylum, published here for the first time.

Neil Belton, my editor at Faber and Faber, threw himself into this project with his customary conviction and enthusiasm, despite the flimsiest of outlines, and has provided invaluable comments over several drafts. Unfailingly generous in his attention and encouragement, he is one of the last great editors. Sara Bershtel at Metropolitan Books has also been tireless, a whirlwind of energy, sweeping away dead wood and thinning overhanging branches. My agent Felicity Rubinstein, at Lutyens and

Rubinstein, has taken care of me in ways that far exceed the bounds of duty. I am truly grateful.

In 2006, I applied to the Authors' Foundation for a grant to tide me along. To my amazement, a cheque arrived some weeks later in the post. Like an unexpected legacy, it opened up the sky to me – and no aunt had to die falling from a horse in Bombay. My thanks to the awards secretary and panel of the Authors' Foundation and K. Blundell Trust for this vital assistance.

Craig Raine published a version of the opening sequence of this book in his tri-quarterly magazine, *Areté*, in 2005. Then and subsequently he has given me help and advice, turning the manuscript around at a point when it was awkwardly skewed. A great mentor and friend. As is Ann Pasternak Slater, a generous provider of intellectual and gastronomic sustenance over many years. Carmen Callil's belief in the importance of telling this story was unflagging. She read and marked up an early draft, and I hope I have done justice both to her editorial wisdom and a great friendship.

For initiating me into the workings of the Lebel revolver, and teaching me everything I now know about guns, my thanks to Jason Abbot (with apologies that I remain as poor a shooter as Violet). For their support and hospitality in Rome, warm thanks to Domitilla Ruffo, Fabio Fassone, Filippo Porcari, Flavia Porcari, Frank Dabell and Jay Weissberg. I was greatly assisted by my brothers: Hugo Saunders, for his promise to read this book, and Alexander Stonor Saunders, for his eternal vigilance over the question of opening lines. I am also grateful to Mary Stonor Saunders, Olivia Jackson Daniels (a budding historian), and to my mother, Julia Stonor, who, in the days before the wondrous arrival of the digitised online archive of *The Times*, elegantly transcribed the relevant articles from the originals, bound in huge volumes in the London Library. A labour of love, one of many.

Finally, thanks to Nick Hewer, Alvin Caudwell, Anna Mike, Roger Thornham, Gavin Houghton, John and Annoushka Ayton, Tom Cotton and Conrad Roeber for love and support; to Timothy Radcliffe OP for a joyous and sustaining friendship, and for being appropriately contrite at handing in his latest book way ahead of me; and to Fiona Burton, to whom this book is dedicated, for her professional insight, galvanising encouragement and the use of a well-appointed shed in her garden. A room of one's own. Priceless.

Sources

ARCHIVAL SOURCES

PUBLIC RECORDS OFFICE, LONDON (PRO)

Ministry of Health. Confidential Registered Files, 'Attempted Assassination of Sig. Mussolini: Detention of Dangerous Lunatics'. PRO/MH79/262

Home Office. Registered Papers, Supplementary Disturbances: Attack on Mussolini by Miss Violet Gibson. PRO/HO144/7950

Foreign Office. Political Departments: General Correspondence from 1906. Italy, Central. PRO/FO371/12195 and PRO/FO371/12196

Foreign Office. General Correspondence. Italy. PRO/FO371/11385, PRO/FO371/11398 and PRO/FO371/11399

German Foreign Ministry Archives: Captured Records. PRO/GFM36/2

ARCHIVIO CENTRALE DELLO STATO, ROME (ACS)

Ministero dell'Interno. Direzione Generale della Pubblica Sicurezza. 'S. E. Mussolini: Attentato, Violet Gibson'. ACS/PS/J5/B.145, ACS/PS/H2/16792 and ACS/PS/H2/16793

Segreteria Particolare del Duce, Carteggio Riservato (1922–43). Gibson. Attentato del 7 Aprile 1926 contro la persona di S.E. Il Capo del Governo ad opera di Violet Gibson. ACS/SPDCR/64/377/R.1 and ACS/SPDCR/64/377/R.2

Tribunale Speciale per la Difesa dello Stato. Violet Gibson. ACS/TSDS/40–41/B.6 and ACS/TSDS/41–42/B.7

MINISTERO DEGLI AFFARI ESTERI, ROME (MAE)

Ambasciata a Londra, 1860–1950. Attentato a Mussolini. MAE/B.616/F2/1 and MAE/B.616/F2/2

PARLIAMENTARY ARCHIVES, HOUSE OF LORDS RECORD OFFICE, LONDON (PA)

Papers of Edward Gibson, First Baron Ashbourne (PA/ASH)
Papers of John St Loe Strachey (PA/STR)

SPECIAL COLLECTIONS DIVISION, GEORGETOWN UNIVERSITY
LIBRARY (GUL)

Sir Shane Leslie Papers: William Gibson Correspondence (GUL/LESLIE/B.1/18
and GUL/LESLIE/B.1/19)

ASHBOURNE FAMILY PRIVATE PAPERS, SUSSEX

Private Collection of Lord Ashbourne. Violet Gibson's travelling case (TC)

ST ANDREW'S HOSPITAL, NORTHAMPTON, ARCHIVE (SAH)

Patient Records: Violet Gibson (SAH/VG).

PART ONE: REVELATION

1: NOW

4 'as if she was trying . . .': Sr Riccarda Hambrough, quoted in Epifanio
  Pennetta to Procuratore del Re, Rome, 10 April 1926, ACS/PS/H2/16792
– 'a half-smile': ibid.
– 'I didn't realise . . .' Violet, quoted in ibid.
5 'red volumes . . .': Edith Wharton, *Italian Backgrounds* (Hopewell, New Jersey,
  1998), p. 85
– 'an age to come . . .': Virginia Woolf, *A Room of One's Own* (London, 1982), p. 98
– 'unmitigated masculinity': ibid.
– 'muscles', 'extraordinary vitality': Lady Asquith, quoted in R. J. B. Bosworth,
  Mussolini (London, 2002), p. 212
6 'quite simple and *natural*': Clementine Churchill, quoted in ibid.
7 'Everyone who came to Rome . . .': D. Darrah, *Hail Caesar!* (Boston, 1936), p.
  100
– 'were constantly trying to catch . . .': Sr Caterina Flanagan, quoted in
  Pennetta to Procuratore del Re, 10 April 1926, ACS/PS/H2/16792
– 'elderly widows . . .': Dino Grandi, quoted in Bosworth, *Mussolini*, p. 304
8 'the muster, the march . . .': ibid., p. 172
– 'Edict Bans Whiskers': 'Rome Cabbies Must Shave', *New York Times*, 10
  March 1926
– 'I wanted to die . . .': Violet, quoted in Epifanio Pennetta to Procuratore del
  Re, 8 April 1926, ACS/PS/H2/16792
9 'Saint Sebastian . . .': Margherita Sarfatti, *Dux* (Milan, 1926), p. 185
10 'in case his political enemies . . .': 'Mussolini Trionfante', *Time*, 19 April 1926
– 'I like to live dangerously': Benito Mussolini, *Scritti e discorsi di Benito
  Mussolini*, vol. V (Milan, 1934–9), p. 390
13 'The poets and the artisans . . .': 'Giovinezza', quoted in Christopher Duggan,
  The Force of Destiny: A History of Italy since 1796 (London, 2007), p. 475
– 'It's nothing . . .': Benito Mussolini, quoted in 'Attentato del 7 Aprile 1926

contro la persona di S. E. Il Capo del Governo ad opera di Violet Gibson',
ACS/SPDCR/64/377/R.2

– 'Don't be afraid . . .': Benito Mussolini, quoted in Richard Oliver Collin, *La donna che sparò a Mussolini* (Milan, 1988), p. 69

14 'flames of fire . . .': 'Premier Hit in the Nose', *New York Times*, 8 April 1926

– 'Leave her! . . .': Ermanno de Bernardini, quoted in 'Attentato del 7 Aprile 1926'

15 '[They] almost killed me . . .': Benito Mussolini, quoted in Collin, p. 70

17 'I don't know anything . . .': Violet, quoted in 'Attentato del 7 Aprile 1926'

II: THEN

18 'catering his way . . .': Norman Rose, *The Cliveden Set* (London, 2000), p. 116

19 'one of the best known works . . .': 'New Publications', *New York Times*, 5 January 1895

20 'attended, of course . . .': *Lady's Pictorial*, 27 February 1897, clipping in PA/ASH

– 'She was the shyest . . .': Elsie to Lord Ashbourne, 10 June 1893, TC

21 'calmly conscious . . .': Roy Foster, *W. B. Yeats, A Life: The Apprentice Mage* (Oxford, 1998), p. 24

– 'love and religion . . .': Virginia Woolf, *Mrs Dalloway* (London, 1976), pp. 112–3

III: OPEN, O YE HEAVENLY GATES

24 'a reputation at twenty . . .': 'St Stephen's Portraits', *St Stephen's Review*, 15 November 1884, clipping in PA/ASH

– 'never had any practice . . .': A. B. Cooke, 'Lord Ashbourne's Political Career', Introduction to 'The Ashbourne Papers 1869–1913' (Belfast, 1974), p. xi

– 'possessed of ample means . . .': ibid.

– 'a man of even temper . . .': 'The Vacancy in the Common Pleas', *The Nation*, 31 August 1878

– 'mellifluous voice . . .': Cooke, p. xii

25 'He never fails . . .': 'St Stephen's Portraits'

– 'unequalled First Class . . .': Advertisement, *Irish Times*, 10 May 1889

– 'minor nuisances . . .': Cooke, p. xii

– 'exceptionally prosperous . . .': ibid.

26 'effective controller . . .': ibid., p. xiii

– 'The houses were ransacked . . .': Wilfrid Blunt, quoted in Declan Kiberd, *Inventing Ireland: The Literature of the Modern Nation* (London, 1995), p. 88

27 'Ireland has been knocking . . .': Charles Stewart Parnell, quoted in R. Barry O'Brien, *The Life of Charles Stewart Parnell, 1846–1891* (Worcestershire, 2008), p. 1

– 'Queen's Irish conscience': 'Introduction to the Ashbourne Papers', PA/ASH

28 'hideous, patronising . . .': Alice James, quoted in Joanne Jacobson, 'Resistance and Subversion in the Letters of Alice James', *Biography* 14/4 (Fall 1991), p. 373

– 'besides landed property': Frances Gibson to Edward Gibson, 9 March 1872, TC

– 'What an awful lot of money . . .': ibid.

– 'a thoroughly domesticated man': 'St Stephen's Portraits'

29 'amusing his little daughters . . .': 'Our Portrait Gallery', *Men and Women*, 4 December 1886, clipping in PA/ASH

- 'a wonderful power of abstraction . . .': 'Celebrities at Home', *The World*, 5 January 1898, clipping in PA/ASH
- 'that great cathedral space . . .': Virginia Woolf, quoted in Peter Dally, *Virginia Woolf: The Marriage of Heaven and Hell* (London, 1999), p. 33
- 'She showed signs . . .': Constance, quoted in 'Mussolini Trionfante', *Time*, 19 April 1926
- 'weep, like geniuses . . .': W. B. Yeats, quoted in Roy Foster, *W. B. Yeats, A Life: The Apprentice Mage* (Oxford, 1998), p. 6
- 'King Lear scenes': James Joyce, quoted in Carol Loeb Shloss, *Lucia Joyce: To Dance in the Wake* (London, 2004), p. 230
30 'the stockade of . . .': Foster, p. 28
31 'delightful alcove . . .': 'Celebrities at Home'
- 'and other less civilised . . .': ibid.
- 'he narrowly escaped . . .': 'H. D. G. Gibson', *The Wellingtonian*, 1906, clipping in PA/ASH

IV: THE PROBLEM OF BEING

33 'tried to sit immovable . . .': Alice James, quoted in Lisa Appignanesi, *Mad, Bad and Sad: A History of Women and the Mind Doctors from 1800 to the Present* (London, 2008), p. 117
34 'Lord Ashbourne generally works . . .': 'Celebrities at Home', *The World*, 5 January 1898, clipping in PA/ASH
- 'mathematics and keeping pets': Frances, quoted in 'Lady of the House', 10 May 1898, clipping in PA/ASH
- 'like a piece of timber': Virginia Woolf, *A Moment's Liberty: The Shorter Diary*, ed. Anne Olivier Bell (London, 1990), p. 138
- 'I seem perfectly grotesque . . .': Alice James, quoted in Joanne Jacobson, 'Resistance and Subversion in the Letters of Alice James', *Biography* 14/4 (Fall 1991), p. 376
- 'an obsession . . .': Florence Nightingale, quoted in Elaine Showalter, *The Female Malady: Women, Madness and English Culture, 1830–1980* (London, 1987), p. 62
35 'Anglo-Saxon fraternity': Norman Rose, *The Cliveden Set* (London, 2000), p. 45
- 'An English headmaster . . .': ibid., p. 28
36 'the social and political showpiece . . .': Thomas Pakenham, *The Boer War* (London, 1992), p. 461
- 'There was a gallant . . .': ibid., p. 462
- 'The utmost anxiety . . .': 'The Captured Irish Yeomanry', *The Times*, 7 June 1900
37 'stated to have been . . .': 'The British Prisoners', *The Times*, 25 June 1900
38 '[He is] a half hatched . . .': Mary Leslie, undated letter, GUL/LESLIE/1/19
- 'It is one of the chief . . .': Willie Gibson, quoted in 'Premier's Assailant is a Sister of Lord Ashbourne', *New York Times*, 8 April 1926
- 'being an Irishman . . .': G. B. Shaw, 'A Note on Irish Nationalism', *New Statesman*, 12 July 1913
- 'indomitable Irishry': ibid.

– 'had but learnt . . .': Oscar Wilde, quoted in Declan Kiberd, *Inventing Ireland: The Literature of the Modern Nation* (London, 1995), p. 37

39 'silk kimonos . . .': W. B. Yeats, 'In Memory of Eva Gore-Booth and Con Markiewicz', *Collected Poems*, ed. Augustine Martin (London, 1992), p. 241

40 'A great red-haired yahoo . . .': Louis Purser, quoted in Roy Foster, *W. B. Yeats, A Life: The Apprentice Mage* (Oxford, 1998), p. 91

– 'petty obligations, genteel rituals . . .': Elaine Showalter, *The Female Malady: Women, Madness and English Culture, 1830–1980* (London, 1987), p. 63

V: THE NEW MYSTICS

41 'the healing Truth . . .': Mary Baker Eddy, quoted in Linda Edwards, *A Brief Guide to Beliefs: Ideas, Theologies, Mysteries, and Movements* (London, 2001), p. 395

– 'scientific certainty . . .': Mary Baker Eddy, quoted in Stephen J. Stein, 'Retrospection and Introspection: The Gospel According to Mary Baker Eddy', *The Harvard Theological Review* 75/1 (January 1982), p. 98

– 'I read the first chapter . . .': Nancy Astor, quoted in Norman Rose, *The Cliveden Set* (London, 2000), p. 40

42 'intense religious indoctrination': ibid., p. 41

– 'Eddygush': Mark Twain, quoted in ibid.

– 'the monumental hysteric': Rose, ibid.

– 'I think she was fond . . .': Elsie to Violet, 25 March 1926, TC

– 'an earnest Christian Scientist . . .': *Liverpool Echo*, 31 May 1913, clipping in PA/ASH

– 'a place of lyrical beauty . . .': Michael Astor, quoted in Rose, p. 132

43 'a small body of utterly . . .': Violet to Frances, undated 1952, SAH/VG

– 'knowledge of the laws . . .': Peter Washington, *Madame Blavatsky's Baboon: Theosophy and the Emergence of the Western Guru* (London, 1993), p. 55

– 'have sold our birthright . . .': Oscar Wilde, *The Artist as Critic*, ed. Richard Ellmann (London, 1970) p. 300

44 'in life and its shadow': George Russell, quoted in Roy Foster, *W. B. Yeats, A Life: The Apprentice Mage* (Oxford, 1998), p. 48

– 'Neither religion nor science . . .': Virginia Woolf, *A Moment's Liberty: The Shorter Diary*, ed. Anne Olivier Bell (London, 1990), p. 361

45 'Do as I do . . .': Cornelius Vanderbilt, quoted in Frances Stonor Saunders, *Hidden Hands: A Different History of Modernism* (London, 1995), p. 9

– 'without distinction of race . . .': Helena Blavatsky, *The Key to Theosophy* (Montana, 1998), p. 371

– 'preaching most unmistakably . . .': ibid., p. 79

VI: LA FEMME QUI CHERCHE

46 'The theological change . . .': 'Perversion', *The Times*, 14 October 1846

47 'The Church of Rome . . .': 'A Pervert Converted', *The Times*, 28 May 1852

– 'deadly [as] prussic acid . . .': 'The Three Priests', quoted in Patrick R. O'Malley, *Catholicism, Sexual Deviance, and Victorian Gothic Culture* (Cambridge, 2006), p. 82

– 'at the intersection . . .': ibid., p. 7
– 'never thought of a convert . . .': Ronald Knox, *Barchester Pilgrimage* (London, 1935), p. 82
– 'I don't believe it's possible . . .': Antonia White, *Beyond the Glass* (London, 1979), p. 92
– 'I can quite see . . .': ibid., p. 93
48 'spokesman for the mind . . .': George Tyrrell, quoted in www.wikipedia.org/wiki/George_Tyrrell
– 'the right of each age . . .': ibid.
– 'to be walking through . . .': Cardinal Merry del Val, quoted in Jeffrey Eaman, *Violet Gibson's Attempt on the Life of Benito Mussolini, Rome 1926* (PhD Thesis, Lancaster University, 2001), p. 273
49 'pestilential human rookeries': Nigel Scotland, *Squires in the Slums* (London, 2007), p. 7
– 'only for operettas': Eileen Gray, quoted in Frances Stonor Saunders, 'The House that Eileen Built', *Guardian Weekend*, 21 July 2001
– 'greatly loved by all': 'New Catholic Peer', *The Universe*, 31 May 1913, clipping in PA/ASH
50 'We consider the Protestant . . .': quoted in O'Malley, p. 46
– 'For a whole year . . .': Violet to Lord Ashbourne, 10 July 1902, TC
– 'I am *very* sincerely sorry . . .': ibid.
51 'Youth . . .': T. S. Eliot, 'Thoughts After Lambeth', quoted in Craig Raine, *T. S. Eliot* (London, 2007), p. 30
– 'network of grudges . . .': Carol Loeb Shloss, *Lucia Joyce: To Dance in the Wake* (London, 2004), p. 58

VII: L'HOMME QUI CHERCHE

52 'the waters of Leman': T. S. Eliot, 'The Waste Land', *Collected Poems 1909–1962* (London, 1986), p. 70
– 'Dostoievskian duds . . .': Ezra Pound, quoted in E. Fuller Torrey, *The Roots of Treason* (New York, 1984), p. 8
– 'child of the last . . .': Benito Mussolini, quoted in R. J. B. Bosworth, *Mussolini* (London, 2002), p. 76
53 '*il tiranno*': quoted in Christopher Hibbert, *Benito Mussolini* (London, 1975), p. 26
– 'sausage-maker's democracy': ibid., p. 23
– 'I was a Bohemian . . .': Benito Mussolini, quoted in ibid., p. 20
– 'two English women . . .': Benito Mussolini, quoted in ibid., p. 22
54 '*apostolo di violenza*': Benito Mussolini, quoted in ibid., p. 23
– 'his philosophical views . . .': ibid., p. 22
– 'No one could see . . .': Angelica Balabanoff, quoted in Richard Lamb, *Mussolini and the British* (London, 1997), p. 17

VIII: HOC EST CORPUS MEUM

55 'I was very naughty . . .': Violet, quoted in Augusto Giannelli and Sante De Sanctis, 'Relazione di Perizia Psichiatrica sull'imputata Violetta Gibson',

ACS/ TSDS/40–41/B.7

- 'My poor, poor brain . . .': Harry, quoted in Victor to Lord Ashbourne, undated November 1905, TC
- 'Poor Harry . . .': Victor to Lord Ashbourne, ibid.
56 'charity and prayer': Violet, quoted in Giannelli and De Sanctis
- 'I'm rather impressed . . .': Antonia White, *Beyond the Glass* (London, 1979), p. 138
57 'painfully aware as I was . . .': John Cumming, quoted in O'Malley, p. 21
- 'in spite of the crowded . . .': Henry James, *Letters*, Volume 1 (Cambridge, Mass., 1974) p. 173
- 'My dearest Father . . .': Constance to Lord Ashbourne, 24 April 1909, TC
- 'never made a crucifix . . .': Giorgio Vasari, *Lives of the Artists* (Oxford, 2008), p. 177
58 'when we read the lives . . .': Violet, notebook, ACS/TSDS/40–41/B.6
- 'moral atmosphere': ibid.
- 'I felt as though I was . . .': Constance to Lord Ashbourne, 24 April 1909, TC
59 'Her legs have gone . . .': Virginia Woolf, *A Moment's Liberty: The Shorter Diary*, ed. Anne Olivier Bell (London, 1990), p. 259
- 'within the bounds of reality': Peter Dally, *Virginia Woolf: The Marriage of Heaven and Hell* (London, 1999), p. 109
- 'tied, imprisoned . . .': Woolf, *A Moment's Liberty*, p. 164
60 'heedless overexertion . . .': quoted in Lisa Appignanesi, *Mad, Bad and Sad: A History of Women and the Mind Doctors from 1800 to the Present* (London, 2008), p. 104
- 'the morbid condition . . .': George M. Beard, quoted in ibid., p. 101
- 'believing or pretending . . .': Henry Maudsley, quoted in ibid., p. 98
- 'perfect examples . . .': ibid.
- 'Sir Roderick Glossop . . .': P. G. Wodehouse, *The Inimitable Jeeves* (London, 2008), p. 74
61 'simple and dignified . . .': Violet to Lord Ashbourne, 13 October 1911, PA/ASH/B/56
- 'Catholicism presented itself . . .': Enid Dinnis, in 'Enid Dinnis, Novelist and Short Story Writer', *Book of Catholic Authors*, First Series, ed. Walter Romig (Detroit, 1942), p. 58
- 'the consonance of wills': Montaigne, quoted in Gifford Lewis, *Somerville and Ross: The World of the Irish R.M.* (London, 1985), p. 217
62 'a solicitor's letter . . .': Virginia Woolf, *A Room of One's Own* (London, 1982), pp. 37–9
63 'I have just now read the news . . .': Violet to Constance, 23 May 1913, TC
- 'The late Baron Ashbourne . . .': 'New Peer Disinherited', *New York Times*, 22 July 1913
64 'old Great Seal of Ireland': 'Will of the Late Lord Ashbourne', *Irish Times*, 27 June 1913
- 'two paintings . . .': ibid.
- 'being confident that . . .': ibid.
- 'comprehended the mysteries . . .': Norman Rose, *The Cliveden Set* (London, 2000), p. 132

IX: HOLY WAR

66 'decided to invite . . .': 'In the Ranks', *The Times*, 11 September 1914
  – 'all of the well-to-do . . .': ibid.
67 'War was the only course . . .': Christabel Pankhurst, quoted in Claire
     Eustace, Joan Ryan and Laura Ugolini, *A Suffrage Reader: Charting Directions
     in British Suffrage History* (London, 2000), p. 111
  – 'proud and delighted . . .': *Punch*, June 1916, quoted in Bernard A. Cook,
     Women and War (California, 2006), p. 238
  – 'the faces of our rulers . . .': Virginia Woolf, *A Room of One's Own* (London,
     1982), p. 16
  – 'above the present hatred . . .': quoted in Leila J. Rupp, 'Constructing
     Internationalism: the Case of Transnational Women's Organizations,
     1888–1945', *The American Historical Review* 99/5 (1994), p. 1576
  – 'to demand that international . . .': quoted in Sybil Oldfield, 'Proposal for a
     Short Collaborative Research Project in British Women's History', *History
     Workshop Journal* 27/1 (1989), p. 176
68 'We worked continuously . . .': Sylvia Pankhurst, quoted in
     www.spartacus.schoolnet.co.uk/wpankhursts.htm
  – 'strong anti-British attitude . . .': quoted in New Scotland Yard to Mr Locke,
     9 April 1926, PRO/HO144/7950
69 'The great reformers . . .': Florence Nightingale, quoted in Elaine Showalter,
     The Female Malady: Women, Madness and English Culture, 1830–1980 (London,
     1987), p. 65
70 'so septic . . .': Dr. R. Courtenay Gayer, 'Notes on the case of The Hon Violet
     Albina Gibson', 3 May 1926, SAH/VG
  – 'all the horrors . . .': Virginia Woolf, *A Moment's Liberty: The Shorter Diary*, ed.
     Anne Olivier Bell (London, 1990), p. 130
  – 'her attitude towards the pain . . .': Gayer
71 'Fr. John O'Fallon Pope . . .': Violet, notebook, ACS/TSDS/40–41/B.6
  – 'precise, sensitive scholar . . .': *Letters and Notices*, vol. I (London, 1935), p. 57
  – 'God, being truth . . .': John O'Fallon Pope, 'A Plea for Scholastic Theology',
     Journal of Theological Studies 5 (1904), p. 185
72 'Unfortunately, the disunion . . .': ibid., p. 188
  – 'The degree of holiness . . .': Violet, notebook, ACS/TSDS/40–41/B.6
  – 'I have no constancy . . .': ibid.
73 'You are not only . . .': John O'Fallon Pope, quoted in ibid.

X: IL MIGLIOR FABBRO

74 'convulsions . . .': Benito Mussolini, quoted in R. J. B. Bosworth, *Mussolini*
     (London, 2002), p. 118
  – 'a rag to be planted . . .': Benito Mussolini, quoted in Christopher Hibbert,
     Benito Mussolini (London, 1975), p. 27
  – 'The Fatherland . . .': ibid.
  – 'that great corpse': ibid.
  – 'gang of robbers': ibid.
  – 'humanity's immortal stigma . . .': ibid.

75 [footnote] 'When I am given . . .': Dorothy Parker, review of *The Cardinal's Mistress*, *New Yorker*, 15 September 1928

- 'I need to orient . . .': Benito Mussolini, quoted in Bosworth, *Mussolini*, p. 90
- 'was his own . . .': Cesare Rossi, quoted in Mark Thompson, *The White War: Life and Death on the Italian Front 1915–1919* (London, 2008), p. 49
- 'mock-heroic madness . . .': Benito Mussolini, quoted in Bosworth, *Mussolini*, p. 85
- 'not an evil-doer . . .': ibid., p. 86
76 'With you, I feel miles . . .': ibid., p. 92
- 'I love you so much . . .': ibid., p. 277
- 'rigid neutrality': Hibbert, p. 35
- 'Revolution is an idea . . .': *Il popolo d'Italia*, 15 November 1914
- 'You hate me today . . .': Benito Mussolini, quoted in Bosworth, *Mussolini*, p. 105
77 'My speciality was . . .': Benito Mussolini, quoted in Philip V. Cannistraro and Brian R. Sullivan, *Il Duce's Other Woman: The Untold Story of Margherita Sarfatti* (New York, 1995), p. 149
78 'In this moment . . .': Benito Mussolini, quoted in Christopher Duggan, *The Force of Destiny: A History of Italy since 1796* (London, 2007), p. 400
79 'maimed victory': Thompson, p. 381
- 'a third-rate club . . .': *L'idea nazionale*, quoted in R. J. B. Bosworth, *Mussolini's Italy: Life under the Dictatorship 1915–1945* (London, 2005), p. 92
- 'those who have been . . .': Benito Mussolini, quoted in Bosworth, *Mussolini*, p. 120

XI: THINGS SNAP

80 'the bursting of people's . . .': Virginia Woolf, *A Moment's Liberty: The Shorter Diary*, ed. Anne Olivier Bell (London, 1990), p. 52
- 'Masked parties . . .': Evelyn Waugh, *Vile Bodies* (London, 2000), p. 104
- 'The dry glare . . .': Antonia White, *Diaries, 1926–1957*, ed. Susan Chitty (London, 1991), p. 16
81 'Are you really a lesbian? . . .': quoted in Philip Nel, *The Avant-garde and American Postmodernity: Small Incisive Shocks* (Mississippi, 2002), p. 21
- 'France is nothing . . .': Nancy Astor, quoted in Norman Rose, *The Cliveden Set* (London, 2000), p. 109
- 'Of all the people . . .': Eileen Gray, quoted in Frances Stonor Saunders, 'The House that Eileen Built', *Guardian Weekend*, 21 July 2001
- 'One must never look . . .': Eileen Gray, quoted in ibid.
- 'driven by loneliness . . .': Virginia Woolf, quoted in Peter Dally, *Virginia Woolf: The Marriage of Heaven and Hell* (London, 1999), p. 142
- 'limited her acquaintances . . .': Enid Dinnis to Italian Consul, London, 16 May 1926, ACS/TSDS/40-41/B.6
- 'extravagant incursions . . .': James Joyce, quoted in Carol Loeb Shloss, *Lucia Joyce: To Dance in the Wake* (London, 2004), p. 91
- 'pearl-buttoned velvet . . .': John Fletcher, quoted in E. Fuller Torrey, *The Roots of Treason* (New York, 1984), p. 105

83 'a pinwheel of affectation': Louis Menand, 'The Pound Error', *New Yorker*, 9 and 16 June 2008

– 'a revolting record . . .': G. B. Shaw, quoted in Shloss, p. 91

– 'a delirious confusion . . .': Carl Jung, quoted in Lisa Appignanesi, *Mad, Bad and Sad: A History of Women and the Mind Doctors from 1800 to the Present* (London, 2008), p. 230

– 'In Paris, before . . .': Zelda Fitzgerald, quoted in ibid., pp. 224–5

– 'like little hooks': Scott Fitzgerald, *May Day* (*The Curious Case of Benjamin Button and Six Other Stories* (London, 2008), p. 121

– 'Christ, William the Conqueror . . .': Scott Fitzgerald, quoted in Appignanesi, p. 248

– 'her great reality . . .': ibid.

– 'lay in bed . . .': Virginia Woolf, quoted in Emily Dalgarno, *Virginia Woolf and the Visible World* (Cambridge, 2007), p. 33

84 'As an experience . . .': Virginia Woolf to Ethel Smyth, 22 June 1930, *Congenial Spirits: The Letters of Virginia Woolf*, ed. Joanne Trautmann Banks (London, 1989), p. 268

– 'a bag of ferrets': Woolf, *A Moment's Liberty*, p. 289

– 'a fire in her brain': James Joyce, quoted in Sean O'Hagan, 'Private Dancer', *Observer*, 16 May 2004

– 'hordes of buxom . . .': John Banville, 'The Sacrifice', *New York Review of Books*, 8 April 2004

– 'I felt her tragically . . .': Kay Boyle, quoted in Shloss, p. 155

– 'takes no account . . .': Friedrich Nietzsche, quoted in ibid., p. 229

– 'o, cripes . . .': James Joyce, quoted in ibid.

– 'eyes peering . . .': Romola Nijinsky, quoted in Joan Acocella, 'Secrets of Nijinsky', *New York Review of Books*, 14 January 1999

85 'I am not an invention . . .': Vaslav Nijinsky, *The Diary of Vaslav Nijinsky*, ed. Joan Acocella (New York, 1999), p. 52

– 'I am weeping . . .': ibid., p. 72

– 'Femmka . . .': Vaslav Nijinsky, quoted in Acocella, Introduction, *The Diary of Vaslav Nijinsky*, p. xxi

– 'a confused schizophrenic . . .': Eugen Bleuler, quoted in Acocella, 'Secrets of Nijinsky'

– 'Why am I locked up? . . .': Vaslav Nijinsky, quoted in ibid.

86 'beyond the frame . . .': quoted in Shloss, p. 113

– 'supreme mode of expression': quoted in ibid.

– 'the germy epoch . . .': Ezra Pound to Laurence Binyon, 30 August 1934, *Selected Letters of Ezra Pound, 1907–1941*, ed. D. D. Paige (New York, 1950), p. 260

87 'of wandering habits . . .': quoted in 'Peer's Son's Death At An Inn', *The Times*, 17 January 1922

– 'You may not know it . . .': Victor Gibson, quoted in 'Dead Man In Inn Was Chancellor's Son', *New York Times*, 17 January 1922

– 'and during periodic . . .': ibid.

– 'no perceptible signs . . .': *The Times*, 17 January 1922

– 'poorly nourished . . .': *New York Times*, 17 January 1922

88 'We were a large . . .': Constance, quoted in *Daily Mail*, 9 April 1926

– 'He died suddenly . . .': ibid.
– 'I was with her . . .': Enid Dinnis to Italian Consul, London, 16 May 1926, ACS/ TSDS/40-41/B.6
– 'nothing of importance . . .': Violet, quoted in Augusto Giannelli and Sante De Sanctis, 'Relazione di Perizia Psichiatrica sull'imputata Violetta Gibson', ACS/ TSDS/40–41/B.7
– 'mischief-maker': Violet, notebook, ACS/TSDS/40-41/B.6
92 'If you went to Paris . . .': Robert Vansittart, *Lessons of My Life* (London, 1944) p. 21
– 'Not until we have . . .': Willie, quoted in 'New Catholic Peer', *The Universe*, 31 May 1913
– '*Beidheadh se i mo . . .*': Willie, 27 June 1918, quoted in *Hansard*, www.mill-banksystems.com
– 'I could go on . . .': ibid.
– 'Thank the goodness . . .': ibid.
– 'that the modern Irishman . . .': ibid.
– 'All I want to do . . .': ibid.
93 'I myself am not . . .': Willie, 1 July 1920, ibid.
– 'picnic in a . . .': Gifford Lewis, *Somerville and Ross: The World of the Irish R.M.* (London, 1985), p. 155
– 'In belonging to a class . . .': ibid., p. 157
– 'the fluxes of temperament . . .': ibid., p. 169
– 'by argument four-squares . . .': quoted in 'Passages on Lord Ashbourne in M. Sheed's book', undated manuscript in GUL/LESLIE/B.1/18
94 'Well, do you exist yet?': ibid.
– 'Moses was little good . . .': W. B. Yeats, *Samhain*, October 1901, p. 9
– 'It seems that . . .': Willie, undated letter, GUL/LESLIE/B.1/19
95 'good pious Catholics . . .': Enid Dinnis to Italian Consul, London, 16 May 1926, ACS/TSDS/40–41/B.6
– 'Every time I saw . . .': Alvin York, quoted in www.wikipedia.org/wiki/Alvin_C._York
– '[Violet] was in . . .': Enid Dinnis to Italian Consul, London, 16 May 1926, ACS/TSDS/40–41/B.6
96 'ad. 9 Oct. 1923 . . .': Copy of the Case Book Entries, File Number 4818, Regarding the Hon. Violet Gibson, PRO/MH79/262
99 'the brain was . . .': Enid Dinnis to Italian Consul, London, 16 May 1926, ACS/TSDS/40–41/B.6
– 'She asked me . . .': ibid.

PART TWO: ACTS

I: THEATRE OF MADNESS

103 'trashily plotted novels . . .': Mark Thompson, *The White War: Life and Death on the Italian Front 1915–1919* (London, 2008), p. 40
– 'was a spectacular case . . .': ibid.
104 'We have no other . . .': ibid., p. 46

- 'In truth, d'Annunzio . . .': ibid., p. 256
- 'stench of peace': Gabriele d'Annunzio, quoted in ibid., p. 374
- 'Two things can be done . . .': Benito Mussolini, quoted in ibid., p. 47
105 'museum of living pathology': Jean-Martin Charcot, quoted in Lisa Appignanesi, *Mad, Bad and Sad: A History of Women and the Mind Doctors from 1800 to the Present* (London, 2008), p. 127
106 'the occult motor . . .': Donato, quoted in unsigned, 'A Great Light Under a Bushel', *The Theosophist* 1/5 (February 1880), p. 27
- 'mechanisms of fascination': Jeffrey Schnapp, 'Fascinating Fascism', *Journal of Contemporary History* 31 (1996), p. 236
- 'interminable speechifying . . .': Sebastian Haffner, *Defying Hitler* (London, 2003), p. 73
108 'The crowd loves . . .': Benito Mussolini, quoted in Christopher Hibbert, *Benito Mussolini* (London, 1975), p. 51
109 'Having lost their power . . .': Umberto Eco, 'Eternal Fascism: Fourteen Ways of Looking at a Blackshirt', *New York Review of Books*, 22 June 1995
- 'I come from the battlefield . . .': Benito Mussolini, quoted in Adrian Lyttelton, *The Seizure of Power: Fascism in Italy 1919–1929* (London, 2004), p. 95
- 'I swear to lead . . .': Benito Mussolini, quoted in Kenneth Scott, 'Mussolini and the Roman Empire', *The Classical Journal* 27/9 (June 1932), p. 646
- 'to save a cabinet . . .': Vittorio Emanuele III, quoted in Richard Lamb, *Mussolini and the British* (London, 1997), p. 27
- 'I could have transformed . . .': Benito Mussolini, quoted in ibid., p. 62
110 'The goal that he . . .': 'The Path of Italy', *The Times*, 8 April 1926
- 'The trouble with Mussolini . . .': quoted in Hibbert, p. 48
- 'The Fascists are . . .': *New Statesman*, 12 April 1924, quoted in Lamb, p. 68
111 'His life . . .': Margherita Sarfatti, *The Life of Benito Mussolini* (Montana, 2004), p. 275
112 'I, and I alone . . .': Benito Mussolini, quoted in Philip V. Cannistraro and Brian R. Sullivan, *Il Duce's Other Woman: The Untold Story of Margherita Sarfatti* (New York, 1995), p. 297
- 'putrid goddess': Benito Mussolini, quoted in Hibbert, p. 62
- 'No one will ever know . . .': Violet, notebook, ACS/TSDS/40–41/B.6
113 'She had been talking . . .': Enid Dinnis to Italian Consul, London, 16 May 1926, ACS/TSDS/40-41/B.6

II: MARTYRS

114 'the stereotyped British . . .': Richard Bagot, *My Italian Year* (Leipzig, 1912), p. 152
115 'just about the rottenest . . .': Scott Fitzgerald, quoted in John Varriano, *Rome, A Literary Companion* (London, 1991), p. 174
- 'The proportion of murders . . .': Augustus Hare, *Walks in Rome* (New York, 1893), p. 675
- 'charitable mission': Statement of Mother Superior Hesselblad, Epifanio Pennetta to Procuratore del Re, 10 April 1926, ACS/PS/H2/16792
116 'When Miss Gibson's friends . . .': Enid Dinnis to Italian Consul, London, 16 May 1926, ACS/TSDS/40–41/B.6

- 'take direction of her soul': Statement of Fedele Stotzingen, Perilli to Procuratore del Re, 12 April 1926, ACS/PS/H2/16792
117 'I would not have received . . .': ibid.
- 'ponderous past . . .': Henry James, *Roderick Hudson* (London, 1969), p. 192
- 'morally corrupted . . .': quoted in Varriano, p. 5
- 'If Roman life . . .': James, *Roderick Hudson*, p. 27
- 'its solitude . . .': Charles Dickens, *Pictures from Italy*, in *The Works of Charles Dickens*, vol. XIV (New York, 1900), p. 475
118 'We have nothing good . . .': Violet, notebook, ACS/TSDS/40-41/B.6
- 'Here we go alone . . .': Virginia Woolf, *On Being Ill* (Ashfield, Mass., 2002), p. 12
- 'dusky arches . . .': Nathaniel Hawthorne, *The Marble Faun* (New York, 2002), p. 141
- 'I wanted to die . . .': Violet, quoted in Pennetta to Procuratore del Re, Rome, 8 April 1926, ACS/PS/H2/16792
119 'very calm and repentant . . .': Statement of Fedele Stotzingen, Perilli to Procuratore del Re, 12 April 1926, ACS/PS/H2/16792
- 'as mad as his sister': Richard Oliver Collin, *La donna che sparò a Mussolini* (Milan, 1988), p. 49
120 'It made me very unhappy . . .': Enid Dinnis to Italian Consul, London, 16 May 1926, ACS/TSDS/40-41/B.6
121 'as she was clearly unwell . . .': Sister Caterina Flanagan, quoted in Pennetta to Procuratore del Re, 10 April 1926, ACS/PS/H2/16792
- 'she was extremely astute': Mary McGrath, ibid.
- 'simple and devout . . .': unsigned review of *More Mystics*, *Times Literary Supplement*, 1924, quoted in Jeffrey Eaman, *Violet Gibson's Attempt on the Life of Benito Mussolini, Rome 1926* (PhD Thesis, Lancaster University, 2001), p. 285
- 'History can tell . . .': Enid Dinnis to Violet, undated 1926, ACS/TSDS/40-41/B.6
122 'time to catch his breath': Giorgio Bassani, *The Garden of the Finzi-Continis* (London, 2005), p. 131

III: GETHSEMANE

123 'If you think . . .': Violet to Constance, undated December 1925, ACS/TSDS/40-41/B.6
- 'I would like so much . . .': Lady Ashbourne to Violet, 22 January 1926, ibid.
- 'goodbye darling . . .': Lady Ashbourne to Violet, 6 February 1926, ibid.
- 'My dearest Vizie . . .': Constance to Violet, 19 March 1926, ibid.
- 'Mother seriously ill . . .': Constance to Violet, 21 March 1926, ibid.
- 'Start at 11:55 a.m . . .': Violet, ibid.
124 'Mother died . . .': Constance to Violet, 21 March 1926, ibid.
- 'My dearest Vizie . . .': Constance to Violet, 21 March 1926, ibid.
- 'I know by now . . .': Elsie to Violet, 25 March 1926, ibid.
- '. . . Your mother went to sleep . . .': Marianne to Violet, 27 March 1926, ibid.
125 'a Christian Science service': ibid.
- 'It is beautiful to live . . .': Benito Mussolini, quoted in 'Mussolini Calls Italy To Discipline In Fighting Speech', *New York Times*, 29 March 1926

– 'with which she covered . . .': Ugo Tavani, quoted in Pennetta to Procuratore del Re, 8 April 1926, ACS/PS/H2/16792

– 'an unusual person': Antonio Ambrosini, quoted in Richard Oliver Collin, *La donna che sparò a Mussolini* (Milan, 1988), p. 59

126 'as one who had lost all . . .': Perilli to Procuratore del Re, 12 April 1926, ACS/PS/H2/16792

– 'There is no pain . . .': Violet, notebook, ACS/TSDS/40-41/B.6

127 'Come. Violet.': Violet to Enid Dinnis, 1 April 1926, ACS/TSDS/40-41/B.6

– 'My dear dear Violet . . .': Enid Dinnis to Violet, 6 April 1926, ibid.

IV: WHAT GOD WANTS

129 'After coming out . . .': Benito Mussolini, quoted in Paolo Palma, *Una bomba per il duce: la centrale antifascista di Pacciardi a Lugano* (Calabria, 2003), p. 5

– 'the Party must fascisticise . . .': Benito Mussolini, quoted in R. J. B. Bosworth, *Mussolini* (London, 2002), p. 216

– 'Hitler and Mussolini . . .': W. H. Auden, 'A Bride in the 30s', *Collected Poems*, ed. Edward Mendelson (London, 1994), p. 129

– 'No danger threatens . . .': Benito Mussolini, quoted in Ronald Graham to Austen Chamberlain, 12 April 1926, FO 371/11398

130 'Live dangerously . . .': Benito Mussolini, quoted in Ronald Graham to Foreign Office, 9 April 1926, FO 371/11398

– 'The people of the future . . .': 'Talk of the Town', *New Yorker*, 3 July 1943

– 'They were what the regime . . .': R. J. B. Bosworth, *Mussolini's Italy: Life under the Dictatorship 1915–1945* (London, 2005), p. 11

– 'It is better not to . . .': Violet, notebook, ACS/TSDS/40-41/B.6

131 'My dearest Benito! . . .': Ugo Guspini, *L'orecchio del regime: le intercettazioni telefoniche al tempo del fascismo* (Milan, 1973), p. 70

– 'clearly protected by God': quoted in Richard Oliver Collin, *La donna che sparò a Mussolini* (Milan, 1988), p. 78

– 'Duce, my most beloved Duce . . .': Clara Petacci to Benito Mussolini, 8 April 1926, quoted in Renzo de Felice, *Mussolini il duce: lo stato totalitario 1936–1940* (Turin, 1981), p. 278

132 '[Mussolini] was wounded . . .': Attilio Bazzan Witness Statement, 10 April 1926, ACS/TSDS/40-41/B.6

133 'After Campidoglio had been . . .': Pietro Martini Witness Statement, 10 April 1926, ACS/PS/H2/16792

V: PROVIDENTIAL ESCAPE

134 'composed of rough-looking . . .': Ronald Graham to Foreign Office, 8 April 1926, PRO/FO371/11398

– 'became enraged at two . . .': 'Younger Fascisti Turn to Violence', *New York Times*, 22 April 1926

– 'It is felt in some quarters . . .': ibid.

135 'Mussolini, the disastrous Italian dictator . . .': *Freiburg Independent*, attachment in Italian Consulate, Zurich, to Minister of Interior, Rome, 14 April

1926, ACS/PS/H2/16792

– 'applause squad': Martin Clark, *Modern Italy: 1871 to the Present* (London, 2008), p. 279

– 'A sensational event . . .': *Freiburg Independent*, Italian Consulate, Zurich, op. cit.

136 *'Telegram.* Sir R. Graham . . .': Ronald Graham to Foreign Office, 7 April 1926, PRO/HO144/7950

137 *'Telegram.* Sir R. Graham . . .': ibid.

– 'Prime Minister had narrow escape . . .': Ronald Graham to Foreign Office, 7 April 1926, PRO/FO371/11398

138 'I am horrified . . .': Austen Chamberlain, quoted in 'Attempt on Mussolini', *The Times*, 8 April 1926

– 'Please express to the . . .': 'King George's Message', *The Times*, 9 April 1926

– 'I have the honour to . . .': William Cosgrave, quoted in 'Miss Gibson's Identity', *The Times*, 9 April 1926

– 'to take all necessary . . .': Luigi Federzoni to Prefects, 7 April 1926, ACS/PS/H2/16792

139 'Fascist squads . . .': Telegrams from Regional Prefects to Minister of Interior, ACS/PS/H2/16792

– 'Despite severe measures . . .': ibid.

– 'News of attempt . . .': ibid.

– 'Local Fascists . . .': ibid.

– 'Congratulations on . . .': ibid.

– 'Energetic measures taken . . .': ibid.

– 'In protest against . . .': ibid.

– 'Il Duce commands . . .': Filippo Turati, quoted in 'Premier Hit In The Nose', *New York Times*, 8 April 1926

– 'something of the saintly . . .': ibid.

140 'something which borders . . .': Arnaldo Mussolini, quoted in Cesare Rossi, *Il tribunale speciale* (Milan, 1952), p. 55

– 'the first flush of dawn': 'Mussolini Sails In Blaze Of Glory', *New York Times*, 9 April 1926

– 'I'm going . . .': Benito Mussolini, quoted in 'Premier Hit In The Nose'

– 'smiled and nodded . . .': ibid.

141 'remember their patriotic duty . . .': Prefetto Reggente La Questura, Perilli, to Uffici di Pubblica Sicurezza, 11 April 1926, ACS/PS/H2/16792

– 'very limit of . . .': ibid.

– 'as if he were . . .': 'Mussolini Sails In Blaze Of Glory'

– 'Tell England . . .': *Daily Express*, 9 April 1926, clipping in 'Gibson: Stampa', ACS/SPDCR/64/377/R.2

142 'My visit . . .': 'Sgr Mussolini in Tripoli', *The Times*, 12 April 1926

– 'The few who know . . .': 'Tripoli All Aglow to Greet Mussolini', *New York Times*, 11 April 1926

– 'Italian Africa is peopled . . .': ibid.

– 'mock-heroic madness': Benito Mussolini, quoted in R. J. B. Bosworth, *Mussolini* (London, 2002), p. 85

143 'We thought . . .': quoted in Christopher Duggan, *The Force of Destiny: A History of Italy since 1796* (London, 2007), p. 384

– 'Mussolini leaves for North Africa . . .': *Il cittadino*, 7 April 1926, clipping in 'Gibson: Stampa', ACS/SPDCR/64/377/R.2

144 'indecent forgetful serenity': Charles Lamb, quoted in Lisa Appignanesi, *Mad, Bad and Sad: A History of Women and the Mind Doctors from 1800 to the Present* (London, 2008), p. 23

VI: QUESTIONS

145 'an assiduous spectator': Gaetani Salucci Witness Statement, 11 April 1926, ACS/ TSDS/40–41/B.7
– 'a poor martyr': ibid.
146 'of anti-Fascist sentiment': Prefectural Report to Chief of Police, Rome, 19 April 1926, ACS/PS/J5/B.145
147 'mysterious undertaking': Statement of Mother Superior Hesselblad, Pennetta to Procuratore del Re, 10 April 1926, ACS/PS/H2/16792
– 'In asking for your advice . . .': Violet, quoted in ibid.
– 'very guarded . . .': Hesselblad, ibid.
– 'a gentle and refined manner': ibid.
148 'STAHLSTECKNADELN . . .': Epifanio Pennetta, Report, 10 April 1926, ACS/TSDS/40–41/B.6
– 'part of a group . . .': Epifanio Pennetta, Report, 7 April 1926, ACS/TSDS/40–41/B.6
149 'made no attempt . . .': Richard Oliver Collin, *La donna che sparò a Mussolini* (Milan, 1988), p. 89
150 'as if in her own . . .': ibid., p. 90
– 'Why did you shoot Mussolini?': ibid.
– 'a meeting place . . .': ibid.
151 'The poor dear . . .': Willie, quoted in 'Premier's Assailant is a Sister of Lord Ashbourne', *New York Times*, 8 April 1926
– 'The Gibson family regrets . . .': quoted in 'Miss Gibson's Identity', *The Times*, 9 April 1926
– 'long sea trip': Constance to Violet, 21 March 1926, ACS/TSDS/40–41/B.6
– 'Sincere congratulations . . .': Constance to Benito Mussolini, 8 April 1926, ACS/SPDCR/64/377/R.1
– 'of a quite ordinary . . .': Constance, quoted in 'Premier's Assailant is a Sister of Lord Ashbourne'
– 'She gave way . . .': 'Woman Went To Italy To Avoid Lunacy Laws', *New York Times*, 9 April 1926
– '[Her] extreme act . . .': Marianne, quoted in Collin, p. 82
152 'I am deeply stricken . . .': Marianne, quoted in *La voce di Mantova*, 9 April 1926, clipping in 'Gibson: Stampa', ACS/SPDCR/64/377/R.2
– 'The jaundiced eye . . .': Violet, notebook, ACS/TSDS/40–41/B.6
– 'Tell Marianne . . .': ibid.
– 'Lord Ashbourne insists . . .': Ronald Graham to Foreign Office, 13 April 1926, PRO/FO371/11398
153 'with probable event . . .': O. E. Sargent, ibid.
– 'He is a crank': ibid.

– 'It seems that the Gibson family . . .': *La voce di Mantova*, 9 April 1926, clipping in 'Gibson: Stampa', ACS/SPDCR/64/377/R.2
– 'the would-be assassin . . .': King George V, quoted in Italian Ambassador Torretta, London, to Benito Mussolini, 17 June 1926, MAE/B.616/F2/2
154 'the Italian Clarence Darrow': 'Culprit's Week', *Time*, 26 April 1926
155 'Miss Constance Gibson . . .': Ronald Graham to Foreign Office, 13 April 1926, PRO/FO371/11398
– 'everything in my power . . .': Andrea Serrao to Constance, 14 April 1926, TC
157 'Violet is quite as much . . .': Willie to Constance, undated April 1926, TC

VII: SECRETS

158 'To Madame Oly . . .': Violet to Madame Oly, 15 April 1926, ACS/TSDS/40–41/B.6
– 'was greatly torn . . .': Violet to Madame Oly, 22 April 1926, ibid.
– '2 night gowns . . .': Violet to Mother Superior, Santa Brigida, 15 April 1926, ibid.
159 'diligent and rigorous . . .': Rosario Marciano to Mother Superior, Mantellate, 14 April 1926, ACS/TSDS/40–41/B.6
160 'My dear Violet . . .': Enid Dinnis to Violet, 9 April 1926, ACS/TSDS/40–41/B.6
– 'Lord Ashbourne . . .': Consul General, Paris, to Minister of Foreign Affairs, 19 April 1926, ACS/PS/J5/B.145
– 'The delicacy of his . . .': ibid.
161 'mysterious': Guido Leto, *OVRA: fascismo e antifascismo* (Bologna, 1952), p. 27
– 'semi-abandoned': ibid.
– 'strange life': ibid.
162 'It seems that she has . . .': Ronald Graham to Austen Chamberlain, 9 April 1926, PRO/FO371/11398
163 'Every evening . . .': *Note*, 22 April 1926, ACS/PS/H2/16792
164 'occult silence': Richard Oliver Collin, *La donna che sparò a Mussolini* (Milan, 1988), p. 104
– 'founded mainly by . . .': ibid.
165 'secrets for privacy . . .': Henry James, quoted in Leon Edel, Introduction to *Henry James, Letters: 1843–1875* (Harvard, 1984), p. xv
– 'a foreign agent . . .': Statement of Antonio David Radoani to Alberto Barbarito, 9 April 1926, ACS/PS/H2/16792
– 'President of the Irish . . .': ibid.
– 'one of the most active . . .': ibid.
166 'a cunning man . . .': Alberto Barbarito to Epifanio Pennetta, 9 April 1926, ACS/PS/H2/16792
– 'dubious Fascists . . .': Franco Fucci, *Le polizie di Mussolini: la repressione del'antifascismo nel 'ventennio'* (Milan, 1985), p. 31
167 'ingenuous programme . . .': Edith Somerville, letter to *The Times*, 9 May 1916, quoted in Gifford Lewis, *Somerville and Ross: The World of the Irish R.M.* (London, 1985), p. 160
– 'senile and slobbering': J. M. Synge, quoted in Roy Foster, *W. B. Yeats, A Life: The Apprentice Mage* (Oxford, 1998), p. 453

- 'bullets to fire . . .': Douglas Hyde, quoted in ibid., p. 454
- 'had a good deal more . . .': Ronald Graham to Foreign Office, 13 April 1926, PRO/FO371/11398
- 'does not mean . . .': Violet to Manager, London and Westminster Bank, 13 April 1926, ACS/TSDS/40–41/B.6
168 'mumble disjointedly': Pennetta to Procuratore del Re, 8 April 1926, ACS/PS/H2/16792

VIII: THE NEW AUGUSTUS

169 'a man with whom . . .': Ivone Kirkpatrick, quoted in Richard Lamb, *Mussolini and the British* (London, 1997), p. 59
- 'strolling musicians . . .': Benito Mussolini, quoted in R. J. B. Bosworth, *Mussolini* (London, 2002), p. 111
- 'a statesman of exceptional . . .': Ronald Graham, quoted in ibid., p. 184
170 'hunched up behind . . .': John St Loe Strachey, 24 April 1924, PA/STR/10/15/1
- 'an opportunist exercise . . .': R. J. B. Bosworth, 'The British Press, the Conservatives, and Mussolini, 1920–34', *Journal of Contemporary History* 5/2 (1970), p. 172
171 'political and mental margarine': Ignazio Silone, quoted in Frances Stonor Saunders, *Who Paid the Piper? The CIA and the Cultural Cold War* (London, 1999), p. 391
- 'I entirely agree with you . . .': Ronald Graham to John St Loe Strachey, 8 May 1924, PA/STR/10/15/4
- 'What a contrast . . .': Hilaire Belloc, quoted in A. N. Wilson, *Hilaire Belloc* (London, 1984), p. 290
172 'All my pleasant impressions . . .': Austen Chamberlain, quoted in Peter Edwards, 'The Austen Chamberlain–Mussolini Meetings', *Historical Journal* 14/1 (March 1971), p. 157
- 'peculiarly close intimacy': Mr Ponsonby, 11 July 1927, quoted in *Hansard*, www.millbanksystems.com
- 'coincidence of purpose': Austen Chamberlain, ibid.
- 'Chamberlain is, in his heart . . .': Benito Mussolini, quoted in Edwards, 'The Austen Chamberlain–Mussolini Meetings', p. 162
- 'handshake was worth . . .': Gaetano Salvemini, *Prelude to World War II* (London, 1953), p. 72
173 'obviously it is a mistake . . .': Harold Nicolson, quoted in Peter Edwards, 'The Foreign Office and Fascism 1924–1929', *Journal of Contemporary History* 5/2 (1970), p. 156
- 'The analogy with . . .': Foreign Office Memo, 5 November 1926, PRO/FO371/11385
- 'It is easy to denounce . . .': Austen Chamberlain, quoted in Edwards, 'The Foreign Office and Fascism', p. 156
- 'If I had been an Italian . . .': Winston Churchill, quoted in Piero Melograni, 'The Cult of the Duce in Mussolini's Italy', *Journal of Contemporary History* 11/4 (October 1976), p. 233

174 'the greatest living legislator': ibid.
- 'The colossal emptiness . . .': Sebastian Haffner, *Defying Hitler* (London, 2003), p. 107
- 'Murder is more common': *The Times*, 21 June 1924, quoted in Bosworth, 'The British Press', p. 173
- 'the most cruel . . .': Giuseppe Bottai, *Critica Fascista* 2/15 (June 1924), p. 495
175 'village ruffians . . .': *The Times*, 6 January 1925, quoted in Bosworth, 'The British Press', p. 173
- 'too horrible to contemplate': ibid.
- 'too sinister an interpretation': quoted in Norman Rose, *The Cliveden Set* (London, 2000), p. 137
- [footnote] 'I shall refuse . . .': Léon Blum, quoted in Bosworth, *Mussolini*, p. 317
- [footnote] 'one Jew who did not . . .': Benito Mussolini, quoted in ibid.
- 'trim handsome . . .': *Morning Post*, 24 October 1927, quoted in Bosworth, 'The British Press', p. 173
176 'in a blaze of glory': 'Rome Welcomes Mussolini Home', *New York Times*, 18 April 1926
- 'Guns boomed . . .': ibid.
- 'the parasitic city . . .': Benito Mussolini, quoted in R. J. B. Bosworth, *Mussolini's Italy: Life under the Dictatorship 1915–1945* (London, 2005), p. 16
- 'at his own expense . . .': quoted in Kenneth Scott, 'Mussolini and the Roman Empire', *The Classical Journal* 27/9 (June 1932), p. 648
177 'We do not want . . .': Gabriele d'Annunzio, quoted in Mark Thompson, *The White War: Life and Death on the Italian Front 1915–1919* (London, 2008), p. 45
- 'in the Roman fashion': Benito Mussolini, quoted in Melograni, p. 229
- 'retrojection of ideas . . .': Mary Beard, quoted in Garry Wills, 'Dark Victories', *New York Review of Books*, 20 December 2007
- 'Symbols of the past . . .': Scott, p. 657
- 'an aesthetic overproduction . . .': Jeffrey Schnapp, 'Epic demonstrations: Fascist modernity and the 1932 exhibition of the Fascist Revolution', in R. J. Golson, ed., *Fascism, Aesthetics, and Culture* (New England, 1992), p. 3
178 'There's no such thing . . .': Ernest Hemingway, *A Farewell to Arms* (London, 2005), p. 154

IX: HIDDEN HANDS

180 'The first appeal . . .': Umberto Eco, 'Eternal Fascism: Fourteen Ways of Looking at a Blackshirt', *New York Review of Books*, 22 June 1995
- 'The infamous . . .': *Giornale della sera*, 8 April 1926, clipping in 'Gibson: Stampa', ACS/SPDCR/64/377/R.2
- 'The Duce is ours . . .': ibid.
181 'a political complexion . . .': Ronald Graham to Austen Chamberlain, 12 April 1926, PRO/FO371/11398
- 'simply the act . . .': ibid.
- 'I [said] that I was . . .': Ronald Graham to Austen Chamberlain, 13 May 1926, PRO/FO371/11398

– 'For the second time . . .': quoted in Richard Oliver Collin, *La donna che sparò a Mussolini* (Milan, 1988), p. 101

182 'irritated and bored': Benito Mussolini, quoted in Collin, p. 102
– 'Mussolini has his own . . .': ibid.
– 'smiling as I have seen him . . .': Enrico Ferri, quoted in ibid., p. 103
– 'Miss Gibson's relatives . . .': Foreign Office Memo, 1 July 1926, PRO/HO144/7950
– 'lucid intervals . . .': ibid.
– 'have another shot . . .': ibid.

183 'Miss Gibson seems . . .': ibid.
– 'it would be extraordinarily . . .': ibid.
– 'It is necessary to add . . .': Foreign Office Memo, 29 June 1926, PRO/HO144/7950
– 'directed that she be . . .': *Insanity and the Insane in Post-Famine Ireland*, Mark Finnane (London, 1981), p. 121

X: LIVES OF THE SAINTS

184 'We cannot always control . . .': Violet, notebook, ACS/TSDS/40–41/B.6
– 'Delight in self contempt': ibid.
– 'Never allow your peace . . .': ibid.
– 'the Sacred Heart . . .': ibid.
– 'It is for God . . .': ibid.

185 'must rise above . . .': ibid.
– 'I did not know for sure . . .': Vaslav Nijinsky, *The Diary of Vaslav Nijinsky*, ed. Joan Acocella (New York, 1999), p. 21
– 'more weak and miserable': Violet, notebook, ACS/TSDS/40–41/B.6
– 'heroic detachment': ibid.
– 'She adopted a religious form . . .': Enid Dinnis to Italian Consul, London, 16 May 1926, ACS/TSDS/40–41/B.6
– 'I came up against . . .': ibid.
– 'the divine possibilities . . .': unsigned review of *More Mystics*, *Times Literary Supplement*, 20 November 1924, p. 778

186 'by acts of friendly . . .': Edith Wharton, *Italian Backgrounds* (Hopewell, New Jersey, 1998), p. 85
– 'There are among us . . .': Violet, notebook, ACS/TSDS/40–41/B.6
– 'white light of piety': W. B. Yeats, quoted in Roy Foster, *W. B. Yeats, A Life: The Apprentice Mage* (Oxford, 1998), p. 96
– 'Words strain . . .': T. S. Eliot, 'Burnt Norton', *Collected Poems, 1909–1962* (London, 1963), p. 194

188 'As Beatrice Ansi . . .': Violet, notebook, ACS/TSDS/40–41/B.6
– 'The Catholics told . . .': ibid.
– 'the battle between . . .': Violet to Enid Dinnis, 11 September 1926, ACS/TSDS/40–41/B.6
– 'the sweetness caused . . .': quoted in Howard Hibbard, *Bernini* (London, 1965), p. 137

189 'I had the greatest . . .': quoted in Robert M. Youngson, *The Madness of Prince Hamlet and Other Extraordinary States of Mind* (London, 1999), p. 168

– 'ecstatic reality': Friedrich Nietzsche, *The Birth of Tragedy*, trans. Walter Kaufmann (New York, 1967), p. 24

190 'disastrous': Prison memo, Mantellate, 5 May 1926 ACS/TSDS/40–41/B.6
– 'only sufficient to prevent . . .': ibid.
– 'that they did not want . . .': Italian Consul De Gaspari, Dublin, to Italian Ambassador Torretta, London, 19 May 1926, MAE/B.616/F2/2

191 'I told her . . .': Frances to Constance, 26 May 1926, TC
– 'in a terrible fright . . .': ibid.
– 'What [the police] want . . .': Enid Dinnis to Mary McGrath, 15 May 1926, ACS/TSDS/40-41/B.6
– 'She seems to realise . . .': Frances to Constance, 26 May 1926, TC
– 'Miss Gibson had at one time . . .': Copy of the Case Book Entries, File Number 4818, Regarding the Hon. Violet Gibson, PRO/MH79/262

192 'Dear Sir . . .': Enid Dinnis to Italian Consul, London, 16 May 1926, ACS/TSDS/40–41/B.6

193 'like the ones . . .': Mary McGrath to Violet, undated June 1926, ACS/PS/J5/B.145

194 'Do you remember . . .': ibid.

XI: MEA CULPA

196 'How big is your heart?': quoted in Acting Crown Prosecutor Marinangeli's report to Examining Magistrates, 21 October 1926, ACS/TSDS/40–41/B.6
– 'Great things tomorrow': ibid.

197 'thought no more . . .': W. R. McClure memorandum, 22 July 1926, PRO/FO371/11398

198 'The Duke had been informed . . .': ibid.
– 'He is not one of those . . .': Ronald Graham to Austen Chamberlain, 23 July 1926, PRO/FO371/11398
– 'The Duke di Cesarò . . .': Oliver Harvey, Foreign Office Memo, 27 July 1926, PRO/FO371/11399
– 'We could not possibly . . .': C. Howard Smith, ibid.

199 'The good God knew . . .': Violet to Enid Dinnis, 11 September 1926, ACS/TSDS/40-41/B.6
– 'How sick one gets . . .': Alice James, quoted in Joanne Jacobson, 'Resistance and Subversion in the Letters of Alice James', *Biography* 14/4 (Fall 1991), p. 372

200 'it was against the will . . .' Violet, quoted in Ronald Graham to Austen Chamberlain, 9 July 1926, PRO/FO371/11398

201 'an extensive somatic . . .': Augusto Giannelli and Sante De Sanctis, 'Relazione di Perizia Psichiatrica sull'imputata Violetta Gibson', ACS/TSDS/40-41/B.7

XII: EXAMINATION

202 'I want to get out . . .': Robert Musil, *Diaries, 1899–1941*, Notebook 7 (New York, 1999) pp. 147–61

203 'Everything is now well . . .': Violet to Sra Bradolini, 6 July 1926, ACS/TSDS/40–41/B.6

204 'which expressed the truth . . .': Violet to Enid Dinnis, undated 1926, ACS/TSDS/ 40–41/B.6

– 'a good Catholic novelist': Violet to Bruno Cassinelli, 13 August 1926, ACS/TSDS/ 40–41/B.6

– 'You can now write . . .': Violet to Enid Dinnis, undated 1926, ACS/TSDS/40–41/ B.6

– 'Those who have given . . .': Enid Dinnis to Italian Consul, London, 16 May 1926, ACS/TSDS/40–41/B.6

– 'My dear Willie . . .': Violet to Willie, 16 August 1926, ACS/TSDS/40–41/B.6

206 'I don't feel up to . . .': Violet to Rosario Marciano, 10 May 1926, ACS/TSDS/ 40–41/B.7

– 'a most remarkable man': Violet to Willie, 16 August 1926, ACS/TSDS/40–41/ B.6

– 'making themselves incompatible . . .': quoted in Jeffrey Eaman, *Violet Gibson's Attempt on the Life of Benito Mussolini, Rome 1926* (PhD Thesis, Lancaster University, 2001), p. 172

– 'the screeching quarrels . . .': Luigi Federzoni, *Diario di un ministro del fascismo* (Florence, 1993) p. 27

207 'a woman of well-developed . . .': Augusto Giannelli and Sante De Sanctis, 'Relazione di Perizia Psichiatrica sull'imputata Violetta Gibson', ACS/ TSDS/40–41/B.7

– 'a closed character . . .': ibid.

– 'great things': ibid.

208 'I gave my life': ibid.

– 'what I say': ibid.

– 'almost always in . . .': ibid.

– 'stubborn dissimulation': ibid.

– 'I hope you are persuaded . . .': ibid.

209 'Blessed John Avila . . .': Violet, notebook, ACS/TSDS/40–41/B.6

– 'He pointed out . . .': Alban Goodier SJ, *Saints for Sinners* (New Hampshire, 2007), p. 47

– 'Some time ago . . .': Violet to Enid Dinnis, 11 September 1926, ACS/TSDS/40–41/ B.6

210 'Each of her discourses . . .': Giannelli and De Sanctis

– 'We are not convinced . . .': ibid.

– 'very very small': Violet to Ivy Orde-Powlett, 25 August 1926, ACS/TSDS/ 40–41/B.6

– 'One remembers that . . .': ibid.

211 'It is the being watched . . .': ibid.

– 'The difficulty here . . .': Violet to Enid Dinnis, 11 August 1926, ACS/TSDS/40–41/ B.6

– 'The ill people are dears . . .': Violet to Ivy Orde-Powlett, 25 August 1926, ACS/ TSDS/40–41/B.6

– 'a great trial to us all . . .': Violet to Enid Dinnis, 26 August 1926, ACS/TSDS/ 40–41/B.6

– 'every day spent here . . .': Violet to Enid Dinnis, 11 September 1926, ACS/TSDS/ 40–41/B.6

- 'In an asylum . . .': Violet to Ivy Orde-Powlett, 25 August 1926, ACS/TSDS/40–41/ B.6
- 'to spoil everything . . .': ibid.
- 'darker imperative . . .': Declan Kiberd, *Inventing Ireland: The Literature of the Modern Nation* (London, 1995), p. 38
- 'No one will know . . . : Violet to Enid Dinnis, 11 August 1926, ACS/TSDS/40–41/B.6
212 'chronic paranoia': Giannelli and De Sanctis
- 'If given her liberty . . .': ibid.
- 'the psychological abnormality . . .': ibid.

XIII: STIGMATA

213 'Women have served . . .': Virginia Woolf, *A Room of One's Own* (London, 1982), pp. 35–6
- 'a doughtily Fascist . . .': R. J. B. Bosworth, *Mussolini* (London, 2002), p. 388
214 'their natural and fundamental . . .': ibid., p. 389
- 'in the correct manner . . .': Christopher Duggan, *The Force of Destiny: A History of Italy since 1796* (London, 2007), p. 466
- 'A woman! . . .': Benito Mussolini, quoted in 'Premier Hit In The Nose', *New York Times*, 8 April 1926
- 'We have always had . . .': *L'assalto*, 9 April 1926, quoted in Jeffrey Eaman, *Violet Gibson's Attempt on the Life of Benito Mussolini, Rome 1926* (PhD Thesis, Lancaster University, 2001), p. 45
215 'enjoyed sexual relations . . .': Augusto Giannelli and Sante De Sanctis, 'Relazione di Perizia Psichiatrica sull'imputata Violetta Gibson', ACS/TSDS/40–41/B.7
- 'many flirtations . . .': Violet Gibson History Sheet, St. Andrew's Hospital, May 1927, SAH/VG
- 'completed the pallid . . .': Giannelli and De Sanctis
- 'the examination of . . .': Augusto Giannelli to Rosario Marciano, 13 August 1926, ACS/TSDS/40–41/B.6
216 'The *furor uterinus* . . .': *Encyclopaedia Britannica*, 3rd edn (1788), quoted in Robert M. Youngson, *The Madness of Prince Hamlet and Other Extraordinary States of Mind* (London, 1999), p. 20
- 'more vulnerable to insanity . . .': quoted in Lisa Appignanesi, *Mad, Bad and Sad: A History of Women and the Mind Doctors from 1800 to the Present* (London, 2008), p. 80
- 'returned humbly . . .': Elaine Showalter, *The Female Malady: Women, Madness and English Culture, 1830–1980* (London, 1987), p. 76
- 'exceeding selfishness . . .': ibid., p. 133
217 'the stigmata of degeneration': Henry Maudsley, quoted in Appignanesi, p. 9
- 'outward defects . . .': ibid., p.98

XIV: HERETICS

218 'no importance': Benito Mussolini, quoted in Paolo Palma, *Una bomba per il*

duce: la centrale antifascista di Pacciardi a Lugano (Calabria, 2003), p. 4
- 'impassiveness of the national . . .': ibid.
- 'gesture of disdainful . . .': ibid.
- 'old *bersagliere*': ibid., p. 6
219 'jaw set . . .': 'Bomb', *Time*, 20 September 1926
- 'This kind of thing . . .': Benito Mussolini, quoted in Palma, p. 6
- 'anarchists, pseudo-anarchists . . .': Jeffrey Eaman, *Violet Gibson's Attempt on the Life of Benito Mussolini, Rome 1926* (PhD Thesis, Lancaster University, 2001), p. 248
- 'clumsy and compromised . . .': Violet, quoted in report by Nurse Flora Vitali, 18 September 1926, ACS/TSDS/40–41/B.6
220 'she had accomplices . . .': ibid.
- 'One's heart sinks . . .': Violet to Enid Dinnis, 1 October 1926, ACS/TSDS/40–41/B.6
- 'As something has just . . .': Violet to Enid Dinnis, 1 September 1926, ACS/TSDS/40–41/B.6
- 'She has cried . . .': Report by Nurse Flora Vitali
- 'Things are being attempted . . .': Ronald Graham to Austen Chamberlain, 3 August 1926, PRO/FO371/11384
221 'There are dragons still . . .': ibid.
- 'on good authority . . .': Ronald Graham to Austen Chamberlain, 29 October 1926, PRO/FO371/11399
- 'the extreme Fascists . . .': Ronald Graham to Foreign Office, 25 January 1927, PRO/FO371/12195
222 'sectarian or political . . .': Report of Procurator General Marinangeli to Court of Appeal, Rome, 21 October 1926, ACS/TSDS/40–41/B.6
- 'demonstrated both cunning . . .': ibid.
223 'a manifestation of . . .': ibid.
- '– first, of having . . .': ibid.
- 'Things being as they are . . .': Andrea Serrao to Constance, 2 November 1926, TC
224 'Blackshirts! Raise high . . .': Benito Mussolini, quoted in 'Bullet, Fired by Youth, Cuts Duce's Shirt', *Washington Post*, 1 November 1926
- 'The shot rang out . . .': Dino Grandi, quoted in Ignatius Phayre, 'Mussolini', *Current History* 45/4 (January 1937), p. 78
225 'Doo-chay! . . .': quoted in ibid.
- 'Be calm! . . .': Benito Mussolini, quoted in ibid.
- 'Maximum indifference': Palma, p. 7
- 'tenacious ballistic attention': Benito Mussolini, quoted in ibid.
- 'corselet of fine Ansaldo . . .': Phayre, p. 78
- 'the cornerstone . . .': Cesare Rossi, *Il tribunale speciale* (Milan, 1952), p. 53
- 'the lubricants that . . .': ibid.
226 'Yes! Du-ce! . . .': quoted in Christopher Duggan, *The Force of Destiny: A History of Italy since 1796* (London, 2007), p. 478
- 'They are but Mary . . .': Edgardo Sulis, quoted in ibid., p. 479
- 'I believe in . . .': quoted in ibid., p. 484
- 'The crowd does not . . .': Benito Mussolini, quoted in ibid., p. 477

- 'It is faith . . .': Benito Mussolini, quoted in R. J. B. Bosworth, *Mussolini* (London, 2002), p. 89
- 'religion of the nation': Emilio Gentile, 'Fascism as Political Religion', *Journal of Contemporary History* 25, 2/3 (May–June 1990), p. 234
227 'suddenly take . . .': Benito Mussolini, quoted in Bosworth, *Mussolini*, p. 218
- 'I had an absorbingly . . .': Lord Lloyd to Foreign Office, 5 November 1926, PRO/FO371/11385
- 'Within twenty-four hours . . .': 'Mussolini Pledges Action To Destroy All Enemies Today', *New York Times*, 5 November 1926
228 'real *coup d'état*': Rossi, *Il tribunale speciale*, p. 52

XV: LOCKDOWN

229 'all those who have . . .': Nathaniel Cantor, 'The Fascist Political Prisoners', *Journal of Criminal Law and Criminology* 27/2 (July–August 1936), p. 169
- 'Publication of the new . . .': 'Opposition to Fascism Grows More Dangerous', *Washington Post*, 7 November 1926
- 'for spreading abroad . . .': ibid.
230 'the Italian genius . . .': Lord Lloyd, quoted in Harold J. Laski, *Reflections on the Revolution of Our Time* (London, 1968), p. 142
- 'any activity whatsoever . . .': quoted in Cantor, p. 174
231 'to obey the orders . . .': quoted in ibid.
- 'in a terrible situation . . .': ibid., p. 176
- 'the occult . . .': Cesare Rossi, *Personaggi di ieri e di oggi* (Milan, 1960), p. 207
232 'calumny and fraud': *Complotti*, 1926, PS/H2/B.6
233 'The Fascist regime . . .': Carlo Rosselli, Letter to *The Times*, 17 December 1932
- 'savage satisfaction . . .': 'The Defence of Fascismo', *The Times*, 8 November 1926
234 'in which neither the ideas . . .': ibid.
- 'It is a pity . . .': O. E. Sargent, Foreign Office, 8 November 1926, PRO/FO371/11385
- 'certainly HERE in Italy . . .': Ezra Pound to Wyndham Lewis, 7/8 February 1939, quoted in E. Fuller Torrey, *The Roots of Treason* (New York, 1984), p. 138
- 'Fine manners will . . .': Austen Chamberlain, quoted in Richard Lamb, *Mussolini and the British* (London, 1997), p. 86
- 'It's useless to fool . . .': Luigi Federzoni, quoted in Richard Oliver Collin, *La donna che sparò a Mussolini* (Milan, 1988), p. 100
235 'one-man show . . .': Ronald Graham, quoted in Peter Edwards, 'The Foreign Office and Fascism 1924–1929', *Journal of Contemporary History* 5/2 (1970), p. 158
- 'There is no doubt . . .': Ronald Graham to Foreign Office, 8 April 1926, PRO/FO371/11398
- 'anguish and profound . . .': quoted in A. Vittoria, 'I diari di Luigi Federzoni: appunti per una biografia', *Studi Storici*, 3 (July–September 1995), p. 741
- 'completely indifferent . . .': Leone Ginzburg, 'Ipotecare il futuro', *Quaderno 10 di Giustizia e Libertà*, February 1934, p. 73
236 'The extreme section . . .': Ronald Graham to Austen Chamberlain, 11 November 1926, PRO/FO371/11399

– 'such offences are not . . .': ibid.
– 'the opportunity of putting . . .': Ronald Graham to Austen Chamberlain, 16 November 1926, PRO/FO371/11385

XVI: SPECIAL JUSTICE

238 'a persistent and incurable . . .': Chief of Police report, 30 December 1926, ACS/TSDS/40–41/B.7
– 'the person in whom . . .': Enrico Ferri to Elsie Gibson, 24 January 1927, TC
239 'Signor Mussolini is anxious . . .': Ronald Graham to Foreign Office, 25 January 1927, PRO/FO371/12195
– 'I could not help . . .': Winston Churchill, quoted in Christopher Hibbert, *Benito Mussolini* (London, 1975), p. 96
240 'not be brought . . .': Ronald Graham to Foreign Office, 10 February 1927, PRO/FO371/12195
– 'the bulky file . . .': Cesare Rossi, *Il tribunale speciale* (Milan, 1952), p. 103
– 'The Case of . . .': 'The Case of Mussolini versus Miss Gibson', PRO/GFM 36/2
– 'Dictator Mussolini': 'Bomb', *Time*, 20 September 1926
– 'Before or after . . .': Ronald Graham to Foreign Office, 10 February 1927, PRO/FO371/12195
– 'I had considerable trouble . . .': Constance to C. Howard Smith, Foreign Office, 16 February 1927, PRO/FO371/12195
241 'My Expeditionary Force . . .': ibid.
– 'I shall be quite ready . . .': Constance to C. Howard Smith, Foreign Office, 8 March 1927, PRO/FO371/12195
242 'the characteristic independence . . .': quoted in Paul Fussell, *Abroad, British Literary Travelling Between the Wars* (Oxford, 1980), p. 40
– 'It really looks . . .': C. Howard Smith to Constance, 17 March 1927, TC. 19 March 1927, ACS/PS/J5/B.145
– 'as soon as it was over . . .': Ronald Graham to Foreign Office, 9 April 1927, PRO/FO/371/12196
– 'They still haven't managed . . .': quoted in Rossi, *Il tribunale speciale*, p. 41
243 'a very graceful act': Foreign Office Memo, 5 November 1926, PRO/FO 371/11385
– 'the man sent to us . . .': quoted in Rossi, *Il tribunale speciale*, p. 38
– 'Mussolini is an impostor!': Tito Zaniboni, quoted in 'Caged Bravo', *Time*, 25 April 1927
– 'the illegal head . . .': ibid.

XVII: LUCID INSANITY

245 'the great sense of horror . . .': Enrico Ferri, 'A Character Study and Life History of Violet Gibson Who Attempted the Life of Benito Mussolini on 7 April 1926', *Journal of the American Institute of Criminal Law and Criminology* 19/2 (August 1928), p. 211
– 'with cruel ferocity . . .': ibid.
– 'the blind instrument . . .': ibid.

- 'a condition of mental infirmity': ibid.
- 'science of psycho-pathology': ibid., p. 213
- 'unconscious frenzy . . .': ibid., p. 211
246 'a slow invasion of the mind . . .': ibid., p. 212
- 'but of her freedom . . .': ibid., p. 211
- 'watchful intelligence . . .': ibid., p. 217
- 'sick will power': ibid., p. 218
- 'her mental state of . . .': ibid., p. 217
- 'lucid insanity': ibid., p. 212
- 'normal intellect': ibid., p. 213
- 'of insane mind': ibid., p. 218
- 'a good thing . . .': Benito Mussolini, quoted in ibid.
247 'History and . . .': ibid., p. 219
- 'the great progress in . . .': ibid.
- 'anthropological profile': Enrico Ferri, 'Mussolini, uomo di stato', quoted in Jeffrey Eaman, *Violet Gibson's Attempt on the Life of Benito Mussolini, Rome 1926* (PhD Thesis, Lancaster University, 2001), p. 237
- 'mystic gesture . . .': ibid., p. 238
248 'a serious form . . .': Augusto Giannelli and Sante De Sanctis, 'Relazione di Perizia Psichiatrica sull'imputata Violetta Gibson', ACS/ TSDS/40–41/B.7
- 'One must accept solitude . . .': Benito Mussolini, quoted in Bosworth, *Mussolini*, p. 243
249 'a misanthrope . . .': Denis Mack Smith, *Mussolini* (London, 1981), pp. 109–12
- 'pathological': Ian Kershaw, *Hitler 1889–1936: Hubris* (London, 1998), p. xxii
- 'mystical vision': Emilio Gentile, 'Fascism as Political Religion', *Journal of Contemporary History* 25, 2/3 (May–June 1990), p. 235
- 'must be considered as . . .': Enrico Ferri, op. cit., p. 216
250 'leave no doubt that . . .': Tribunale Speciale per la Difeso dello Stato, Sentenza Numero 41, 6 May 1927, ACS/TSDS/41–42/B.7
251 'well fed': Condition on Admission, St Andrew's Hospital, May 1927, SAH/VG
252 'a large quantity . . .': *Elenco dei corpi di reato che dalla Cancelleria del Tribunale Civile e Penale di Roma si trasmettono alla Tribunale Speciale per la Difesa dello Stato*, 27 June 1927, ACS/TSDS/41–42/B.7
253 'Dear Mother Superior . . .': Violet to Mother Superior, Mantellate, undated 1927, ACS/TSDS/40–41/B.6

XVIII: EXODUS

255 'Legally she will not . . .': Constance to C. Howard Smith, Foreign Office, 16 February 1927, PRO/FO371/12195
- 'We beg to make it . . .': Thomas Cook & Son Ltd to Constance, 18 September 1926, TC
256 'I won't be staying . . .': quoted in Richard Oliver Collin, *La donna che sparò a Mussolini* (Milan, 1988), p. 134
257 'nervous prostration': quoted in Lisa Appignanesi, *Mad, Bad and Sad: A History of Women and the Mind Doctors from 1800 to the Present* (London, 2008), p. 357

- 'it is impossible to define . . .': Maurice Craig, *Psychological Medicine* (London, 1905), p. 19
258 'such derangement . . .': Henry Maudsley, quoted in ibid., p. 24
- 'goddess of proportion . . .': Virginia Woolf, *Mrs Dalloway* (London, 1976), pp. 88–9
- 'delusional insanity . . .': Diagnosis on Admission, St Andrew's Hospital, SAH/VG
- 'hysterical and suspicious . . .': Violet Gibson History Sheet, St Andrew's Hospital, May 1927, SAH/VG

PART THREE: LAMENTATIONS

I: MANSION OF DESPAIR

263 'destination kept rigidly . . .': 'Paranoiac', *Time*, 23 May 1927
- 'Was there any cause . . .': Violet Gibson History Sheet, St Andrew's Hospital, May 1927, SAH/VG
264 'release practically without . . .': C Howard Smith, Foreign Office, to Constance, 18 May 1927, PRO/FO371/12196
- 'The family of Violet . . .': Ashbourne family letter, 19 May 1927, TC
265 'She is afflicted . . .': 'Paranoiac'
- 'the realist's landscape': George Levine, quoted in Elaine Showalter, *The Female Malady: Women, Madness and English Culture, 1830–1980* (London, 1987), p. 35
266 'the weary . . .': quoted in Arthur Foss and Kerith Trick, *St Andrew's Hospital, Northampton: The First One Hundred and Fifty Years (1838–1988)* (London, 1989), p. 111
- 'fitting receptacles': Showalter, p. 33
267 'special apparatus . . .': ibid.
- 'In the façades . . .': ibid., p. 34
- 'pauper idiots': ibid.
- 'chronic ladies and gentlemen . . .': ibid.
- 'anxiety, trouble . . .': quoted in Foss and Trick, p. 193
- 'apoplexy, brain disease . . .': ibid., pp. 193–4
- 'objects of interest . . .': ibid., p. 85
268 'especially one who . . .': Showalter, p. 38
- 'first-class patients': Foss and Trick, p. 202
- 'regaled themselves . . .': ibid., p. 98
- 'Dance: Hands Across . . .': ibid.
269 'nervous diseases . . .': 'Mental Disorders', *The Times*, 8 October 1927
- 'not only the largest . . .': ibid.
- 'hydrotherapy centre . . .': ibid.
- 'The most modern . . .': ibid.
- 'By means of the handsome . . .': ibid.
- 'Mansion of despair': Mary Wollstonecraft, quoted in Showalter, p. 1
- 'Such a step will . . .': quoted in Foss and Trick, pp. 94–5
270 'He would one day . . .': Hugh Kenner, *The Modern Irish Writers: A Colder Eye* (London, 1984), p. 150

- 'the gate to the prison . . .': Dominique Maroger, quoted in Carol Loeb Shloss, *Lucia Joyce: To Dance in the Wake* (London, 2004), p. 417
- 'How would you like . . .': Antonia White, *Beyond the Glass* (London, 1979), p. 241

II: THE ABSENCE OF GOD

271 'If this is a hospital . . .': Ezra Pound, quoted in E. Fuller Torrey, *The Roots of Treason* (New York, 1984), p. 200
272 'expansive delusion': M. R. Phillips, 27 May 1927, SAH/VG
- 'Abnormally self-satisfied': M. R. Phillips, 19 May 1927, SAH/VG
- 'no regrets': M. R. Phillips, 16 June 1927, SAH/VG
- 'So, let's talk . . .': Violet to unidentified correspondent, undated June 1927, SAH/VG
273 'devotes time to reading . . .': M. R. Phillips, 1 July 1927, SAH/VG
- 'the silenced world beyond': Roy Porter, *Social Studies of Science* 12/3 (August 1982), p. 472
- 'and look at . . .': ibid.
- 'acting as a strange . . .': Note in file, 18 September 1927, SAH/VG
- 'attack of acute . . .': ibid.
274 'The conversation drifted . . .': Frances to Medical Superintendent, St Andrew's, 5 December 1927, SAH/VG
- 'despite not shouting out . . .': ibid.
- 'impaired judgement': Note in file, SAH/VG
- 'dangerous and highly . . .': Note in file, 4 March 1928, SAH/VG
275 'I cannot keep my . . .': John Clare, quoted in Foss and Trick, p. 130
- 'It is getting to be . . .': Charlotte Perkins Gilman, *The Yellow Wallpaper* (London, 1973), p. 21
- 'I it is im possible . . .': Vaslav Nijinsky, *The Diary of Vaslav Nijinsky*, ed. Joan Acocella (New York, 1999), p. 123
- 'The world feels less . . .': Violet, notebook, ACS/TSDS/40–41/B.6
- 'the devil was . . .': Note in file, 4 April 1928, SAH/VG
- 'was a full . . .': John Clare, quoted in Arthur Foss and Kerith Trick, *St Andrew's Hospital, Northampton: The First One Hundred and Fifty Years (1838–1988)* (London, 1989), p. 127
- 'wildly excited . . .': Note in file, 24 April 1928, SAH/VG
- 'Why did you hit . . .': ibid.
- 'actually seen the devil . . .': Note in file, 1 May 1928, SAH/VG
- 'while the devil . . .': Note in file, 10 September 1928, SAH/VG
- 'no apparent reason . . .': Note in file, 24 April 1928, SAH/VG
276 'to an asylum where . . .': Violet to Enid Dinnis, 11 September 1928, SAH/VG
- 'to fall into wicked . . .': ibid.
- 'once again I have seen . . .': Violet to Constance, 11 September 1928, SAH/VG
277 'yet in that unbearable . . .': 'Biography of St John of the Cross', Christian Classics Ethereal Library, www.ccel.org/j/john__cross
- 'strengthened with tapes . . .': Note in file, 17 April 1930, SAH/VG
278 'Red mark around neck . . .': ibid.
- 'Nullity had charms . . .': Antonia White, *Beyond the Glass* (London, 1979), p. 121

III: BURIED ALIVE

279 'melancholy degeneration': Hugh Kenner, *The Modern Irish Writers: A Colder Eye* (London, 1984), p. 149
 – 'world-wide increase . . .': 'Lunacy in 1926', *The Times*, 23 September 1927
 – 'Napoleonic march . . .': Roy Porter, *Social Studies of Science* 12/3 (August 1982), p. 472
 – 'The devoted attention . . .': Arthur Foss and Kerith Trick, *St Andrew's Hospital, Northampton: The First One Hundred and Fifty Years (1838–1988)* (London, 1989), p. 185
280 'closely confined . . .': 'Alleged False Imprisonment In An Asylum', *The Times*, 23 June 1922
 – 'for suicide should Hitler . . .': Virginia Woolf, *A Moment's Liberty: The Shorter Diary*, ed. Anne Olivier Bell (London, 1990), p. 476
 – 'DEFENCE COUNSEL: Do you . . .': 'Alleged False Imprisonment In An Asylum'
 – 'HIS LORDSHIP: Talks volubly . . .': ibid.
281 'frightened to death . . .': ibid.
 – 'I have been suffering . . .': ibid.
 – 'Harley Street is not . . .': ibid.
 – 'Moral therapists were . . .': Roy Porter, 'Being Mad in Georgian England', *History Today* 31 (December 1981), p. 46
282 'very closely supervised . . .': Note in file, 15 April 1931, SAH/VG
 – 'the rain, needle . . .': Dr. Daniel Rambaut, quoted in Foss and Trick, p. 217
 – 'CHESNEY ALLEN: Lovely melody . . .': Bud Flanagan and Joseph McCarthy, 'Underneath the Arches', www.lyricsplayground.com
283 'fond of reading history . . .': Note in file, 19 April 1944, SAH/VG
 – '17 September 1930 . . .': Note in file, SAH/VG
 – 'the choking knotweed . . .': Hilary Mantel, 'Author, Author', *Guardian*, 6 September 2008
284 'I hope Violet continues . . .': Constance to Medical Superintendent, 23 October 1934, SAH/VG
 – 'I have no doubt . . .': Report of Dr Henry Yellowlees, 4 September 1935, SAH/VG
 – 'technique for living': Georg Simmel, quoted in Caroline Douglas, 'Precious and Splendid Fossils', *Beyond Reason* (London, 1997), p. 39
286 'a very clever letter . . .': Constance to Dr Rambaut, 9 June 1936, SAH/VG
287 'still in a state . . .': Note in file, 2 September 1935, SAH/VG
 – 'Now I know she is mad': James Joyce, quoted in Carol Loeb Shloss, *Lucia Joyce: To Dance in the Wake* (London, 2004), p. 222
288 'You're the top! . . .': Cole Porter, 'You're the Top', www.lyricsplayground.com
 – 'the greatest lawgiver . . .': Winston Churchill, quoted in Richard Lamb, *Mussolini and the British* (London, 1997), p. 76
 – 'the defence of race': *Regio Decreto, Legge No. 1390* and *Legge No. 1381*, 5 and 7 September 1938, www.anpi.it/documenti_espulsi.htm
 – 'Among the rest . . .': Benito Mussolini, quoted in R. J. B. Bosworth, *Mussolini* (London, 2002), p. 340
289 'tell the Italian press . . .': Galeazzo Ciano, quoted in Lamb, p. 21

- 'rough beast ...': W. B. Yeats, 'The Second Coming', *Selected Poetry* (London, 1974), pp. 99–100
- 'Things fall apart ...': ibid.

IV: COMETH THE HOUR

290 'wanted war ...': R. J. B. Bosworth, *Mussolini* (London, 2002), p. 358
- 'Mussolini had chosen ...': ibid., p. 369
- 'against the plutocratic ...': ibid.
291 'in case they have ...': Violet to Winston Churchill, 19 May 1940, SAH/VG
- 'Each enemy ...': ibid.
292 'with pen rather than ...': Note in file, 19 April 1940, SAH/VG
- 'her special knowledge ...': Note in file, 23 October 1939, SAH/VG
293 'glorious navy ...': Benito Mussolini, quoted in 'The Attempt on Mussolini', *The Times*, 9 April 1926
295 'a progressive unbalancing ...': 'Why Mussolini Failed', *Picture Post*, 11 January 1941
- 'he violated every ...': quoted in Bosworth, *Mussolini*, p. 374
- 'a failure of preparation': Giuseppe Bottai, quoted in ibid., p. 374
296 'crafty, cold-blooded ...': Winston Churchill, quoted in 'Mr Churchill On Next Phase', *The Times*, 10 February 1941
- 'As things are today ...': Constance to Dr Tennent, 10 February 1941, SAH/VG
- 'the opportunity of escape ...': Note in file, 23 October 1939, SAH/VG
- 'I feel the lack ...': Violet to Dr Tennent, undated, SAH/VG
- 'conditions under which ...': Note in file, 5 November 1939, SAH/VG
- 'in bed and taking ...': Note in file, 3 January 1935, SAH/VG
297 'breathlessness, attacks of ...': Dr Rambaut to Constance, 11 June 1936, SAH/VG
- 'cardiac insufficiency': ibid.
- 'worst heart attack': Note in file, 30 October 1936, SAH/VG
- 'rude and overbearing ...': Note in file, 5 March 1937, SAH/VG
- 'Studies physical condition ...': Note in file, 12 March 1938, SAH/VG
- 'I am suffering from ...': Note in file, 20 March 1939, SAH/VG
- 'the wonder of ...': Note in file, 19 April 1940, SAH/VG
- 'Her pulse and circulation ...': Note in file, 11 March 1943, SAH/VG
- 'she claims to have been ...': Note in file, 4 September 1944, SAH/VG
- 'which alters the nature ...': ibid.
298 'the mecti ...': ibid.
- 'heart attack': Note in file, 5 March 1941, SAH/VG
- 'definite evidence ...': W. R. Ashby, X-Ray Department, St Andrew's, 4 March 1941, SAH/VG
- 'I am seriously ill ...': Violet, quoted in A. W. Forbes, Board of Control to Medical Superintendent, St Andrew's, 19 November 1941, SAH/VG
- 'a report on her complaint ...': ibid.
- 'As you know ...': Medical Superintendent, St Andrew's, to Board of Control, 24 November 1941, SAH/VG

299 'Violet was resident . . .': Constance to Dr Tennent, 21 January 1943, SAH/VG
300 'I turned away . . .': Willie, undated 1937, GUL/LESLIE/B.1/19
301 'I need not recapitulate . . .': Medical Superintendent, St Andrew's, to Lord Ashbourne, 21 May 1942, SAH/VG
  – 'poor': ibid.
  – 'at some time . . .': ibid.
302 'I hear that my nephew . . .': Violet to Dr Tennent, 5 July 1942, SAH/VG
  – 'led to nothing . . .': Violet to Dr Tennent, 26 October 1942, SAH/VG
  – 'We have suggested . . .': Constance to Dr Tennent, 21 January 1943, SAH/VG
  – 'little fortune': Violet to Lord Ashbourne, 13 October 1911, PA/ASH/B/56
303 'Your Royal Highness . . .': Violet to HRH Princess Elizabeth, 18 November 1944, SAH/VG
304 'born mentally impaired': www.thepeerage.com/p949.htm
  – 'She appears to have . . .': 'Nieces Abandoned in State-Run Mental Asylum and Declared Dead', *Sunday Herald*, 7 April 2002
305 'Her name doesn't . . .': ibid.
  – 'She's a lovely person . . .': ibid.
  – 'Went to Rome . . .': *Burke's Peerage and Baronetage* (London, 2009), p. 152

V: BY THE HEELS AT MILANO

306 'Fascism is not only . . .': quoted in Christopher Duggan, *The Force of Destiny: A History of Italy since 1796* (London, 2007), p. 476
  – 'companions dead . . .': quoted in Duggan, p. 486
  – 'Quite leisurely from . . .': W H Auden, 'Musée des Beaux Arts', *Selected Poems* (London, 1984), pp. 79–80
307 'You virtually need . . .': quoted in Duggan, p. 498
  – 'baggy, unpressed . . .': Franco Maugeri, quoted in R. J. B. Bosworth, *Mussolini* (London, 2002), p. 402
  – 'I shan't go . . .': Tito Zaniboni, quoted in Christopher Hibbert, *Benito Mussolini* (London, 1975), p. 237
  – 'Nonsense . . .': quoted in ibid., p. 246
  – 'It isn't nonsense . . .': ibid.
308 'the highest prison . . .': Benito Mussolini, quoted in Bosworth, *Mussolini*, p. 402
  – 'a filthy apologist . . .': Charles Olson, quoted in E. Fuller Torrey, *The Roots of Treason* (New York, 1984), p. 226
  – 'Only blood can cancel . . .': Benito Mussolini, quoted in Bosworth, *Mussolini*, p. 403
  – 'Duce! Duce! . . .': Adolf Hitler, quoted in Hibbert, p. 271
  – 'Italy be treated . . .': Benito Mussolini, quoted in ibid., p. 184
  – 'but always as slaves': Galeazzo Ciano, quoted in ???
309 'stand erect . . .': Benito Mussolini, quoted in ibid., p. 409
  – 'Hitler and I . . .': Benito Mussolini, quoted in Hibbert, p. 274
  – 'The bullets pass . . .': Benito Mussolini, *My Rise and Fall* (New York, 1998), p. 249
  – 'I'm convinced I shall die . . .': Benito Mussolini, quoted in Ignatius Phayre, 'Mussolini', *Current History* 45/4 (January 1937), p. 77

- 'Aim at my heart!': Benito Mussolini, quoted in Duggan, p. 531
310 'Make a speech now!': quoted in ibid., p. 532
- 'The breathless, bloody . . .': Philip Hamburger, 'Letter from Rome', *New Yorker*, 19 May 1945
- 'misshapen because of . . .': quoted in Sergio Luzzatto, *The Body of Il Duce: Mussolini's Corpse and the Fortunes of Italy* (New York, 2005), p. 70
311 'There were no roars . . .': Hamburger
- 'There is too much future . . .': Ezra Pound, quoted in Torrey, p. 148
- 'Brother Benito': ibid.
- 'jovial comrades': Ezra Pound, 'Pisan Cantos', Canto 84, quoted in 'Saved by the Ant's Fore-Foot', David Trotter, *London Review of Books*, 7 July 2005
- 'the slime and filth . . .': Robert L. Allen, quoted in Torrey, p. 5
312 'It is unfortunate . . .': Norman Rosten, quoted in ibid., p. 200
- [footnote] 'categorically that he is not . . .': quoted in ibid., p. 196
- 'the arms for ten million . . .': Benito Mussolini, quoted in Phayre, p. 80
- 'vomit death at all . . .': ibid., p. 81
313 'Fascism is not insanity . . .': Nancy Cunard, quoted in Hugh D. Ford, *Nancy Cunard: Brave Poet, Indomitable Rebel 1896–1965* (Philadelphia, 1968), p. 358
- 'one man and . . .': Winston Churchill, quoted in Piero Melograni, 'The Cult of the Duce in Mussolini's Italy', *Journal of Contemporary History* 11/4 (October 1976), p. 236
- 'autobiography of . . .': Piero Gobetti, quoted in David D. Roberts, 'Frustrated Liberals: De Ruggiero, Gobetti, and the Challenge of Socialism', *Canadian Journal of History* 63 (17), p. 46
- 'Fascism only regiments . . .': Ezra Pound, quoted in Torrey, p. 154

VI: CASTING OFF

315 'during a recent illness . . .': Countess Winterton to Dr Tennent, 28 November 1946, SAH/VG
- 'a great friend': Fanny Esterházy to St Andrew's, undated December 1947, SAH/VG
- 'With advancing years . . .': Dr Tennent to Fanny Esterházy, 17 December 1947, SAH/VG
- 'not too late . . .': Note in file, 4 October 1949, SAH/VG
- 'a miracle': ibid.
- 'the result of the treatment . . .': Note in file, 7 March 1947, SAH/VG
316 'there would always be . . .': Violet to Dr Tennent, 19 July 1948, SAH/VG
- 'return some of . . .': ibid.
- 'I am not strong enough . . .': Constance to Dr Tennent, 22 November 1946, SAH/VG
- 'There is no one . . .': ibid.
317 'Miss Gibson is now . . .': Medical Superintendent, St Andrew's, to the Official Solicitor, 29 April 1950, SAH/VG
- 'To start in new . . .': Constance to Dr Tennent, 29 March 1950, SAH/VG
- 'a very distinguished . . .': Dr Tennent to Dr J. O. F. Davies, 27 March 1951, SAH/VG

- 'to less expensive quarters': Constance to Dr Tennent, 17 March 1951, SAH/VG
318 'suffering from influenza . . .': Deputy Medical Superintendent, St Andrew's, to Constance, 9 February 1951, SAH/VG
- 'general physical health . . .': Dr Tennent to Constance, 30 April 1951, SAH/VG
- 'pay an early visit . . .': ibid.
- 'doubtful if she will . . .': Dr Tennent to Constance, 16 May 1951, SAH/VG
- 'I think Violet enjoyed . . .': Constance to Dr Tennent, 11 May 1951, SAH/VG
- 'I am sure she will . . .': Dr Tennent, to Constance, 16 May 1951, SAH/VG
319 'as they break . . .': Constance to Dr Tennent, 3 December 1951, SAH/VG
- 'Mrs Corner nursed me . . .': Violet Gibson, Will, undated 1943, SAH/VG
- 'Violet and I . . .': Constance to Dr Tennent, 3 December 1951, SAH/VG
320 'Dear Frances . . .': Violet to Frances, undated 1943, SAH/VG
321 'a crossword puzzle': Lucia Joyce, quoted in Carol Loeb Shloss, *Lucia Joyce: To Dance in the Wake* (London, 2004), p. 8
- 'hors d'oeuvre': Samuel Beckett, quoted in Brian Dillon, 'The Drowned Life of a Writer's Daughter', *Independent*, 29 July 2004
- 'sinister choreography . . .': Shloss, p. 182
- 'The poor child . . .': James Joyce, quoted in ibid., p. 226
- 'Lucia's self-understanding . . .': ibid., p. 31

VII: DEATH IN EXILE

323 'It is a statutory . . .': Dr Tennent to Lord Ashbourne, 15 October 1952, SAH/VG
- 'a quarter of an hour . . .': Lord Ashbourne to Dr Tennent, 23 October 1952, SAH/VG
- 'I am at once alive . . .': Note in file, 10 November 1953, SAH/VG
- 'regards herself as . . .': ibid.
- 'she has become much . . .': Dr Tennent to Lord Ashbourne, 11 September 1955, SAH/VG
- 'a small cerebral . . .': Note in file, 19 February 1956, SAH/VG
324 'somnolent and confused . . .': ibid.
- 'now very frail . . .': Dr Tennent to Lord Ashbourne, 21 March 1956, SAH/VG
- 'still bright . . .': ibid.
- 'visit her at your early . . .': ibid.
- 'I would be grateful . . .': Lord Ashbourne to Dr Tennent, 23 March 1956, SAH/VG
- 'where she went . . .': Nanette Bewly to Dr O'Connell, 22 March 1956, SAH/VG
- 'to think there is nothing . . .': ibid.
- 'In the event of . . .': Lord Ashbourne to Dr Tennent, 27 March 1956, SAH/VG

EPILOGUE

325 'I am . . .': John Clare, 'I Am', *John Clare, Major Works* (Oxford, 2008), p. 361
- 'with all the rights . . .': Violet Gibson, Will, undated 1943, SAH/VG

326 'Fortunately, she did not . . .': Dr Tennent to Lord Ashbourne, 4 June 1956, SAH/VG

 – 'Violet Gibson, 1876–1956.': Violet's gravestone, Kingsthorpe cemetery, Northampton

327 'What is life?': John Clare, 'What is Life', *Major Works by John Clare* (Oxford, 2004), p. 26

Picture Sources

Index

Gibson, David (nephew of VG), 151

Gibson, Edward (brother of VG): birth, 28; death, 300; education, 35; father's funeral, 65; inheritance, 63–4; marriage, 18, 37; political views, 161; relationship with VG, 241, 264

Gibson, Elsie (Elizabeth, sister of VG), *see* Bolton

Gibson, Frances (sister of VG), *see* Horsbrugh-Porter

Gibson, Harry (Henry, brother of VG): birth, 28; death, 55, 61, 66; education, 35; illness, 52, 55; shooting, 31; tobogganing, 19–20, 52

Gibson, Liliam, 141, 160

Gibson, Marianne (née de Monbrison, sister-in-law of VG): in Compiègne, 62, 88, 89, 300; family background, 88, 161; father-in-law's funeral, 65; husband's death, 300; marriage, 37; mother-in-law's death, 124–5; portraits, 88, 90; relationship with VG, 88, 90–1, 94–5, 116, 125, 151–2, 163, 206, 286; religious beliefs, 88, 319; response to shooting, 151–3

Gibson, Mary (née Wood, sister-in-law of VG), 55, 61

Gibson, Victor (Ernest, brother of VG): birth, 28; Boer War, 36–7, 66, 285; brother's death, 55; death, 86–8, 151; education, 35; father's death, 63, 65; political views, 87, 167; wife's death, 55; WWI service, 66, 87

Gibson, Violet: family background, 3, 18–21, 23–4, 212; childhood, 29; education, 29–30, 207; debutante, 18, 32; bridesmaid at brother's wedding, 18, 37; conversion to Catholicism, 46, 47, 49, 50–1; social work, 49; in Switzerland, 52, 54, 55; social life, 55–6; engagement, 56, 61; in Rome, 56–7; in Devon, 61–2; father's death, 63–4; father's funeral, 65; war work, 68–70; studying in Switzerland, 68; operations, 70, 149; brother Victor's death, 88, 151; at Compiègne, 88–91, 94–5; knife attack on servant, 95–6; in mental home, 96–9; in Rome, 114–18; suicide attempt, 8, 17, 118–20; mother's death, 124–5, 185; shooting of Mussolini, 3, 13–14, 49, 128, 136–7, 214, 275–6; arrest, 14–17; imprisonment at Mantellate prison (Regina Coeli), 15–17, 130, 144, 158–9, 190, 200–1, 221, 237–8; police investigation, 145–9, 162–8; conspiracy theory about shooting, 148, 162, 163–5,

179–82, 201, 250–1; medical investigation, 149; interrogation, 149–50, 222; confession, 195–200; at San Onofrio lunatic asylum, 201, 203–12, 219–21, 237; analysis of intellectual capacities, 207–10; gynaecological examination, 215–17; prosecution, 223–4, 236; at Villa Giuseppina clinic, 238, 239, 251, 252; case presented to Special Tribunal, 244, 245–50; return to England, 251–3, 254–6; Harley Street examinations, 257–9; committal to St Andrew's asylum, 259, 263–4; life at St Andrew's, 272–4, 277, 282–4, 296–300, 315–16; suicide attempt, 277–8; request to be moved to convent, 284, 298, 303, 317; letters smuggled out, 285–6; letters unsent, 290–2; request for discharge, 298–300; campaign for release, 316–18; death, 324; will, 319, 325, 326; grave, 319, 325, 326–7

APPEARANCE: beauty as a girl, 29; as bridesmaid, 18, 20; cartoon depiction, 180; as debutante, 32; eyes, 217; at Holloway Sanatorium (aged 48), 97; medical examination in Rome, 207; prison mug shots, 15–16; religious dress, 81–2; in Rome after mother's death, 126; in Rome after shooting, 15–16, 193, 251; scars, 97, 149; at time of shooting, 3, 11;

CHARACTER: as a child, 29, 34, 51; Dinnis's account, 193; dossier on, 207–8; Ferri's profile, 245–8; psychiatric investigation, 207

FINANCES: alms-giving, 115–16, 252; annual income, 167, 317; bank credit arrangement, 116, 167–8; cheque book, 159, 190, 252; cost of nursing care, 301–3, 317; private income from father, 50, 52, 61, 62, 64, 167, 303; trust fund from mother, 303;

GUNS: access to, 120, 150, 196; brother Harry's shooting, 31; bullets, 148, 252n; Lebel revolver, 5, 17, 128, 162, 180, 252n; small revolver, 113, 114–15, 120; suicide attempt, 118–19

HEALTH: appendicitis and peritonitis operation, 70, 71; attitude to pain, 70, 73; breast operation, 70; childhood illnesses, 34; Christian Science, 42–3, 50, 320; death, 324; diet in prison, 189–90, 193–4, 237–8; examinations in Rome, 149, 201, 207–10, 215–16; gynaecological examination, 215–16; heart problems, 297, 298, 299, 301; illness in Milan, 57–9; influenza, 318; mental state after mother's death, 125–6;

'nervous crisis' after brother Victor's
death, 88; nursing care, 302–3, 316–17; old
age, 315–19, 323–4; removal of teeth, 16;
self–diagnosis, 297–8; suicide attempts, 8,
17, 118–20, 278, 283; tuberculosis, 296;
weight loss, 190, 237–8, 239, 251;
HOMES: Buckfastleigh, Devon, 61–2;
Kensington, 86, 96, 112; lodgings, 52;
Merrion Square, Dublin, 30–1, 42–3;
Putney Hill, 63
MADNESS: assessments at St Andrew's,
271–2, 273, 282–3, 287, 292, 298–9; attack on
fellow inmate, 200–1; attack on guard, 237;
attack on servant, 95–8; attacks on fellow
patients, 275, 277, 299; case for, 191–3; certified insane, 96, 192, 258–9; crises in St
Andrew's, 273, 275–7; definition, 188;
descriptions of, 84; Dinnis's account, 185,
192–3; family views of, 274, 299–300;
Harley Street examinations, 257–9, 284; in
Holloway Sanatorium, 96–9, 191–2; hysteria, 216–17; in padded cell, 275, 276; psychiatric examination in Rome, 207–10; religious mania, 160, 188, 192, 197, 246, 249,
287; Special Tribunal finding, 250; suicide
attempts, 8, 17, 118–20, 278, 283; *Times* article, 265; violence, 95–8, 192, 200, 208, 237,
275, 277, 299;
PERSON: belongings from convent, 158–9;
chess, 273; jigsaw puzzles, 121, 159, 203,
206; notebooks, 70–2, 184–9; 'secret',
206–7, 210–12, 223, 246, 263–4; title, 29, 49;
POLITICS: advice to Churchill, 290–2; conspiracy theories about her connections,
164–7; Irish politics, 167, 273–4; Italy's need
to be rescued, 112, 263, 287; Labour supporter, 112; pacifism, 68, 69–70, 95;
Radoani's deposition, 165–6
RELIGION: attitude to Pope, 94–5, 163; burial, 319, 325; Christian Science, 42–3, 50,
320; conversion to Catholicism, 46, 47, 49,
50–1; family views, 49–51, 183, 319; imitation of saints and hermits, 185–9;
Modernist belief, 49; relationship with
birds, 283–4; religious mania, 160, 188, 192,
197, 246, 249, 287; self–mortification, 71–3;
spiritual director, 71–3, 112, 184; theme of
sacrifice, 45, 70, 112, 117, 120, 184, 188, 189,
192; Theosophy, 45, 62; view of soul, 273;
vision of the devil, 275, 276
RELATIONSHIPS: with brother Willie, 49,

50, 90, 125–6, 241, 256, 286; engagement,
56, 61; with father, 29, 34, 50–1, 55, 57, 61;
flirtations, 215; friendships, 50, 55, 61–2, 185;
with mother, 42–3, 123; sexual, 215; with
sister Constance, 57–8, 241, 276–7, 283, 301,
318, 324
Gibson, Willie (William, brother of VG), *see*
Ashbourne, second Baron
Gilman, Charlotte Perkins, 257, 275
Ginzburg, Leone, 235
Giolitti, Giovanni, 104–5
'Giovinezza' (Fascist anthem), 13, 129, 169, 247
Giuseppina Segatini, Sister, 179
Gladstone, William, 25
Gobetti, Piero, 175, 313
Godfrey, Martha, 183
Golden Dawn, Hermetic Order of the, 44
Gonne, Maud, 35, 37, 39–40
Goodier, Alban, 209
Gore-Booth, Eva, 39
Graham, Sir Ronald: on Ashbourne, 152;
audiences with Mussolini, 200, 236; deal-
ing with Lloyd case, 230; dealing with
Slater case, 243; dealing with VG case,
153–5, 162, 181, 198–9, 200, 235–6, 239–40,
252; opinion of VG, 182–3; opinions of
Mussolini, 169–70, 171; reports on Fascist
regime, 173, 220–1; response to shooting,
136–8; on *squadristi* groups, 134
Graham, Lady Sybil, 6
Gramsci, Antonio, 233
Grandi, Dino, 7, 11, 128, 224
Gray, Eileen, 35, 49, 62, 81
Griffith, Arthur, 37
Grosvenor Crescent, London, 63, 64, 256
Guidi, Augusta, 77

Haile Selassie, 293
Hall, Radclyffe, 80
Hamburger, Philip, 310, 311
Hare, Augustus, 115
Harley Street, 257–9, 281
Harrow School, 35
Hart, Dr Bernard, 258–9
Hasek, Jaroslav, 83
Hawthorne, Nathaniel, 118
Hemingway, Ernest, 178
Henry VI, King of England, 121
Henry III, King of France, 95
Hesselblad, Mary Elizabeth, 4, 146–7, 158
Hitler, Adolf, 106, 129, 289, 292, 308–9
Hoare, Sir Samuel, 78